The
Journal
of
Irreproducible
Results
II

The Journal of Irreproducible Results II

Selected and Edited by
George H. Scherr Ph.d. and Jim Glenn

BARNES
&NOBLE
BOOKS
NEW YORK

Contents

ARTS & LANGUAGE

Romantism in Pathology ✎ *Ray Past* 3

How to Make Your Way through Almost Anything: A Simple Mechanical Guide
✎ *Betty H. Zisk* 5

Why U.S. Folk Eat Turkey on Thanksgiving ✎ *Daniel M. Berry* 6

Taking the Mystery Out of Mozart K Numbers ✎ *Ronald P. Cody & Jan R. Cody* 10

A Critique of Omar Khayyam's Economics ✎ *Eli Schwartz* 12

Linguistic Notes: The Pseudessive Mood ✎ *Eric Chevlen & Daniel Temianka* 13

The Quantitative "Facts" of Art History: Painting ✎ *John F. Moffitt* 14

Graphsmanship III: The High Energy Coloring Book ✎ *J. Lipkin* 17

Limerick Contest 20

BEHAVIOR

Unrecalled Falls ✎ *Jeff Brone* 23

Advice to Mice: A Commentary on the Reward and Punishment Game
✎ *Dominic Recaldin* 24

Be Nice to Bloomingdales ✎ *Walter J. Kent* 26

"Harzmountain-Liederkranz: Eine Neue Fundstelle der Grouchomarxkomplex"
✎ *Diane P. Gifford* 27

Computer-Generated Offspring ✎ *Frederick V. Malmstrom* 29

Emotion in the Rat Face ✎ A. *Daniel Yarmey* 31

Inner Turmoil ✎ *Naomi Fein* 33

Is Less Really More? Grazing the Logic of Bovine Collective Action ✎ *Paul W. Turner* 35

Prince of Petomane ✎ *Peter Lennon* 37

Error-Free Behavior: The Discovery of Orthobehavioralism
✎ *Walter B. Reid & Cameron K. McKinley* 39

CONSUMER STUDIES & ECONOMICS

Beyond Reaganomics:
Some Pseudo-serious Answers to Big Questions No One Is Asking
✎ *Tod Roberts* 43

Foamy Beer ✎ *Organization of Undetected Consumer Hazards* 45

On Shoe Buckles, Pulley Blocks, and Things ✎ *D. Zuck* 46

Brew-Blaster ⌁ *Benjamin L. Schwartz* 49

Comment: A Gratifying Deregulatory Initiative at the Confluence of Technology,
    Safety, and the Graphic Arts ⌁ *Michael B. Jennison & Kip Tourtellot* 50

The Art and Science of Preventative Neglect ⌁ *Denis R. Benjamin* 52

. . . And Cast the Surly Bonds of Earth Asunder . . . Sometimes ⌁ *R. R. Jeffels* 54

A Visceral Approach to Economic Policy: Lessons from the Laugher (sic) Curve
    ⌁ *Paul E. Greenberg & James A. Haley* 57

On Cancer-Causing Agents ⌁ *Organization of Undetected Consumer Hazards* 59

ENVIRONMENT

National Geographic: Doomsday Machine Revisited ⌁ *Victor Milstein* 63

House Plants and How to Stop Them ⌁ *Calvin Tomkins* 65

Futterman Scale of Sunrises ⌁ *David K. Lynch* 67

The Historical Novel and Its Value in Trees ⌁ *Scientific American* 68

Cooking with Potential Energy ⌁ *R. C. Gimmi & Gloria J. Browne* 69

Meteorological Determinants of Electoral Contests ⌁ *J. Randolph Block* 71

Patterns of Distribution and Frequency in the Coca-Cola Bottle
    ⌁ *David T. Bell, Forrest L. Johnson, Stanley K. Sipp, & Stephen G. Pallardy* 72

Environmental Pollutants and Prey Density Effects May Induce Suboptimal
    Foraging Behavior in Man-Eating Space Aliens
    ⌁ *Michael W. Hart & D. Spencer Adams* 73

European Geography Revised (by the Department of State) ⌁ *Sergey M. Shevchenko* 75

A Refutation of the Proof That Heaven Is Hotter Than Hell ⌁ *Tim Healey* 76

Magnetically Aligning Your Garden ⌁ *Jim Ballard* .78

LAW

Service of Process in Merry Old England ⌁ *David V. Stivison* 83

The Literature of Medieval European Law in a Nutshell ⌁ *T. G. I. F. Kearley* 84

Of Civil Leghts ⌁ *Saadyah Maximon* 86

Legal Reasoning—A New Tool for the Hard Sciences ⌁ *Barry Blyveis & Debbie Blyveis* 88

The Envelope Please ⌁ *David V. Stivison* 91

Special Deterrence, the Death Penalty, and Crime ⌁ *Martin D. Schwartz* 93

The Course of True Time in Albany Never Did Run Smooth ⌁ *James M. Rose* 95

MATHEMATICS

The Large-Cake Cutting Problem ⌁ *D. R. Olander* 99

Assignment of Fault in Complex Systems: The Calculation of Blame ⌁ *R. J. Halbert* 102

The Rational Number Shortage ⌁ *Robert K. Bender* 104

A Theory of 4 Physical Dimensions ⌁ *Jordan Levenson* 105

A Graph Theorist Looks at Peripheral Canals ⌁ *Phyllis Zweig* 107

On Some Little Known Results of Real Analysis ✎ *Michael Gering* 109
Countdown to Linkage: A Numerical Analysis of the Gulf War ✎ *Ronald R. Stockton* 110
The Re-emergence of Tautologies ✎ *Paul E. Greenberg* 112
An Investigation into the Time-Keeping Accuracy of Stopped Clocks ✎ *T. A. Mielke* 114
The Department of Parking and Alternate Reality ✎ *Jeff Rasmussen* 115

MEDICINE

Siamese Twinning in Gummy Bears ✎ *C. Robert Campbell* 119
A Dictionary of Pharmaceutical Research: Comments and Excerpts, Continued
   ✎ *Robert L. Iles* 120
Milestones in Medical Education: Selecting the Correct Medical Profession
   ✎ *David H. Gutmann* 122
How We Die ✎ *Francis Levy* 124
The Short-Pants Syndrome: Preliminary Clinical Findings of "Trousers Disease"
   ✎ *Richard L. Holloway* 126
Annals of Emergency Medicine: Public Area ✎ *Francis Sullivan* 127
Occasional Notes: Cost Containment by a Naval Armada
   ✎ *James V. Maloney Jr. & Keith Reemtsma* 128
All of Ob-Gyn ✎ *Alfred J. Padilla* 130
To Marrow and to Marrow and to Marrow . . . North American Adventures in
   Postgraduate Haematology ✎ *David Orchard* 131
On Hirsutism in a Doll Population
   ✎ *A. Nicole Scofield, Amanda K. Scofield, & R. Hal Scofield* 133
Milestones in Modern Medical Education: The Ultimate Synthesis
   ✎ *David H. Gutmann* 135

PHILOSOPHY & THOUGHT

A Small Thought ✎ *Richard Lilienthal* 139
Being a Short Excursus into the Origin of Western Philosophy, from the Time
   of the Greeks until the Time of the Greeks Some Two and One-Half Centuries Later
   ✎ *Howard Zaharoff* 140
The New Science of Quantum Semantics ✎ *Roman Laskowski* 143
Time for Divine Intervention ✎ *Leonard X. Finegold* 145
An Investigation of Hassell's Modified Maxim: Hard Work Never Hurt Anyone,
   But Then Neither Did a Whole Lot of Good Rest ✎ *Pamela Cochrane Tisdale* 146
Artificial Stupidity: An Introduction ✎ *Wallace Marshall* 148
Webbèd Footnotes: The Duck in Contemporary Western Thought ✎ *Philip N. Lawton Jr.* .150
Musings of an Aging "Scientist" ✎ *Russele de Waard* 153
Management Interaction: The Pedagogy of Group Process in Middle Management—
   A Xenophobic View of THE Meeting ✎ *William J. Tobin* 154

PHYSICS

Physics Non-Department First to Photograph New Element ∽ *Ellin Beltz* 159

Static Electricity ∽ *Richard L. Sutton Jr.* 161

Ineffective Lagrangians and the Big Ba(n)g ∽ *Harry J. Lipkin* 162

The Short-Lived Phenomenon of the Piezo-Photic Effect ∽ *Bobby Matherne* 164

The Feline Moment: Phenomenon Notes ∽ *R. J. Allen* 165

Forming a Simple Quad Latch ∽ *Bill Sacks* 169

The Theft Hypothesis ∽ *Nathaniel S. Hellerstein* 170

Invisibility: Theory and Practice ∽ *Jordan Levenson* 171

The Return of Maxwell's Demon? ∽ *Ron Birkhahn* 173

The Fly as an Aeronautic Force ∽ *Tim M. Sharon & Richard D. Brewer* 175

SCIENTIFIC METHOD

Irreproducible Results—A World Record Claimed ∽ *Ted Gerrard* 179

Saga of a New Hormone ∽ *Norman Applezweig* 182

The Noble Art ∽ *R. Keith Hanson* 183

Experimental Approaches to the Date of Origin of Koopmans' Theorem
   ∽ *Wanda A. St. Cyr, L.N. Domelsmith, & K. N. Houk* 185

Radiocarbon Dating: A Bootstrapping Fallacy ∽ *D. J. Huntley* 187

Common Sense Adjustments of Stellar Parallaxes ∽ *Jan Paul Dabrowski* 189

Jost Joshin'! Or, Application of a New Psychometric Method to an Old Tried and Untrue
   Experimental Design to Improve the Validity of a Tailor-Made Scoring Key
   ∽ *Warren S. Blumenfeld & William L. Godbey* 190

Significantly Entitled ∽ *Stephen Kaufman* 193

Double-Blind Crossover: A Metaphorical Parable ∽ *Nathaniel Haynes* 194

SOCIOLOGY

Belle's Constant ∽ *D. McIvor & Oslen Belle* 197

Psychotics for Reagan: New Hope for the Republican Party ∽ *Laurence B. Guttmacher* . . .199

Non Relatives ∽ *Kenneth Kaye* 201

Hope It's Fresh: The Armadillo and Late-Pleistocene Hunters ∽ *Richard L. Stromberg* . . .203

Notes on the Sociobiology Fracas ∽ *David Weinberger* 205

On the Incidence of Contra-Stripe Ties in the Transportation Consulting Industry
   ∽ *Diane Kravif* 207

Food As a State System ∽ *A. M. Ruder & C. T. Ruder* 208

Heggie's Objection to the Peter Principle ∽ *Jack Heggie* 210

A Social Science Experiment Designed to Assess the Effect of Degrees
   of Acculturation upon Musical Oicotypification ∽ *Keith Cunningham* 213

Preface

The *Journal of Irreproducible Results* was established as a publication in 1956. Although the subscribers at that time primarily were members of the scientific community, the *Journal* soon established a broad format of general interest to those who might enjoy satire and humor. Articles are submitted from countries throughout the world and are reviewed by an editorial board of distinguished members of over forty different professions.

The broad expanse of business, government, and academic interests that contribute to the *Journal* merely emphasizes the fact that no phase of endeavor is immune from being flawed with "irreproducible results." How else could one explain such ignoble pursuits as the complex engineering required to fabricate a strapless evening gown; the effect of playing gentle music on a farm to influence the rate of growth of a cornfield; housing rats in cages with tennis balls as a model to study infidelity in man; the inevitability of the U.S. East and West Coasts sinking into the sea unless people desist from accumulating vast hoards of *National Geographic* magazine; and numerous other observations that have been generously funded with tax money. The observations of *Discover* magazines that "the *Journal of Irreproducible Results* is the funniest thing to happen to science since Archimedes ran naked through the streets of Syracuse" has been enhanced by the remarks of Senator Proxmire who said "The *Journal of Irreproducible Results* is the funniest thing he has read since seeing the president's budget message to Congress."

—GHS

ARTS
&
LANGUAGE

Romantism in Pathology *

Ray Past

Dear Brother Wally:

A copy of your recently published piece *"The Histologic Demonstration of Iron in Osseous Tissue"* has fallen into my hands, and I know you will both understand and approve if I exercise an older brother's prerogative and offer you a few constructive thoughts on it.

First of all, lest you think some of my remarks overly critical, let me hasten to say that generally speaking, yours is a fine piece of work. You have a good idea and you carry it through from its beginning to its logical conclusion, the death of the principal characters and their contribution to our way of life. So if some of my observations seem to you a little severe, let me ask you to think them over in the

---

* Reprinted From *The American Journal of Pathology*

spirit in which they were offered. You will, I am sure, see that they are sound and will agree that they could go far toward getting you published in a periodical of wider and livelier circulation than *American Journal of Pathology* which is, let's face it, somewhat stodgy.

As a general suggestion I recommend that you lighten your style. Not that it doesn't have its bright spots. Referring to the demise of the rats as a "sacrifice" is masterfully delicate word handling. But all too often you come up with something like this, which I select at random:

> "Since iron was incorporated at the epiphysis and also at the periosteal surface, it may be said that iron participated in both endochondral and membranous types of bone formation."

Now, I ask you, who's going to read stuff like this? Practically nobody, that's who. If you keep on writing in this way, your whole audience will be reduced to a handful of MD's. I'm really sorry to have to say this, but your addiction to multisyllable, obscure words is almost pathological. You'll have to conquer it.

For example, consider your title. Since your basic plot deals with iron in bones you would of course want the title to reflect it. The one you have selected does that, but what a pale reflection! Also, it's too long. What you want is something short, with a snap to it: **"THE IRON BACKBONE;"** **"SPINES OF STEEL."** I don't offer these as real titles but as ideas, suggestions of the direction your thinking ought to take. At least they have some life. **"The Histologic Demonstration of Iron in Osseous Tissue"** indeed!

Now, I mentioned plot above. Generally, as I say, yours is good. But you overlook the value inherent in suspense. As far as one can tell, all the characters in your piece — that is, the rats — make the same sacrifice with the same degree of willingness and with the same success. Wouldn't it obviously be better if rat after rat failed — some of them chickening out, some flunking their physicals, some meeting some horrible premature end — and then of that crisis one rat comes through? Or you have two rats triumphant, one of each sex. There are any number of possibilities really. But this monotonous succession of uniformly successful rats that you have, why, it takes all the interest out of it. Where's the sense of victory? There isn't any. Where the accomplishment is too easy there is little virtue in it.

As for character development, I regret that you've shown no imagination whatsoever. Don't you see that you can't get your reader interested in some nameless, impersonal, vaguely realized rat? The harm isn't that the main character is a rat. That's OK. Animal stuff has gone over big for centuries. Look at Aesop. No, what's wrong is that you haven't give your rats any personality! The simplest thing in the world would be to give them names at least. Maybe your main rat could be "Charlie." And to give it a little sex angle he could have a girlfriend, "Edith." (If you decide later to aim at the *Saturday Evening Post* kind of market, the names could easily be changed to Derek and Karen.) Give them some lines to speak; don't just be jerking them around like puppets; let their natures reveal them. Thus Charlie (Derek) could speculate darkly on the sacrifice he sees casting a dreadful cloud over the future. And Edith (Karen) fearfully pleads with him, not to throw himself away, as she sees it:

"Oh, Charlie (Derek) darling, why must it be <u>you</u>? Oh, God! <u>God</u>! Let it be some other rat's husband!" etc.

And Old Charlie (Derek), dedicated to the cause of osseous tissue or whatever the hell all the foofaraw's about, gently but firmly disengages himself from her embrace and explains why he has to do it. ("Louie failed. Jim failed. Even Jarvis failed. Don't you see, dear? The whole American Association of Pathologists and Bacteriologists is counting on <u>me</u>. I'm the only one left!") This could be moving. It could have real punch. You might even bring in some little ratlets. Maybe Edith (Karen) could be preggie. This could be tremendous. Will it be a boy or a girl? Will it be six of each? Is Charlie (Derek) to die (i.e. sacrifice himself) without even seeing their furry little faces, without ever knowing how many of which he got from whom? (Edith? Charlotte? Lucille?)

Do you see? I don't mean to push this too hard, but don't you see? How flat your anonymous rats are against Charlie (Derek) and Edith (Karen). It hurts me to see yours so insipid when it would be so easy to inject a little life into them.

Finally, boy, you ought to get yourself a new illustrator. Nine cuts for a six page story is pretty lavish illustration, I'll admit — but frankly it would be better to have no art at all than what you have. Consider the dramatic situations your artist overlooks! Of course I don't mean he should reveal the climax, pulling the plug on the plot — I hate that kind of thing as much as you do — but heavens, with all the drama you have, what with the noble rat's devotion to duty, the love angle, the heartbreaking failure of all the other rats - with all this, surely he could get something better than "At one week there is an iron-positive "line' beneath the periosteum of the cortical diaphysis.x 100." This is hardly worth doing. In fact, what the hell is it? You might as well have your stuff illustrated by Jackson Pollock or some of those guys. Contrast this with a drawing, probably done in melancholy shades of blue, of Charlie and Edith, hand in hand, ascending the seemingly endless steps toward the sacrificial altar, behind which a reddish tinge suggest the setting sun, symbolizing life's end. The redness would also hint at the horror of Charlie's deathblood and that all, y'know. You can get lousy with symbols here.

Charlie and Edith would be mostly in silhouette, but their ears and their tails bravely erect would indicate with what courage they confront the end. Another nice thing about this kind of illustration is that if *The American Journal of Pathology* is too cheap to use color it would be almost as effective in black and white.

I don't think it would be too corny to have Charlie's tiny rat soul ascending into heaven, like little Eva on wires, and perhaps Edith waving a tear-drenched handkerchief in her right forepaw, her left clutching a *Bible*.

I know that nowadays many would think that too sentimental, but a little sentimentality never hurt anybody in my judgment. Besides, if you're going to have this noble sacrifice, you might as well go all the way. Or did you intend for Edith to be a sacrifice too? In that case, maybe a couple of simple graves with a few bereaved rats moping around. I've got it! The graves could be marked with <u>iron</u> crosses! Wouldn't that subtly underscore your theme, though! Maybe "Iron Crosses" would even make a title, with the rich load of connotations the phrase has.

Anyhow, you have to jack up that illustrator. I wouldn't pay him a dime for what he's already done.

I hope when you've slept on these few points I've raised you'll accept them in the proper manner. Remember that I wouldn't take the time or trouble to offer criticism at all if I didn't think your stuff basically good. It just needs a little jazzing up if all.

Above all don't get discouraged. Just keep working. Work is what makes a writer. That and a few gimmicks. Don't hesitate to send me your next piece for a critique. I'll be glad to offer you any suggestions I can. It would be helpful if you'd send it before publication rather than after. And send it directly to me. Don't rely on my accidentally stumbling across it as I did this one. God, you might as well have buried it! Oh, one more thing. Don't count too much on the editor of *The American Journal of Pathology*.

How To Make Your Way Through Almost Anything[1]

a simple mechanical guide

Although it may have gone unnoticed by all except a few curmudgeonly old school teachers and some cranky exnewspapermen, the English language is in large extent being replaced by jargon.

DIFFERENCES EXPLORED

Jargon is not slang. Slang is sometimes witty. It is also usually understandable, within the context that it is delivered.

A logger who lays down his chain saw and picks up an axe is understood when he announces that he is about to operate on the tree by the Armstrong Method. So is the man on the tide flats who calls his shovel a Clam Gun or the mechanic who drops his wrench, grabs a ball-peen hammer and announces that he is going to use his Persuader to Christianize a piece of machinery.

PUT-DOWN FOR THE GREAT UNWASHED

Slang is used for amusement. Jargon is used for confusion. Jargon words are heavy and ponderous. They are presented as the language of an elite.

Unlike slang, jargon is considered to be much too good for the common people. It is the code of exclusive classes whose members use it to communicate with one another while politely putting down the unwashed masses who cannot understand the words.

Having observed the growth of jargon as a replacement for English during most of my lifetime, I confess that even today I hesitate to suggest which class of society relies most heavily upon it.

THE FOUNTAINHEADS

Armies make extensive use of jargon. (In army jargon, a target is not a target. It is a Pre-selected Impact Area). Jargon almost always takes longer to write than English, for which reason it is used by people to whom time and money are of little consequence.

Government bureaucracies dispense jargon in fountains.

Academics, particularly those in economics or sociology, emit it in geysers and baptize one another in the thundering torrents.

Businessmen and unionists are awed by the stuff and frequently hire people to write it for them under their own names, so that they may be confused by their own language instead of somebody else's.

FORMULA PROVIDED

Might I therefore put forward the suggestion that the cause of simple, Churchillian English has long since been lost and that those who love the language as a means of communication should accept their defeat gracefully and learn the jargon.

This is the purpose of this column.

Here is the Handy Guide to Jargon. A simple formula. A child could use it. Many do.

Please clip and save the following columns of words. The key to their use is provided at the bottom of the column.

HANDY GUIDE TO JARGON

0. integrated	0. management	0. options
1. total	1. organizational	1. flexibility
2. systematized	2. monitored	2. capability
3. parallel	3. reciprocal	3. mobility
4. functional	4. digital	4. programming
5. responsive	5. logistical	5. concept
6. optional	6. transitional	6. time-phase
7. synchronized	7. incremental	7. projection
8. compatible	8. third-generation	8. hardware
9. balanced	9. policy	9. contingency

To use the Handy guide to Jargon, it is not necessary to have any thought whatever nor any understanding of the words. Just think of a three digit number. Let's say 913. Read across the columns. 'Balanced organizational mobility.' Pretty impressive, wouldn't you say?

Drop that into any letter, any speech, and your words will have the sonorous tone of authority.

Try 268: systematized transitional hardware, and 074: integrated incremental programming.

With the Handy Guide to Jargon, any Canadian who can write three figures on a piece of paper is equipped to deal with the highest mandarins of government, business, science, the arts or the radical left. In fact, you can cope with anybody. They won't understand what you're saying, but they will recognize you to be an intellectual and social equal.

---

[1]This article is a copy of a column in the Williams Lake Tribune written by Paul St. Pierre, M. P. He in turn lifted the guide from an unsigned photocopy circulated among the inmates of Parliament Hill. He later learned the originator is Betty H. Zisk of the Western Political Quarterly. To her, our thanks; to him, our thanks along with the hope that the guide will travel far and wide.

Why U.S. Folk Eat Turkey On Thanksgiving

Daniel M. Berry
Technion, Haifa 32000, Israel

This paper attempts to determine the origin of the U.S. custom of eating turkey on Thanksgiving day from manuscripts that were found in an archaeological excavation near Salem, Massachusetts.

Introduction

One question that has plagued U.S. Thanksgiving day celebrants for years is why turkey is eaten in the traditional Thanksgiving day meal. This author has managed, with a great deal of difficulty and personal expense, to obtain an old Hebrew manuscript that was found in a recent classified[1] archaeological excavation near Salem Massachussets. A bit of historical and Hebrew linguistic analysis applied to this manuscript has finally answered the plaguing question. This answer is given following descriptions of the background leading to the discovery and of the analyses.

Holidays and Food

On a holiday, it is quite traditional to eat foods that remind us of the purpose of the holiday. For example, on Passover (פסח), Jews eat matza (מצה) to remind them that the Hebrews left Egypt so hurriedly that they did not have time to let the dough rise to make bread. The question naturally arises, "Why does one eat turkey on the U.S. Thanksgiving?". Indeed, part of the religious service, called the *Seder* (סדר), that is read before the festive meal on the first night of Passover, consists of the youngest at the table asking the *four questions*, which ask why matza and other special foods are eaten on Passover.

International Bird

However, before getting into this question, let us observe something about the bird itself. The name of the bird is very international, despite the fact that the bird is truly native to North America; its name seems to be the name of another country in a lot of languages.

1. English: *Turkey*[2]
2. Portuguese: *Peru*
3. French: *Dinde* (from D'Inde, literally "from India")
4. Hebrew: *Tarngol Hodu* (תרנגול הודו, literally "Indian fowl")
5. Arabic: *Deek Rumi* (ديك رومي, literally "Roman or Romanian fowl")
6. Russian: *Indyuska* (Индюшка), literally "from India"
7. Turkish: *Hindi,* literally "Hindi" a language spoken in India
8. Hindi: *Peru Pakshi*, literally "peru bird", where it is believed that the word "peru" is the same as in Portuguese.[3]

Perhaps the reader can supply other examples in languages not known to the author.[4]

NOTES:

[1] Therefore, there are no papers about the dig that I can cite, and security laws prohibit me from mentioning the archaeologists by name. Even the reason for classification is classified.

[2] According to *Webster's Ninth New Collegiate Dictionary*, published by Merriam-Webster in 1989, the origin of the English word "turkey" is from confusion with the Guinea fowl, supposed to be imported from Turkish territory.

[3] The evidence that "Peru" has a Portuguese origin comes from the fact that the Portuguese explorer Vasco da Gama is considered to have discovered India for the West and Portugal colonized India before the French and British did. It seems reasonable to assume that the bird was introduced into India by the Portuguese and hence was called "peru pakshi" by the local folk as their rendition of what the Portuguese were calling it.

Since so many languages name the bird after India, it was interesting to determine what the bird is called in India. Each person I asked gave me a different answer. Besides the answer cited above, one Hindi speaker, Malini Kanth, a software consultant at Atlantic Duncans International, said that in Hindi, turkey is called "shuturmurg". "Murg" means "chicken", but it is not known what "shutur" means. A related word "shuta" means "little" but that does not sound right given the relative sizes of turkey and other fowl. Harsh Varma, from Bear Steams & Co., a native speaker of Hindi, pointed out that in India there is a cousin of the turkey called the "Lalsar" (literally "red head"), and many Indians use that term for the turkey as well. Rivka Best, a Hindi scholar, points out that the reason for the variety of names is the rich diversity of languages and dialects in India. She observes that English serves as a lingua franca to bridge this linguistic diversity, and offered that most Indians call the bird by the English word "turkey" since the bird is not native to India.

MASSACHUSETTS

Archaeological Excavations

In excavations near Salem, Massachusetts, an old Hebrew manuscript was found that sheds some light on why one eats turkey on Thanksgiving. This manuscript was titled *Haggada Shel Hodaya*[5] (הגדה של הודיה, literally "Telling of Thanksgiving"), reminiscent of the book used during the Passover *Seder* titled *Haggada Shel Pesach* (הגדה של פסח, literally "Telling of Passover"). It prescribes that someone at the table ask why turkey is eaten at the festive meal, it gives the story of thanksgiving that is familiar to every child in the U.S. today, and then suggests eating a festive meal containing at least turkey. It, unfortunately, does not really give a direct answer to the *why* question, leaving the reader to figure the answer out from the story.

It is clearly not surprising that a manuscript dealing with the origins of Thanksgiving was found near Salem, Massachusetts. However, it may be surprising that a *Hebrew* manuscript was found near Salem, Massachusetts. It should not be; the influence of the old testament, written in Hebrew, on the pilgrims and their descendants in Massachusetts is well known. Just look at the maps of Israel and Massachusetts. The Massachusetts cities of Salem, Rehoboth, and Hebronville are clearly named after the ancient Israeli cities of Jerusalem (ירושלים), Rehobot (רחובות) and Hebron (חברון).

Hebrew in the U.S.A.

Moreover, Benjamin Franklin once proposed that Hebrew be the national language of the nascent U.S.A. After all, why keep English if the U.S.A. is breaking away from England? Franklin felt that every educated person should be able to read the Old Testament of the Bible in the original language. Moreover, Hebrew was a required course at Harvard and Yale. It went so far that Hebrew is in the seal of Yale, *Urim v'Tumim* (ארים ותמים).

Can the reader imagine what would be today and the future if Benjamin Franklin had his way?

- Everyone would be speaking Hebrew in the U.S.A.

- Hebrew would be the international language of diplomacy, science, technology, commerce, etc.

- Everyone in the world would call a computer *machshev* (מחשב).

- In the 23rd and 24th centuries, the standard language of the United Federation of Planets would be Hebrew; Humans, Vulcans, Klingons, and Romulans would all be speaking Hebrew!

ISRAEL

NOTES:

4 Please send any examples to the author at dberry@cs.technicion.ac.il on the Internet.

5 This document is not to be confused with *Mishlei Hodaya* (משלי הודיה, literally "Psalms of Thanksgiving)", which are songs of more general thanksgiving, found in Qumrun. It is clear, however, that the Hebrew name of the holiday, *Chag Hahodaya* (חג החודיה, literally "holiday of the-thanksgiving") is derived from this ancient name of these psalms.

Key Discovery

Analysis of the manuscript showed that the pilgrims evidently knew that the Hebrew word *hodu* (הודו) means both:

- thank (plural imperative)
- India

The other name for turkey in those days was *Indian chicken* because Columbus thought he was in India when he saw turkeys for the first time! Indeed, in modern Hebrew, the phrase for turkey is precisely *tarngol hodu* (תרנגול הודו, literally "Indian fowl or chicken),[6] and this is often shortened to simply *hodu* (הודו), especially in contexts in which it is known that one is speaking about a fowl to be eaten. What better way to have the holiday dinner remind people to give thanks!

An Old Quotation

The reader's curiosity may be demanding to know precisely what was found in the *Haggada Shel Hodayah* manuscript? The manuscript contained a very curious wish for the holiday that alerted us to the above conclusion, and it clarified the origin of a Thanksgiving day greeting that is given to this very day. The wish is quoted below with a phrase by phrase transliteration and translation given below. Do notice the play on the word hodu (הודו), which means both "thank" and "India".

בחג ההודיה:
הודו שאתם לא תרנגול החודו

בחג	ההודיה:
b'chag	ha-hodaya:
On-holiday-of	the-Thanksgiving:

הודו	שאתם	לא
HODU	she-atem	lo
Give-thanks	that-you	are-not

תרנגול	החודו
tarngol	ha-HODU.
fowl	the-indian.
	the turkey,

or in more colloquial English, "On thanksgiving, give thanks that *you* are not the turkey!"

So now, the origin of eating turkey on Thanksgiving day is clear.

More Haggada Details

There was still more in the *Haggada Shel Hodaya* manuscript. The *Haggada* also specifies a number of thanksgiving prayers after the meal and ends with a single sentence that is reminiscent of the last sentence that is said after the Passover meal, which is aimed mainly at Jews in the diaspora, *L'shana habaa b'irushalayim* (לשנה הבאה בירושלים, literally "Next year in Jerusalem"). The last sentence of the *Haggada Shel Hodaya* is *l'shana habaa b'shalayim* (בשלים לשנה הבאט, literally "Next year in Salem").

Evidently, those planning the Thanksgiving holiday celebration anticipated a future diaspora of U.S. citizens, such as this author! For some reason, yet to be discerned, this prayer has fallen into disuse along with most of the rest of the *Haggada Shel Hodaya*.

Conclusion

This paper has examined an old Hebrew manuscript found in an archeological excavation near Salem, Massachusetts, that answers the age-old question of why one eats turkey on the U.S. thanksgiving holiday. Besides answering this question, the manuscript clarified the origin of a greeting given to this day and gave another prayer that is not said today, despite its intention to be said today.

Bon Apétit, (בתאבון)

Acknowledgements

The author thanks the archaeologists who performed the excavations that yielded the manuscript discussed in this paper. As mentioned, the dig was classified and security laws prevent me from mentioning the names of the people involved. The author also thanks Rivka Best, Prof. Zeki Berk, from Food Engineering at the Technion, Prof. Nachum Dershowitz, from Com-

---

NOTES:

6   One astute reader of an earlier draft of this paper asked why modern Israeli Hebrew adopted Columbus's terminology since it is known today that Columbus was *not* in India, but was rather in America, i.e., why is not the Hebrew name for turkey the equivalent of "American fowl"? Perhaps it has to do with the well-known fact that Columbus was Jewish and was perhaps on a voyage to find a new home land for the Jews being kicked out of Spain in the 1492 Inquisition. Modern Israel wished to honor this early Zionist by keeping his terminology.

puter Science at the University of Illinois at Urbana, Anela Apollos, Dr. Dorab Patel from Twin Sun, Prof. Azaria Paz, from Computer Science at the Technion, Prof. Peter Wegner, from Computer Science at Brown University, and Medha Yodh, an Indian and a dance instructor formerly associated with and teaching at the Department of Dance at the University of California at Los Angeles, for their invaluable assistance in analyzing the manuscript and Prof. Daniel Jackson, from Computer Science at Carnegie Mellon University and Prof. Dick Kemmerer, from Computer Science at the University of California at Santa Barbara for their comments on an earlier draft of this paper.

From The United States Department Of Agriculture:

CROP FAILURE

If a planted crop fails and you are unable to replant by the end planting date, you should file for failed acreage credit.

Consequently, if your chicken crop fails due to disease and you are unable to start up again as a result of having dead chickens, you should file for a failed chicken credit.

Also, if your hogs contract a disease and die before you are able to go to market, you should file for a failed hog credit.

Taking The Mystery Out Of Mozart K Numbers

LA MUSIQUE, by George Braque.

If you have often wanted to convert easily from Mozart K (Koechel) numbers to conventional numbering of Mozart Symphonies or Piano Concerti, then-by all means-take this article and burn it. If you would like a little fun, read on!

Ronald P. Cody
University of Medicine and Dentistry of New Jersey
Rutgers Medical School

Jan R. Cody
Blanche and Irving Laurie Music Library
Rutgers, the State University of New Jersey

Have you ever listened to a Mozart Piano Concerto or Symphony on the radio and tried to guess the number, only to have the announcer identify the music as Mozart Piano Concerto in d minor, K466? Now, I don't know about you, but I haven't yet memorized all the Mozart Piano Concerto and Symphony K numbers and their commonly accepted enumeration. I suppose that announcing Mozart's Piano Concrto number 20 in d minor does not carry with it sufficient snob appeal. I'm sure that purists will claim that the K numbers will avoid any confusion that may result from ambigious numbering systems. But, don't you know what I'm talking about when I say, "Mozart Piano Concerto number 20 in d minor?"

Since we will probably not be able to convert radio announcers to our way of thinking, we need to apply a modicum of modern mathematics to the problem. A simple solution would be to carry around a piece of paper with a table of PC (piano concerto) numbers, symphony numbers, and their corresponding K numbers in one's wallet or pocketbook. Ah, but that takes up too much space and it clearly lacks that indefinable *je ne sais quoi*. (You could, alternatively, carry around your Groves which shows some scholarly instincts on your part but might be too fatiguing.)

Here is where modern statistics and high speed computers come to the rescue. We'll teach those announcers who can be snobs! Let us first investigate the relationship between the Mozart K numbers and the Mozart Piano Concerti. If we plot the K numbers on the x-axis and the PC numbers on the y-axis, we will obtain a plot like that in Figure 1.

Now we can attempt to find a regression line so that we can predict a PC number given a K number. Figure 1 shows such a line. Now, by using only a simple formula

$$PC \text{ number} = .05784K - 7.955673$$

we can predict the PC number given a K number. Even though the linear regression line is statistically significant (p = .0001), our prediction can be several PC numbers away from the true value. Well, let's see if we can improve the situation.

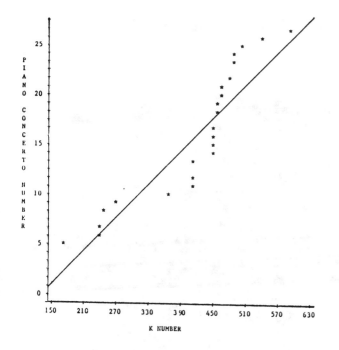

FIGURE 1.

With the wonders of modern computers, we can investigate non-linear curves to fit our data. A fairly good fit results from a 4th order polynomial solution.

Now all we need to remember is a single equation:

$$PC\ number = -121.195 + 1.656701K - .00765258K^2 + .00001285727K^3 - .0000000100378K^4$$

This isn't perfect, but it does a good job. This equation will never be more than 3 concerti off in the range of PC numbers from 5 to 27. Also, it will be within 2 numbers 95% of the time. (The adjusted multiple correlation coefficient is .9575 if that means anything to you.)

If you think this is impressive wait until you see the symphony results! Mozart was kind enough to be more linear (or Koechel was) with his symphonic output over his life. Why, with a mere 2nd order polynomial regression, we can achieve an adjusted multiple R^2 of .9705! We can be within 2 numbers from the correct symphony number 85% of the time. This equation is shown below:

$$Sym = .027465 + .157692K - .000159446K^2$$

So now you have a way of putting those snobbish radio announcers in their place. Just remember two simple equations, do some mental arithmetic, and arrive at a nearly perfect result. What could be simpler!

REAL JUSTIFICATION FOR TRAFFIC ACCIDENTS[1]

Thomas E. Gill
Davis, CA

Many people who experienced the misfortune of an automobile accident were asked to summarize exactly what happened to them in a few words on accident or insurance forms. The following quotes were taken from these forms. Published in the Toronto *Sun*, July 26, 1978.

The other car collided with mine without giving warning of its intentions.

A truck backed through the windshield into my wife's face.

The other guy was all over the road: I had to swerve a number of times before I hit him.

I had been shopping for plants all day, and was on my way home. As I reached the intersection, a hedge suddenly sprung up obscuring my vision. I did not see the other car.

I was sure the old fellow would never make it to the other side of the roadway, so I ran over him.

I saw the slow-moving, sad-faced old gentleman as he bounced off the hood of my automobile.

The cause of this accident was a little guy in a small car with a big mouth.

A Critique Of Omar Khayyam's Economics

Eli Schwartz
Bethlehem, PA

There has been a tendency for scholars of the history of economic thought to dismiss much of the earlier medieval writers as not being informed by a commercial society. (For example, see R.L. Heilbroner's The Worldly Philosophers Chapter II.[1]) But in fact, the usual dating of modern economic analysis as starting with Adam Smith and his immediate predecessors is largely the result of an ignorance of much of the earlier writings in the non-Western countries.

A case in point may be found in the works of Mr. Omar Khayyam, an eleventh century Persian mathematician and writer best known to us through the English translation of his commentaries by Edward Fitzgerald first published in 1859. Mr. Khayyam's quatrains purvey in general a hedonistic philosophy; the economic commentary is brief, trenchant, and highly sophisticated. Thus in Quatrain XII, line 3, we have "Ah, take the Cash and let the credit go." This maxim may be taken as the departure point for the modern concepts of liquidity preference and net risk avoidance.

To be fair, Mr. Khayyam does not always understand the full subtlety of the economic problem he poses. Thus in Quatrain XXI, he muses, "I often wonder what the Vintners buy, one half so precious as the goods they sell." Here he misses the point of diminishing marginal utility or, in modern terms, the change in the rate of the marginal substitution between available consumer goods. No matter how high the gross value of their wine, at some point, the vintners will wish to sell part of their supply to obtain other goods or services. In Walrasian terms, the wine sellers would find the utility of other goods rising relative to their own use utility.

This error is all the more surprising because in the earlier Quatrain XI, Mr. Khayyam offers a correct solution. He opines, "A loaf of bread beneath the bough, a flask of wine—and thou beside me singing in the wilderness; and the wilderness were paradise enow!" This is one of the earliest examples in the literature of a clear delineation of an optimum mix of goods within a budget constraint.

---

[1] Heilbroner, R,L., The Worldly Philosophers, 4th Edition, Simon & Schuster 1970.

LINGUISTIC NOTES: THE PSEUDESSIVE MOOD

Eric Chevlen, M.D.
Daniel Temianka, M.D.
Palos Verdes Estates, CA

Research in Mideastern paleolinguistics[1] has recently brought to light the existence of a special form of the subjunctive mood. This set of verb forms, the "pseudessive", was frequently used in Ugaritic and other ancient languages of the Levant*. But while the subjunctive mood expresses hypothetical or wishful ideas in general, the pseudessive is used more specifically to express *things that might have been true, were it not for facts or beliefs which have subsequently been found to be false.*

The pseudessive should not be confused with the *jussive,* employed for orders or commands, nor the *Jurassic,* which refers to dinosaurs. (The dinosaurs are examples of entire species that would still be true were it not for the ice age.)

As a convention in this discussion, the pseudessive form will be indicated by use of the notation § . For example, "Heshmeh § went to the marketplace § to buy some marshmallows, but § found that they § had been recalled by the health department." Note that all four verbs in the sentence are inflected in the pseudessive mood, since (1) the Akkadian Health Department had no authority concerning marshmallows,[2] and (2) there were neither health departments nor marshmallows in ancient Akkad. Or again, quoting the Phoenician *bon mot,* "Samyah § wants to go jogging, but Samyah's wife § has not washed the family jockstrap." This sentence is written in the pseudessive mood, of course, because Samyah is a feminine name.

In contradistinction to the subjunctive, which applies only to verbs, the pseudessive may also be applied to interjections. For example, if you go into the bathroom late one night to brush your teeth, but find that the lightbulb has burned out, your oath will take the form of the *expletive pseudessive* if you are both blind and edentulous.

The pseudessive may also be applied to queries. An associate recently asked us, " §Is it necessary for me to § understand your question in order to § give an inappropriate response?" (The answer was, of course, no.) This is termed the *interrogative pseudessive.*

We remember a television episode in which William Bendix was on vacation in Hawaii. It rained suddenly every time he went outdoors—*but there were no clouds in the sky!* He spent his entire holiday in the pseudessive mood. Many international travelers have had similar experiences. Consider the angry expressions used by tourists who find it impossible to purchase Ex-Lax in Mexico. That these comments are necessarily in the pseudessive mood is ironic testimony to the power and influence of foreign grammar.

One frequently encounters clumsy attempts to reintroduce the pseudessive into modern speech[3]—efforts stymied by the fact that it has never been used before in those languages. This produces such semantic treacheries as the modern German practice of forming very large words, e.g., Missverständetunangemessenantwort (the "inappropriate answer" cited above). Regrettably, the pseudessive mood has also found use in political rhetoric: Eldridge Cleaver once used it in a California Senate campaign when he said, "If elected, I'll §lower your taxes."

The pseudessive pervades the world of modern advertising too—for instance, the commercial wherein a housewife goes to her refrigerator to make a gourmet meal, only to find that her jar of Miracle Whip is empty; or the one in which a fancy bridge party would have been perfect but for the improperly managed odor of household cat dung.

Finally, the etymology of the term "pseudessive" is itself an example of pseudessive semantics: it would have been derived from the Greek root *pseudo* ("false") and the Latin *esse* ("to be"), were it not for the fact that it is actually a corruption of the Canaanitic phrase, *"Sod 'os sif,"* which means, "My orange cat has a gray hairball in its throat." As always, it loses in translation.

<The End (so to speak)>

---

*Not Oscar.
[1] Eco, Umberto, *Lost Wax Paleolinguistics: Theory and Practice.* Rome: Semiotics Press, 1987.
[2] Allegro, John, *The Sacred Mushroom and Glossolalia.* Henley-on-Thomas: Food of the World Press, 1979.
[3] Göpper, Felix, "Semitics and semantics—the influence of triliterate roots in post-hegelian philosophy," *J Amer Solipsist Assoc.* 34:358-367, 1961.

The Quantitative "Facts" Of Art History: Painting

John F. Moffitt
Las Cruces, NM

The "facts" resurrected below (at great, and probably pointless, effort on my part) represent the *measurable (quantifiable) attributes* of certain man-made objects that might, and very often are, called *"Art."* For purposes of defining what follows, this gravid term, "Art," signifies a material artifact thought up by the ever-fertile human mind, so producing a wholly cerebrated ("imaginary") object which is taken to be, even on this material plane, UNIQUE, one-of-a-kind: in short, IRREPRODUCIBLE! That notwithstanding, it is significant to note that (for the most part) in what follows little reference has been made here to subjective — thus unquantifiable and so unscientific — considerations of inherent "QUALITY," that is either of aesthetic motivations and/or cultural significance. Accordingly, the intrinsic value of such a labored compilation mainly resides in its sheer irrelevancy and jocular non-utility. If there is any positive purpose that might attach itself to this objectified (*aber gegen-wissenschaftliche*) project, this would be to stifle further proliferation of the reigning spiritual (*gesitige*) and/or mythic (*irrsinnliche*) perceptions of *"Art."*

Earliest Schematic Imagery

A number of truly ancient rock engravings ("petroglyphs") with colored patterns of circles, dots, lines, and arcs (made with ochre and hematite) have been found at the Malunkunanja II site in northern Australia. By thermoluminescence and other analytic methods, the human-made marks have been dated as being perhaps 50,000 years old. But the petroglyphic doodles, with some very similar but considerably *later* examples being found in North America, are not (at least, not yet) considered "ART" in the full-blown sense. As most experts now believe, the oldest known examples in Europe (vs. Australia) of apparent attempts at two-dimensional (semi-) representational "art" are dated in the Paleolithic ("Old Stone") period, perhaps beginning as far back as ca. 60,000 B.C. Some of the earliest discoveries appeared at La Ferrassie, near Les Eyzies, in the Perigord, France. These materials, rocks decorated with incised symbols and animal forms with black and red pigments, are ascribed to a period called the Aurignacian III, of ca. 25,000 B.C. (see below: "II. Sculpture. Oldest...").

Earliest Representational Paintings

Initially fragmentary evidence of Paelolithic imagery, as "cave art" — the first recorded human impulses towards what can be properly called "visual art" — first turned up in 1834 at Chaffaud, Vienne; unfortunately, the number of examples encountered at this French site which can (even now) be reasonably dated by stratigraphy is very limited. The first Paleolithic "painting gallery" to become widely publicized belongs to the cave of Altamira (Santander, Spain), first discovered by don Marcelino Santuaola in 1875. Other magnificent examples of extensive "mural-paintings" have since been found, for instance (as discovered in 1940), the perhaps surprisingly lively cycle of game-animals displayed in the famous cave at Lascaux (in the Dordogne, France). As has been argued by a few academic diehards, circumstantial paleo-zoological evidence (i.e., that the animals so depicted are presently and long since, extinct) suggest to them that the earliest, or most rudimentary and underlying examples of "paintings" found at Lascaux might be pre-Gravettian (or *pre*-pre-Cro-Magnon), i.e., possibly dating — umm, maybe NOT after all — even earlier than ca. 65,000 B.C.

Better informed opinion now however attributes this momentous "invention of painting," and that of music as well (as attested to by what appear to be flutes), to the inappropriately disparaged Cro-Magnon peoples. The mature period of the rupestrian (cave) art was between 13,000 and 10,000 B.C., but it did begin in a rudimentary fashion perhaps much earlier, possibly even 30,000 B.C. (or *maybe* even 50,000 years ago; see previous entry: "Earliest Schematic Imagery").

For reasons only to be guessed at, the illusionistic-zoomorphic cave-painting phenomenon was restricted to a limited region within Europe, one mostly facing the Atlantic: northern Spain and southwestern France for the most part. Perhaps significantly, this is essentially the same area now embracing the traditional frontiers of the truly ancient and completely autonomous Basque peoples, still having their very own, rampantly mysterious, language-group and genetic peculiarities. Are, in short, the present inhabitants of *Euskadi* neo-Cro-Magnons?

Largest "Old Master" Painting

This must be *Il Paradiso*, painted between 1587 and 1590 by Jacopo Robusti, alias Tintoretto (1518-94), and his son Domenico. As seen today on Wall "E" o f the Sala del Maggior Consiglio, in the Palazzo Ducale (Doge's Palace) in Venice, Italy, the work is 72.2 feet long, and 23 feet high, and contains more than 350 human figures. All in all, it is very well done.

Largest "Painting" Ever (at least at this date)

The largest (but certainly not the "best") "painting" ever known measured 72,437 square feet (after allowing for the schrinkage of the canvas). Unfortunately, its subject matter and ideological purposes were less than transcendental. Made up of brightly colored squares, upon which was superimposed an immense "Smiley Face," it was executed, in May 1990, by school children and older (if not more profound) art students

from Robb College, Armidale, New South Wales, Australia. In this instance (with some other examples following shortly), the real goal was scarcely "aesthetic"; instead, we may believe that the intention was wholly quantifiable. However rudimentary in thought or form, if this (or any other) artifact proves to be *measurably* "the biggest" (whatever), then it achieves instant fame: IT WILL THEN BE RECORDED IN THE *GUINNESS BOOK* OF RECORDS.

American Biggies (Destroyed)

Previously credited (under the rubric of "serious art") with having been the largest painting in the world, was a massive *Panorama of the Mississippi*, completed by John Banvard (1815-91) in 1846. Banvard's indefatigable composition showed the river scene for 1,200 miles in a gradually unfolding fluvial panorama and as depicted upon a continuous strip of canvas which was probably 5,000 feet long and 12 feet wide, thus with an accumulated gross area of more than 1.3 acres (60,000 square feet). Banvard's epic painting is believed to have been destroyed when the rolled canvas, stored in a barn at Cold Spring Harbor, Long Island, New York, caught fire shortly before Banvard's death on May 16, 1891 (thus perhaps precipitating Banvard's own, one-way trip across yet another river, the Lethe).

American Biggies (Extant):

The largest (if not "best") American painting now still in existence is probably *The Battle of Gettysburg*, completed in 1883, after 2 1/2 years of work, by Paul Phillippoteaux (France) and 16 assistants. It, too, was another American "panorama painting" but this one was immobile, i.e., did not unroll. Weighing six tons, Philippoteaux's painting (a proto-"stabile": see below) is 410 feet long, 70 feet high — mere 28,700 square feet, as compared to Banvard's epic effort. It depicts the climax of the Battle of Gettysburg in central Pennsylvania, as fought on July 3, 1863. In 1964, the painting was bought by Joe King of Winston-Salem, North Carolina (and one wonders if it is presently exhibited in Mr. King's living-room).

The instrinsic art historical significance attachable to this now-obsolete genre — the American "panorama-painting" — is typically ignored. Such panoramas were, in fact, once commonplace, particularly before the Civil War, and so they represent a once ubiquitous feature of the American *mental* landscape. Typically, they were presented to the general public in the context of a scrupulous visual encyclopedia of enlightening travel "fact." Then (as now), such ordered assemblages of "facts" were shaped (more or less consciously) by *myth*, mainly (then) in character either nationalistic ("Manifest Destiny") and/or religious (America as an *"Opus Dei"*). Whereas they were presented to eager consumers an "educational" experience postulated upon an exposition of documentary, specifically geological and geographical, scientific certitudes. In actual fact, their physical means of presentation shows their true function to have been simply populist *entertainment*. Then, as now, to be truly palatable in America, "education" must be coated with a thick but transient sauce of entertainment.

Typically, these more or less massive panoramas (as noted previously, Banvard's *Panorama of the Mississippi* was "the biggest" of all) were offered to public view at commercial theaters following vigorous advertising campaigns in the popular press. Seats were made available — that is, sold — at a box-office. For one such performance (in 1849, in Louisville, Kentucky) seating in the dress circle and parquet went for 50 cents, and the second tier of boxes for 25 cents; customers were advised that this nocturnal performance commenced at "8 1/2 precisely." The gradual unrolling of the painted panorama usually took several hours. The temporally extended, slowly unfolding, visual experience was provided with generous rest-stops at designated picturesque vistas and/or historically significant sites scattered along the way, and all the while the fictive travelogue was complemented, even sensuously enhanced, by more or less extemporaneous verbal commentary with pianoforte music accentuating the emotional rests and highpoints properly belonging to selected topographical-historical features. Typically, members of the audience brought opera glasses with them, so allowing for detailed, private and psychologically isolated, inspection of particularly interesting detailed bits belonging to the extended *paysage moralisé américain*.

The art historical results in late American culture arising from the panorama-painting phenomenon are (or should be) perfectly obvious. In the first place, here we see the actual physical foundations, as a kind of perceptual convention, leading to a well remarked native propensity for the oversized painting, obviously a physical-mental trait well ingrained within the national character long before the advent of the oversized canvases belonging to the so-called Abstract Expressionists. More fundamental is the procedural contribution of American panorama-painting to *the* quintessential — and so typically mechanized or *industrialized* — "American art-form," the (literally) *moving picture*. Like the "movies," the panorama-painting provided gradual, *communal and passively received, revelation,* so conveyed by means of a cumulative and extended, and above all kinetic, experience. In its most effective moments, the American panorama-painting was simultaneously intimate yet distant, presenting a congress of glittering disparate parts, a delirious compendium of exciting, provocative, and often exotic effects. This was a perceptual experience made up from so many, more or less instantaneous and isolated, mosaic-like fragments, and the total significance of each bit could not be thoroughly grasped until the entire sequence, qua psychological *montage*, was completed. Like the movies — *and late modernist entertainment in general* — in the end, the American panorama-painting-performance-piece-educational-experience represented disposable experience — and a literally disposable "art."

GRAPHSMANSHIP III THE HIGH ENERGY COLORING BOOK

H. J. LIPKIN

This is an experimental curve. Theory says there is no peak at point B. Color the Peak Red.

This is an experimental curve. Theory says there is a peak at point B. Color the Peak Grey.

This is an experimental curve. It is in complete disagreement with theory. Color the error bars BLACK. Make them bigger, BIGGER! BIGGER!

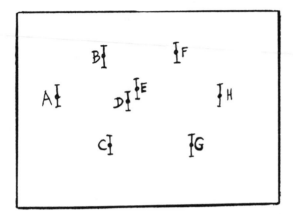

This is a Dalitz plot. Draw a map of the world on the plot. The points tell you where you may find Dalitz.

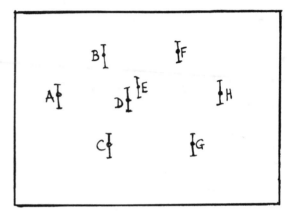

These are experimental points plotted as an idiot-gram. If you are an idiot, color them all colors of the rainbow. If you are not an idiot, do not color them. Just take an anti-histogram pill and go to bed.

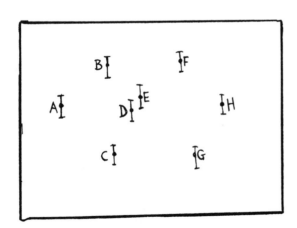

This is a spark chamber picture. An interaction at A produces three tracks, ABF, ACG, and ADEH. Draw in the tracks. Color them any colors you wish, and interpret the event.

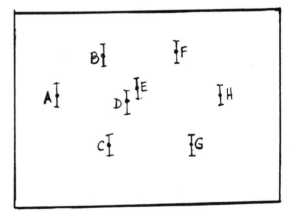

These are experimental points on a Feynman Diagram. Connect the points by appropriate solid, dashed and wavy lines. Color them in a gauge invariant way. Calculate the contribution of the diagram to all orders and disorders.

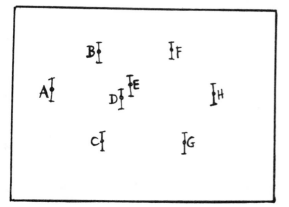

These points are experimental evidence for a new unitary symmetry octet. There is no time to color this picture. Send it to *Phys. Rev. Letters**, right away!

_____

*or New York Times

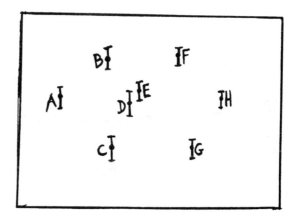

These are experimental points in the non-physical region of the complex angular momentum plane. Only Chew knows what they mean. If you are a Believer color them gold. If you are not a believer, put a cut from point A to infinity. Do the same for points B, C, D, E, F, G, and H. After you have cut the paper to pieces, throw it away.

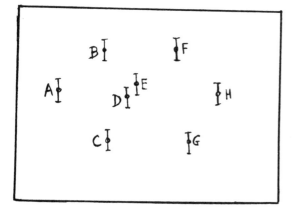

Can you find the Intermediate Boson in the picture?

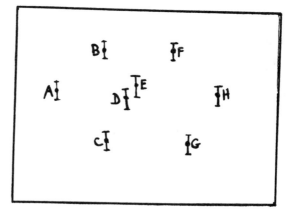

These are experimental points. The values are all finite. The theory gives infinite values. So the experiment is wrong. Do not color this page. Throw it away. Design an experiment to give the correct infinite value.

Limerick Contest

Twelve year ago the *Journal of Irreproducible Results* sponsored a limerick contest in which the last word of the limerick was to be "Irreproducible." Following are some the examples of limericks that we received.

We are now are responsoring this contest. Years ago the prizes consisted of a $1.37 and a lifetime subscription to the *Journal of Irreproducible Results*. Because of inflation, we will now be offering a grand prize of $1.86 and a life-time subscription to the *Journal Of Irreproducible Results* (our lifetime, not yours). Please submit all entries to J.I.R. - Limerick, Box 234, Chicago Heights, IL 60411.

Receipts of the limericks will not be acknowledged, but all entries submitted to a committee of our Editorial Board and the three winning entries will be published in a subsequent issue of the Journal.

The genus is clearly deducible
Horse and Ass are interseducible
And the offspring lives
But invariably gives
Results which are Irreproducible

D.B. Mac Lachlan

Conception is now found inducible
By in vitro detente in a crucible
But the act is maligned
Though the product's in kind
As the honeymoon's Irreproducible

Nancy Raymond

The act of Van Gogh was excusable
When he cut off his ear that was usable
For he had a belief
That he could find relief
If he got a new Irreproducible

Roger Brandt

Gold nuggets from paydirt are sluiceable
And chocolate not carob is mousse-able
A high quality thing
Has a certain true ring
Like your journal, that's Irreproducible

Stuart A. Copans

While pondering equations reducible,
A chemist knocked over a crucible.
This caused quite a flap,
For it spilled in his lap,
And rendered him Irreproducible

Edward P. Hughes

My entries were all inexcusable
None had meaning deducible
I tried and I tried
'til out loud I cried
Nothing rhymes with Irreproducible

Linda A. Hearn

BEHAVIOR

Unrecalled Falls

Jeff Brone
Annapolis, MD

On November 1, 1995, the Arkansas Journal of Medicine reported that one out of every five people does not remember having fallen down a flight of stairs. This article is on the heels of the reports from Darris Solvang, a noted hypnotherapist and meat inspector of Skyridge, WY, who has helped many of his patients recall long repressed episodes of falling down stairs. A disturbing trend, or a long overdue problem.

It's true. You may have fallen down a whole flight of stairs and not even remember it. Call it Selective Trauma Affective Internalized Repression Syndrome, or STAIRS for short, and it can affect anyone. Daniel Truesdale, an acute sufferer, was once rolled down 150 foam rubber stairs (for his own safety), and only could recall three of them (numbers 5, 74 and 108). There are several reasons why you might not remember such an encounter:

1. You're really, really preoccupied.

2. You're a senior citizen. Your memory might be failing, and selectively your brain remembers only vital information, like who didn't call you on your birthday, while forgetting things like falling and the like.

3. You have associated it with a childhood trauma and blocked it out. This one is usually most lucrative for the hypnotherapist.

Dr. Robert Narry, of the National Falling Down Institute in Darbyville, GA, makes the point that people should not be overly alarmed by this syndrome. There is every chance that you haven't fallen down stairs recently. He offered this simple advice in his latest symposium entitled "The Humpty Dumpty Syndrome." He urged us to ask ourselves these questions. A yes answer may mean that something is wrong:

Are people saying things like "Are you OK?" and "Nice tumble there, Wallenda" and "You clumsy imbecile"?

Do you have unexplained bruises, head pains and the urge to be "helped up"?

When you get to the bottom of some stairs, do you break into an uncontrollably joyful version of Barry Manilow's "Looks Like We Made It"?

When descending stairs, do people insist that you "go first"?

If you answered yes to any of these questions, you may have fallen down stairs recently. If so, there is a chance to bring back the memory and make peace with the stairs down which you fell. The institute has established a hotline; 1-800-555-I Think I Broke Something. Operators can suggest doctors and things. Call. There's nothing to be afraid of — except stairs. You clod.

Advice To Mice: A Commentary On The Reward and Punishment Game

Dominic Recaldin

There are all manner of opportunities for white mice today. When I was young, it was either straight into a petshop, or try to scratch a living off the corporation rubbish dump. Neither was exactly a bed of roses. Pet shops were doss-houses for down-and-outs—stray cats, stolen dogs, and so on. But they were a darn sight better than a rubbish dump. Wild albinos never stood a chance there. Every dump had its population of "pinkies." You'd see them begging by piles of old tin cans, shuffling off to spend whatever they could get on surgical spirit and orange juice.

Getting about in the day-time was purgatory on account of their eyes. And as for moving about at night, they were like searchlights in a blackout: the owls couldn't believe their luck. And then science came, and life changed almost overnight. After generations of persecution, white mice were suddenly "in." Scientific research changed us from being the most untouchable into the most hutchable animals in the history of Man.

The boom began, I suppose, with medical research. This is still a tremendous career outlet these days, but it is not without its attendant risks, of course. You pay your penny and take your choice. You could be lucky and be part of a skin-grafting team. Apart from finishing up like a harlequin quilt you come to no real harm. On the other hand, you may end up in toxicology tests at Porton Down. Even so, by following the age-old rule "Never Volunteer," you could stay there all your life and never have a day off sick. When they start to fumble around for

test animals' - just fade quietly away into a corner of the cage. The ones they can't catch they invariably leave as controls. Never rush or panic, as this will draw their attention. And above all, don't attack them: a cornered scientist can be vicious. If all else fails and they grab you anyway, pee on their hand.

I would like to say a word here about accommodation in research labs. By and large it is very good. The meals are regular and the food is excellent. There is

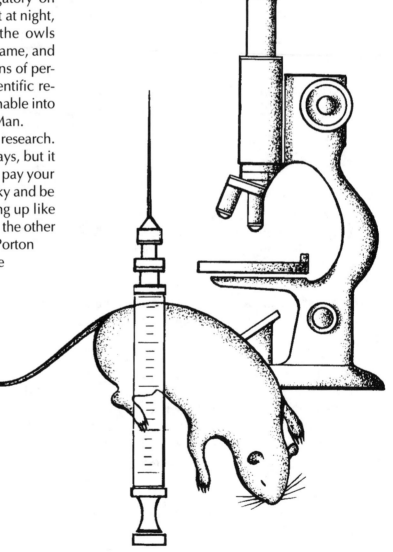

room for improvement in other directions, however. I wish they wouldn't persist in putting down sawdust. It gets all over your fur. You keep thinking you've got systemic dandruff. Newspaper would be better. None of your *Daily Sketch* rubbish though. Most of us prefer a heavy daily—*The Times* is favourite—especially if the crossword is on view. But for God's sake change the paper every day. Never mind the hygiene: what were the answers to yesterday's clues?

Although the level of treatment at senior research institutes is second to none, the conditions at the school laboratory level leave a great deal to be desired. Indeed, I have seen some of my toughest colleagues go to pieces on learning that they were to be posted to one particular secondary modern school in south-east London. The softening-up process in schools is pretty nasty but if you can get through that you may be adopted as the form pet, and there are worse ways of earning a living.

Their favourite trick is the bell-jar torture. In this "experiment," you are placed on a platform surrounded by water, and an inverted bell-jar is put over you, After a while, you find that the water level is rising and lapping around your paws. Whatever you do don't panic. Any undue exertion will only make the water rise faster. Just sit perfectly still and sweat it out. You'll find the water level slowly stops rising and ceases altogether after a while. When it does, they take you out. Their nerve always cracks before yours does.

The trendy thing is space research, but like everything else it has its ups and downs. I made only one trip myself and I can't say I enjoyed the feeling weightlessness overmuch. They forgot to strap me for a start. Every time I breathed out I jetted across the cage and bashed my head against the bars. I got taken short, too, before we reentered. That didn't make me any too popular with the rest of the crew, you can imagine.

I found my own metier in psychology. I run mazes and things. Psychologists are pleasant, simple-mind souls, and life is pretty good. Mind you, you need be a cut above the average with the old gray matter. They don't like dim animals doing intelligence work: it takes them far too long to get any results you see. They'd never use rabbits, for example. They're as thick as two planks. Naturally, it doesn't do to be too smart either. Most mazes are ineptly easy. It's all you can do sometimes not to nod off in the middle of a run, paralyzed with boredom. But you must appear to play the game and act as though the entire thing is straining the frontiers of your intelligence. You scratch their back and they'll scratch yours.

Reward-punishment games present a bit of a problem. You'd think psychologists would know better. I am not altogether unknown in the trade as a cheese gourmet. I like nothing better than a rich, ripe wedge of Stilton. And what do I get? That same old indestructible cube of New Zealand Cheddar, day after day. The first time I saw it I nearly had a blue fit. If that's the *reward*, I thought, what's the bloody punishment? Quite frankly, some mornings I prefer to press the wrong button on purpose. Anything is preferable to *that* pig's breakfast, even twelve volts up the hooter.

Reprinted with permission from *The New Scientist*.

M. C. Bourne Dept. Food Science, N.Y. Agric. Exp. Station. Geneva. N.Y.
SQUEEZE ENGINEERING
Washington Science Trends, 1967 18/8, 52 (May 22).

"The force exerted by the human hand in a food squeezing test is partly dependent upon the person making the test and partly on the softness of the food according to recently published research. Force distance curves were plotted for firm and flabby apples squeezed by a testing machine. The firm apples provided a fairly steep curve disclosing that it does not deform very much when it is squeezed. The flabby apple gave a curve with a much greater slope at first indicating deformation to a considerable extent. However, as the force continued to rise, the shape of the curve obtained from the flabby apple gradually approximated the shape obtained from the firm apple. Similar results were obtained with jumbo sized marshmallows. The studies led researchers to the conclusion that gently squeezing is a superior means of testing quality. However. whether firmness is a desirable or undesirable characteristic depends upon the food being squeezed."

BE NICE TO BLOOMINGDALES

Walter J. Kent
Wyckoff, NJ

If physicists are right, the ultimate state toward which the universe is heading will be one without form, pattern, hierarchy or differentiation. In a word: chaos.

But that is so far in the future that contemplating such a condition should hardly affect the price of a cup of coffee. However, it should influence our attitude toward organizations and individuals we encounter today. Consider the following:

Every effort contains degrees of order and disorder, known as the order/disorder ratio, abbreviated o:d.

An effort exerted by one person, for example a dentist working alone, is well under his control. It's to his best interest to waste as little time and energy as possible, and he may reach an o:d as high as 3:1, which means he's confused only one quarter of the time—a charitable assessment, considering the population at large.

Using 3:1 as an admittedly arbitrary and generous standard for a single individual effort, it has been our observation that the ratio decreases as the square of the number of persons involved. For instance, the shoemaker whose wife helps him in the shop has an o:d one forth as high as our dentist friend, or 3:4, which means he is confused six hours out of eight. When his two sons come in to help out, the o:d changes to 3:16, which means that in two eight hour days, the soles and heels go on correctly for only an hour and a half each day. But extend this to large organizations, like Bloomingdales or Blue Cross Blue Shield, with thousands of employees. The o:d then reaches numbers which drive my word processor bananas, expressing them with large negative exponents that I don't understand. Order for all practical purposes approaches zero. It becomes an extremely rare event, like a flight departing on schedule. It doesn't disappear completely because even Bloomingdales does occasionally get orders right and Blue Cross Blue Shield does pay a claim. This is because they have so many employees that even though each is working at 3^{-7}% efficiency, their sheer numbers get the work done.

This is not news to anyone who has dealt with a large organization. It is merely a cosmological explanation for a ubiquitous experience.

Realize then, that if the universe is advancing toward utter chaos, the organizations demonstrating a higher degree of disorder are by definition the more developed ones. They are the future. Perhaps we can find it in our hearts to honor them with the respect, reverence, and awe that more advanced life-forms deserve.

"Laws and institutions are constantly tending to gravitate. Like clocks, they must be occasionally cleaned and wound up and set to true time."

Henry Ward Beecher
1947

"Harzmountain-Liederkranz: Eine Neue Fundstelle der Grouchomarxkomplex" (A Translation and Synthesis)

Diane P. Gifford
Santa Cruz, CA

Harzmountain-Liederkranz is a highly significant but little-known Middle Palaeolithic site in Northern Germany. It is little known in English-speaking circles—or in any other for that matter—for basically linguistic reasons. The main problem is that Dr. Heinrich Tripper, the principal excavator, in a fit of regional chauvinism, wrote the entire report in Furglian, an obscure Prussian dialect (Tripper et al., 1968). The matter is further complicated by Furglian orthographic peculiarities—the language is written entirely in Arabic script. This bizarre development goes back to an edict of Furglia's twelfth-century ruler, Duke Otto the Perverse, who was renowned for his practical jokes.

I happened to learn Furglian during a sojourn in a very progressive grammar school. So, without further ado, the report.

Harzmountain-Liederkranz is located in the picturesque Dreckflusse Valley in northern Germany. The area receives 5 to 7 meters of rain per year, and it has a mean July temperature of 1° Centigrade. This bizarre combination, supposedly the result of an ancient curse, makes the area the ice cube capital of Germany and a real political white elephant. The East and West German governments are continually at each other's throats over who has to administer the area, and are currently negotiating to have it annexed to Poland.

Liederkranz is a small town with little to recommend it except the local flannel factory. The town experienced a wartime boom in the 30's and early 40's when designated the official Hitler Youth Camp pajama supplier. Postwar trends toward skimpy nighttime attire have once again turned Liederkranz into a sleepy hamlet.

The Dreckflusse River and the smaller Schlemiel join at the head of the valley, and the conjoined waters head vaguely for the North Sea. In Pleistocene times the Schlemiel ran the opposite way, emptying, after several spectacular cataracts, into the Persian Gulf. This apparently has no significance at all, except that it led a couple of geological experts on quite a merry chase. In the words of Carlos Bitzer, in his massive work, *Everything and Archaeology* (1971), "It sure ruined a perfectly good Sunday afternoon."

The site itself was discovered by workmen digging a hole for a water purification plant in the winter of 1963. During the trenching operation an observant foreman noticed four workmen had been impaled by falling mammoth tusks. The quick-witted official called someone to get that stuff out of there before they had to pay any more workman's compensation. The call went out to Dr. Heinrich Tripper, curator of national antiquities and knickknacks for the George Gobel Museum. Subsequent excavations were carried out at great hardship, mainly for the 5,000 Liederkranzers who suffered thirst and cholera during the delay in construction of the water purification plant.

Geology and Geomorphology—Axel Klimmerfinger & Rainer Kreutzersonata

The peculiar periglacial phenomena recorded in the stratigraphy result from the activity of the local ice sheet, the Scheisskopf Glacier. This phenomenal 12' by 2 mile behemoth mistakenly advanced down from the Jura during an exceptionally warm August in the Eem Interstadial and expired miserably in local pits and depressions. This prompted Tripper's famous remark, "It didn't know its ice from a hole in the ground."*

Sedimentological studies were carried out on deposits and on skulls of a horse and a bison. These indicate that seasonal meltwaters at the site flowed from east to west in the spring occasionally meandering to the left on cloudy days and during Holy Week, and furthermore that the animals in question never cleaned their ears.

Botanical Evidence—Dr. Milo Mindelriss

Dr. Mindelriss was not able to present full pollen spectra for publication, since he was still learning to do long division at the time. He was, however, able to make some general remarks on proportions, "Oh, a little of this and a pinch of that..." He provided a species list which includes the following plants: 3 species of pondweed, 4 species of water-loving sedges, marsh willow, waterlilies, Sago palm, and dandruff. Macrobotanical remains included thousands of willow twigs, a couple of berries, three nuts, and two grams of hashish. Dr. Mindelriss was at a loss to explain the last occurrence, except to put forth the theory of cultural contacts with the Near East (see Solucki 1969 for a related note).

Botanical evidence, taken as a whole, would seem to indicate that the Neandertalers sojourning at Liederkranz were semi-aquatic, and that the area was more than simply a *cultural* backwater.

Faunal Remains—Wolfgang Grebe

The faunal remains generally indicate a cold and wooly fauna, with reindeer and mammoth predominating. Based

---

* See Dr. Tripper's article in *American Journal of Salvage and Demolition Archaeology* entitled "Rip It Out."

upon a count of legbones, he described the reindeer *Rangifer tarandus pessinister*, the Left-footed Reindeer. In addition to this he established a new species: *Mammuthus non-nasalis*, the Trunkless Mammoth. Dr. Grebe was about to publish four more descriptions of this new taxa when he disappeared mysteriously during an international congress of mammalogists held in Venice. Several of the participants, in fact, rather nervously insist no one of that name ever existed.

Animals also found at the site include a wolf, a vulture, and a desman. This last creature was described as *Desmana moschata*, not to be confused with *Desmana morris*, the Naked Desman. Desmans, for those who are not familiar with them, are rather nasty little insectivores which live in the water and eat bugs, crustaceans, and the toes of hapless swimmers. They live in holes in stream banks, have bare tails, and are thought to be the prototypes for a number of unappetizing characters in European folklore (see also Lauss, 1976).

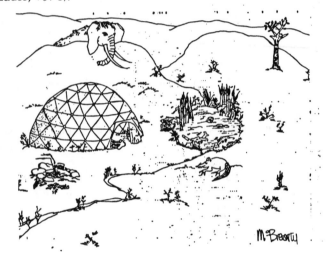

HARZMOUNTAIN-LIEDERKRANZ - Artist's Reconstruction

Radiocarbon Dates

Radiocarbon dates were run by Doppelgänger Laboratories, which is actually a front name for Dr. Tripper's mother, who uses a pressure cooker, some cheesecloth, and a candy thermometer. The dates were:

    44,000 ± 300 B.P. (2100 B.C.)
    52,000 ± 2 B.P. (1984 A.D.)

Dr. Tripper comments in Radiocarbon: "Not what I'd been expecting, but for $1.98 whaddya want?"

Paleoanthropology

Turning finally to palaeoanthropological matters, Dr. Franz Rinderpest of the Bavarian Institute for Aversive Conditioning has recently published a paper entitled "Was gibt bei dem Liederkranzer Hippies?" (Rinderpest, 1978). In it he argues that the Basidio-mycete fungal remains from the hearth were not, as Dr. Tripper alleged, "kindling materials," but fragments of the related *Amanita muscaria*—or

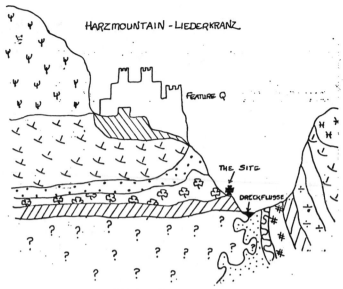

HARZMOUNTAIN-LIEDERKRANZ

magic mushroom. "Dose guys wuz gettink more dan feuers going up dere," he says. He pictures the site as a Palaeolithic Woodstock, with the inhabitants frolicking on the herbaceous tundra and hallucinating under Northern Lights.

Rinderpest further argues that this provides the only believable explanation of the abrupt *neandertalensis-sapiens* shift in Europe. Massive chromosomal damage, he contends, could produce a big change in people in only a few generations.

(At this point, I offer my own modest insight into a possible connection, hitherto not noted in print, between the *Feuersteinputzen* (or "fooling around" with flint) diagnosed by Tripper and Rinderpest's site formation scenario.)

CONCLUSIONS

Obviously, many critical questions about the nature of this site remain unanswered. They are likely to stay that way too, since Dr. Tripper is no longer around to discuss his information on the site.

So, sadly, this very interesting, if a bit confusing site is destined to remain somewhat mysterious. I can only hope that readers, as I, are even less enlightened about it now than they were prior to this. Descartes once said, "Not enough said is sometimes more than adequate." ∎

REFERENCES

Bitzer, Carlos 1971 *Everything and Archaeology.* City Lights Press, San Francisco.

Lauss, Marcel 1976 Ethnos, logos, et bozos dans la préhistoire. Essai sur les determinants de la variation stylistique des utiles de Grotte du Grot. *Problémes Semiologiques sur les Problémes Semiologiques.* 34(II-2-a): 115- 267

Rinderpest, Franz 1978 Was gibt bei dem Liederkranzer Hippies?

Solucki, R. 1969 What else we found at Srednivashtar Cave, wherever... *Hashrunners' Digest* volume who cares...

Tripper, H., *et al.*, 1968 Harzmountain-Liederkranz, eine neue Fundstelle der Grouchomarxkomplex. *Eiszeiteltern und Ruckwarts* 5:22-707.

COMPUTER-GENERATED OFFSPRING

Frederick V. Malmstrom
Seattle, WA

WOMAN IN AN ARMCHAIR, by Pablo Picasso, Chicago Art Institute

ABSTRACT

Twelve undergraduate surrogate couples participated in an 18-week experiment raising simulated, computer-generated offspring (CGO). Contrary to predictions that all twelve couples would subsequently elect to raise their own natural offspring, results were mixed. Although all couples considered the experiment to be realistic, nationwide application of the technique could, instead, point the way to celibate religious orders as a growth industry.

Computer-Generated Offspring

To prospective parents who have ever considered raising offspring, the inevitable question has been, "What will it be like?" Unfortunately, as most actual parents have later found out, there are no realistic simulations of true parenthood, even though there have been innumerable attempts to simulate what would otherwise be irreversible process.

Historically, there have been well-documented attempts to create life in the laboratory, either from synthetic or recycled parts, all with varying degrees of success. Perhaps the first was a well-publicized experiment by Shelley (1818). Informative as this heroic effort was, the experiment can only be regarded as a limited success because the offspring had contained several uncontrolled-for variables. Other successful attempts at creating the offspring include those of Collodi (1881), Shaw (1912), and Rorvik (1978). A limitation of these experiments, besides their uncontrollability, is the permanence of the offspring; at present, there are neither convenient nor ethical means of disposing of the end product.

Use of animals as surrogate offspring has, likewise, met with varying degrees of success. One of the first efforts to answer, "What will it be like?" with animals was made by Caligula (0038). Reputedly, this experiment, like Shelley's was not well-received. Other pioneering efforts, such as those of Lilly (1968), the Gardners (1973), Patterson (1981), and Reagan (1951) have added enormous valuable information as to the practicability of the methodology. In fact, the use of people as surrogate offspring has successfully been attempted by reversing the independent and dependent variables (viz. Romulus & Remus, B.C. 752; Burroughs, 1915). Nevertheless, the question of the external validity of such experiments remains as yet unanswered.

Finally, the use of inanimate objects for offspring, such as dolls, have the disadvantage of total passivity. While this quality may, indeed, be a desireable characteristic in offspring, the effect is simply not realistic. Nevertheless, the total inadequacy of dolls as an experimental technique does not negate their great successes as either therapeutic (Bandura, 1965) or applied (Flynt, 1977) commodities.

The use of synthetic, animal, and inanimate offspring, furthermore, has now become unnecessary. Recent successes in the flight simulation industry in the uses of computer-generated imagery (CGI) have shown great promise. For example, by use of CGI, a pilot can now "fly" a previously unseen airspace without fear of unscheduled impacts. Unlike viewing a motion picture which is "flat," with CGI if a pilot moves the controls to the right, for example, the view will correspondingly move to the left. The effect is, according to pilots, "total visual realism." And, of course, the cost-effectiveness compared to that of flying an actual aircraft is enormous. The final advantage of CGI is that as a training device, it permits one to make recoverable errors.

Hence, we were inclined to ask ourselves whether this technology of CGI could be used as a training and/or research device to screen prospective parents? In effect, if one could be responsible for the raising of computer-generated offspring (CGO), the learning process might be a remarkably efficient method of simulating, "What will it be like?"

In conducting such an experiment, there are several hypotheses to be entertained. First, would prospective parents consider such an experiment to be realistic? If so, then the results of such experiments might be reflected in the parents' willingness to have natural offspring. If the result can be validated, then would there be any therapeutic or applied benefits to be derived?

METHOD

Subjects

The subjects were 12 volunteer, childless, heterosexual, surrogate couples who were selected from a pool of 1,200 USC psychology undergraduates who received an extra five points course credit for participation in the experiment.

Materials

Prior to the experiment, the couples attended a counseling session during which they selected both the physical and personality characteristics of their desired offspring. The list of traits and their strengths were drawn from a pool of those set forth by Sheldon (1938) and Cattell (1961). In addition, previous pilot work with natural parents had suggested that an additional offspring trait of Gratitude (P.F. 17) ought to be added to Cattell's list. The entire list of offspring characteristics was then programmed into a computer-generated imagery (CGI) program supplied by the Boeing Company (Elson, 1981) and projected holographically into a flight simulator (Singer) head-up display. These holographs were then transmitted via modem to the surrogate couple's personal computer.

Design and Procedure

The entire 18-year childhood and adolescence of the CGO was then compressed into an 18-week experimental sequence, one week representing one year of the offspring's life. Further realism was incorporated into the experiment by effecting total impoverishment of the surrogate parents. Impoverishment was simulated by lavish payroll/allowance deductions paid directly to orthodontists, boutiques, ballet instructors, private universities, etc.. In addition, substantial, frequent, and random billings were made to appear on the surrogate parents' monthly MasterCard/Visa bank statements. The couples were then otherwise left unattended to raise the CGO with instructions to call a crisis control number in case any problems developed. (The number was a placebo, and no calls were ever returned.)

RESULTS AND DISCUSSION

All couples filled out an end-of-course critique at the completion of the 18 week period. Even though all surrogate parents considered the experiment "curious" and "not uninformative," more specific comments attesting to the realism of this child-rearing experiment were:

"Like having all my teeth drilled at once."

"Felt like a non-stop pro hockey game, body checks and all."

"It was swatting gnats in a Louisiana bayou. I found it frustratingly difficult to strike a holographic image."

"Sort of like no-win Donkey Kong."

Aside from the verbal feedback of the parents, the following tabulations of their follow-on behavior is shown below:

(a) 4 couples elected to have subsequent natural children. This compares with 12 out of 12 prior to the experiment.

(b) 3 couples, at the time of this writing, decided not to have natural children but were, instead, considering choosing between a celibate religious order and voluntary sterilization.

(c) 1 couple had had the experiment terminated. It should be noted that this separation was terminated by the CGO itself on the grounds that he/she would not again participate unless it could select its own parents. This CGO is presently on file at the National Archives (Case #82-11, floppy disk) awaiting readoption.

(d) 1 couple separated during the experiment and are now involved in a child custody contest in the U.S. Patent Courts. We are informed that the loser will, however, gain possession of PC Junior.

(e) 3 couples elected to have no subsequent natural offspring and, instead, adopted the CGO outright. It is of particular interest that these three CGO's were preprogrammed exceptionally high on the Cattell P.F. 4 trait (Humble-Assertive), indicating they had a high tendency towards an absence of humility. One CGO is now a cadet at the U.S. Air Force Academy, and the other two are psychology graduate students at Stanford University.

CONCLUSION

While all surrogates described the experience as valuable, the results must be interpreted as having mixed implications. It is possible once surrogates experience, "What will it be like?" that the national birth rates could drop precipitously. On the other hand, the resounding realism of the experiment could signify the start of a new growth industry—Prospective Parental Assessment Centers. An additional benefit might be that, in light of the decision of the 3 couples to adopt their CGO's a substantial percentage of childless couples, especially the gay, could at last realize their goal fulfillment of offspring. ∎

REFERENCES

Bandura, A. (1965) Bad time for Bobo. *Journal of Personality and Social Psychology, 1,* 589-595.

Burroughs, E.R. (1915). *Tarzan.* New York: Classic Comics.

Caligula, E. (0038). My kingdom for my horse: conversations with Incitatus. *Journal of Empirical Studies, 2,* 111-117.

Cattell, R.B. (1961). A methodology for analyzing personality in 16 dimensions. *Journal of Factor Analysis, 16,* 16-1616.

Collodi, C. (1881). *Pinnochio* (E. Bergen, Trans.). Naples: Woodstock & Son.

Elson, B. (1981, December 14). Boeing studies new imagery technique. *Aviation Week & Space Technology,* pp. 78-85.

Flynt, L. (1977, June). 1001 creative uses for Barbie. *Hustler,* pp. 46-49.

Gardner, B. (1973). *Hand sign for Washoe.* Reno: Troglodyte Press.

Lilly, J. (1968). *Fun time for Flipper.* La Jolla: Bottlenose Books.

Patterson, F. (1981). Tea-time for Koko. *Science, 211,* 86-87.

Reagan, R. (1951). *Bedtime for Bonzo.* Hollywood: Universal Flicks.

Romulus, K. & Remus, U. (B.C. 752). Mother, what big teeth you have. *Journal of the American Dental Association, 1,* 1-12.

Rorvik, D. (1978). *In his image.* New York: Lippincott.

Shaw, G. (1912). *Pygmalion.* London: Lerner & Loewe.

Sheldon, R. (1938). Ectomorph, endomorph, & mesomorph: the case of Larry, Curly & Moe. *Journal of Multiple Multiple Personality Personality, 9,* 8.

Shelley, Mary Wollestoncraft (1818). *Frankenstein.* London: IEEE Transactions on Systems, Man, and Cybernetics.

FOOTNOTES

Requests for reprints should be sent to: F.V. Malmstrom, Ph.D., C.G.O. M/S 9F-40, P.O. Box 3999, Boeing Aerospace Company, Seattle, WA 98124.

The ultimate blame for this study must, of course, rest with Vincent and Jean Malmstrom.

Emotion In The Rat Face

A. Daniel Yarmey
Guelph, Ontario, Canada

ABSTRACT

This study showed that rats differ in their expressiveness of facial emotions as a function of personality differences between internalizers and externalizers. Internalizers demonstrated few signs of facial emotionality and were indistinguishable from each other. In contrast, externalizers expressed variable facial emotions and were easy to differentiate. It was concluded that Darwin was on target in his descriptions of emotions in man and animals.

Very few of us have forgotten Darwin's (1872) classic work, *The Expression of the Emotions in Man and the Animals*. All of us are in his debt for showing that primate facial expressions are universally recognizable. Darwin's contributions laid the scientific foundations for such contemporary research as the study of emotions in the human face (Ekman, Friesen and Ellsworth, 1972), and the detection of deception (Ekman and Friesen, 1969). Nevertheless, Darwin's reputation as a critical observer of emotions in animals may be at risk if the scientific community is to believe the findings of Davis and Simmons (1979). These investigators report that their experimental judges and artists were unable to differentiate among facial expressions of rats. When rats were induced to produce 12 separate and distinct mood states such as: tiredness, ecstasy, confusion, fury, and so on, judges could not discriminate one facial expression from another. Although these findings may be empirically sound, several different interpretations must be considered and tested.

One hypothesis is that the subjects, chosen from the University of Guelph colony of laboratory rats, came from a visible minority, such as an Asiatic strain, and as all occidentals know "All Orientals look alike." It's also possible that the artists and observers showed a response bias and were "anti-rat", and recognized fewer emotions than would observers who were more objective. Another explanation and one that was tested in this investigation is that Davis and Simmons were insensitive and did not really know their subjects. It is likely that they failed to discover the true identities of these rats. Without testing for personality differences it is not surprising the obtained results were found. Rats are not just a bundle of conditioned responses and habit strengths, they have feelings too!

The present experiment tested the hypothesis that rats differ in their expressiveness of facial behavior as a function of personality differences.

METHOD

Subjects. Ten subjects came from the University of Guelph laboratory used by Davis and Simmons and ten came from the local psychiatric center which was reputed to have many different personality types. Volunteers were paid $3.00 per hour as subjects.[1]

Procedure. All subjects were given a battery of personality tests: the RAT (Rat Apperception Test); the Draw-A-Rat Test; the Ratashack Ink Blot Test; and the Rat-Facs Test (Rat-Facial Affect Coding System). Subjects also were observed for three months. The experimenter watched the rats and the rats watched the experimenter and both *really* got to know each other. On conclusion of the observation period an artist drew portraits of each rat as the experimenter induced subjects to produce 12 separate and distinct mood states. The artist was not aware of the personality scores of subjects.

INTERNALIZERS

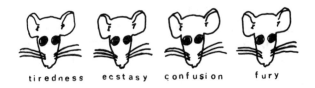

tiredness   ecstasy   confusion   fury

EXTERNALIZERS

tiredness   ecstasy   confusion   fury

RESULTS AND DISCUSSION

The personality scores were analyzed with Rat - statistics, i.e., range, *rho*, regression analysis, right skewness, and rapid eye movements (not really a statistical test). All scores from the "R" analyses were transformed and summed to yield a measure of internalizers - externalizers.

The transformed personality scores revealed that all of the rats selected from the University of Guelph animal colony were internalizers (p<.00001), whereas the psychiatric rats were all mixed up (p>.00001). Some are best described as internalizers (N = 3), others as externalizers (N = 4), and the remainder as "wild and crazy guys" (N = 2.5, one rat was half alive). Internalizers revealed very little signs of facial emotionality, but they showed a lot of internal emotions such as a rapid heart rate. On the other hand, externalizers showed many different facial expressions. Their little bodies, however, were quiet. Heart beats, for example, were very slow (see also Buck, Miller, & Caul, 1974).

These results support the observations and conclusions of Darwin and show that his results may be generalized to include the rat. The rats used by Davis and Simmons probably were internalizers which may account for their findings. However, no interpretation is available to explain why all of the University of Guelph rats are up-tight internalizers. ∎

REFERENCES

Buck, R., Miller, R.E., and Caul, W.F. Sex, personality and physiological variables in the communication of emotion via facial expression. *Journal of Personality and Social Psychology,* 1974, *30,* 587-596

Darwin, C. *The expression of the emotions in man and the animals.* London: John Murray, 1872

Davis, H., and Simmons, S. An analysis of facial expression in the rat. *The Worm Runner's Digest,* 1979, *21,* 81-82

Ekman, P., and Friesen, W. Nonverbal leakage and clues to deception. *Psychiatry,* 1969, *32,* 88-106

Ekman, P., Friesen, W., and Ellsworth, P. *Emotion in the human face.* New York: Pergamon Press, 1972

[1]No thanks can be given to the Natural Sciences and Engineering Research Council of Canada who refused to support this project.

Why The Spider Did Not Eat The Fly

Science News, Volume 131, No. 17, April 25, 1987

In the dog-eat-dog world of the wild, a disguise can mean the difference between freedom or being some other creature's luncheon special. Some prey animals, for example, copy the coloration and patterning of animals, plants or rocks that many predators find extremely unappetizing or even toxic.

Ecologist Erick Greene at Princeton (N.J.) University's Department of Biology and his colleagues obtained similar results but took a slightly different tack. They worked with the *Zonosemata vittigera* fruit fly and 11 jumping spider species. Greene's group recorded the behavior of the spiders when they were put in the same enclosure with one of the following: a normal *Zonosemata*, a normal house fly, a house fly onto which *Zonosemata* wings had been transplanted, a *Zonosemata* with house fly wings (which are about the same size and shape of *Zonosemat's*) or a *Zonosemata* with wings from another *Zonosemata*. (Wings were attached with Elmer's White Glue. According to Greene the transplanted flies flew and behaved normally).

The first and last of these groups survived with flying colors; when they waved their wings, spiders stopped stalking and began to wave their legs at the flies. Most of these flies were then able to back away, zigzagging and wing-waving, and fly off. The other groups of flies did not fare as well.

Submitted By:
Christine Crawford-Oppenheimer
Poughkeepsie, NY

Inner Turmoil

Naomi Fein
New York, NY

There is a paucity of literature on the clinical entity inner turmoil—or emotional turmoil, as it is sometimes termed (by the layman). (1) Why are we so afraid of it, of *saying it?* Inner turmoil. There. It is an overdetermined phenomenon: one hears almost constantly such expressions as:

—I'm just falling apart
—Look at me, I'm actually wringing my hands and femurs
—My psychiatrist says I'm having a walking nervous breakdown, he doesn't know how I even function, if it were anybody but me, any patient but me, he'd have to hospitalize him
—I'm *very* perceptive, I sense color auras, I'm sensing very cerise auras at this point in time
—Drippy
—Blurky
—Grotty
—In pieces and bits
—I'm just a Mess (2)

This observation is socio-culturo-anthro-political, sure, but can we not consider such a personal approach valid in a discussion of Person? Yes we can. These above indented greasy-spoon gleanings are the harvest-hour indications that one of the most neglected, yet strangely prevalent problems in contemporary (American) life is the dysfunction which we call 'IT': inner turmoil (3) (along with the plague that rots wheat, that word that shows up in crossword puzzles.

Diagnosis

Senslare says (4) we can be..."pretty damn sure of ITs if we feel damn fidgety in a room with a patient who has 'em." (Oh, Sanslare, not *again* with that!)

Soucurates feels somewhat differently. "We can determine a diagnosis of IT when the patient transmits waves of fidget for a period exceeding the duration of the session." (5) (He's such a dip, that Soucurates. And *derivative..?!)*

Strump tends to subsume, gather, heap and dump inner turmoil under the rubric 'anxiety.' "It's all the same bloody thing, why are we making such a bloody thing of it, anyway, then?" (6) (Strump, of course, is from Ohio). Gee, did we *sneer* at Strump.

Causation

Of course, basically anything can cause IT: outer turmoil and unknown fears are prominant causes. Crazy thinking is, perhaps, an oustanding difficulty that pre-or even antecedes IT. Past experiences seem to fuel it, while irrational dreads are the bellows, oddball instincts the match, aggravations and agita the tinderbox, low self-esteem the striking hand, low blows the...

Occasionally, parenting (pro or con) can be tossed into the pot, while childhoos (past, present, future) spices the brew. Waiting for things that never happen; things that do happen but aren't really as, I *mean*, this ain't the *apocalypse,* come *on!* Portents. Portents are big. Kitchen odors. Petty flicks of the eye and tense, pseudo-cheery smiles of significant others. Weird hugs in which significant other doesn't bother to look into my eyes—your eyes, I mean—but is seeing something more significant over my—your shoulder. Fully explained absences of significant:...detailed presences of—

Waiting for a significant someone who—most unfortunately—*is* going to happen.

The list of causes is overdetermined (I don't know what that means, either) (7).

Experiential Data

Physical locality (somatic spatiality)—the pit of the tummy. A cold prick of a shivery sort of unspeakable terror begins it and then zap!—the unpleasantness spreads in shuddering spirals. Brr, brr. When it's bad (aargh) but not yet horrid (eeeee!) it stabilizes between the belly-button and the sternum, between which two fences it cuts up the grass and makes a hell of a ruckus. The sensation of imminent bad stuff and hard times. Churning, chugging, sweating pores, bursting skin, taut and pulsing eyeballs. The teeny hairs on the back of the hand ache.

Some people complain:
—I don't know, I can't breathe, IT must be heartburn.
—I don't know, I can't breathe, I'm having heart spasms.
Some people cry—
—IT hurts, IT hurts, IT doesn't hurt, I don't know, I can't breathe.
People become inarticulate. Words, rationality flee:
—Something terrible's going to happen, I feel like a *muffin.*
—IT hurts:
IT affects breathing:
—I can't
People are so boring.

Anguish; the knife hangs by a thread over the neck. (That's not too colorful but what the hell, this is strictly clinical language.) Time slows, stops. An irresistable desire to rush around the room and go nowhere appears. Time heads backwards. Rush around the walls, slapping significant objects that stick out; check the clock. No time. Sink to knees and beg piteously for relief. Belief in a paternalistic god and magic rituals: "If I bang the wall three times and scream 'Pease porride,' all will pass." Deals are made with dieties. (8)

The second stage comes rapidly after nothing much happens in the first stage. The sensations expand, moving up toward the shoulders and down beneath the groin. As of yet the knees, calves and feet remain free of IT, as do the neck and head. There is an intense throbbing as the heart threatens to break. Beneath this, the lower colon presents the (re?) articulate illusion that it is doubling back within itself and folding into the upper colon where "those little food-eating finger-shaped biologic things that stick out" are. (9) The body has begun a rather witty *somatometaphor* (10): it pretends it is chewing itself.

The person who has the misfortune to share this body now perceives his options:

Death

Occasionally there is a third stage—a rare achievement: horridity. (11, 12)

Case History

J.K.'s husband left her in the lurch one morning because he had to go to work as usual. He was not due back until 5:35 PM. J.K. went immediately—at 9:35 (somewhat significant)—into ITs. She passed smoothly from stage one—the bads—into stage two, which she characterized as "the worses." (Terms that patients coin during sessions imediately become the property of the therapist.) And then the ultimate: "IT, I don't know, went past my knees and into my feet. IT, I don't know, got itself into my head. I just felt, I don't know, like my skin was a plastic baggie puffed up with someone else's *geist*. (J.K. is Mittel European.) This *geist* I don't know, had swallowed up al my organs and spat them out and there I was, organless, full of a nasty *geist*. I don't know." J.K. had reached *IT Horridity*. It ended at %34. Had her husband been late from the office, her husband might have had to hospitalize her one way or the (significant) other. (J.K. is a *total* pain.)

Prognosis and Therapeutic Methodology

the ITs are (lousy but) self-l;imiting. Psychotherapy performs absolutely fabulous miracles. Several practical suggestions that one can offer one suffering from ITs:

—Talk about it to yourself, calling yourself ugly names. (13)
—clean out hairbrushes, dirty Scrubbies, et al. (14)
—change clothes every few minutes. (15)
—Whack all clocks until the plastic splinters and screams. (16)
—Dope yourself up with anything you've got lying around the house: grams of cocaine, Fantastik fumes, chicken feathers, etc. (17)
—Go to sleep until a significant other arrives or there's a rerun on TV of "The Mary Tyler Moore Show." (18) ∎

REFERENCES

(1) Spart EG: "Pain in the Neck," in: *Poetics*, Ligonier, 1974.
(2) Personal eavesdropping in fast food joints, 1968-1984.
(3) Author: Intimate individuated intense conversations with 56 intensely interested and intellectual friends, Nov. 29, 1979.
(4) Senslare EG: "The Patient-Healer Fidget Transmission," Daily Mirror, p. 75-75, Vol XXV/3, 1776.
(5) Soucurates EG: *The Twelve Minute Hour*, New York, 1980.
(6) Strump EG: "Lumping," J. of Crit. Crp., p. 1-2, Vol V/3, 1976.
(7) Author: "Honest confusion as a psychotherapeutic technique," Chapter DXI, In: *Confusion*, unpublished ms.
(8) Author: *Diety Dealing: Ineffecitive Coping Techniques That Cope by Coping Out*, El Paso, 1975.
(9) Stark EG: "Colonic Function In The Adult," N. Eng. J. of Med., p. 857-921, Vol XII/88, 1978.
(10) Author: trademark term and used since by anyone who's anyone in the field.
(11) Stormp, EG: "New Words As Praxis, Not Pathology," J. of Pysch. Geek, p. 12-89, vol IX/1, 1972.
(12) Author: "Neologisms As Process Not Phooey," J. of Me, p. 88-77, Vol X/3, 1973.
(13) STimme EG: "Self-pathonomenclature," J. of Ladies Home, Apr., 1979.
(15) Susie, E(lsie) G(igi): "Strip 'n' Save," WWD, July 28, 1973.
(16) Story EG: "Time and Linear, Plastic As Perfect," In Press.
(17) Sid: "Death of a Sales(man)," CBS docu-drama, 1981.
(18) The honest opinion of the masses.

Is Less Really More?
Grazing The Logic of Bovine Collective Action

Paul W. Turner
Bloomington, IN

In his groundbreaking work on collective action, Mancur Olson (1965) argued that the ability of groups to achieve their goals varies in proportion to their size. Larger groups, he claimed, are more difficult to organize for collective action because they are more prone to problems of *free-riding* (where some individuals benefit from, but do not contribute to, the group effort) and because the marginal benefits that accrue to group members decrease with increases in group size; in other words, the pie is divided up into smaller and smaller pieces. Because of these two conditions, larger groups will often fail to achieve their goals because rational individuals will be less likely to contribute to groups where others benefit freely from their efforts and where the net returns to themselves are conspicuously small.

Organizing in smaller groups, on the other hand, is a somewhat simpler task because free-riders are easier to detect and punish and because the benefits that accrue to individuals as a result of their actions are not dispersed across a large group. Under these circumstances, Olson argued, rational individuals will be more willing to contribute to the group effort. Smaller groups, therefore, are thought to be easier to organize and better suited for success in terms of realizing their goals.

Beefing Up The Argument

To this author's knowledge, this argument has yet to be applied to species other than humans. In an effort to fill this gap in the literature, this research examines a current collective action problem of particular importance to the global cow population—the proliferation of McDonald's franchises across the globe. Currently, McDonald's franchises can be found in 79 countries, up from 51 countries just five years ago (McDonald's Corporation 1994). Franchise locations include the formerly socialist bastions of Bulgaria, China, the Czech Republic, Poland, and Russia, as well as such exotic locations as Brunei, Kuwait, Morocco, and Trinidad. If this trend toward global McDonaldization continues, the future for the world's cow population could become increasingly medium rare.

The Rational Cow Model

To properly analyze this urgent problem, we assume a rational cow with the following preference ordering:

1) stay alive
2) move to greener pasture
3) chew cud that is high in fiber
4) kick the guy with the branding iron where it counts
5) get in a Far Side cartoon

From this preference ordering, we deduce that cows will organize in protest against the establishment of new McDonald's franchises in their home countries as the founding of such franchises threatens preference #1 above by increasing the demand for Quarter Pounders, Big Macs, Happy Meals, etc. However, given the hypothesized relationship between group size and collective action success outlined above, would expect that smaller cow populations will be more successful in this protest effort. That is, countries with smaller cow populations will have fewer McDonald's franchises while countries with larger cow populations will have more McDonald's franchises. Put another way, it is hypothesized that less *is* more when it comes to the dynamics of bovine collective action (see Figure 1).

Figure 1. *The Less-Is-Moo Hypothesis*

Testing for Cow Causality

To assess the Less-is-Moo Hypothesis, data were gathered on national cow populations and number of McDonald's franchises by country. Cow population data on 163 countries were drawn from *World Resources 1994-95* (World Resources Institute 1994). Data on McDonald's franchises were graciously provided by the Customer Satisfaction Department at McDonald's headquarters in Oak Brook, Illinois (McDonald's Corporation 1994). The number of McDonald's franchises by country was then regressed on national cow population, yielding the following results:

Table 1. Regression Analysis of the Less-is-Moo Hypothesis

Variable	Coefficient	Standard Error	t
COW	.0000104	.00000244	4.247***
constant	10.90866	60.61914	0.180
*** p < .0001			n = 163

As indicated by the results of the regression analysis, national cow population was found to have a statistically significant relationship with the number of McDonald's franchises in a country and this relationship was in the expected positive direction. Interpreting the results substantively, for each additional 100,000 cows in a given country, that country can expect to have approximately one additional McDonald's franchise within its borders (100,000 multiplied by the COW regression coefficient of .0000104 = 1.04).

Thus, it does appear that cows suffer from some of the same collective action problems as humans. Where cow populations are large, cows appear to have a difficult time of organizing themselves to protest the estab-lishment of first-time or additional McDonald's franchises. If the world's cow population hopes to stem the tide of global McDonaldization, it may want to consider either a migration policy that would relocate cows from countries with larger populations to those countries with a smaller bovine presence or a birth control policy that would slow cow population growth in the future.

This paper has demonstrated that the argument of Olson (1965), originally formulated with humans in mind, may be equally applicable to cows. To discover if other animal species have difficulties in organizing for collective action in large groups, further empirical tests are needed. One such test might adopt the methodology similar to that used here to look at the relationship between national chicken population and the number of Kentucky Fried Chicken franchises present within a country. As the number Kentucky Fried Chicken franchises is also growing throughout the world, such a study would provide yet another timely opportunity to test the pluck of Olson's thesis.

REFERENCES:

McDonald's Corporation. 1994. *Performance at a Glance.* Oak Brook, IL: McDonald's Corporation.

Olson, Mancur. 1965. *The Logic of Collective Action.* Cambridge, MA: Harvard University Press.

World Resources Institute. 1994-95. *World Resources 1994-95.* Data Base Diskette. Washington, D.C.: World Resources Institute.

Banghart, Bachrach and Pattishall
(Division of Educational Research, University of Viriginia, Charlotteville, Virginia)

STUDIES IN PROBLEM SOLVING
Contract No. 474 (8) Office of Naval Research Sept. 1959

"In other words, for this particular tax, intelligence did not seem to interfere with problem solving performance."

****

ACADEMIC GRAFFITI

Notice taped to electric hand dryer in medical faculty washroom:

"Push button for a one-minute message from the Dean."

PRINCE OF PETOMANE

PETER LENNON

For July 14, the time when Parisians give voice with petard and brass-band to whatever dry store of joy is still left in them, a publisher, M. Jean-Jacques Pauvert, has very appropriately produced a handsome tribute to one of the most celebrated noise-makers the European stage has ever known: M. Joseph Pujol. At the height of his career as star of the Moulin Rouge, Marcel Pagnol in his book "Notes on Laughter" tells us that Joseph Pujol could draw matinee gates worth 20,000 francs, while Sarah Bernhardt the same week only managed 8,000. Eye witnesses claim that he was one of the greatest amusers of all time. His career spanned more than twenty years.

Why then does the name Pujol mean nothing to us today? Because to perpetuate his name it is necessary to describe what he did, and for a couple of generations this simply could not be done in print. (Perhaps it still can't.) Dear me, how styles of entertainment have changed! Pujol described himself as "Le Petomane." Not to beat about the bush Pujol's talent was that he could fart like nobody else in the world, before, then, or since.

He could fart tenderly (le petit pet timide de la jeune fille) or aggressively (le pet rond du macon); rapidly like a machine gun; or he could produce a deep, slow cannon-roar lasting up to ten seconds. He could give a very good account of a do-ra-me-fa *derriere*-wise, imitate a violin, a bass, or the timbre of a trombone.

Pujol was no scurvy, back-street, perverted farter. He only farted in the very best places, and for considerable sums of money. Eyewitnesses insist on the gravity and impassibility of his performance, and the essential seriousness of this father of ten buxom children.

In 1887, the year Mallarmé published "L'Apres, midi d'une Faune," Pujol, aged 30, appeared for the first time on a public stage in Marseilles. His talent had already been the envy of his schoolmates, the admiration of his regiment, and evoked the solicitous respect of his family. Within a week Marseilles was crowding to see the *Petomane*. For the next twenty years, in Marseilles, Paris, Brussels, North Africa, all over Europe Pujol presented an unchanging ritual. Dressed in a red coat and black satin knickerbockers, he would approach the ramp and announce gravely:

"Mesdames, Mesdemoiselles, Messieurs, I have the honour to present to you a performance of petomania . . ."

He would then stoop and begin his finely graded, escalating performance. In his history of the "Caf 'conc'," Jacques — Charles describes the scene at the Moulin Rouge. "At first the audience would remain astounded. Then someone would be stricken with a crazy laugh. In a moment people would be howling and staggering with laughter. Some would stand paralysed, tears pouring down their cheeks, while others beat their heads and fell on the floor. Ladies would begin to suffocate in their tight corsets, and for this reason there were always a number of white-coated nurses in attendance."

MLLE YVETTE GUILBERT wrote: "It was at the Moulin Rouge that I heard the longest spasms of laughter, the most hysterical cries of hilarity that I have ever heard in my life."

The King of the Belgians travelled *incognito* to Paris for a private demonstration by M. Pujol.

But it was not only an audience in search of a belly laugh who flocked to see Pujol; the Academy of Medicine in Paris was, so to speak, hot on his tail. Pujol, partly to prove the authenticity of his performance (which he could hardly do on the stage of the Moulin Rouge), submitted to a number of elaborate medical examinations which are described in "La Semaine Medical" of 1892 by a Dr. Marcel Baudouin with a zest and enthusiasm for detail which unfortunately cannot be reproduced here.

Pujol finally broke with the Moulin Rouge and opened his own theatre, the Pompadour. Then in 1898, the year Pierre and Marie Curie discovered radium, Pujol discovered that the Moulin Rouge were going to present a rival female *Petomanie*. He brought an action for unauthorized imitation. Lawyers had to attend the theatre and note the range, quality and form of the lady's performance. But before the case actually came to court the lady was exposed as a fraud (she had whistles hidden in her skirts).

Pujol, who lived to be 88, was an outstanding example of man's ingenuity in making the best of whatever gifts natue bestows — be they ever so curious. With extraordinary courage, and by the sheer quality of his performance he imposed the fart on a stupefied but defenceless Europe.

He was a star until 1914 when the countries of Europe decided to get together on a roaring orgy of petomania of their own which was no doubt distasteful to this gentle and scrupulous performer. (By the way, he claims never to have suffered from stagefright).

How has his name come to light again? Simply because his family of honest bakers and masons in Marseilles were pained that their famous ancestor had become so neglected. Around July 14 (last year) they had the idea of appealing to a pair of well-known journalists on the ORTF pointing out the injustice that: "France has done nothing for the memory of its Petomane!"

Now justice has been done. But, alas, given the standards of our time the tribute could neither be aural or visual.

Taken from The Guardian, Thursday, July 13, 1967

'Tis The Season For Folly

By Barney Brantingham, Santa Barbara, CA, News-Press, Sunday, December 18, 1983

Dale Lowdermilk of the sarcastic Not-Safe ("Protecting everyone from everything—at any cost") wants to warn us about Christmas.

Yes, Christmas.

"Adults must be extremely careful NOT to give (children) gifts which are:

1. Flammable.   2. Non-digestive.   3. Illegal. 4. Fattening. 5. Erotic. 6. Too scary. 7. Allergenic (fur/feathers).   8. Requires assembly. 9. Squeaks. 10. Melts. 11. Chokes 12. Explodes. 13. Crawls. 14. Bites. 15. Was born in a cabbage patch. 16. Requires batteries. 17. Makes noise. 18. Has sharp edges. 19. Is painted, pressurized or has a cord. 20. Too expensive."

For adults, Dale recommends auto safety items, such as:

1. Oatmeal-filled bumpers (will provide emergency food supply following any collision).

2. A third, fourth and fifth rear taillight.
3. A speed-control electrode (fits under driver's seat and is activated when excessive speed is encountered.
4. A state-of-the-art one gallon gas tank (will reduce fire hazard of ordinary size auto tanks.)
5. A "DO NOT TALK TO DRIVER" card for your dashboard (to reduce the risk of distractions).
6. Special air bags which inflate when you turn on the ignition.

Dale also recommends getting your vehicle a safety inspection once a year and having pollution control devices checked monthly. "Instead of driving to 'Grandma's house,' put Grandma on the bus.

"Christmas shoppers are warned to dress warmly, carolers should not strain their vocal cords and everyone is cautioned about over-spending, overeating or over-thinking. MERRY CHRISTMAS."

Thanks, Dale. And be careful. After all, you ARE an air traffic controller at the Santa Barbara Airport.

ERROR-FREE BEHAVIOR: THE DISCOVERY OF ORTHOBEHAVIORALISM

Walter B. Reid
Miami, FL
Cameron K. McKinley
Weisbaden, Germany

Man is exhorted to strive for perfection (Walk before me and be thou perfect. Genesis 17:1), but so far his ambition is not fulfilled. The consequences of error often are severe (But if you do not harken to me, and will not do all these commandments ... then I will chastise you again sevenfold for your sins. Leviticus 26:14), and we are warned to take care (Beware lest you be carried away with the error of lawlessness. II Peter 3:17) that our errors do not become overwhelming. Clearly then mankind is at a crossroads regarding the problem of the proliferation of errors. The enormity of the problem becomes clear in the microcosm of psychology: for example, most psychologists will accept results as meaningful when there is a statistical significance of 5%, that is, a 5% error. Apply that reasoning to scientific journal publication. For a monthly publication schedule, one issue every other year is utter hogwash. Translate this to everyday professional life and we have a frightening implication. Five percent of our time is spent in erroneous behavior. For the total population this is the equivalent of 15,000,000 people who do everything wrong all the time. With the exponential increases in populations capable of behaving and new areas in which to behave, mankind needs to reassess his position and plan a way out of this chaos.

Our method out of this chaos is to do away with the prosthetic approach to life and any tolerance of error. No more Bugger factors, no more safety factors, no more structural or linguistic redundancy. In place of the patchwork prostheses of

everyday life, we propose an Orthobehavioral approach: error-free behavior. Man is however not yet skilled at developing perfect behavior but we propose a modest beginning. Buried in the quagmire of life, one finds pearls of behavior (orthobehavior) that can be correctly done every time. The authors succeeded in collecting these pearls and subsequently constructed a hierarchy of orthobehavioral items during the years 1967-1970 when they were involved in activities clearly beyond their levels of competence as the co-managers of the Dry Prong (La.) Hammer Factory and Glue Refinery.

The following list of items was found to be error-free 100% of the time:

LEVEL I

1. Breathing voluntarily while awake.
2. Identifying current U.S. coins (in daylight).
3. Growing head (or facial) hair (any length, any color).
4. Tearing single sheets of any newspaper.
5. Removing eyeglasses without poking ear pieces in eyes.

LEVEL II

1. Scribble with ball-point pen (any color).
2. Chew gum (at least 6 bites).
3. Break pencil lead (No. 2 pencil).
4. Stare at something (anything, more than 3 seconds).

5. Operate household light switch (light need not operate).

LEVEL III

1. Lick postage stamp without cutting tongue.
2. Put on shoes. (Anyone's shoes. Need not be tied).
3. Operate an ordinary zipper. (Open or shut. Must be intact).
4. Sleep. (Any duration, anywhere, anytime, no drugs, dreaming optional).
5. Close zipper in 3 above so as to catch a sensitive bit of skin.

LEVEL IV

1. Operate dial telephone (any number).
2. Stand on one foot. (More than 3 seconds).
3. Walk. (Anywhere, any speed. More than 3 steps without falling. No canes, crutches, etc.).
4. Talk. (Any words. Any language. No one need listen).
5. Hold lighted cigarette more than 30 seconds without burning fingers. (Anyone's fingers. Regular or King size. No filters).

Novices may practice items sequentially from each list as applicable to make sure one is not starting with too difficult an item and progress through to the end. Upon reaching the end of the list, novices may continue to produce increasingly complex behavior until they have achieved the goals reached by the authors in 1971, that of behavior which is purfekt. ■

ADAPTIVE SOCIAL BEHAVIOR

Videotaping Session #22

(Client approaches Doctor A, looking a bit unsure. Dr. A is busy behind a desk, but finally looks up quizzically.)

Client: (nervously) Er... Dr. A? My case manager, er, uh, told me to see... you... about...er...

Dr. A: (kindly) Why, of course, yes, no worry. (taking command) You *do* appear to be a bit anxious, don't you?

Client: (confused at this) Well...well, I...uh...

Dr. A: (confidently) No problem. (produces a bottle of pills) Take two of these pills, three times a day. Your anxiety will no longer be of concern to you. (pause) Take four now, to get you started. (hands four pills to Client) Now, remember: three pills, two times a day. (gives bottle to Client) Have a good day.

(The good Dr. A returns to work. Client, ever-so-slowly moves on--to Doctor B.)

Client: (slowly) D-o-c-t-o-r B-? A-r-e y-o-u D-o-c-t-o-r B-?

Dr. B: (looking up) Why, of course! Who *else* would I be? (examining Client visually) Now you *do* look a little slow! Tired? Depressed? Down in the dumps?

Client: (slow as ever) W-e-l-l...

Dr. B: (quickly) *Of course* you are! I could see it in a minute. I *am* the doctor, aren't I? Here, just take *several* of these. (produces a bottle of pills)

Client: (the same) B-u-t...

Dr. B: (insistant) Just take these. (places bottle in Client's hand) Everything will be OK. (pause) On second thought, maybe you should take some now. I'll check up on you in a week or two. (pause) Have a nice day.

(Client reluctantly takes several pills and immediately reacts! Jittery. Nervous. Hyperactive. Client jogs up to Doctor C.)

Client: (speedy) Dr. C! Dr. C!

Dr. C: (with languid disinterest) Yes?

Client: (quickly) Dr. C! Dr. C! I'm so jumpy! So jumpy!

Dr. C: (nonplussed) Why do you say that?

Client: (running in place) Why? Why? Dr. C! Dr. C! Because! Because! I can't stop! Can't stop this!

Dr. C: (blandly) Anything else?

Client: (pleading) Dr. C! Dr. C!

Dr. C: (begrudgingly) All right. (pause) You clients are all alike, always asking for unnecessary medication! (pause) Take two of these (produces a bottle) and be done with it. (pause) And, have a nice day.

(Client gathers up the bottle, takes two pills, and immediately returns to normal speed. Client approaches Doctor D.)

Client: (nervously) Er...Dr. D? My case manager, er, uh, told me to see.. someone... about...er...

Dr. D: (soothingly) Why, of course, yes, no worry. (pause) All you really need to do is set up an appointment with Dr. A!

END OF VIDEOTAPING SESSION

Richard F. Kennedy
Columbus, Ohio

CONSUMER STUDIES & ECONOMICS

BEYOND REAGANOMICS:
OME PSEUDO-SERIOUS ANSWERS TO BIG QUESTIONS NO ONE IS ASKING

Tod Roberts
Cleveland, OH

By the Celebrated Lecturer at Large, Professor Hans Heinrich, University of Torshavn, Iceland

Place: La roche College
Science Center
Room 103 (Demo. Theatre)

Time: Friday, Nov. 20, 1984, 8:00 PM

Seating available on a first come, first serve basis.

ADMISSION FREE

Professor Orr's Introduction of Professor Hans Heinrich

Prof. Hans Heinrich, whose previous appearance on this campus about two and a half years ago in a lecture on "Time from the Philological Perspective" stirred one of the most memorable outbreaks of lethargy, narcolepsy and Tourette's Syndrome ever witnessed in the history of this college, calls himself "a lecturer at large."

Professor Heinrich's Lecture, So To Speak

This evening I would like to welcome myself to the topic Prof. Orr has just announced. Let me first please review a little of the background with you.

Never before in mankind's history has the science of economics commanded such attention as today. The reasons for this are innumerable, and I shall therefore limit myself to two:

1. The apparently ceaseless installation of 24-hour automatic bank teller machines, which have spread across the landscape of Western economic life like an oil-spill from a Japanese supertanker, and
2. The continuity of human greed.

Such heavy attention on economics has necessitated a fresh new voice in the cacaphonous debate we hear around us. We are daily bombarded with propaganda from Marxists, socialists, monetarists, Reaganomists, Galbraitheans, Neo-Keynesians, Friedmanics, and an unheavenly host of others. Two explanations of economic behavior that appear especially odd are "micro-" and "macroeconomics." Let me briefly summarize these theories so as to reveal their pathetic weaknesses early in this lecture. I shall, of course, be as open-minded as possible in reducing them to the intellectually paltry blips on the economic radar screen which they clearly are.

"Micro": the very word conjures images of cheapness, narrowness, meretriciousness, and small-mindedness. Though the originators of this view doubtless see themselves as dispassionate, objective researchers unswayed by a scintilla of feeling, their manifestos belie such high self-regard.

Listen for a moment to one of their key principles, couched in the language of pseudo-science:

The oven with a memory...cooks a whole meal... cooks three foods at once, by time or temp. Variable power settings...defrost, roast, more. Delay start. Memory recall. Sale price of $399.95 in effect November 1 to November 25 unless otherwise indicated.

Na, does this, I ask you, demonstrate objectivity? Science? Good sense? Bosh!

As if "micro" weren't enough to lead us down the primrose path of economic chaos, the microeconomists' opposite numbers—a staunch band of post-bourgeois, rotund ladies and gentlemen, dressed (respectively, one hopes) in heavy tweed suits and morning coats with cumberbunds—present, on first glance, a more rational approach to man's economic behavior. I refer, as you perhaps can easily surmise, to those advancing the "macro" view. Briefly, this holds that modern man's economic behavior is such a big, complex subject that we're better off just avoiding it completely. The macroeconomists originated one slogan which tells us a great deal about their approach: "Don't confuse us with the facts."

Though I personally admire such an attitude for its honest admission of futility, it has some serious weaknesses, of course. For one thing, if you're an academic depending on a publishing record for promotion and tenure, this type of leisurely, even apathetic approach makes it very hard to produce anything good enough even for an academic journal. For another, these theorists' general lackadaisicality makes them very unattractive to newspaper reporters, Nobel Prize committees, and similar observers who can notably influence the likelihood of your face appearing on a million covers of *Time Magazine*.

But beyond micro, macro, Reagan-o, and all the other views heretofore advanced, there's one that's bound to grab you and make you sit in one place long enough to hear it out...Velcro Economics, or, as it has inevitably been shortened by journalists eager to save space, *Velcronomics*.

What is Velcro?

In a nutshell, which is (metaphorically speaking) where this theory got its big start, Velcronomics poses three tenets that set it apart from all its competitors:

1. First, far from being the root of all evil, money is a pleasant possession indispensable to one who truly wants to be a steady, reliable consumer.
2. The second tenet—which, like much of Velcronomic thinking, allows a wide choice of assent, dissent, and ignorance among its followers—may be stated thus: supply and demand are always functions of demand and supply.

3. And third, neither man nor his economic behavior makes much sense.

Velcronomics and the Supply-Siders

And now we may turn to some of the ramifications and effects of Velcronomics in light of other theories and ejaculations from contemporary economic thinkers and, in passing, glance at some of the historical figures who helped bring about these modern-day notions.

One hears frequently nowadays of "supply side" economics, and Velcronomists have not sat idly by listening to such rubbish. The supply siders claim that real growth...as a percentage of A&P...comes about through the revolution of rising expectations—that is, offering tantalizing consumables to an entire class of persons who have as much chance of obtaining such baubles as you and I have of breaking the casinos in Las Vegas—and through flooding the marketplace with worthless objects that no one really wants but which will automatically be purchased because money moves as naturally from consumer to seller as water seeks its own level in a sewer system.

Velcronomics' answer to the supply siders is *blind-side* economics, which holds that producers and consumers both move about in a shadowy labyrinth of misinformation, thwarted material desires, and unenlightened self-interest, frequently bumping into one another as they race toward the elusive reward they've been promised by battalions, if not whole divisions, of clever hucksters who use the sophisticated persuasive techniques of television and other mass-media advertising vehicles to trap unwary consumers totally ignorant of the *caveat emptor* doctrine. Blind-side economics, though not generally recognized under that name, finds a cynically enthusiastic audience among every paranoid liberal's favorite boogey men, the Trilaterialists. Consequently, blind-side economics has many powerful enemies, not least of whom are those who would like to force greater freedom onto an already chaotically free-market economy.

What Velcro Has to Say about Adam Smith

Let us turn now for a moment to another phrase which, though originating many years ago from the pen of Adam Smith...a man some call the putative father of economics-...carries a currency that leads to its frequent repetition in contemporary gatherings of econobabblers. I refer to Smith's famous words with which he describes the motivation leading every individual unconsciously to advance the good of society whilst pursuing his own interest. In Smith's words, this individual is led by "an invisible hand to promote an end which was no part of his intention."

Though I, like many others who have labored long in the oft-times inhospitable—and even hostile—climate of economics, greatly respect Smith, I believe the Velcronomic analysis of this motivation is more to the point today. The Velcronomist views this influence *not* in terms of Smith's "invisible hand" but rather in terms of a highly "visible foot."

That is, the "foot" of monopolistic forces—whether capital, labor, or the secret police—has so rudely marched across the modern landscape that none of us remains untromped by its terrible power.

The Velcro Laws

Velcronomics eschews such cleverly casuistical terms as "money supply" or "seasonally adjusted unemployment figures" because they fly in the face of the indisputable idea that such elegant fictions, though of great delight to both academics and men of commerce, inevitably founder on the shoals of two basic laws that I hope you will all feel privileged to hear publicized for the first time in this lecture:
1. The Law of Diminishing Returns on Non-Existent Capital, and
2. The Law of Investors' Panic Precipitated by Over-Reliance on Fictitious Statistics

Briefly, these Velcronomic laws may be elucidated thus: the law of diminishing returns on non-existent capital states that if you have no capital to begin with, you will have even less than nothing after you have invested it.

The law of investors' panic precipitated by over-reliance on fictitious statistics shows essentially that *all* measurements on which non-Velcronomic solutions projections and solutions are normally based deserve the jaundiced eye of pyrrhic skepticism because they are invented, stated, and confirmed by the very same basic tribe of prevaricators whose pronouncements succeed on the basis of the investing public's naive good faith.

America's daily business press tells us constantly of the nation's need to "reindustrialize" its economy. But Velcronomics asserts that this alone is inadequate. America should be aiming not for a strengthening of its industry but for a whole new economic era, an age for which we have not yet established even a vocabulary that describes the economic relationships of man to machine, man to job, man to man, or (for that matter) or man to woman. And Velcronomics, though admittedly still in its formative—it not infantile—stages, offers a way out of this narrow thinking, a way ...beyond Reaganomics. ∎

---

*This lecture was originally published in the SECRET PAPERS of the Stephen Duck Society, 2339 S. Taylor Rd., Cleveland, Ohio 44118.

ORGANIZATION OF UNDETECTED CONSUMER HAZARDS

A consumer-oriented organization devoted to problems that are not readily discernible but have become costly to the consumer.

P.O. Box 85
Tippecanoe, Indiana 46570

FOAMY BEER

It is all too familiar for us to see advertising in magazines, newspapers, on television and billboards showing a mug or glass of beer with the foam head constituting more than a third of the volume in the glass. In fact, the high head of foam sitting on top of the beer has been immortalized in advertising as if the quality of the beer has a relationship to the amount of foam that stands thereon.

Having implanted this image of desirability of a mass of foam, most manufacturers include into their formulation of beer a chemical derivative of alginate, in order to insure that the viscosity of the beer is increased to a degree so that the foam will hold its form for a reasonable period of time.

Alginates are extracted chemicals from seaweeds and derivatives of these are specifically designed for the beer industry. This makes possible the drinking of foam which constitutes bubbles of carbon dioxide which when dissolved in water results in carbonic acid.

The American public in particular, and probably much of the world in general, has acquired the practice of toasting their bread before it's eaten which has the effect of freeing the toast of carbon dioxide trapped therein during the baking process. The carbon dioxide in bread is exactly the same gas liberated by essentially similar yeasts as are utilized in brewing beer. Why we have become susceptible to a drinking habit of swallowing carbon dioxide bubbles in beer and carefully remove the carbon dioxide bubbles from bread by toasting is a little difficult to comprehend except that it may be explained by the enormous amount of promotional impact that directs our daily eating as well as social habits.

We doubt that our modest message will effect any serious change in beer-drinking habits but it somehow strikes us that the public should be informed so that at least those of us who may not wish to swallow derivatives of alginates could choose those beers which are free of these chemical additives.

THE SHOOKJONG SHAKES

Singapore is just emerging from a 12-day epidemic of fear.

It flashed through the Republic when it was rumoured that meat from pigs vaccinated against swine fever was spreading "Koro," a marked refraction of the penis which Chinese believe will vanish completely into the abdomen if unchecked, killing the victim.

All over the island desperate men, beset by a sudden shrinking feeling, have abruptly exposed and seized their retiring natures, and then held them captive with chopsticks, a loop of wire, a bit of string or their bare hands while anxious bystanders have run for the doctor or dialled 999. At least 600 sufferers have hurried to hospitals and private clinics.

"Koro" was first mentioned in traditional Chinese medical treatises 3,000 years ago and has passed down in warning tones from generation to generation ever since. Senior medical experts here call it the "cultural disease," since it is an inbuilt Chinese phobia. But it has also been found among Malaysian peoples and Sudanese, and both Indians and Malays have been among its victims this week.

Known as "shookjong" by the local Chinese, "Koro" seems to come from the Malay for tortoise and has no scientific Latin name. Western medicine regards it as a purely psychological affliction, an hysterical condition producing a real or imagined contraction of the male organ. But since anxiety can cause this shrinking, and the shrinking in turn causes anxiety, Singapore has been caught on a rising spiral of alarm.

Chinese healers have been curing cases with massage and herbal medicines (in one instance a mixture of pepper and brandy, half to be drunk, half to be rubbed into the affected part). Western-trained doctors have mainly talked the patient out of his panic...

Two successful press conferences by the Ministry of Culture have now cut the flow of "Koro" cases to a trickle. But although the people of Singapore were told that the shrinkage was a harmless phenomenon and that pig vaccine and pork had nothing to do with it, many still clung to their old-fashioned fallacies. Slaughter in the abattoirs fell from about 1,300 pigs a day to 100. The pig trade is now very slowly reviving.

—From the LONDON OBSERVER

ON SHOE BUCKLES, PULLEY BLOCKS, AND THINGS

Augeas*
Middlesex, EN2 8JL

Regular visitors to Kenwood will have studied with enjoyment the exhibition of eighteenth century shoe buckles that forms part of the Lady Maufe collection; and what better time than this Jubilee Year to remind ourselves of the origin of the industry for which our country is famous? On the evidence of Samuel Pepys, who, on January 14th, 1659, noted in his diary, "This day I began to put buckles on my shoes," it can be asserted that they came into fashion in that year; indeed it could be said that the introduction of these objects of adornment presaged the end of austerity and the Commonwealth, and the restoration of ostentation and the Monarchy.

Throughout the eighteenth and early nineteenth centuries, almost everybody wore shoe buckles, and the present exhibition demonstrates, in the words of the catalogue,[1] to which we are much indebted, "the astonishing inventiveness of the British craftsman before the age of mass-production". For a century and a half, "a man's social position could be determined by the quality of his shoe buckles, ranging from the diamond-studded gold of the flamboyant dandy to the sober silver of the merchant or master craftsmen who might change to silver-gilt for ceremonial occasions". The manufacture of shoe buckles became a major industry, and many jewellers and silversmiths announced on their trade cards that they were specialists in the art. Silver buckles were often marked with the maker's name, and there is a long list of manufacturers, many located in and around the City of London, from St. Paul's Churchyard to Holborn and St. Martin's Lane. Provincial centres also were active; Matthew Boulton was, among many other things, a buckle-maker, and in evidence to a House of Commons Committee in 1760, he stated that 8,000 people were employed as buckle-makers in the Birmingham area alone.

But the thriving and prosperous buckle industry was threatened with a sudden end when in the 1790s shoe buckles were swept out of fashion by the "effeminate shoe-string". This caused distress, according to the buckle-makers' petition to Parliament, to more than 20,000 people engaged in the industry, "who could find little comfort in supplying the limited needs of Court dress, legal officers, and the kilted Highland regiments". Happily, as every schoolboy knows, the threat of massive unemployment was averted by the prompt, courageous, and unprecedented action of the then Home Secretary, Lord Benwood Wedge, who, by the insertion of an inconspicuous and obscurely worded sentence into the middle of the Navy estimates, brought the whole industry into public ownership. A bemused nation awoke to find that the half-million pounds that ostensibly had been voted to double the size of the Navy in the face of the Napoleonic threat, had been annexed instead for the nationalisation, as it came to be called, of shoe buckle production. It is reported that when the news reached the Prime Minister, he said, "Roll up the map of Europe; it will not be wanted again in our life-time". Then, turning his face to the wall, he cried out for one of Bellamy's veal pies, and expired.

With the changes of government that resulted, the expansion of the industry was soon put in hand. A Department of Shoe Buckle Production and Marketing was set up with Benwood Wedge at its head, but the vigorous and thrusting export drive that he initiated soon resulted in continental accusations of 'dumping', and led directly to the resurgence of the Napoleonic Wars and the famous but since distorted gibe that the British were 'a nation of shoebucklers'. The denial of overseas markets threw the nation back on its own resources, and led, in an attempt to increase internal consumption, to government-inspired manipulation of fashion, the most notable being the reintroduction of the shoe buckle as an ornament for the top-boot, to which the popular military hero, Wellington, allowed his name to be attached. But voluntary action soon proved inadequate to absorb the rapidly increasing output, and Parliament was forced to introduce the first of many legislative measures, the Shoe

*Dr. D. Zuck.
Chase Farm Hospital. Enfield.

Buckle (Protection) Act of 1812. This made the wearing of shoe buckles compulsory, while at the same time prohibiting the import or manufacture of buttons and bows[2]; as a result the traditional gear of the Englishman, belt and braces, became de rigueur, while the weaker sex played their part by adopting the many-buckled stays and corsets. In the light of later events, this measure is now regarded by historians as "the thin end of the Wedge", for it was soon followed by further legislation. To provide the resources for the powerful and rapidly growing workers' organization, the Association of Shoe Buckle Producers, or A.S.P., the levy on the paste glass that was widely used for buckle decorations, which, under the Glass Excise Act of 1777 already stood at the high level of £ 1-1-5½d. per cwt., was raised to an incredible £ 5; and at the same time a swingeing shoe-buckle inheritance tax was imposed. An ill-advised, if short-lived, attempt to regulate shoe-buckle output, was effective only in stirring up the industrial strife that culminated in the Manchester Massacre, after which successive governments resigned themselves to tackling the problem from the consumer end. Much ingenuity was expended in seeking out new uses for shoe buckles. With simple modifications it was found that they could serve as door-knockers, handles, pendulums, weights, vanes for windmills, and, with the coming of the age of steam, ships propellors. It was, of course, Faraday, who, while idly turning a shoe buckle between the poles of a permanent magnet, discovered how to generate electricity; and even the great 1851 Exhibition was held in a building in the plan of an enormous buckle. By the mid-century it had been found accidentally that buckles, if made of wood, could be burned as fuel, a most valuable find for a country that was rapidly becoming impoverished; but the breakthrough that, even if it was not the beginning of the end, might justly be said to herald the end of the beginning, was the discovery that none of the various Shoe Buckle Acts had regulated the material from which buckles might be made.

As larger and larger areas of the country were taken over to store the vast mountain of shoe-buckle products that sixty-five percent of the working population were now engaged in turning out, attempts to export them forcibly to the colonies led to the progressive loss of the British Empire as one dependency after another sought its freedom. The discovery that small sharpened shoe buckles packed into mortar shells, grenades, and other projectiles, inflicted hitherto inconceivable injuries, temporarily brought this movement to a halt, but before long the problem of storage of a product that the rest of the world did not want again reared its ugly head. The Shoe Buckle (Transfer) Act of 1889 made it illegal to bequeath buckles, and subsequent legislation regulated the gift of buckles, and required the replacement of shoe buckles initially five yearly, and then at progressively shorter intervals until the current period of three months was arrived at. Associated with these enactments came the establishment of the Department of Shoebuckle Registration and Licensing, and the introduction of regula-

tions that required the stamping of buckles, and authorised the police to inspect them. This responsibility has, of course, been transferred to the Inspectorate and Corps of Shoe-buckle Wardens.

The reduction of output necessitated by two World Wars and the intervening slump provided temporary relief, but by the end of 1946 production was again in full swing, and the situation was rapidly becoming desperate. The Shoe Buckle (Storage) Bill of 1947, which sought to empower the Secretary of State for Shoe Buckle Storage to introduce regulations requiring the occupiers of all premises with a capacity greater than one thousand cubic feet to devote one half of the volume to the storage of shoe buckles brought protests from a cross section of the population, and for once the three estates of the realm, the Lords, the Church, and the Publicans, spoke with one voice. The discovery that all the almost new Victorian workhouses, that were to be the hospitals of the new National Health Service, were already packed to the doors with shoe buckles, almost led to the resignation of the Minister of Health; and the decision taken at a stormy Cabinet Meeting to remove them and store them in the mines instead, resulting in the disastrous coal shortage of the Winter of 1947 and the resignation of the Minister of Fuel; and required also for its implementation the nationalisation of the railways and the road transport industry.

STOWING THE SAIL, by Winslow Homer, Art Institute of Chicago

For the first time in one hundred and fifty years, voices were heard to ask, softly at first, and then more clearly, "Are all these shoe buckles really necessary?" A promising young professor at the London School of Economics was sent to Coventry by his colleagues for raising the question on a radio discussion programme, and eventually had to seek political asylum in the United States.

Fortunately, the situation had been eased somewhat by the great technical advances of the last ten years, that have enabled the problem to be tackled at both ends. The introduction of that brilliant innovation, the three-day week, has reduced output to the level where such developments as the storage of shoe buckles in concrete caissons in mid-Atlantic and steel cannisters in lunar orbit can just keep in step; and a most promising idea is the pilot plant for the recycling of shoe buckles. This, if successful, will allow the export of valuable processed shoe buckle waste to the industrialised manufacturing countries of Europe and the Third World. The importance of the buckle as a constituent of camel harness has recently been realised by the Department of Trade, and a marketing delegation is shortly to set out to the Middle East.

It is not generally realised that as early as the year 1800 an enormous number, estimated by one authority as over one million, wooden pulley blocks were being produced annually for the maintenance and refitting of the ships of the British Navy alone.[3] This immense requirement stimulated the design and setting up of machinery at Portsmouth for the mass production of pulley blocks; which innovation is associated with the names of those great engineers, Brunel and Maudsley.[4] But when the development of the steam engine for naval propulsion appeared likely to displace sail, and the livelihood of the pulley block workers was threatened... ∎

NOTES AND REFERENCES

1. **Hughes, B. and T.** (1972). Georgian Shoe Buckles. London, G.L.C.
2. Such protective measures were not an innovation. Tim Healey, M.B., F.F.R., writing on the protection of the wool trade in *John Peel Jottings*, *No. 62* (Wigton, S. Redmayne and Sons Ltd.), states, "Many curious protective Acts were passed of which those insisting upon woollen cloth as the only permitted material for a shroud are an example. An Act of 1666 first laid this down and after the Restoration this was reinstated in 1678. "An Act for Burying in Woollen" starts "For the encouragement of the Woollen Manufactures and prevention of the exploration of money for the importing of linen, it is enacted that no corps (sic) of any person shall be buried in any shirt, shift, sheet or shroud, or any thing whatsoever made or mingled with flax, hemp, silk, hair, gold or silver, etc., in any stuff or thing, other than what is made of sheep's wool only; on pain of £5". It finishes, most appropriately, "Provided that no penalty shall be incurred by reason of any person that died of the plague". The intervening clauses give details as to who is to attest to all this, and to whom the fines were to be paid. An informer received his share of the fine. The minister of every parish was required to keep a record of all burials within his parish and of the affidavits brought to him attesting to the material of the burial garment. These oaths were generally made by the woman who laid out the body and by a relative".
3. **Cardwell, D.S.L.** (1972). Technology, Science and History. London, Heinemann, p. 118.
4. **Armytage, W.H.G.** (1970). A Social History of Engineering. London, Faber & Faber, p. 117.

CONTINUING EDUCATION COURSES FOR 1984

Self Improvement

s1101   Creative Suffering
s1103   Guilt without sex
s1105   Ego Gratification Through Violence
s1108   Whine your Way to Alienation

Business & Career

BC-1   "I made $100 in Real Estate"
BC-5   How to Profit From Your Own Body
BC-6   The Underachievers Guide to Very Small Business
        Opportunities
BC-7T   Tax Shelters for the Indigent
BC-8   Looters Guide to Cities

Crafts

C102   How to Draw Genitilia
C105   Gifts for the Senile

Home Economics

EC401   How You Can Convert Your Family Room into a
        Garage
EC406   1001 Other Uses for your Vacuum Cleaner
EC408   How to Convert a Wheelchair into a Dune Buggy

Health & Fitness

11203   Exorcism and Acne
11212   Suicide and Your Health
11213   Biofeedback and How to Stop It
11216   Tap Dance Your Way to Social Ridicule

Submitted by:
Louis Herzberg
Nedlands, Western Australia

CONGRATULATIONS!

On your new, industrial quality, combined coffee maker and anti-armour missile launcher.
It's EASY to use the sensational

BREW—BLASTER

Just follow these simple directions

I Getting Started

1. Locate the cover plate on the ON-OFF switch. This is at the lower left corner on the back of the unit. CAUTION: If the BREW-BLASTER has been installed up against a wall, *do not attempt to move it away by hand.* Any unequal push on either side will warp the casing, making the unit permanently inoperable. If such a move is necessary, use your regular household Fork Lift Truck.

2. Remove the cover plate. Notice that the recessed receptables are *metric* size. Use a 4 mm Allen wrench. If you mistakenly try to use a standard American tool of the wrong size, it will break off and block the process until a machinist is called to drill out the broken pieces.

3. Depress the ON-OFF switch to turn the unit on. To discourage accidental activation, e.g. by curious children, the switch positions are not marked. The plate has been left blank. The ON position is along the bottom of the plate, two thirds of the way to the left corner.

II Preparation for Use

1. Load a missile into the gun barrel. The barrel is marked MISSILE HERE. Missiles may be procured from your local international arms dealer. CAUTION: Do not use any munitions of Syrian origin. (These may be identified by the "MADE IN KOREA" logo.) Syrian missiles often omit the safety shield on the detonator. They may fire accidentally during loading, resulting in embarrassment or decapitation.

2. Insert coffee beans into hopper marked COFFEE BEANS. This label has been provided to clarify even further the simple process of operating your BREW-BLASTER. CAUTION: Use only green unroasted coffee beans. If ground coffee is inserted instead, it will clog the mechanism, lock the motor, and blow the fuse. If this should happen, replace the feed mechanism, motor, and fuse. Replacement kits may be obtained from your dealer.

   Coffee beans should not be roasted prior to use in the BREW-BLASTER. When the missile fires, the heat of the exhaust gas is used in the ingenious design of this revolutionary new product to roast the beans to the exact degree for perfect coffee.

   Green coffee beans are imported regularly from Belize and may be purchased from your international food and drug dealer.

III Operating the Unit

1. Check the control panel. All lights should be green if instructions have been followed carefully. If any lights are red, discard missile and coffee beans, and start again. CAUTION: BREW-BLASTER should not be operated by color-blind persons. CAUTION: Do no expose discarded missile to extreme heat.

2. Pull sharply on the combined operation handle labeled FIRE/BREW. The unique design of the BREW-BLASTER permits one single action to activate both functions. CAUTION: Pull the handle hard. If it should stick halfway down, the unit must be disassembled by a repairman. CAUTION: Keep all body parts well clear of flame exhaust vent when pulling handle. (Flame exhaust vent is located 4 inches directly above the combined operations handle.) During operation, high temperature exhaust gas from the missile launch stage is discharged from the vent. This toxic discharge may be hazardous to your health.

3. PROMPTLY release combine operation handle. Although it rarely happens, there is a remote possibility that ionized gas in the missile reaction chamber may create a short circuit. In this case, dangerously high voltage levels may occur briefly on the combined operations handle. CAUTION: BREW-BLASTER should not be operated by individuals with cardiac weakness. Before first use of your unit, we recommend that you have a comprehensive physical examination.

4. A perfectly brewed pot of fragrant fresh coffee is now available in the container marked COFFEE DISPENSER. *Pour yourself a delicious cup and ENJOY!*

THAT'S ALL THERE IS TO IT!

Benjamin L. Schwartz
Reading, MA

COMMENT: A Gratifying Deregulatory Initiative at the Confluence of Technology, Safety, and the Graphic Arts

Michael B. Jennison*
Kip Tourtellot
Washington, DC

We have long been troubled by the rigidity of federal regulations requiring that the horn symbols on automobile steering columns and control stalks face from right to left, *viz*:

S5. *Requirements.* (a) Except as provided in paragraph (b) of this section, each passenger car, multipurpose passenger vehicle, truck and bus manufactured with any control listed in S5.1 or in column 1 of Table 1, and each passenger car, multipurpose passenger vehicle and truck or bus less than 10,000 pounds GVWR with any display listed in S5.1 or in column 1 of Table 2, shall meet the requirements of this standard for the location, identification and illumination of such control or display.

TABLE 1. Identification and Illumination of Controls

Column 1	Column 2	Column 3	Column 4
Hand Operated Controls	Identifying Words of Abbreviation	Identifying Symbol	Illumination
Horn	—	[4]	—

[4]Identification not required for vehicles with a GVWR greater than 10,000 lbs., or for narrow ring type controls.

S5.1 *Location.* Under the conditions of S6, each of the following controls that is furnished shall be operable by the driver and each of the following displays that is furnished shall be visible to the driver. . .

Hand-Operated Controls

(b) Horn.

S5.2.1 Vehicle controls shall be identified as follows:

(a) Except as specified in S5.2.1 (b), any hand operated control listed in column 1 of Table 1 that has a symbol designated in column 3 shall be identified by that symbol. . .

S5.2.1.1. . .The identification of a horn control need not appear to the driver perceptually upright except when the vehicle, aligned to the manufacturer's specifications, has its wheels positioned for the vehicle to travel in a straight forward direction.

49 C.F.R. ● 571.101 and Table 1 (excerpted) (1984). Imagine our delight, then, when we learned that the competent authority is planning to allow use of horn symbols facing to the right as well. We could only respond appropriately with the following modest draft memo:

MEMORANDUM

RE: Homeosonic Orthotubular Repercussive Noisificater (HORN) Deregulation

Reply to Att'n of: CFFE**
From: General Counsel, Avuncular Agency
To: Chief Counsel, Subsidiary Administration

Thank you for your analysis of the difficult issue of the proper placement of the Homeosonic Orthotubular Repercussive Noisificator (HORN)[1] symbol in new automobiles. On the margins of our last departmental colloquium, you mentioned that your admnistration was taking the bold step of allowing manufacturers of automobiles for the U.S. market to display HORN symbols facing either left or right on steering columns or control stalks, as the case may be. We share your view that deregulating, within limits, the directional orientation of such symbols is consistent with this Administration's policies.

With regard to your position that the symbol must continue to be displayed horizontally, we would like you to consider the following issues:

1) Is this requirement effective only when the plane of wheels is perpendicular to the standard datum plane and parellel to the longitudinal axis of the vehicle? If not, what performance standards are required to keep the HORN symbol properly oriented when, for example, the steering wheel is rotated or counter-rotated or the car is on its side or otherwise akimbo? (We note that proper orientation could be maintained through the use of a gimbal-mounted gyroscopically stabilized platform or a laser-based inertial orientation system, but we recommend avoiding promulgation of design standards.)[2]

*Mr. Jennison and Mr. Tourtellot are international lawyers with the U.S. Department of Transportation. The views expressed are their own and not those of the Department.
**The Committee of Fifteen Engineers.
[1]Known in the vernacular as Hand-Operated Remote Noisemaker.

2) Should there be a requirement forbidding the inverted display of the HORN symbol? If, what performance standards should be used to determine the lawful orientation of a bilaterally symmetrical, and thus directionally ambiguous, orthographic depiction? How can the reasonable disinterested observer tell if it is indeed upside down (topsy-turvy)?[3]

Finally, we pose two questions with respect to the truth-in-symbology issue:

1) Must the HORN symbol reflect accurately the appearance of the particular automobile's HORN device?

2) If not, what limitations are there on choice of symbol?[4] May, for example, a flugelhorn, euphonium, or basset horn be employed in place of the customary bugle? In this vein, you should consider permitting an *end-on* depiction (either anterior or posterior). As well as promoting anonymity and genericity,[5] this approach would, given the ergonomic propensity toward bilateral rather than radial symmetry, rectify many of the earth-center/base-plane reference problems enumerated *supra*.

We believe that resolution of these issues will expedite review by the Office of Management and Budget of this important, significant, major, environmentally sensitive, and small-business, minority-business, and disabled-person[6] impactive rulemaking.

---

[2]Similar problems are posed by positioning the HORN symbol on "tilt wheel" steering wheels. However, an inexpensive laterally balanced for-and-aft walking-beam counterweight device would rectify the problem. It would also remove any need for a companion rulemaking to require the installation of attitude and/or horizontal situation sensor/directors in passenger automobiles.

[3]Consider also the consequences of accidental or intentional airbag inflation, which obscures the HORN symbol(s) on the steering wheel. We suggest embossing the HORN symbol on the appropriate location on the airbag corresponding to the steering wheel location(s). You might also address the problem of providing braille HORN symbols for blind drivers.

[4]We perforce note the desirability, nay the necessity, of achieving the maximum possible international harmonization of technical standards relating to automobiles, of which this is ineluctably an example, among our Group B trading partners. See, e.g., Trade Agreements Act of 1979; General Agreement on Tariffs and Trade, Standards Code; organic documents of Working Party 29; *et al.* In this regard, we note with approval your agency's statement in Lamps, Reflective Devices, and Associated Equipment, Docket No. 81-11, 46 Fed. Reg. 43719 (1981).

Behind this Notice lies the continuing agency participation with such groups as the International Standards Organization (ISO) and the Group of Rapporteurs on Lighting and Light Signalling (GRE) of the Economic Commission for Europe in a cooperative effort to standardize motor vehicle lighting systems. A primary goal of these groups is to remove unnecessary differences between countries that tend to serve as barriers to international trade. With the increasing trend towards international harmonization, both domestic and foreign manufacturers are advocating a new look at automotive headlighting.

Dare we gainsay that HORN symbols are no less important?

[5]The nature, state, or condition of being generic, i.e., nonspecific.

[6]See the last sentence of note 3, *supra*.

LUMINESCENT PHENOMENA OF THE EXTERNAL FEMALE GENITALIA

P.A. MacDonald and M. Sydney Margolese
Radiation Laboratories, the Manitoba Cancer Institute,
Winnipeg, Canada
Fertility and Sterility, 1950, 1:26

Submitted By
Rick Vetter
Riverside, CA

The authors have made a study of the luminescence of the vulva in normal and abnormal physiologic states. It has been found that luminescence appears pre-puberally, is always present thereafter, and varies in character with cyclic fluctuations of the ovarian hormone levels.

Knowing nothing of the scientific aspects of this study, my only comment pertains to the intriguing potentialities of the "luminescent vulva." While I am sure that the learned authors did not wish to convey any such idea, I'll bet that the vision which leaped to the wicked minds of some readers of this paper, was that of a vulva glowing in the dark. I can imagine that such depraved readers might visualize the fairylandish picture of a colored picnic extending into the night, with luminescent vulvas twinkling like fireflies among the trees. I can also hear such low-minded persons remark that the luminescent vulva might serve better than a candle in the window to draw the weary wayfarer home to shelter, rest and romance, or crudely remark that where there is light there is heat. Endless possibilities along this line suggest themselves, but they have no place in a staid and dignified family publication like the Survey. The Editor apologizes to the authors for even the few above excerpts from the subconscious gutters of the minds of a few of his friends who have offended his delicacy by thinking such thoughts as have been quoted. **Ed: Fertility and Sterility.**

The Art and Science of Preventative Neglect

Denis R Benjamin M.B.,B.Ch.
Seattle, WA

I recently attended a seminar on the care and feeding of the marine diesel engine. I hoped to learn a little basic maintenance and disabuse myself of the mystique that diesel engines have always held for me. My sailboat, understand, is powered by a small single cylinder diesel engine. My previous boat had run flawlessly for six years without the change of a single filter, or, come to think of it, even a change of oil. I knew that my good luck with engines was due to run out. Moreover "preventative maintenance" had become the watchword of our mechanical civilization.

By the end of the seminar I was terrified. I had learned a hundred ways the machine could die. I left with a long list of regular tasks I was now mandated to perform on the engine to stave off its premature destruction. And what about my automobile?? Twelve years and 150,000 miles with only the occasional oil change and even rarer tuneup! No one could accuse me of practicing preventative maintenance. A blasphemous thought came to mind, "Is there any evidence that preventative maintenance has any value?" It is a catchword that makes good intuitive sense, but our intuition has let us down enough in the past. Might not the gurus of the mechanical world be making the same mistake that many physicians have in the recent past — assuming that every healthy organism is on the verge of self destruction unless we constantly prod, replace, clean, scrape, lubricate and purge various components on a regular basis? And might we not be producing more iatrogenic disease or even be creating new disease by our obsession?

The following study was performed with these thoughts in mind. It was supported by grants from an oil-recycling conglomerate.

Sixty (60) associates were questioned in the hospital cafeteria between 9.00 a.m. and 2.00 p.m. in a relaxed informal atmosphere. None had consumed more than 3 lattes or 2 espressos. Interviews were only conducted on partly sunny days, to limit the effect of weather on their outlook. Being Seattle, the study took two years to complete. Two questions were asked:

How frequently do you service your car?

How much trouble does it give you ? (estimated as the number of days lost driving and yearly expenditures on car repairs)

We discarded the results from all the surgeons since their chauffeurs handled all these trivial details. Another small group of responses were excluded. These were from a few environmentally aware health addicts who only ride bicycles. A number of these individuals don't even believe in engines. After exclusion of these data, and suitable hot oil massaging, fifty evaluable responses remained. Results are graphically displayed in Figure 1.

The results appear stunning. They are in fact perfectly predictable. A machine functions as an entire unit. It is more than the sum of its parts, each component being dependent on another. As it works, parts wear in a distinct pattern, until it "gets in the groove." Replace a part and what happens? You disturb the balance. New stresses are created on their components, inviting failure. Soon you get into the cycle of constant replacement, bank overdrafts and extreme frustration.

The answer to surviving in this technological age is so simple — preventative neglect. Do just enough to keep the system running. To steal a maxim from medicine — "above all do no harm." Other terms applied to this technique include "watchful waiting" and the more crass "if it ain't broke, don't fix it." This theory has wider application than simple mechanical devices. It was successfully employed in politics and public policy planning during the Reagan years, during which time it was known as "benign neglect." We challenge the promoters of obsessive and elaborate maintenance schedules to produce sound documentation disproving our theory. In the meantime we are pursing funding from a couple of local auto-wrecking companies to continue the studies and develop quantitative techniques to measure just how much neglect is optimal.

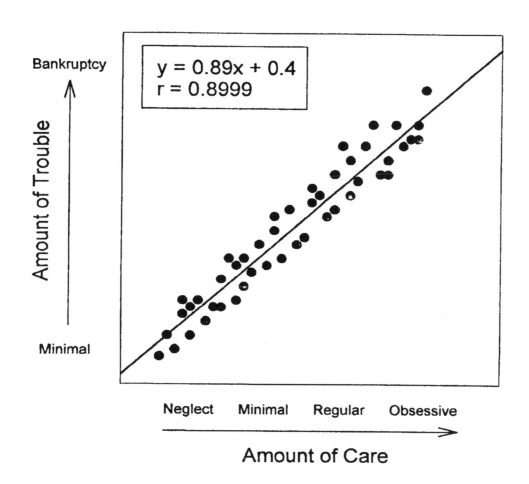

$$y = 0.89x + 0.4$$
$$r = 0.8999$$

Bankruptcy

Amount of Trouble

Minimal

Neglect   Minimal   Regular   Obsessive

Amount of Care

.. AND CAST THE SURLY BONDS OF EARTH ASUNDER
...SOMETIMES

R.R. JEFFELS, Principal
Okanagan College
1000 KLO Road
Kelowna, B.C., Canada V1Y 4X8

There is a languid, friendly, almost lovable informality about airline schedules these days, as though a new race of Luddites were throwing bits and pieces of rusty scrap-iron into the gleaming gullet of the computer. Things don't always go as they should.

Now, I have no real knowledge about how airline schedules are created, tested, and put into operation. But I see a vast team of young men with MBAs (transportation option) — trained in Cartesian logic, probability theory and critical-path planning — coagulated somewhere outside Toronto in a converted rubber-mat factory. The eyes are narrow, knowing, calculating: those eyes have seen everything, including the spectral image of Time Future. They talk ceaselessly and knowingly about input, bits, bytes, software, hardware, garbage-in-garbage-out, and the relative merits of COBAL vs FORTRAN vs WATFIV. And they spend their lives writing endless variants on depVan0830hrsarrTor1515hrsexcSatSunandstathols.

But somewhere along the line, a vast and consuming ennui overtook them. They yawned in their collective lassitude and said: "What the hell! All we really need is a general approximation of TOT and ETA." And a clever one trained in the philosophies of the East reflected: "In the divine order of things, in the black rolling reaches of infinite space, on the further frontiers of the eternal mind, what is this moment in 1978? A mere flashing spark in the roaring fire of Time. Let 'em wait."

It's an imperfect world, I know: God is perhaps an absentee landlord, and Man a mere mote in His eye. But still and all, these little delays can be annoying: an extra day in Toronto, three in London, an hour lost in Saskatoon . .. it tests a man's patience, courage and resolution. We all understand what can go wrong and we're sympathetic: strikes (pick today's job classification), mechanical failure, weather, acts of God, the slow delivery of bonded stock from the Sky Shop, overbookings, geese on the runway.

There was a new one the other day in Vancouver. The nice young lady called the flight, admonished us about lighted tobacco, mentioned the inviolability of the first eight rows, described the sanctity of the blue boarding pass, ordered us to enjoy the flight, opened the swinging door, listened to whispered intelligence from a fellow-worker, then closed it again abruptly. "There will be a short delay, ladies and gentlemen. Please have a seat. We can't find the pilot." Eventually the pilot turned up, of course, and we cheered him as you do the runner who comes last in the marathon. It's a matter of honouring acts of bold courage and noble intention.

I know something about waiting in airports, especially in the endless tundra of Toronto's Terminal 2. When it was opened, the senior project architect referred to it with perverted pride, I thought, as a *People-mover.* A bit churlish and demeaning, you will agree. Not the same homey feeling we used to get in the Greyhound bus-station in East Edmonton or the old kiosque on the platform at Sioux Lookout. It seems to reduce me to a mere particle in motion, some kind of wobbling social molecule in a dark, endless void, and the idea strips me of wholesome thoughts about myself, my fellows, the universe, and certainly about the architect.

A man needs a lot of native craft and guile to amuse himself in an airport these days; and university courses in Slavonic Studies, Comparative Religion, and the Taxonomy of Vascular Plants don't seem to help. So much for spending your life furnishing the mansions of the mind. To begin with, there's always the brooding malaise that comes from being set aside from the mainstream of life, hermetically sealed in a chrome, plastic, and concrete bubble, sequestered twenty or thirty miles from an established centre of civilization where people still smile and move cheerfully among their stones.

And perhaps, just perhaps, there's some kind of brilliantly-contrived plot by a malevolent spirit to make you play the lead in Outward Bound: in reality, if the truth were known, you are booked on a flight that does not exist, for a destination unknown, with a spectral crew, and gray ghosts for traveling companions. Ever get the feeling? Time no longer exists in the concrete bubble, but yet it's not the placid timelessness of an old-fashioned ocean voyage. Usually you measure the wait in hours not days so the opportunity does not exist to chronicle the tragic story of your life, dine with the captain, slosh down duty-free Scotch, lose at the bridge table, or begin a darkly-productive liaison.

The question, as the French say, poses itself: what to do? You can spend just so much time passing and repassing through the electronic scanner at the security check. Not that I don't enjoy it: testing whether or not the musical note of the cattle-prod changes with each succeeding entry. By the way, it does. But the attendants are knowing coves and they soon get to recognize you. There are muted snickers about your aberration. *Volvophilia,* I suppose you'd call it. And you may be more psychologically resolute than I am in finding decent pastimes, but I can't watch the baggage carrousels turning in their quiet, monotonous despair for more than ten minutes at a stretch. I get too emotionally involved with that last, lost valise from London. It waves its multi-coloured, tattered travel tags heroically but forlornly. It's on the verge of surrender . . . like a lost patrol in a desert fort under siege. It's not coming out alive, and the captain knows it.

I've put in some profitable hours examining, in parallel and comparatively, the rates offered by Avis, Hertz, Budget, and Tilden. It's the supreme test of clerical skill. Is there really a difference between the 12-cents-a-mile levy plus the basic per-diem rental charge plus insurance against the no-mileage charge, flat-rate, all-in, drop-any-where, pay-for-gas-and-oil imposition? Except on weekends, of course. I may be a mathematical illiterate (a non-quantitatively-oriented person, as my friend the professor of mathematics puts it), but let me tell you there isn't the thickness of a cigarette paper of difference between the lot.

Mutual of Omaha wants to bet me — and the odds are fairly decent — that I won't die, physically, before I reach London. I refuse the bet. I never could stand the thought of my own death, not even for insurance purposes.

The little foreign exchange bank, just over there, speaks 29 different languages; and each has slurring, contemptuous remarks to make about the Canadian dollar. Say *sound as a dollar* these days and it means *having a hollow ring.* It stands, this black and dismal day, at 84.25 American. I hear full scorn in the voices of Italy, Spain, Germany, Greece, Luxembourg, and Sweden, but I turn a deaf ear to Peru, Bolivia, Tanzania, and Iceland. A nation can stand just so many insults and indignities. Anyway, to hell with it, I need neither zloty nor drachma. I'll take my exchange in solid pounds sterling . . . only they're not solid, pounds, nor sterling any more. I tell you . . . we have seen the death of Empire. Now we're pallbearers at its funeral.

Eating and drinking eventually sate you. In any case, the Fort-Knoxian prices are enough to turn bread to brick in your mouth. You've read everything in the bookstore, at least everything that doesn't bring the hot blood of guilt to your cheeks. You grow ashamed of your own pulsing avarice as you watch the overseas travellers in the Duty Free Store ordering bottles of Grant's Best Procurable, cartons of Rothmans, fistfuls of Seikos . . . and all the perfumes of Arabia. The genuine seal-skin change-purses bearing the blazon Toronto no longer excite me, and I've had it up to the third man with totem poles. The Hummel

figures — once chaste and chubby children — now wear knowing leers. I don't want a specially-reduced official souvenir nylon-and-plastic carry-all from the Edmonton games. I didn't want one even before they were specially reduced: my taste runs to top-grain leather. The local hand-crafted pottery looks suspiciously oriental, and the all-Canadian maple sugar candies come in boxes stamped *Made in USA.*

I have gleaned the ground, here and there, for discarded newspapers from across the world, read the headlines, scanned the editorials, agonized over the astrological columns, picked the least offensive: "Scorpio (October 24 — November 22) Stay close to home. Travel is risky. Expect delays and frustrations. There is unexpected expense and your stars repeat certain cautions. Your health should improve slowly. Virgo and Pisces persons show influence."

By now I have exhausted the cultural resources of Terminal 2, and I take up my position in one of those concrete and naugahyde in-out trays that pass for easy chairs: the ones with short back and sides to discourage loitering. Across the aisle a woman of middle years ruminates on chocolates and knits, mouthing the count, like a method-actor in the wings waiting to go on. I examine the nails of my left hand intently and wonder if anything of value is buried there. I attempt a cross-word puzzle, boldly, in ballpoint, but I give up almost immediately on two across which has a clue involving a knowledge of the hierarchy in the Moorish army at the time of Charlemagne.

Suddenly I feel the need to communicate with some one, anyone. There is a woman on my right — a big, handsome, worldly woman of about 40 —with crushed red velvet for a mouth and hair as black as the inside of midnight. She is bored. We are all bored . . . divinely bored. She stares into endless space, eyes narrowed in existential anguish, smoking a cigarette Bogart-style, lighted end cupped close against the palm. She lives in solitary confinement within the frozen syntax of her private thoughts.

I lean over casually and say politely: "Don't you think they ought to give college courses on how to wait in airports?" The honey-glazed eyes turn towards me momentarily. In them I read either quiet contempt or controlled fear. My pride rejects the former, accepts the latter. Controlled fear . . . as though somehow I had attempted an assault on her virtue . . . there, in the middle of Terminal 2, under the watchful eyes of men in uniform, in-law-visiting grandmothers, Baptist ministers, and women who knit. She says nothing. The head swivels slowly back to its original position, and she returns to war-time Casablanca with Ingrid and Humphrey. To preserve the last remnants of my tattered dignity I wait a decent length of time, get up, and let myself be carried downstream by a freshet of passengers who are just in from Mexico – sombreros, ponchos, espadrilles, tooled-leather bags: accoutrements destined for the next Rotary auction in Yahk, B.C., or Birch Bark, Ontario.

I find a second in-out tray further down the terminal. And just to hear another human's voice, I ask a man the time. He gives it to me without looking at the Timex, without removing his eyes from the centre-fold of Playboy. For a moment, I share Miss April with him over his shoulder: a brief *ménage à trois*. But he knows and shows pride of possession by slowly folding the magazine until Miss April goes into the pre-natal crouch. I turn away to my left.

I am looking straight into the yellow-green eyes and open smile of a man who is obviously from Britain: suits at a hundred quid a time, Rex-Harrison narrow-brimmed, one-edge-up-one-edge-down hat, three inches of white cuff, striped Guards tie, slip-on moccasins, tightly-rolled bumbershoot. Look, I know an Englishman when I see one. I ought to, I spent a decade there. I say something about North Sea oil and the decline of the value of shares in Rolls-Royce. The mouth and eyes continue to smile blandly, even obediently, but he says nothing. He is obtusely indifferent to my overtures,. We sit looking and smiling at each other, thoroughly compromised. Then I notice he's wearing an ordinary luggage tag on a string through the button hole of his topcoat. It identifies him as a *restaurateur* from Athens on his way to Moose Jaw. He has access to no language but his own. I nod briefly in his direction and begin my wanderings again.

Vaguely, through the leaves of an artificial rubber plant, I watch the crews coming in to take command of aircraft. They look lean, rested, bronzed, carefree and, my God, *young*. At today's prices, the traveller has the right to men who look like aging philosophers, not Olympic runners. A pilot, any pilot, should be at least as old as your father. Not one of them is wearing the 1939-45 Star. They look as though they should be driving Formula 5 cars in Monaco, not shepherding Boeing 747s through troubled skies and across clouded moons. I want my pilot to be a Moses, recently descended from the mountain, bearing with him the Laws of Flight inscribed on tablets of stone. What do these beardless youths really *know* about yaw, torque, negative dihydral, forced landings, and dead reckoning . . . I mean what with everything being done by cybernetics these days? Personally I prefer the baling-wire-and-pink-sealing-wax days of aviation. At least you knew when the damn things were moving: you could feel the wind on your face.

A remote, sepulchral voice comes on the loudspeaker: it has a vast *mal du siècle* quality about it. In four languages, including my own, it proclaims the imminent departure for London of my delinquent aircraft. The long crocodile of passengers moves towards the gate. Up ahead I see the worldly lady with the crushed velvet mouth talking animatedly to my sullen stranger with the Timex watch and the special option on Miss April. So much for human fidelity. I cling to the boarding pass as though it were my special pink blanket, and I'm on my way to the next adventure in flight.

Injuries caused by the cold include all those due to lack of warmth

International Civil Defence Organization
I.C.D.O. Monographic Serial No. 5

"Sudden death, though fortunately it is rare, is frequent..."

British Medical Journal (No. 6119, April 22, 1978, P. 1010)

"AsTable 1 reveals, the variability in licking due to the differences between the two confederates is not significant nor does the confederate variable interact with any of the other variables."

Holstein, Carolyn M., Goldstein, Joel W., Bem, Daryl L. The importance of expressive behavior, involvement, sex, and need-approval in inducing liking. *Journal of Experimental Social Psychology*, 1971, 7, 534-544.

USDA reports *negative* DES findings at 10 days withdrawl. Now for the forthright fortnight and month residue analysis. If it isn't there after 10 days, why would it still be there after two weeks and thirty days?

A VISCERAL APPROACH TO ECONOMIC POLICY: LESSONS FROM THE LAUGHER (SIC) CURVE

Paul E. Greenberg
James A. Haley
Ottawa, Ontario Canada

In the late 1970s, advocates of supply-side economics argued that taxes could be reduced and budgets balanced simultaneously. Perhaps the most prominent proponent of this Panglossian paradigm is the polemicist, Arthur Laffer, who reportedly first expounded his now-legendary theory on the back of a cocktail napkin[1] in a Washington bar.[2] Laffer demonstrated to an amazed David Stockman that, beyond some level, further tax increases actually lead to a reduction in government tax revenues as individuals engage in unproductive activities designed to shelter their income. In 1980, Laffer's imaginative analysis enabled Candidate Reagan to assert, with theoretical justification, not only that the deficit could be eliminated by reducing the tax rates of the well-to-do, but also that the subsequent explosion in the productive effort of the private sector would create the wealth required to restore the once proud military to its previous position of strength.[3]

Laffer concluded that marginal tax rates were too high on the basis of an exhaustive process of visceral analysis[4] in which he "discovered" that the economy was on the downward sloping portion of the Laffer curve. Implicit in Laffer's analysis is the assumption that the wealthy are more productive than other socio-economic classes in the economy.[5] He was then able to prove that tax revenues could be raised with lower marginal tax rates on the wealthy by showeing that when starting on the downward sloping portion of the Laffer curve, the *maximim maximorum* could only be reached by creating private incentives to above-ground economic activity through lower tax rates.

Our own work in this area focusses on the backward-bending labour supply curve, which can be easily derived from a simple model of the work/leisure tradeoff. Following Laffer, we undertook an extensive visceral analysis[6] which led us to the conclusion that the rich are situated on the downward-sloping portion of this curve.[7] From this, of course, it follows directly that raising the marginal tax rates of the rich would result in increased work effort on their part as after-tax income is reduced, thereby stimulating output and employment, and

THE RAG PICKER, by Edouard Manet

increasing government tax revenues.[8] Nirvana could not possibly be more easily accessible, even with a super-saver ticket.

The importance of our analysis, while self-evident, may require further explanation to supply-side economists. What we have clearly proved on an intuitive level is that the government can achieve two important macroeconomic policy objectives simultaneously; it can eliminate budget deficits, and reduce unemployment in the economy merely by raising the marginal tax rates of the wealthy.[9] Their increased desire to work will create new wealth in the economy which will, of course, trickle down to everyone's benefit.

---

[1]The well-known economist, John Kenneth Galbraith, has remarked that the napkin would have been better left to its original purpose.

[2]The importance of food and drink in shaping the modern world should not be dismissed. Napoleon, for instance, accounted for the early success of his armies with the credo: ''An army marches on its stomach''. See: Ham Sandwich, *Modern History: A Gastronomic Interpretation* (Unpublished Doctoral Thesis, Universite de Cordon Bleu), and Biff Wellington, *The Role of Lettuce in the Industrial Revolution* (Papers and Proceedings, ''The Leafy Vegetables Lecture Series'', Culinary Institute of America).

[3]Ronald Reagan has, for quite some time, recognized the stifling effects of a burdensome tax policy. While he was an actor in Hollywood, he apparently would complain that excessive income taxation seemed to act as a major disincentive to making additional movies. However, since Reagan is loathe to make bold assertions based solely on visceral sentiments, he did not run for President until Laffer's theoretical breakthrough provided him with substantive support for his intuitively supply-side position.

[4]The process leading to this revelation is described by another prominent proponet of the supply-side paradigm, former quarter back and current Congressman Jack Kemp, who remarked: ''When you look around and see so much evidence of unemployment and underemployment. . .you sense that the (tax rates are too high.'' The importance of introspection in economic policy-formation has, for too long, been overlooked by the mainstream of the profession.

[5]This proposition stems from the writings of the famous 19th century social critic, Herbert Spencer, who was once privately heard to argue: ''If the rich are not more productive than the rest of society, whey then are they rich?'' It can be shown that the rich are the most productive members of society, for they reveal their inherent productivity through the accumulation of wealth.

Futher support support, on a metaphysical level, can be found in the teachings of John Calvin, who preached that the deity rewarded those who worked hard with worldly riches. Consequently, if God favoured you with riches, it could be inferred that you were more productive. One need only recall the attempt by the Hunt brothers to monopolize the world silver supply to convince oneself of the validity of this proposition.

[6]Our technique is described in greater detail in a forthcoming essay entitled ''Proper Uses of the Entrails of Ruminants in Forecasting Economic Behaviour'', in *Zoological Econometrics*.

[7]We relied on extensive anecdotal evidence as well.

[8]The observant reader will realize that our policy recommendation depends, as does Laffer's, on the superior productivity of the rich. We believe that it is important to impose onerous taxes upon these individuals in order to force them to work more. Under these conditions, failure by the rich to undertake more economic activity in response to a tax rise would jeopardize the lifestyle to which they have grown accustomed.

[9]Actually, it has been shown at various times that a government can achieve no more than two objectives in a given time period, or three if it has enough money.

Bug in-ear theories are finally decided

Submitted By:
Alan Tyler
Jackson, MS

Clarion-Ledger-Jackson, MS, p. 1A - May 3, 1985

BOSTON — When a patient walked into the emergency room with a cockroach hiding in each ear, doctors knew they had a once-in-a-lifetime chance to settle one of the uncertainties of medical science.

''We recognized immediately that fate had granted us the opportunity for an elegant comparative therapeutic trial,'' they wrote in a letter in Thursday's New England Journal of Medicine.

The proper way to remove a cockroach from someone's ear, it seems, has been the subject of little-publicized disagreement. The time-honored method is to drop some mineral oil in the ear, then try to pull the little critter out. A newer, competing technology is to squirt it with lidocaine, an anesthetic, to make it bug out on its own.

The doctors did a comparative experiment. In one ear went some mineral oil.

''The cockroach succumbed after a valiant but futile struggle, but its removal required much dexterity on the part of the house officer,'' they reported.

In the other ear, they sprayed some lidocaine.

''The response was immediate,'' they wrote. ''The roach exited the canal at a convulsive rate of speed and attempted to escape across the floor. A fleet-footed intern promptly applied an equally time-tested remedy and killed the creature using the simple crush method.''

The experiment was conducted by Drs. Kevin O'Toole and Rick Martinez at Charity Hospital in New Orleans, and it was written up for publication by Dr. Ronald D. Stewart, director of emergency medicine at the University of Pittsburgh School of Medicine.

''This is not an uncommon problem,'' Stewart said in an interview. ''We in emergency medicine see this quite frequently. It usually happens to children who are sleeping. Cockroaches like warm, dark places. There are no warmer, darker places, with few exceptions, than the ear canal.''

However, this case of double cockroach ear blockage appears to be a first in the annals of medicine, he said.

Organization Of Undetected Consumer Hazards
(O.U.C.H.)

A consumer-oriented organization devoted to problems that are not readily discernible but have become costly to the consumer.

ON CANCER-CAUSING AGENTS

In 1958 the United States congress passed the Delaney Amendment, which required that any substance found to be carcinogenic, literally under any circumstances of testing, be banned as a food additive. Thus, as a result of the Delaney Amendment, the government has mandated that packets of artificial sweetener such as those containing saccharin or derivatives of saccharin be labeled:

"Use of the product may be hazardous to your health. This product contains saccharin which has been determined to cause cancer in laboratory animals".

What the legend fails to indicate is that the amount of saccharin that had been previously found to cause cancer in experimental animals, would require the intake in a human of almost a third of an adult's full weight; in other words, one would literally have to be eating nothing else but saccharin by the spoonful, in order to simulate the experimental design which was found to cause cancer in a single animal and in a very restricted animal study.

Nevertheless, because of the Delaney Amendment, saccharin containing products are so labeled, and we would expect that other agents which have been found to be carcinogenic would be so labeled and these are:

Nitrites:

It has been found that high doses of sodium nitrite, a common ingredient in many foodstuffs, increases the incidence of benign and malignant liver neoplasms in rats (1). Nitrites have been shown to be converted to nitrosamines in many situations and nitrosamines have clearly been demonstrated to be highly carcinogenic (2). There has been no labeling to our knowledge on any foodstuff containing nitrites that they have been shown to be carcinogenic, or that they may be modified into nitrosamines which are carcinogenic.

Safrole:

Safrole may be found in many spice flavorings, such as anise oil, sassafras oil, or cinnamon leaf oil. Safrole has been shown to be carcinogenic (3). Again we have not found safrole labeled as a potential carcinogen when it is found in any food ingredient or spice flavoring.

Phenacetin:

Phenacetin is an aniline derivative which has been associated with human cancer, and was formerly widely used as a component of aspirin and caffeine (4). We have not seen phenacetin-containing preparations marked as being carcinogenic or even potentially carcinogenic.

Chromium:

It is possible to walk into almost any pharmacy these days and buy a bottle of tablets containing chromium salts. Chromium compounds are also a component of sugar and cigarette tobacco. Chromium compounds have been clearly shown to be carcinogenic (5). We have not seen any products on the shelf either in foodstores or pharmacies that contain chromium salts that have been labeled as carcinogenic or potentially carcinogenic.

Cigarette Smoke:

The number of compounds, some merely toxic and others markedly carcinogenic, which have been found in cigarette smoke are literally legion (6). One of the most active carcinogenic chemical in cigarette smoke is benzopyrene (7). Yet we have not found any cigarettes or any other products which contain these potent carcinogenic substances, labeled as clearly causing cancer.

Perhaps an explanation should be forthcoming to the American people to determine why the Delaney Amendment has not been implemented for these and a plethora of other products as it has been for saccharin where the cancer causing activity is more minimal than any of those cited above (8).

(1). Lijinsky W, Kovatch RM, Riggs CW (1983) Altered incidences of hepatic and hematopoietic neoplasms in F344 rats fed sodium nitrite. Carcinogenesis 4:1189-1191

(2). Chemical Carcinogenesis and Mutagenesis I, C.S. Cooper and P.L. Grover, Springer-Verlag, New York, 1985, p 76

(3). Chemical Carcinogenesis and Mutagenesis I, C.S. Cooper and P.L. Grover, Springer-Verlag, New York, 1985, p 395

(4). IARC(1980) Phenacetin. IARC Monogr 24:135-161

(5). U.S. EPA (1984) Health assessment document for chromium. Final report. EPA-600/8-83-014F. Environmental Criteria and Assessment Office, Re search Triangle Park, North Carolina

(6). Chemical Carcinogenesis and Mutagenesis I, C.S. Cooper and P.O. Grover, Springer-Verlag, New York, 1985, pp 67-68

(7). Benzopyrenes, Martin R. Osborne and Neil T. Crosby, Cambridge University Press, 1987

(8). The Final Report on Saccharin, Dr. Morris Cranmer, Orbital Advertising, P.O. Box 134, Park Forest, IL 60466

PRESS RELEASE

Baghdasarian Receives "Stir-the-Pot Award"

The National Organization Taunting Safety and Fairness Everywhere (NOT-SAFE) is proud to announce that it has selected Uxbridge, Massachusetts "do-it-yourself" plumber, Peter Baghdasarian to receive the 1987 "STIR-THE-POT" Award.

In 1974, after notifying authorities that he intended to install his own plumbing (in the house he was building for himself), officials knew they were dealing with a radical "plumbing pirate", indeed a *"Toileteer"* of the first degree. By challenging the monopolistic and intimidating Massachusetts plumbing laws, Mr. Baghdasarian has inspired hundred, perhaps thousands of other would-be *Gardeners* (who might dare to landscape their own yards), *Mechanics* (who might risk imprisonment for cleaning their cars spark plugs), do-it-yourself *Doctors* (who might remove a splinter from their child's finger), or self-proclaimed *Professors* (who might provide unlicensed educa-tonal instruction to friends, relatives of even total strangers!).

After enacting many of the nations strictest tax, gun control and building code laws, the Massachusettes legislature seems oblivious to the fact that their state coincidentally (?) has one of the highest deliquent taxpayer and per-capita murder rates in the country. . .and of course there are many more "Baghdasarian-types" still lurking among the pipes, waiting silently with wrenches and unlicensed blow torches in hand.

Mr. Baghdasarian now faces criminal charges for recently installing a faucet at his home while inspectors, union officials and even the town patrolman watched. This Doubly-Defiant act of intentional and unmitigated "plumbing" deserves just recognition and reflects highly upon one man with a backbone, Mr. Peter Baghdasarian, our *"Taunter of the Year"* for 1987.

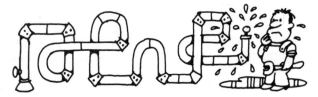

Cautiously,

Dale Lowdermilk
Founder NOT-SAFE
Montecito, CA

ENVIRONMENT

NATIONAL GEOGRAPHIC: DOOMSDAY MACHINE REVISITED

VICTOR MILSTEIN, Ge. 01
Academy of Appurtenant Analyses

Kaub's excellent article (JIR, 1974, 20:22–23) was the first organized warning of imminent disaster. Unfortunately Jones' recent response to this is quite erroneous and dilutes the efficacy of the alert. The same issue of the Journal (JIR, 1974, 20, No. 4) contains a letter by Koosman (page 31) which reports a directly validating experience of Kaub's hypothesis but then goes on to deny the generalizability of it.

Allow me to dispose of Koosman's ready acceptance of his Texan's explanation first. Texas will sink (sic) and is in fact sinking (sic) at present. The reason for this has nothing to do with the accumulation of the magazine Kaub described as beautiful, educational and erudite, since these qualities usually are not considered in relation to oil in Texas. While it is true that the oil that is being pumped out of the ground is replaced by the brine pushing it out, this will not save Texas. Everyone knows that oil floats on water; even salt water. (Remember the oil-soaked gulls and other birds after the oil-spills in the Gulf of Mexico and along the Atlantic and Pacific Coasts?) This means that the light oil that Texas is floating on is being replaced by brine. This heavier brine will compress the material under it and sink deeper into the earth. *Quod erat demonstrandum,* Texas will continue to sink (sic).

To return to Jones' whitewash of the impending catastrophe. He makes eight assumptions in arriving at his conclusion that it will require 24.92×10^9 years to depress the crust of the United States 100 feet. Of these eight assumptions, two are completely incorrect and three are irrelevant (numbers 1, 3 and 6). The two crucial, incorrect assumptions are numbers 2 and 4. Number 2 assumes that the monthly circulation of National Geographic will remain constant. Since the population of the United States and especially the population of children in the U.S.A. is increasing, it is clear that the monthly circu-lation of National Geographic will also increase since the magazine is subscribed to mainly for school children. (The initial subscription is taken out with the intent of allowing the child to cut-up the magazine. However, the beauty of each issue is such that parents never permit such sacrilege.) Thus, since the population of the United States is increasing, the monthly circulation of the Magazine will also increase. This will be a lower bound estimate since both standard of living and degree of pretentiousness have been increasing at a more rapid rate than the population of the United States. This pretentiousness is an important motivating factor in subscribing to National Geographic.

The other critical assumption, namely number 4, is that the magazine is evenly distributed over the 48 states is false. In truth, the 23 states comprising the Eastern one-fourth of the country in land area (in fact 23.8%) comprises more than half (56.4%) the population. Thus, it is clear that more than 50% of the density of the increasing numbers of the magazine is accumulating in less than one-fourth of the land mass.

These figures necessitate a recomputation of the ultimate effect of accumulation of National Geographic Magazines. The most likely result, taking account of the increasing population density of the West Coast as well, is that subsidence will occur at both the East and West Coastal ends of the United States. The probability is that both coasts will sink, and the West Central portion of the United States (with the exception of Texas, as noted above) will be raised up an average of 217 meters. And, Jones to the contrary, this will take place in much less 24.92×10^9 years. It will occur in 457.247×3^7 years! Clearly Kaub's warning must be heeded if we are to avoid disaster.

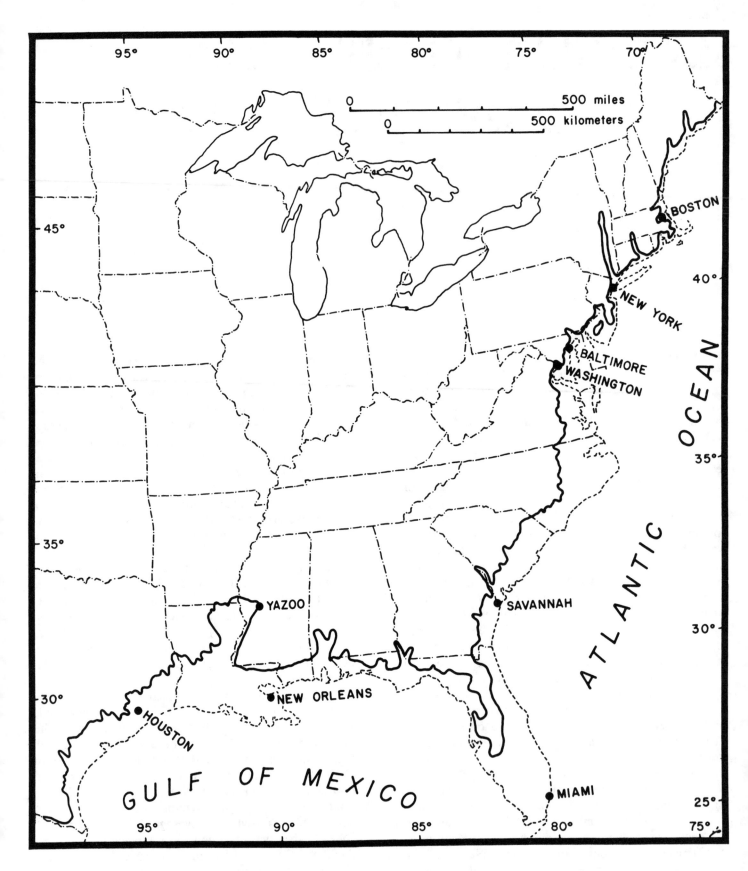

FIGURE 1.

The eastern coastline of the conterminous United States. The
present-day coastline is indicated by the dashed line. The
heavy, solid line represents the coastline following depression
of the continental landmass 100 feet (30.48 m.) upon extensive
accumulation of the National Geographic Magazine.

House Plants and How to Stop Them

CALVIN TOMKINS

Of conspiracy and clammy tendrils.
Notes from a counter-revolutionary

Three months ago I agreed to look after the apartment of a man who lives in my building while he was out of town on business. Looking after it meant watering the plants, which sounded innocuous enough. He had promised to leave a watering schedule and he had also rambled on a bit about "trouble signs" and "misting" and other arcana, but I didn't listen very hard, and, never having been in his apartment, was in no way prepared for what I found when I let myself in the door, squeezed past the large, spiny *Anthraxia dementis* that took the place of an umbrella stand and surveyed the infestation within.

Plants of every size and description obscured the windows, encroached on the walls and furniture and drooped menacingly from overhead supports. An odor of rotting vegetation made breathing difficult. Suppressing a shudder, I made my way to the kitchen, thinking I would moisten a handkerchief and hold it to my nose, but the sink was so thoroughly clogged with wandering arab and bridalclaw that I was unable to find the taps. The bathroom, when I got to it, was even worse—tangled, sawtoothed *Detestia woodii* filling the tub and spilling over in dangerous profusion on the floor.

In the bedroom, where I ventured next, the shades were drawn and I could see nothing. As I groped for the light a clammy tendril of *Travestia malens* wrapped itself around my neck and I gave way to panic. Flailing wildly at the fronds and creepers that sought to hold me back, I fought my way through thickets of smugrose and lampbane, banged my head painfully against a low-lying branch of *Ficus horribilis* and stumbled, gasping for breath, out the door and down the stairway to the street.

It took me an hour or so to get hold of myself. I walked around the neighborhood, drinking in the light, tangy smog and feeling underfoot the reassuring solidity of concrete and refuse. Somewhere along the way, though, I started to notice something I had never quite absorbed before. Every block seemed to have at least one store and sometimes two or three stores selling house plants. Not only that—every bar, every restaurant, every drugstore and grocery and massage parlor had its own interior jungle through which customers, grown oblivious from habit, poked and shouldered their way to get at the merchandise.

In my local bookstore I found, to my mounting dismay, an entire section devoted to volumes on how to grow plants indoors, all of them written by fierce-looking authors with suspiciously elongated earlobes. Could it be possible that a vast and sinister conspiracy was taking shape under our very noses? A quick glance through the Yellow Pages in a nearby Walgreen's confirmed my worst fears. The pathological spread of the house plant industry, far from being localized in my neighborhood, was out of control in every part of town. It was then that the full horror of the situation struck me. What we faced, I realized, was nothing less than the most serious case of ecological backlash yet uncovered. Nature, everywhere trampled and subverted in its own habitat, was striking back with a terrible vengeance, and it was doing so in that soft and vulnerable underbelly of our culture, the American apartment.

What to do about it was the question. I considered moving to the suburbs but that would have been the act of a coward, and besides, my intuition told me that things were no better out there. No, my civic duty was clear. Boldly seizing the initiative, I sat down and wrote urgent letters to my local congresspeople, demanding that they appoint an urban task force with powers of subpoena. Pending their official action, several friends has asked what they can do, individually, to help meet the foliage threat. Here, then are some practical suggestions for concerned citizens— interim measures that will not reverse the green counter-revolution, to be sure, but which may slow it down while more drastic measures are undertaken:

• Indirect Approach: Do not attempt to talk plant owners into throwing out their plants. They simply won't listen.

From GARDEN magazine
Published by The New York Botanical Garden

But you may be able to sow small seeds of discontent that will grow large on reflection. "How do you manage to keep anything alive with that poisonous *Torporosa* in the room?" is a useful gambit. Imply that they have invested far too heavily in yesterday's plants, thus missing out on *Peaflor jimmiana* and other trendy new species. Pinch up a little soil from around their most luxuriant *Bostonia strangulus,* sniff it, hold it close to your ear while rubbing between thumb and forefinger, wash your hands and leave hurriedly.

• Going Them One Better: This technique has proved effective in apartments where the owner talks to the plants, plays music to them and has them on demand feedings. "Not Mahler, for God's sake!" you might exclaim, as you rush to switch off the hi-fi. "Do you want to rootbind your *Streptocarpus*" A neighbor of mine reports that he got into a shouting argument with a large *Dracaena dubium* at a cocktail party recently; a drink was thrown, and both of them were asked to leave. I myself have had fine results from leering wolfishly at a hanging pot of creeping japonica over a period of an hour.

• Tips On Succulents: Cacti and succulents are particularly hard to combat. Overwatering alone is no guaranteed solution, and my own experience has shown that three vodka martinis actually caused a supposedly dormant *Comatosa terminalis* to bloom. Cigar ash, dropped skillfully on a monoecious node, appears at this writing to be a good bet, but the results are not yet conclusive. Small specimens such as *Flagrens discolor* and kick-me-not can be pinched back at the base when your hostess is not looking. Be alert for toxic spines.

• Natural Allies: Carry with you at all times a small bottle of Dichlorobenyldril, available at most drugstores and supermarkets under the trade name of 6-12. When other methods fail, a few drops of this odorless ichor, surreptitiously applied to a plant's root system, will soon attract aphids, mealybugs, red spider mites, scale, sowbugs, pillbugs and thrips in overwhelming numbers. These tiny but marvelously adroit creatures are still our best hope in the uphill struggle against house plants. They thrive in light, humusy soil or sphagnum moss. Keep away from direct sunlight and water daily.

Gerre: The Computer Typed Letter

Dear Mr. K.H. Leverly:

You and the other residents of 444 Undine Ct. in beautiful Glendale, CA. 90554 are especially aware of the importance of a nice green lawn along the streets of Glendale, CA. 90554. Yes, Mr. K.H. Leverly, what is more important to you, Mr. K.H. Leverly and to your city of Glendale, CA. 90554 than a good civic appearance. It means more pleasure for you, Mr. K.H. Leverly, and your neighbors on 444 Undine Ct. Your business, Mr. K.H. Leverly, too, will prosper if your area and all of Glendale, CA. 90554 looks green and beautiful.

Because of your evident civic pride we are sending you, Mr. K.H. Leverly, a special introductory offer for your lawn at 444 Undine Ct. Yes, for only $5.95, Mr. K.H.

Leverly, a 25 pound package of TALL TREES GARDENS special CUSTOM LAWN FEED, compounded just for your, Mr. K.H. Leverly, lawn at 444 Undine Ct. Yes, we have already gone ahead and approved credit for you, Mr. K.H. Leverly so if you Mr. K.H. Leverly return the enclosed card within 5 days we will send you Mr. K.H. Leverly free to 444 Undine Ct. our special CUSTOM LAWN FEED RAKE especially designed for use in Glendale CA. 90554. So hurry, Mr. K.H. Leverly!

Sincerely,
Thomas Youngman, for
TALL TREES GARDENS INC.

From The Offices of
TALL TREES GARDENS, INC.
of PASADENA CALIFORNIA

Futterman Scale Of Sunrises

David K. Lynch
Topanga, CA

1. Thick overcast, no colors, gradual brightening. Of no interest except to insomniacs, recent parolees and lower life forms with little photosynthetic capability.

2. Thick overcast, occasional thin areas. No color except a dull blue lasting a few minutes. Gradual brightening. Occasional stirring in the underbush. Damp breeze. Of interest only to roosters. No threat to Vampires.

3. Thin overcast, uniform grey. Color limited to dull blues with minor reds and yellows. Birds show some interest. Graveyards seem cheery. Vampires worried.

4. Thin overcast, some high clouds visible. Colors faded pinks and oranges, pleasant but unremarkable. More energetic birds take flight. First appearance of shadows and pale sunbeams.

5. Thin high clouds, scattered low clouds. Colors light pastels and airy, with occasional electric oranges accompanied by pink and yellow rays. Larks are heard and whole flights of wrens take to the skies. Much activity in the bushes. Distant violins can be heard. Breeze fragrant. Many promise to get up and enjoy the dawn more often.

6. Crisp air with cartoon animals in the clouds amid a backdrop of cerulean blues and aquamarines. Sunbeams spring from every cloud. Positively aromatic breeze, warm and motherly. Grazing cows stop and look up. Birds harmonize with cats. People stop and stare, bouncy violin quartet heard even indoors. Bambi and Thumper seen. Most sensitive people feel faint and must sit down.

Taken from: ULYSSES DERIDING POLYPHEMUS, by Joseph M.W. Turner, Tate Gallery, England

7. Clouds billow with multicolor pulsating fringe lace, sunbeams dance and sparkle. First cherubs appear around loftier buildups. Great sense of well being. Golden horns sound from above and drown out full orchestra. Fragrance of ambrosia quite pronounced. Bluebirds and robins fly sweeping formations and nocturnal bats remain aloft. Cats and dogs dance jigs. Great nations agree to discard weapons. Most people swoon if looking directly into sunrise. Artists drop like flies. Even southern Californians admit that it's far out (sic).

8. Clouds resemble Venus de Milo, David, Pieta. Colors almost indescribable as entire celestial vault throbs sending out wave after wave of shimmering color. Cherubs everywhere. Cupid seen darting between great trumpets. Music swells and approaches climactic crescendo, drowning out the pandemonium in the bushes, and audible in deepest coal mines. Few people remain standing, and many pass out, even those indoors and not directly illuminated. Breeze overpoweringly fragrant and carries all known species of birds aloft. Only one out of ten poets still conscious. Continental drift and evolution momentarily stop. Photographs impossible.

9. Details sketchy. Only eight such sunrises reported and only two verified. Eye witnesses limited to hardened criminals who saw sunrise relfected from bulletproof glass. #9 sunset suspected of causing dinosaur extinctions.

10. Theoretically possible. Probably fatal to most life forms, even those with little photosynthetic capability.

from The Scientific American May 16, 1903

The Historical Novel And Its Value In Trees

The flood of novels which has incessantly poured in upon us of late years, more than ever emphasizes the truism that of the making of books there is no end. A decade ago it was the so-called "psychological novel" that enthraled us; now it is the judiciously advertised historical novel that holds our rapt atention. Through the ingenious refinements of modern advertising the sales of fiction have been increased so prodigiously that a novel can hardly be called a "success" unless it has been sold to the extent of a hundred thousand copies.

The newspaper tales of the enormous editions of historical novels are by no means as fantastic as they may read. A list, carefully complied from publishers' returns which are absolutely without reproach, shows that the sales of nine recently published novels have reached astounding proportions. Of one book, over 400,000 copies have been sold. Another is in its 325 thousand. Less successful books have attained only a paltry sale of 100,000, while a few minor ones hardly exceed a disappointing 80,000.

It is not our purpose to dilate upon the relative merits of these volumes of fiction, but simply to show what it costs to satisfy the public appetite for tales of wild adventure.

Books are made of paper. Paper in turn is made of cellulose, of which the chief source of supply is timber. In order to describe the romantic career of a seventeenth century gentleman of the rapier, it is necessary to fell a few hundred trees; the publication of many narratives in which the exploits of other cavaliers are dwelt on, may therefore entail the destruction of a forest.

The nine novels to which we have referred had a total sale of over 1,600,000 copies. Since the average weight of each book sold was probably twenty ounces, a little calculation will prove that these 1,600,000 books contained approximately 2,000,000 pounds of paper. We are assured by a manufacturer of paper that the average spruce tree yields a little less than half a cord of wood, which is equivalent to about 500 pounds of paper. In other words, these nine novels swept away 4,000 trees, and they form but a small part of the fiction so eagerly read by the American public. Some books are worth more than 4,000 trees. What may be the tree-value of the modern historical novel it is not within our province to decide.

■

68

Cooking With Potential Energy

R.C. Gimmi
Gloria J. Browne,
Tucson, AZ

The obvious solution to any future energy crises is the development and use of potential energy. This form of energy is ubiquitous in nature; it is renewable; and, to date, it has largely been untapped.

All elevated objects possess potential energy. When an object is dropped from a height, its, potential energy is converted into kinetic energy. Upon impact with the ground, this kinetic energy is converted into heat. This phenomena may be described with the energy balance $\Delta Z \dfrac{8}{8\frac{}{c}} = C_p (\Delta T)$.

If the change in height (ΔZ) can be made sufficiently large, significant amounts of heat can be generated. Everyday tasks such as cooking could be made safe, simple, and energy efficient.

In our experiment, we proved that this can be done. In six hours, we partly cooked a 25 pound turkey with potential energy.

There was considerable debate among the investigators as to what we should cook. A goose was suggested but we finally settled on a 25 pound, defrosted, Greaseball ® brand turkey.[2]

At 9:00 in the morning, an undergraduate carried the bird tip the stairs to the tenth floor of the University of Southern Arizona administration building. From this vantage point, he flung the bird from a ledge.

Immediately after the turkey impacted on the pavement, the investigators inserted a thermometer into the carcass and recorded the temperature. The assistant then ran back down the stairs and retrieved the bird.

This process was repeated 72 times in six hours with the same turkey.

The world's supply of combustible energy resources, such as wood and fossil fuels, are rapidly diminishing. If civilization is to continue, we must quickly develop alternative non-combusting energy sources that can be used for basic human needs. Heating, transportation and cooking will be of paramount concern.

This new energy must be cheap, safe and of such low technology that it can be easily understood by the layman.[1]

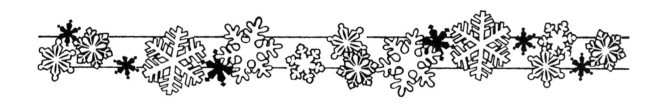

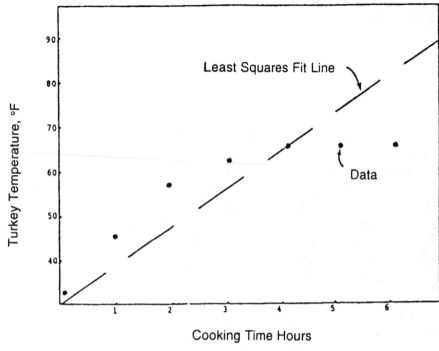

Figure 1. Rate of cooking for turkey. Initial turkey temperature, 32°F; Final turkey temperature, 65°F. Ambient temperature, 68°F.

Data are supplied in Fig. 1. A least squares fit was used on the data. The rate of temperature increase for the turkey was 8°F/hr.

At 3:00 pm the last of our funding[3] was consumed and the experiment was halted.

By extrapolating from our existing data it was obvious that the turkey would have reached a temperature of 400°F in approximately 46 hours. While this is admittedly a "slow cook", our critics will have to concede that we did not burn any fuel.

The principal investigator sampled some of the partly cooked bird. He found it was "somewhat cool" but comparable to any of the cooking his spouse has done at home. He also reported that the meat was very tender.[4]

The scientific community has known about potential energy for hundreds of years. So, why aren't we funding more research on it? If we had developed our potential energy reserves in the 1950's, the energy crises of the past two decades would have been avoided.

We believe that a board of inquiry should be convened by Congress to determine why this information has been suppressed by other scientists.[5] What did each scientist know and when did they know it?

This board will probably uncover a conspiracy of researchers, enamored with money for high-tech projects, who are hiding simple answers from the public.

---

[1] Fonda, Prof. J., "No Nukes is Good Nukes" 1. Eschatological Sci. of Tannu Tuva, 1595.
[2] Our consultant, Prof. S. Hoenig remarked, "This experiment would be a turkey, even with good results."
[3] $11.07 for the turkey; $1.93 for bananas that were periodically given to our assistant.
[4] Viscosity 94 centipoise.
[5] We will testify in return for a small consideration.

METEOROLOGICAL DETERMINANTS OF ELECTORAL CONTESTS

J. Randolph Block
400 E. Randolph
Apt. 2224
Chicago, IL 60601

This article presents some preliminary findings from a study of the relationship between the characteristics of the social-psychological environment and voter turnout. An underlying assumption of the study is that voting, as an individual's act, is determined in the main by an individual's lack of motivation as produced by factors causing inconvenience. Specifically, in any election, an individual's attitudes toward the candidates, parties, and issues are almost completely unrelated to his decision whether to vote. Rather, an individual votes only to preserve his right to complain about the results of the election; when the value of his "bitching rights" (which isn't much) is exceeded by the inconvenience associated with voting, that individual will not vote. This view falls in the mainstream of the so-called "rational" theory of voting behavior, as set forth by Anthony Downs[1] and others. Some scholars have linked voter turnout to factors related to convenience, thereby plagiarizing this study in advance.[2] Still others have studied the relationship between the decision to vote and such political factors as ballot format and polling hours.[3]

The individual and institutional factors analyzed in these studies belong to what might be called the "political" environment, in that they are subject to the control of policymakers. My study, however, focuses on a factor neglected by these scholars because it is not thought of as being under the control of policymakers. Nevertheless, common sense tells us that the factor which is the subject of this paper is perhaps the most important determinant of voter turnout. I am referring, of course, to the weather.

Everybody complains about the weather, but nobody studies its political importance. To analyze its effect of voter turnout, I decided to look at California, since they're always bragging about their weather. Voter turnout for the presidential election of 1968 was compared to precipitation on election day as reported in climatological data published by the U.S. Department of Commerce. This comparison was difficult since climatological data are reported by observation stations of which California has over 600, and not by counties. Station precipitation figures were accordingly organized by county and averaged to give a precipitation figure for each county. These figures were then plotted against voter turnout (as % registered voters) using ordinary least-squares regression.

The results were astounding, even when one considers how much effort went into selecting data that would support my hypothesis. A simple bivariate model yielded the following results:

$$\text{Voter turnout} = 85.57 - 13.54^* \cdot \text{rainfall (in inches)} \quad R^2 = .32$$

$$\text{\# observations} = 58 \ (= \text{\# California counties})$$

$$^* = \text{significant at 1\% level}$$

These results confirm our a priori expectations. As can be seen from the sign of the coefficient of rainfall, the more it rains, the less people vote. Profound, isn't it?

Nonetheless, there is good reason to suspect that the relationship between rainfall and voter turnout is nonlinear. In Fig. 1, for instance, average voter turnout by county is plotted against average rainfall by county for the presidential election years 1960 through 1972. Evaluated according to the

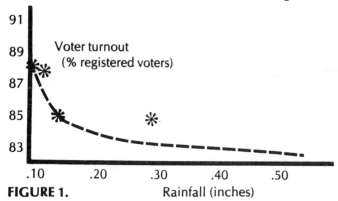

FIGURE 1. Rainfall (inches)

inter-ocular trauma test, these data suggest an exponential relationship of some sort, which matches our a priori expectations as well: there must be a critical amount of rainfall (the "soak factor") beyond which the outcome of the decision whether to vote is unaffected by additional rainfall. At that point, the prospective voter is so thoroughly soaked that any more rain can't make him any wetter. Fitting such an exponential curve to the data represented in Fig. 1, we get the dashed-line curve of that figure, which represents the following:

$$\text{Voter turnout} = 83.36 \cdot \text{Rainfall} -.006796 \quad R^2 = .60$$

A glance at the graph of this curve should convince the reader that the "soak factor" for California is between 0.1 and 0.2 inches of precipitation.

The importance of these findings for political scientists is obvious. First, this study shows that weather is so important in determining voter turnout as to make November a silly time to have an election: why not July 4th? Nice weather, a parade, a couple of beers, then you go vote. Second, the results of this study are extremely relevant for those yo-yos NBC hires to predict election results. Finally, this study proves beyond dispute something that we Midwesterners have known for a long time: Californians are sissies who can't stand even a teensy-weensy bit of rain.

NOTES

1. See Anthony Downs, *An Economic Theory of Democracy* (New York: John Wiley & Sons, Inc., 1960), but don't read it.
2. Stanley Kelley, Jr., Richard E. Ayres, and William G. Bowen, "Registration and Voting: Putting First Things First," *The American Political Science Review*, LXI (June, 1967) pp. 359-379.
3. Jack L. Walker, "Ballot Forms and Voter Fatigue: An Analysis of the Office Bloc and Party Column Ballots," *Midwest Journal of Political Science*, X (November, 1966), pp. 448-463.

Patterns of Distribution and Frequency In the Coca-Cola Bottle

DAVID T. BELL, FORREST L. JOHNSON
STANLEY K. SIPP and STEPHEN G. PALLARDY
Department of Forestry
University of Illinois
Urbana, Illinois 61801

Introduction

With the current administrative pressure to "publish or perish," members of academia are driven to utilize the 25 h of the day to the utmost. The "All-American Coke Break," is beginning to feel the pressure of the increased priority of research in the daily activities of university research personnel. To relieve the guilt feelings of the "secret coke break," an analysis of frequency and distribution of the coke bottles was initiated. Because outside funding was unavailable the research effort was achieved entirely through the personal sacrifice of the authors.

Methods

On the bottom of most Coca-Cola bottles, a city name, assumed to be the location of the plant producing the bottle, is imprinted into the glass. For the two year period, August 1972 - July 1974, an accurate count of these locations of origin and the number of occurrences for each location was diligently recorded by standard scientific methods.

Data on the number of bottle-producing locations and the total bottles per state were compared by stepwise multiple linear regression, using an IBM 360/75 computer, against (1) State Population, (2) State Geographic Area, (3) Distance from Urbana, Illinois, (4) Distance from Atlanta, Georgia, and (5) the State's Average yearly Accumulated Degree Hours Above 80°F (Heat Sum).

Results

Of the 656 bottles consumed by the authors and anonymous associates, every state except New Hampshire and Hawaii was represented (Figure 1). Linear regression analysis between the number of bottle producing locations per state and the total number of bottles sampled per state proved significant at the 1% level. Because of the similarity in the data, the following discussion will emphasize results from data on total bottles per state, but similar results were achieved by using the data on number of bottle producing locations per state.

FIGURE 1. Map locations of Coca-Cola bottle producers. A listing of the locations can be obtained from the authors.

The stepwise multiple linear regression analysis revealed that population accounted for 51.6% of the variance in the distribution of the Coca-Cola bottle sample. When Heat Sum was added to the analysis, a total of 65.44% was accounted for in the coke bottle population variance. Distance from Atlanta, Distance from Urbana, and State Area accounted for only an additional 5.322% of the population variance.

Discussion

It was assumed at the outset of the recording period that Distance from Urbana, and Distance from Atlanta (the home of Coca-Cola) would play major roles in the distribution of coke locations. It is apparent, however, that refilling the bottles swamps any distance-related phenomena in the analysis of variance. The distribution of coke bottle producing locations is skewed in the direction of warmer climates as proven by the significant linear correlation coefficient (r = .380) between coke locations and heat sum. Human population distribution correlated most strongly (r = .516) with the number of bottles consumed by our research group. It is suggested that the U.S. Census Bureau conduct the 1980 population census by renting a coke machine and donating the money to research.

Environmental Pollutants and Prey Density Effects May Induce Suboptimal Foraging Behavior in Man-Eating Space Aliens

Michael W. Hart
Seattle, WA

D. Spencer Adams
Seattle, WA

Patterns of demographic change and environmental pollution in post-war North America have received a great deal of attention from both physical and social scientists. Put simply, our industrialized urban areas have become increasingly polluted and less fit for human habitation. At the same time, economic and social changes have caused large numbers of people to abandon the urban centres and rural hinterlands in favor of moderately crowded but economically prosperous suburban areas. The negative effects of these two patterns (increased industrial illness and disease; aggressive behavior in crowded communities; economic instability of corporate farming) have been the subject of much concern. We describe here a previously unrecognized—and potentially catastrophic—interactive effect of these patterns: altered feeding behavior by optimally-foraging man-eating space aliens (MESAs).

The invasion of our planet by MESAs is apparently imminent[1], but the consequences of such invasion are unexamined (beyond the immediate implication that at least a few folks will be invited for lunch). Assuming optimal patterns of search behavior and prey selection by the invaders, MESAs will presumably forage most intensely in areas where favored prey items are concentrated at the highest densities[2]. Our data

MY EGYPT, by Charles Demuth

suggest that these foraging areas will coincide with preferred areas of human habitation, setting the stage for large-scale decimation of North American human populations.

Methods

We chose sampling locations by throwing darts at a pin-up map of the continental United States while blindfolded. For each dart, the nearest urban (>500,000 persons), suburban (10,000 - 100,000 persons), or rural (<5,000 persons) settlement was chosen for study. Since we had only 20 darts, six urban, six suburban, and eight rural

[1]Donovan, D. "Gigantic UFO that shocked the world! (Incredible story the government is trying to cover up: Alaskan UFO shocks the world!)." *Weekly World News,* Vol. 8, 1986, 5.

[2]Charnov, EL. "Optimal foraging: attack strategy of a mantid." *American Naturalist,* Vol. 110, 1976, 141-151.

locations were chosen (their names are being withheld on the advice of our solicitor). For each sampling location, an estimate of human prey density was calculated from figures provided by the U.S. Census Bureau. Urban locations were arbitrarily assigned a distance of 1 km from the nearest major urban centre. Distances for suburban and rural locations were estimated from the pin-up map.

Since accurate experimental data on prey preferences was not available, three indices of environmental pollution which would likely affect prey taste, and therefore prey preference, were measured: accumulated heavy metals in liver tissue (AHML), including Pb, Hg, Al, Fe, and Zn; total epidermal particulate carbon (TEPC); and whole-body accumulated organochlorides and polychlorinated biphenyls (WBAO CPCBs). These data were collected by methods best left to the imagination.

Differences in pollutant content among urban, suburban, and rural prey were tested by one-way analysis of variance (ANOVA), using Bonferroni *a posteriori*[3] paired contrasts with a critical value of 0.05/2 = 0.025 for two contrasts. The relationship between log-transformed prey density and distance from the nearest major urban centre was examined using simple least-squares linear regression.

We found large differences among sampling locations in two of three prey preference indices (Figure 1). Prey in rural locations had lower liver heavy metals (F=7.971, p=.013, ANOVA) and lower epidermal carbon (F=5.886, P=.033,

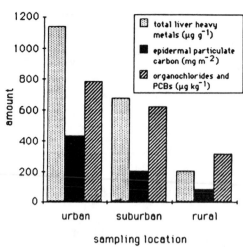

FIGURE 1. Mean accumulated heavy metals (AHML) (Pb, Hg, Al, Fe, Zn) in liver tissue, epidermal particulate carbon (TEPC), and accumulated organochlorides and PCBs (WBAOCPCBs) in human prey from urban, suburban, and rural sampling locations.

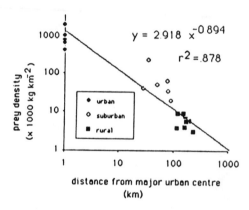

FIGURE 2. Linear regression of log-transformed human prey density at urban, suburban, and rural sampling locations against log-transformed distance from the nearest major urban centre. Assorted meaningless statistics are shown above the plot.

ANOVA) than either urban or suburban prey. Similar differences in mean organochloride and PCB accumulation were evident, but these differences were not significant due to the large variation within sampl-

ing locations (these seem to be ubiquitous pollutants[4]).

We also found an excellent relationship between distance from the nearest major urban centre and human prey density (Figure 2), described by the equation:

$$\log(\text{density}) = \log(2.918) - 0.894 \log(\text{distance})$$

This relationship explains approximately 88% of the observed variation in prey density. Interestingly, the relationship underestimates prey densities slightly in suburban locations, compared to urban and rural areas.

As our cities become more polluted, and small communities and family farming operations wither economically, a larger part of the population is accumulating in relatively clean, moderately dense suburban areas. Our results suggest that continuation of these trends could lead to catastrophic devastation of human prey populations by man-eating space aliens. Because the greatest concentrations of prey consist of nasty-tasting, low-preference prey types (eg: accountants, lawyers, construction workers), while more delicious, preferred prey (eg: gentleman farmers, aging hippies) occur at very low densities, patterns of human environmental pollution and demographics may lead to suboptimal foraging by MESAs in these growing suburban regions.

Mounting economic and biological pressures have failed to influence politicians to deal with these environmental and social problems. We hope that the forecast destruction of suburban populations by MESAs will galvanize our political leaders to take action. 🗑

---

[3]We decided afterwards which differences we wanted to look significant.

[4]A technician mixed up the samples.

European Geography Revised (by the Department of State)

Dr. Sergey M. Shevchenko
Athens, GA

In the official U.S. document on the diversity immigrant (DV-1) Visa Program for the fiscal year 1995 the following countries are classified as European:

> Kazakhstan
> Kyrgyzstan
> Tajikistan
> Turkmenistan
> Uzbekistan

In Asian capitals this is considered as a reaction of the U.S. Government on Michael Fay's caning in Singapore. On the basis of strict anonymity, an official in Washington, D.C. (actually, it was a guard, but a highly informed one) suggested that if caning of American delinquents will become a routine procedure in Asia, its territory may be decreased further by ascribing Afghanistan and Iran to Australia.

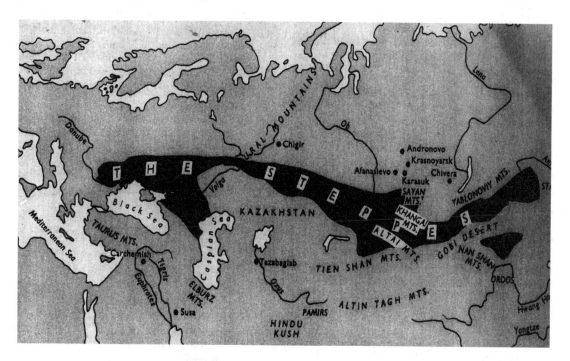

A.J. Ryan and C.L. Thomas
SPORT PARACHUTING AND SKY DIVING
J.A.M.A. 1965, <u>194</u>, 259-263 (p.262 - line 37)

"Difficulties occurring during descent can be responsible for serious injuries but these do not occur until the parachutist hits the ground."

A REFUTATION OF THE PROOF THAT HEAVEN IS HOTTER THAN HELL

DR. TIM HEALEY, F.R.C.R.; M.I. Nuc.E.

In Applied Optics (1972, *11* A14) there appeared a calculation of the respective temperatures of Heaven and Hell. That of Heaven was computed by substituting the values given in Isaiah 30 26[1] in the Stefan-Boltzman radiation law,

so that $(H/E)^4 = 50$,

where E, the absolute temperature of the Earth, is 300°K, whence the temperature of Heaven, H, is 798°K or 525°C. This is hard to find fault with.

The assessment of the temperature of Hell stands, I suggest, on less firm ground. As authority we use the data provided in Revelations 21 8[2], so that the temperature of Hell *seems* to be 444.6°C - the temperature at which liquid sulfur is in equilibrium with its vapour - a temperature indeed which is sufficiently reliable to be used in the secondary calibration of pyrometers.

Now this last reckoning fails to follow the argument through. 444.6°C is the temperature at which liquid sulfur is in equilibrium with its vapour *at normal atmospheric pressure*. Have we any data as to the pressure likely to be found in Hell?

The answer is "Yes". A nineteenth century mathematician has already provided the groundwork for us[3] and we may feel confident that by the year 2000 the total number of the damned will be at least

29,422,641,251,519,917,000 souls.

Yet the area of the valley of Gehinnom[4] is only

7,000,000 square meters.

We can now apply these figures in the Ideal Gas Equation to calculate what the pressure will be in the valley of Gehinnon. Since surely some souls must have been damned since 1877[5], the pressure can only have increased since these calculations were made and the equilibrium point on the phase diagram of sulfur must have shifted still further, so that if we can show that at a temperature of 525°C sulfur would still be liquid at the pressure calculated (which is a minimum value, remember) Hell (Gehinnon) is now cooler than Heaven.

Certain corrections must be applied first, however.
1. Neiht based his calculation on a date of creation of 1658 + 2326 - 1877 = 2107 BC (minimum). Counting generations in the Bible gives a date for the Creation of 4004 BC. However, atomic dating has shown that Olduvai man is at least 2×10^6 years old[6].
2. We should use a Fibonacci series for the expansion, not a simple doubling series[7]. The ancient Jewish laws against inbreeding also act in the same direction[8].
3. By a fortunate coincidence, the effects of 1 and 2 cancel each other exactly[9].
4. The human body is not an ideal gas, but
5. A good deal of it is gaseous at 525°C, and in any case,
6. It could well be that at very great pressures the external pressure may well exceed the pressure of electromagnetic repulsion, when different "gas" laws would apply. This merely explains how the Lord works in fitting so large a number of damned souls into so small a space[10] and it need not be quantitative.

In the calculation the following assumptions are made:-
1. The average height can be taken as one meter. This seems a fair figure between the newborn babe and the fullgrown man.
2. The average space needed is about 30 cm x 20 cm. It seems unlikely that any closer packing could be achieved. Neiht uses a figure of 1/20 cubic meters per person, which is nearly identical with my independent assessment. Mine allows a neat cancellation, later.
3. I have assumed that not more than two layers of damned persons can be accommodated, since otherwise those in the middle layers would escape the full rigours of Hell.

So that,

The volume available in Gehenna is $60 \times 10^6 \times 2$ m³ and

The original volume of the damned is $0.06 \times 29.422641 \times 10^{18}$ m³

Then, at constant temperature (which we assume, taking equilibrium)

$$P_1 V_1 = P_2 V_2 \text{ or } P_2 = P_1 V_1 / V_2$$

Substituting,

$$P_2 = \frac{29 \times 6 \times 10^{16}}{2 \times 6 \times 10^7}$$

$$= 14.5 \times 10^9 \text{ atmospheres} \ldots\ldots\ldots\ldots\ldots(1)$$

Now let us see what pressure is needed to liquefy sulfur vapour at 525°C.

We have, using the Clausius-Cleypeyron equation in its integrated form,

$$\text{Log } P = 7.43287 - \frac{3268.2}{T}$$

where P = pressure in mm Hg

and T = the elevated boiling point in °K,

so that

Log P = 7.43287 - (3268.2/798)

=3.3373813

whence,

P=2174.607 mm Hg

$$= 2.86 \text{ atmospheres} \ldots\ldots\ldots\ldots\ldots\ldots(2)$$

(1) is so much greater than (2) that Revelations 21 8 indicates a temperature very considerably higher than 525°C.

Thus, Hell is hotter than Heaven (which remains deucedly hot).

REFERENCES

[1] "---the light of the moon shall be as the light of the sun and the light of the sun shall be sevenfold as the light of seven days - - -" The light of the moon is negligible in comparison with that of the sun.

[2] "- - - the lake which burneth with fire and brimstone: which is the second death".

[3] *A Mathematical Proof of the Non-Existence of Hell* from the writings of the free-thinker Neiht, born in Brussels, 1877. "The area of the valley of Jehoshaphat is 60,000,000 sq. ms. - - - Supposing that each race originated with one couple only, one has five couples or ten people, and applying to them the principle of compound interest, up to the Flood there were 9,289,000 births in 1,658 years. Since the Flood up to our epoch 2,326 years have passed, during which, if only five couples survived, they would have produced 2,213,867,610,000 children. If these calculations are extended up to the year 2000, the resulting number is 34,326,414,259,-675,172,000 which, together with the 9,289,000, makes 34,326,414,-259,684,461,000 offspring. If one concedes, charitably, that all papists are saved, their number today being 1/7th of the population of the earth, that of the damned would be made up of those born before the Flood plus those born since the Flood up to the year 2000 minus the 1/7th of those born since the year 44, that of the birth of Christ: this number is 4,903,773,008,164,544,000, and the total of damned would be 29,422,-641,251,519,917,000.

"The mean cubic area between a new-born infant and an adult is about 1/20th metre; the bulk of the damned above is equal to the mass of a sphere of radius 705,504 metres; that of the earth is 6,366,200 metres.

"If one puts back the origin of man, following certain German naturalists, to 80,000 years, the number of damned would form a cube three times the size of the earth.

"Now, how does one assemble the 34,326,414,260 millions risen on a surface of 60,000,000 sq. metres to judge them and how does one sink this mass of damned, through all manner of rock, to a depth of 5,660,660 metres?"

[4] The valley of Jehoshaphat is the Gehenna of the Jews (Jehennam in the Koran) - the place of eternal torment. The word is derived from Gehinnom = the valley of Hinnom where sacrifices were offered to Moloch (2 Corinthians 33 6) (= Adremmelech - the God of Sepharvaim). In later times, all manner of refuse was dumped there and fires were constantly maintained to consume it. The sulfurous stench and the fire was the original of the Christian concept of Hell. (The estimate of Nieht of Gehenna's area 60x10⁶ sq. m. is wrong, according to measurements taken on the spot by the Editors).

[5] eg Dzhugashvili, Iosif and DeSalvo, Albert H.

[6] Curtis G.H. and Evemden, J.F. in *Nuclear Clocks* USAEC Pp40-41.

[7] Leonardo da Pisa *Liber Abaci* 1202 (Out of print).

[8] Leviticus 18 6 et seq.

[9] Westfall, R.S. *Newton and the Fudge Factor Science* 1973 751-758.

[10] "In my father's house are many mansions: If it were so I would have told you. I go to prepare a place for you." John 14 2. Also, "Those things which are impossible with men, are possible with God" - Luke 18 27, and " . . . with God all things are possible." Matthew 19.26.

EUPHEMISM

Robin Wolfson
219 Roundtree Court
Sacramento, California 95831

In times of drought, the wise apply
The maxims of Leibnitzian laws:
Before you flush, a moment's pause
To verify, as specified,
The presence of sufficient cause.

THE FAR-SIGHTED GEOLOGIST

Tog Jackson
Adjunct Professor of Soil Science
University of Manitoba
Winnipeg, Manitoba, Canada

That his bodily image might last,
A geologist had himself cast
In a tub of cement,
For it was his intent
In the future to be in the past!

MAGNETICALLY ALIGNING YOUR GARDEN

Jim Ballard
Everett, WA

FORCES OF THE EARTH, by Fritz Winter.

Fertilizers, soil treatment techniques, special watering systems and numerous other methods for harvesting the most from your organic garden have all overlooked one kind of application that will *always* produce larger, healthier yeilds.

It's a method I call "*Magnetic Zone Planting*". I discovered, after eleven years of controlled experimenting, that there seems to be a way of realigning magnetic currents throughout a garden plot. It is easy to perform, is inexpensive, and brings immediate results.

Most gardeners plant rows of seeds with the position of the sun in mind. That's commendable, but they haven't gone quite far enough. Planting the rows of seeds should be just the first step. Magnetizing most of the rows in a true north/south direction is the next step, and a vital one.

How do you magnetize the rows? Having experimented with a number of different sized magnets, I can assure you that a horseshoe shaped magnet between five to six inches long, is ideal. Smaller ones produce only feeble results; larger ones cause the plants to bolt and seed too quickly.

Do *not* use the bar type magnets because they tend to produce an odd effect where the tops of the plants flourish, but the base tends to either remain the same size or grows smaller. Vegetables like corn become too top-heavy and fall over.

Also, it is important that each prong on the horseshoe magnet remain exactly parallel to the garden's surface as you magnetize the rows. Don't pivot or turn the magnet as you make each pass.

Which Vegetables Respond?

Fortunately, almost all vegetables—and virtually all herbs—improve under the magnet's current. Likewise, most plants' growth skyrockets if the magnet's sweep is made in a north/south direction. But, there are some exceptions.

The following chart lists various vegetables and how the magnetic alignment should be made.

VEGETABLES	MAGNETIC ALIGNMENT
Acorn squash	N/S
Beets	N/S
Beans	*E/W
Beets	N/S
Broccoli	N/S
Cabbage	*(See text)
Carrots	N/S
Celery	N/S
Corn	N/S
Cucumbers	(Currents don't seem to work)
Endive	N/S
Kohlrabi	*Diagonally between N/S and E/W
Lettuce	N/S
Onions	N/S
Peas	N/S
Radishes	N/S
Spinach	N/S
Zucchini	*(See text)

Cabbage is another exception to the north/south orientation rule. Cabbage will grow much larger when *circular* passes are made just a few inches above either the seeds or the plants. Also, be sure to point the prongs downward—rather than parallel to the earth—for more successful growth.

Don't even bother trying to magnetize the zones around cucumbers. They just won't improve that plant's growth cycle. I am completely at a loss to explain why. Perhaps nearby plants rob magnetic currents from the cucumbers.

Kohlrabi is a beautiful vegetable that has warranted a great deal of experimenting. After numerous failures, I hit upon the current charging method of "double diagonal sweeps." Put simply, instead of moving the magnet in a north/south or east/west direction, I make dual passes diagonally over each kohlrabi plant. This produces a succulent, deeply colored vegetable that I'm sure is loaded with minerals.

A different process is required for zucchini. After planting the seeds, make north/south passes immediately. After about two weeks, make east/west passes over the new growth. Repeating this process every two weeks will ensure numerous and beautiful squash. This method never fails.

The vegetables listed in the chart above are ones I've worked with, and certainly doesn't imply that the magnetic zones, properly set, won't work on other plants like leeks, cantaloupe or parsnips. I'm sure they will. If you enjoy vegetables other than the ones covered, experiment on your own, determining appropriate magnetic current orientation for those species.

Aligning the Magnetic Currents

Regardless of the shape of your garden, all rows should be planted in a north/south direction to make it easier to magnetize the space. Seeds should be planted at the indicated depth and with proper spacing between other seeds. Of course, fertilizer—unless it's totally organic compost material—need not be used. These currents will far out perform any of the 10-20-20 vegetable fertilizers commercially available!

You should wait two days after planting the seeds before you align the currents. Early morning is the very best time, and preferably at a time when dew is still on the ground. At any rate, this process should first be done before the sun comes up. I've discovered that sunlight seems to weaken the currents during the first week or two, so you should magnetize the ground at an early hour until the plants become established.

With the horseshoe magnet's ends facing true north, slowly move over each row, making a single pass above each type of vegetable. Never go back and repeat a row! It will befuddle the currents so much that some plants will stop growing. (Of course, when kohlrabi gets large enough, the "double diagonal sweeps" should be used. But this plant's the exception).

Remember to keep the magnet parallel to the ground. Take your time. Enjoy this early morning outing because you are getting an edge over the other gardeners in your area. You are taking the normally unaligned magnetic currents in and around the ground and aligning them for your plants. Don't concern yourself with what others may say or imply if they see you working. Just keep repeating this early morning activity daily for the first week and then taper it off slowly. After about one month, you should be realigning currents approximately twice a week.

When you first skim over the seeds, keep the magnet about three inches from the dirt. As time elapses—say in two weeks hence—move out to about six inches. Gradually, throughout the vegetables' entire life, move the magnet higher until you are making passes about eighteen inches above the tops of the plants.

Aligning the magnetic currents in your garden has other benefits besides improving the size, nutritional value and taste of your vegetables. Slugs won't go near correctly magnetized soil! It's true. My gardens used to be a mecca for these critters, but once I started setting up the magnetic currents, they've stopped visiting. No doubt their nervous system is sensitive enough to pick up the currents and they stop in their tracks. I haven't used slug bait in years, and I suspect you won't have to either once you magnetize the soil.

Another side benefit of correctly aligned magnetic currents is the complete elimination of garden insect pests. My gardens have no aphids, flea beetles or other damage-producing insects. The currents seem to attract the pollinating bees and lady bugs can be seen wandering all over the lettuce greens and carrot tops.

A gardener friend of mine took my experiments a few steps further. He nailed magnets from stakes that were driven into the ground at either end of the garden. He had nine stakes each on the north and south side of the plot. He strung twine between each stake and over each row. He also hung magnets—spaced about two feet apart—from the twine so that the ends faced downward.

To the neighbors, it looked slightly funny, I suppose, with all those magnets hanging from the string and on the stakes, but, boy did it work! His garden flourished, and it would have produced a tremendous yield if the neighborhood kids hadn't stolen all the magnets and trampled every last plant he had.

But, I digress. Buy yourself a magnet and align your garden magnetically at your next planting. I guarantee that the vegetables and herbs you grow will surpass in size and quantity any harvest you've made in the past.

February 28, 1987

The Honorable Bill Archer
Washington, D.C.

Dear Congressman Archer:

My Brother, Russ Vanderslice, up in Tulsa, Oklahoma, received $1,000 check from the Government this year for not raising hogs. So I am going into the "not raising hogs business" next year.

What I would like to know is. . .in your opinion. . . what is the best kind of farm not to raise hogs on, and what is the best kind of hogs not to raise? I would prefer not to raise razorbacks, but if that is not a good breed not to raise, I will just as gladly not raise the Berkshires or Durocs.

Brother Russ, is very joyful about the future of the business. He has been raising 100 hogs for more than 20 years and the best he ever made was $400 in 1981, until this year when he got that check for $1,000 for not raising hogs.

If I can get $1,000 for not raising 50 hogs, than will I get $2,000 for not raising 100 hogs, etc.? I plan to operate on a small scale at first, holding myself down to about 4,000 hogs, which means I will have $80,000.

Now another thing. . .these hogs I will not raise will not eat 100,000 bushels of corn. I understand that you also pay farmers for not raising corn. So will you pay me anything for not raising 100,000 bushels of corn not to feed to the hogs I'm not going to raise?

I want to get started as soon as possible as this seems to be a good time of the year for not raising hogs.

Your Constituent,

R.E. Vanderslice
Katy, Texas

P.S. Can I raise 10 to 12 hogs, on the side, while I am in the "not raising hog business". . .just enough to get a few sides of bacon to eat?

March 12, 1987

Mr. R.E. Vanderslice
Katy, Texas

Dear Ron:

I agree. The "not raising hogs business" sounds like the next best thing to a currency printing press—but, before you go hog wild with it (so to speak) you need to be a little careful. It seems that the only people eligible to go into the "not hog raising business" are those who are already in the "hog raising business".

I'll admit that sounds like a pretty inefficient way to do it, since it would be far easier for someone who is not now in the "hog raising business" to make the transition into the "not raising hogs business".

Unfortunately, efficiency has not been a hallmark of our federal agriculture programs. That's why you'll see me continue to vote against this kind of ridiculous effort to stabilize farm prices by paying farmers not to plant crops or raise animals. Obviously, you agree with me.

Thanks for your most entertaining—and yet poignant—letter.

Sincerely,

Bill Archer
Member of Congress

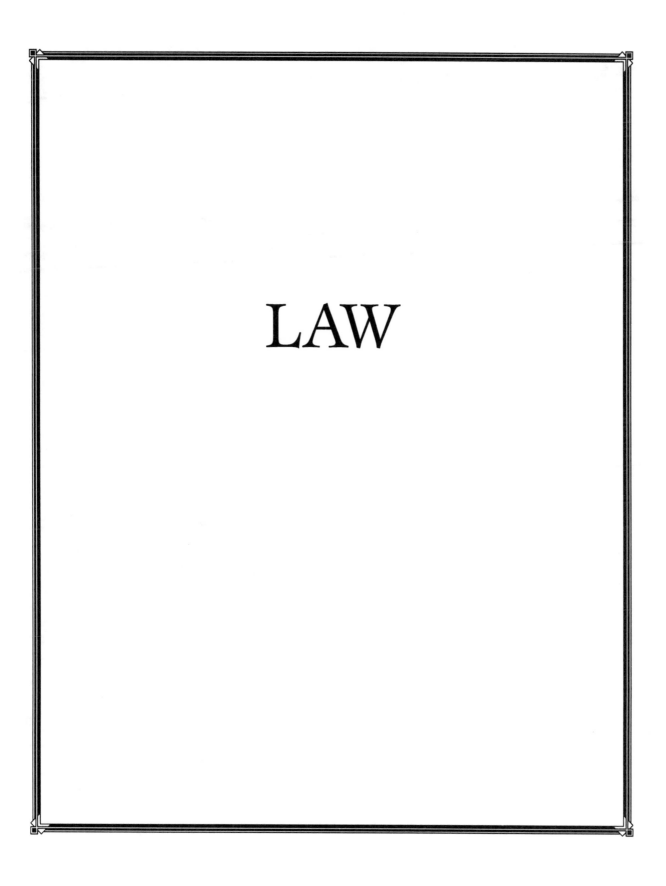

LAW

Service of Process in Merry Old England

David V. Stivison, Esq.
Philadelphia, PA

Trying to serve judicial papers on a reluctant recipient ranks as Excedrin headache number nine. If you have ever had this experience, take heart: You are not alone. In fact, early English cases show that the same problems plagued our English legal predecessors fully two centuries ago. In a case where a mother had hidden her children, who were defendants in a lawsuit, the English courts allowed the frustrated plaintiff to serve the papers on Mum. *Baker v. Holmes,* 21 Eng. Rep. 173 (1705). If the wife is in hiding, the husband can be served, and if the husband is nowhere to be found, the wife can be served. But when the wife received service, it had to be accompanied by a careful explanation of the importance of giving the papers *to her husband!* Clark v. Greenhill et us., 21 Eng. Rep. 202 (1743), *Pulteney v. Shelton,* 31 Eng. Rep. 516 (1799). Service was even allowed upon a father-in-law. *Thompson v. Jones,* 32 Eng. Rep. 306 (1803). A person's agent to receive mail, or his clerk could he handed the documents. *Hunt v. Lever,* 31 Eng. Rep. 517 (1799); *De Manneville v. De Manneville,* 33 Eng. Rep. 78 (1806). And if the clerk has died and the defendant "refused to be spoke with," a court could require appointment of a new clerk by issuing a subpoena *ad faciend' attornat,* although the Court failed to explain how this subpoena could be served any easier than the original one. *Ratcliff v. Roper,* 24 Eng.

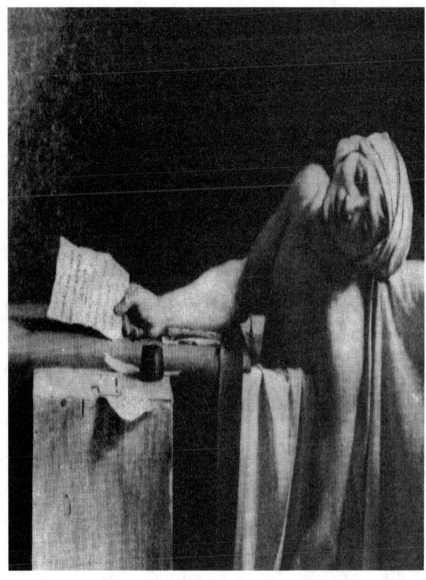

Rep. 453 (1718). One women's clerk was served in her stead after "repeated attempts in vain to serve her, and her constant habit of keeping her door locked, and only appearing at the window," no doubt making interesting observations on the process-server's ancestry and eternal habitation, *Henley v. Brooke* (1803, quoted at 33 Eng. Rep. 78). Ordinarily, if a litigant showed contempt for the court's orders, he or she would be hauled in by the Sergeant, imprisoned, and have his or her property sequestered. If the party could not be found, the Sergeant marked the order "non est inventus," and the property was seized anyway. This was not enough, however, for one enraged plaintiff, who had tried repeatedly to serve papers on a man who stayed locked up in his lodgings every day but Sunday-the one day on which service could not be made. The plaintiff sought a *commission of rebellion* from the Court, which would have allowed him to break the door down and serve his opponent, even on Sunday. Luckily for the defendant, the Court had more patience, and told him to just keep trying, *Edwards v. Pool,* 21 Eng. Rep. 441 (1788). May YOU all have better luck finding your foes than these hapless litigants of Merry Old England!

THE LITERATURE OF MEDIEVAL EUROPEAN LAW IN A NUTSHELL

T.G.I.F. Kearley
Urbana-on-Boneyard, IL

The nature of European law and legal literature during Middle Ages is certainly obscure enough to merit scholarly attention, yet relatively little has appeared on the topic recently in our professional literature.[1] That appalling oversight will be remedied here. Although this article will deal with a great many forms of medieval legal literature, such as diplomata, capitularia, cartae, and the like, it will not examine other documents which, though indicia of a legal relationship, are more commercial in nature. I am, of course, alluding t such writings as hotel and taxi bills, and restaurant checks. While the latter figured quite prominently in Nineteenth Century studies on this subject, recent scholarship suggests that many, if not most, of these documents were in fact forged—perhaps for tax purposes. Space constraints prevent me from going into the "Pseudo-Essenische Falschungen" further, but I refer your to Herr Professor Doctor Max Schlimmst's pioneering work "Sind diese nicht komisch, oder...?"[2]

Before discussing European medieval legal literature, however, it is necessary to briefly summarize the Roman legal writings which preceded them. The *Theodosian Code* of 438 had a great impact on Germanic tribes that encountered it in their conquests and, in fact, on all subsequent Western law. Had the barbarian chieftains not been exposed to this code, they might have continued to have their simple peoples live in accordance with old, orally transmitted customs rather than drafting for them legislation written badly in a foreign language—as we still do to this day. (Contrary to common belief, little was written in this era not because most people were illiterate but because they could not find pens that worked.)[3]

The best known Roman legal writings, however, are those works created under Justinian's order by Tribonian's commission of scholars. Though today we call these works the *Corpus Juris civilis* or *Corpus Juris Civilis*, depending on the depth of our understanding, at the time the collection was simply known as "the law" and was just something to be gotten around.[4] It caused quite a stir when it was rediscovered in late 11th Century Italy, though, because the law schools were just then reopening after a semester break of several centuries and campus bookstores were desperately looking for texts. This synthesis of Roman jurisprudence was given its modern name by Denis Godfroy or Dionysius Gothofredus—it was certainly one of the two—who was sick of having people ask him what he was talking about when he referred to "those old Roman law books" and who thus dubbed Justinian's work *Corpus Juris Civilis* for want of a better name.

In any event, the Germanic tribes that settled in former Roman territories after the Western Empire's dissolution became quite nettled at constantly being referred to as barbarians and decided that putting their laws into writing would show some class. Thus we find such law books as the seminal *Lex Salica*, dating probably from the 5th Century, which embodies early Frankish jurisprudence with provision such as "If any person shall strike another on the head so that the brain appears, and the three bones which lie under the brain shall project, he shall be sentenced to 1200 denars.... If anyone shall have called a woman a harlot, and shall not have been able to prove it, he shall be sentenced to 1800 denars...." It is unclear whether such written laws enhanced the status of these tribes with their subject Roman populations, but they do show that the behavior of the Salic Franks was not much different from that of ours today.[5]

The next real advance in European legal literature arose in the Frankish kingdom of Charles the Great, or Charlemagne, whose appended title of honor stemmed from "the great" numbers of Saxons, Lombards, and others he killed for their reluctance to accept the Carolingian Renaissance. (His brand of statesmanship is said to have resulted from listening to *The City of God* read aloud for hours at a time.) Charlemagne continued the Merovingian practice of using "cartae", or charters, to confer rights and duties upon his subjects. One of the most famous Carolingian cartae—the "Rhonese Palimpset"—has recently been called into question by modern scholarship, however. This well preserved charter purports to bestow upon the ancestors of its discoverer—one Pierre Malfaire—a huge area of land containing, among other things, the Saint-Etienne vineyards. Uncovered in 1959 under an eviction notice to Mr. Malfaire's uncle Marcel, the carta's authenticity was brought into doubt when a chemical analysis of the paper on which it was written showed it to be of the same composition as E-Z Race typing paper and very likely made far fewer than the necessary 1150 years ago.[6] This incident should not be allowed to overshadow the step forward made by Charlemagne in his applying the principles of cartae to a more broadly applicable type of law known as the "capitularia", through which he helped reestablish the notion of the territoriality of laws. Of these weighty laws which applied throughout the Empire, one of the best known concerns penmanship—"On Scribes, that They Should Not Write Corruptly".

After Charlemagne's death the Carolingian government was maximally decentralized. Law became localized with regional lords and courts enforcing rules based on feudal relations and ancient usages. With control of education returned to the localities along with law, few people could read or write, so judges "remembered" prior decisions and gave their own orally (a state of affairs to which modern judges might not be entirely opposed but to which modern law publishers certainly would be).

A substantial body of law was created in this way, however, and some of it did find its way into writing. About 1150, Obertus de Orto, a.k.a. Gerard "The Black" Capagisti, or perhaps many people, synthesized Italo-Germanic feudal law into a work known as *Libri Feudorum,* or *Conseutudines Feudorum,* or *Usus Feudorum,* or *The Book of Fifes.* (It is not without reason that this era is known as the age of uncertainty. Much of this trouble could have been avoided had a good set of cataloging, or cataloguing, rules been available at the time.[7]) Another compilation of feudal law, the *Assizes of Jerusalem,* was created in the early 12th Century by the Europeans who had made themselves at home in Palestine after the Crusades. Unfortunately, the text was lost in 1187 along with their lease on

Jerusalem; the Europeans had fallen behind on their rent and Saladin, acting on behalf of the landlords, made a forced entry and seized all their property, including the *Assizes,* to satisfy the debt. As memories were much better in those days, though, new editions were reconstructed for the territories from which the Crusaders had not yet been evicted. Fortunately, a still later edition was translated into Italian in 1531, and a French translation of that was done around 1840 so that modern lawyers have a source to turn to if faced with a client whose cause of action arose in Asia Minor during the 14th Century (assuming the problem of laches can be avoided).

Space does not permit a discussion here of the many other species of medieval legal literature. We have not even mentioned that most noble of all types of legal literature, the form book, which was well known as early as the Sixth century and which was raised to a popular art form in the later Middle Ages by English scriveners. (It has been suggested that modern American attorneys, who owe so much of their bounty to the form book, ought to take the medieval scribe as their patron saint and place statuettes bearing his likeness on the dashboards of their BMWs.) A full discussion of the form book and other related subjects—such as the story of West Publishing Company's origins in a Twelfth Century English Cistercian monastery must await the second special law issue of this journal. 🗑

---

[1]This may be yet another ill to be laid at the doorstep of our permissive educational system; a firm grasp of Latin is simply no longer expected of educated persons—to say nothing of attorneys. Even Berlitz does not offer a basic Latin conversation for tourists course. The author suggests that the best way of guaranteeing that in the future at least lawyers will know Latin is to offer the LSAT in that language only.

[2]Schlimmst. "Sind diese nicht komisch, oder. . .?" 52 *Zeitschrift für Quittungs- Rechnungs- und Prosopographischestudien* 309 (1958) [Hereinafter reffered to as Kleinwort]

[3]The first reliable evidence supporting this thesis was uncovered by the archeologist Professor Charles Renault who discovered mounds of cracked, bent and broken quills on the coast of Sardina in the course of his fourteen year mandatory sabbatical there. See C. Renault, *Ex ubi haec Styli venerunt?* (1938).

[4]The three original parts were the *Code,* the *Digest* or *Pandects,* and the *Institutes.* (The term Pandects, derived from the Greek root "Pan", pertaining to the Greek god of pastures and forests, and "decter", a verb meaning to strike to the ground; the *Digest* was often referred to by this name because of the harsh penalties it contained for Pan worship, which virtually "knocked out" that religion.) Later "the *Novels*" were added to the first three parts in order to make the whole set easier to read and more marketable.

[5]Perhaps their rationale for the curious differential in fines for these two acts was an early example of applying economic principles to law; the person whose brain was projecting would likely not be in much of a position to spend his denars (medical knowledge being what it was) whereas the falsely accused woman would probably give the local economy quite a boost after her ordeal. At the time the denar was worth about two gulpens.

[6]McDougal, supra n.5 at 43-45 no. 14; but cf p.2 infra, et seq. & res ipsa.

[7]See generally, Hotchkiss, "The Strange Inaction of Medieval American Academic Libraries: A Failure of our Library Education?", 16 *Journal of Pedantic Librarianship* 441 (1979).

Saadyah Maximon
Migdal haEmeq, Israel

Prejudice is naturally at the root of the suspicion in which we leght-handers are held. As old as civilization, the suspicion is attested to[2] by *dexter*[3] which to this day implies skill of hand and cleverness of mind, and by *sinister*[4] which to this night implies witches astride broomsticks.

This prejudice is deep-rooted; even we leght-handers are unwitting[5] subscribers to it: Prestigious leght-handed women's liberationists demand their "rights"; leght-handed writers describe a hero's heart in the "right place" when everyone knows nature planted it on the leght.

To add insult, the Arabs use the right hand only at dinner. True, water is scarce in the desert, but must it be the leght exclusively that is to do the wiping?

Nor have we exhausted the prejudice. Consider *adroit*[6] for skillful, or deft under stress, and *gauche*[7] for tactless, or awkward. "Right" intrudes pervasively into all facets of language. *Correct*[8] and *direct*[8] are some common representatives. They extend into geometry[9] and anatomy[10]. None of these "right" derivatives satisfies the definition, "pointing East when facing North". Even in sports parlance[11] the up-and-down postures of North and South on the conventional map seem to have dictated the term "South-paw".

Minorities of the world coalesce round flags of movements proclaiming their "rights", so-called[12]. Most minorities are smaller than ours, and only two are proven to exceed ours in size: one defies the conventional definition of "minority" by exceeding fifty percent of the general population[13]. We leght-handers do constitute ten percent of the population in any land whose laws permit us to exist[14].

Now we leght-handers have organized the Third Minority[15]. Let us state our modest program for reforms—following our campaign for the Amendment making the handshake[16] unconstitutional.

The LEGHT[17] Program

ONE: We will fly the flag of the Tribe of Benjamin[18], when it is discovered at our dig on Tel Ehud[19].

TWO: We challenge the authority of any lexicon[20] that slurs the leght as "awkward" or "witchlike" and/or[21] curries the right with "rectitude" or "might is right".

THREE: We call for revision of all education in order to restore to leght-handers all that right-handers have for millennia arrogated to themselves. We have engaged the best legal staff[22] to institute a class action against all educators, schools, manufacturers of classroom supplies, publishers with their authors and artists, school boards, and politicians. . .on behalf of leght-handers[23] who have suffered educationally, professionally, socially, or traumatically from:

A. . .writing with the right[24] when one is naturally leght-handed. . .obviously leading to psychic trauma;
B. . .writing with the leght on equipment designed for the majority right[25] with a resultant illegible backhand.

FOUR: We demand that industry[26] commence with design, manufacture, and distribution of tools, instruments, and furnishings suitable for the leght-hander—notably the leght-handed teakettle, the leght-handed screwdriver, the leght-handed ballpoint pen, and the long-neglected leght-handed waterbed. Distinctions here between leght and right may seem to be obscure, but the wording on the respective product labels[27] will help.

FIVE: We note that manufacturers of pianos are perpetuators of the chauvinist convention that relegates the accompaniment of music to the leght hand. We insist that pianos be made optionally with the treble keys on the leght.

SIX: In line with measures achieved by other minority groups, we insist that for a time[28] leght-handers be hired beyond our ten percent share in occupations where prejudice has been blatant—outstandingly in courts of law, where truth may be attested to only by the right hand. As a corrective more leght-handed witnesses must be recruited.

SEVEN: We are lobbying for revision of the obsolescent spelling of "left" into realistic "leght". The old is associated with negative meanings including "left disease'' for paralysis and ''left side of the bed'' for morganatic marriage[29]. The new spelling equates both hands with graceful ''gh''[30].

EIGHT: We shall carry on till our ten percent is established in all phases of industry, science, society, education, and the arts. In religion too: Let the clergy not intone, ''Thou holdest my right hand''.

NINE: We reserve our options with respect to retroactive damages[31].

TEN: We shall not be satisfied till our tithe is carried to its coast-to-coast limits, when fully one-tenth of the highways shall be subject to the rule of ''Keep to the Leght''.

---

[1]''GH'' is pronounced as in ''rough''.
[2]If not indeed codified.
[3]Latin for ''right''.
[4]Latin for ''leght''.
[5]If not witless!
[6]Derived from French *droit* for ''right''.
[7]French, literally ''leght''.
[8]The Romans lacked the elegance of ''gh''.
[9]*e.g.,* ''right'' angle and *rectangle.*

[10]Rectum— a ''straight'' passage.
[11]In the game most susceptible to leght-handed advantage!
[12]The snideness is aimed at the prejudicial use of ''rights'', not at the cause, which we would naturally call ''leghts''.
[13]*i.e.,* the ''fair sex''.
[14]Hysterical?—consider the law of Saudi Arabia that amputates a thief's right hand on the assumption that only the right is capable of theft.
[15]After women and blacks, but probably ahead of homosexuals.
[16]Right-handed.
[17]Not a conventional acronym, LEGHT means L for Leght, E for lEght, G for...
[18]A leght-hander: Judges iii,15, *q.v.*
[19]These excavations have never been acknowledged by the right-handed archeological world.
[20]Regardless of its reception at the courts of law or the quadrangles of academe.
[21]You've got the ''legal'' point: we're going to the Supreme Court.
[22]Leght-handed by *default; see what we're up against?*
[23]Living or departed.
[24]By force—probably of a ruler.
[25]By implicit force—nonetheless real.
[26]Not merely ''specialty houses''.
[27]A further argument for truth in product labelling.
[28]To be negotiated.
[29]We would eschew political implications.
[30]Which is more meaningful in ''leght'' than in ''right'' because it is audible.
[31]Reasonably, to extend to the Biblical Judges who first gave leght-handers recognition.

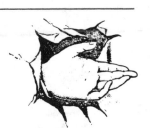

Jury Finds Westhoff Not Guilty

A jury accepted without question the plea of insanity entered by Father Frank Westhoff of Jefferson City, Missouri. There was a problem with the insistence by the defendant that the insanity was "temporary." The majority of the jury felt otherwise.

The defendant was charged with the death of his parakeet and cruelty to animals. He claimed that the Parakeet "cussed me out," and that his reactions were triggered by this event. The defendant claimed he was administering discipline to the bird with his solid brass belt buckle and belt. The death of the bird was said to be instantaneous, since as the Humane Society charged, the belt buckle weighed "exactly twenty-eight times the body weight of the parakeet." Westhoff is said to have done four to six thousand dollars worth of damage to the furnishings in the home, before the belt buckle actually made contact with the bird.

The spokesperson for the Humane Society said that this was an act of unspeakable barbarity committed by a depraved maniac with chronic homicidal tendencies toward wholesale depravity." the defendant would only admit that this was not 'his finest hour,' but did say that he was glad the trial was over, and now he would be getting some pigeons for entertainment. "They're bigger than parakeets," said Westhoff, "and if they cuss at me, it'll even the odds a little more." He expressed no regret at the loss of his parakeet.

Reprinted from the *Columbia Daily Tribune*

Legal Reasoning - a New Tool for the Hard Sciences

Barry and Debbie Blyveis
Columbia, MD

This article will enhance scientists' critical skills by teaching them legal reasoning. Our starting point is the etymology of the word "lawyer." The phonetic resemblance of "lawyer" and "liar" is not mere coincidence. "Liar" was originally a Neanderthal word whose meaning has remained virtually unchanged for 65,000 years.[1] Neanderthals revered liars. Lying was a critical survival skill designed to mislead one's tribemates as to the location of prime hunting and gathering spots. However, in this and many other ways the Neanderthals were outperformed by their CroMagnon competitors, who were such accomplished liars that they continually sent their Neanderthal neighbors on wild goose chases searching for nonexistent nourishment. Ultimately, this

caused the almost complete extinction of the Neanderthals.[2] The most honored CroMagnon liars later came to be known as "liers," then as "liwers," and still later as "lawers." The word completed its final evolution into "lawyer" at about the time that lawyers discovered that they could lie on behalf of a tribemate and charge him a fee.[3]

Lawyers soon learned that specialized lying yields even larger fees. The earliest recognized legal specialty was shyster, soon followed by corporate and anti-trust law.[4]

Much of scientists'[5] unjust criticism of lawyers is attributable to the former's lack of familiarity with legal reasoning. Legal and scientific methods of reasoning are two different but equally valid methods for achieving their objectives. Scientific reasoning proceeds thusly:

Hypothesis → experiment → conclusion

Legal reasoning in its pure form proceeds thusly:

Assumption → conclusion

Pure legal reasoning is observed only in vitro. The reaction proceeds in vivo only with the aid of the catalyst

$$\$\text{-}\$=H\text{-}S=\$\text{-}\$$$
$$||$$
$$\$=\$\text{-}H\text{-}S=\$\text{-}\$$$

---

1   For those readers cognizant of the continuing debate as to whether Neanderthals had the ability to speak, we are unfortunately unable to offer a meaningful contribution. Anthropologists do not know whether Neanderthals utilized their extensive vocabulary to communicate by vocalizing, by signing, or by smoke signals.

2   Although the remaining subspecies, *Homo Neanderthalis U.S. Congressis,* is listed as threatened, contributions to preserve and protect the remnant population are not encouraged.

3   The alpha liar, later called the alpha lawyer, enhanced his breeding success to the extent that today the proliferation of lawyers is overtaxing available resources.

Lawyers bitterly resent being labeled as parasites on society. Actually, the legal profession benefits society in numerous ways, such as providing employment for the physically and ethically handicapped. For example, one of us (not you) was asked how he could be a trial lawyer when his hearing is so bad. One of us (Id.) replied by explaining that when one physical sense is deficient, it is compensated for by increased acuity in other senses, i.e., although unable to hear the witness' answers to his questions, the lawyer can smell fear.

Perhaps it is easier to explain the workings of the law to scientists by selecting a particular area of law as illustrative - the law of seizures[6] and forfeitures[7] which is much in the news these days. Civil forfeiture cases are brought against property, not persons. The concept of suing a lawn chair is as incomprehensible to scientists as quantum electrodynamics is to lawyers, and is best left to legal minds. Because the property is the defendant, civil forfeiture cases bear peculiar titles such as U. S. v. Five Parcels Known as 64 Lovers Lane[8], and U.S. v. one Afghan Urial Ovis Orientalis Blanfordi Fully Mounted Sheep).[9]

In the eyes of the law,[10] the property committed the crime, e.g., the house in which the cocaine was stashed is guilty.[11] Lawyers proudly denominate this kind of astute reasoning "legal fiction." Legal fictions could fruitfully be adopted by hard scientists to create useful chemical, physical and biological fictions, enabling those scientists to realize their age-old dreams of lead-from-gold, perpetual motion, and life-from-mud. In the eyes of the law, civil forfeiture does not punish the owner of the forfeited property. The genesis for this viewpoint is a passage from a renowned work: LOVE IS HATE - WAR IS PEACE - FORFEITURE IS NOT PUNISHMENT[12]

What happens if someone else uses your property to violate the law without your knowledge or consent and the government seizes it for forfeiture? Well, the Supreme Court, in a recent celebrated case[13] ruled, in a five to four decision, that you are out of luck.[14] However, in another celebrated case[15], the Supreme Court decided that the Eighth Amendment prohibition of excessive fines applies to civil forfeiture, so that a criminal's property cannot be forfeited if the forfeiture is excessive in comparison with the crime he committed. Combining the holdings of the Bennis and Austin cases yields the resultant rule that all the property of an innocent person can be forfeited, but only some of the property of a guilty person, an example of almost pure legal reasoning.

Forfeiture lawyers are justly proud of their successes, as evidenced by their most popular bumper stickers: "Kiss your assets goodbye," "Your assets   ours," and "Your assets cheerfully returned — not."[16]

The hard sciences could profit immensely from the assistance of lawyers in the study of natural laws. Take the Law of Gravity. Physicists have from time immemorial[17] sought to alter or suspend the Law of Gravity, with no success. Lawyers are better trained and more adept[18] at discovering loopholes in and exceptions to laws. Only with the aid of the legal profession can man evade gravity and explore the galaxy.[19]

In summary, the right to remain silent and the right to have a lawyer present are fundamental laws. In contrast, scientific laws are not considered fundamental.

---

4   There is some evidence for the view that what has been observed is not the specialization of lawyers, but, rather, their speciation. The evidence is thin because lawyers, averse to empirical methodology, do not yield samples for genetic analysis (Code of Legal Ethics Rule 7B.39). However, Guanine, A.T.C., and Strauss, Levi (1998), "Legal Genes," Journal of the Genomes of The Professions, 3 (4), 18, posit persuasive evidence for the existence of Homo Lex and at least suggestive evidence for Homo Lex Shyster and Homo Lex Patents and Trademarks. Also, reports abound of a Lost Tribe of Lawyers, famous for their annual throat-clearing ceremony, but they seem to have disappeared when their habitat was desertified by a maximum fee schedule. They may have been the subspecies Homo Lex Troglodyte, which has not been observed in the wild or the courtroom since 1747.

5   "Scientist" is another word of Neanderthal origin. Unfortunately, as to its meaning those poor beasts were clueless. Brow, Og (1985), "Heritability of Neanderthal Communicative Characteristics," Journal of Jargon, 15, 73-81. Lawyers acknowledge the immense Neanderthal contribution to the practice of law by making Neanderthals the exclusive referent of "The Party of the First Part."

6   For a definition, see Unskroopulous, I.M., (1996) "Seizures and Other Convulsive Disorders," Journal of Forensic Invoicing 5 (3) 19.

7   Forfeiture is the transfer of title to property from a person to the government, as result of an infraction of the law. This article treats only of civil forfeiture because criminal forfeiture isn't funny.

8   830 F. Supp. 750 (S.D.N.Y. 1993).

9   964 F.2d 474 (5th Cir. 1992).

10 The reference invariably is, "in the eyes of the law," and never, "in the mind of the law," an oxymoron.

11 Only in the field of forfeiture law are lawyers able to perform laboratory experiments at the Bell Laboratory for Inanimate Criminology. In this regard, while the authors are not bucking for an IgNoble Prize in Inanimate Criminology, neither would they refuse one if offered.

12 Orwell, G., Forfeiture Farm, 336.

13 The case is Bennis v. Michigan, 64 USLW 3708 (3/4/96) but the meaning of "celebrated case" is obscure at best. The Bennises celebrated neither the decision nor the forfeiture of their car.

14 The five to four vote does not mean that you are out of luck five times out of nine. Probability analysis is not offered in law school. You are in fact out of luck nine times out of nine.

15 So-called because it was heard on Justice Ginsburg's birthday. The case is Austin v. U.S., 113 S. Ct. 2801 (1993).

16 Incidentally, the footnote was a development of an amphibious ancestor of Homo Lex.

17 Fisic, J.P. (1991), Journal of Immoral Physicists, 4(3) 33.

18 Blackstone Himself (1994) "The lawyer as God - Using Legal Reasoning to Prove the Divinity of Lawyers," Journal of Legal Introspection 13522(39) pp. 13,567-19,981.

19 Of course, when enforcement of the Law of Gravity is required, the job is also best left to lawyers.

Graf Hilgenhurst

"Refresh my memory, Lowenstein...exactly what kind of law do you practice...?"

The Envelope Please

David V. Stivison
Philadelphia, PA

Oscars, Obies, Emmys - Every profession has its award for conspicuous effort. Surely attention must also be paid to the efforts of the stalwart interpreters of the law, those lawyers and judges whose pronouncements fairly stun the reader when first encountered. Now that need will be met! Let the spotlight now shine on these paragons of their profession. And now, the envelope, please!

The Most Creative Trial Tactic Award had many able challengers, including:

●The litigation attorney who asked a plaintiff to "identify all of his relatives within the fourth degree computed according to the civil law;" *Griffin v. Memphis State and Manufacturing Co.*, 38 FRD 54 (DC Miss 1965).

●The closing arguments in a trial involving sales of unregistered stock: "The trial was hotly contested throughout. Perhaps the prosecuting attorney's allusions in his argument to violent crimes, specifically bank robbery, murder and Ruby's shooting of Oswald were somewhat extreme. But counsel for the appellants went to the other extreme of likening their clients' purported offense to parking too close to a fire hydrant;" *U.S. v. Wolfson*, 405 F.2d 779, 785 (2nd Cir. 1968).

The Spiro Agnew Award for eschewing polysyllabic obfuscation had four nominees. The runners-up are:

●Justice Taft, for his unforgettable observation, "Without a driver, a truck cannot move." *Van Meter v. Pub. Util. Comm. of Ohio*, 165 Ohio St. 391, 397 (1956).

●Justice Bramwell's immortal, "The matter does not appear to me now as it appears to have appeared to me then." *Andrews v. Styrap*, 26 L.T. 704, 706 (1872).

●Arkansas Public Public Utility Commission for its insight that, "Pipe hangers are, roughly speaking, devices from which pipe hangs." *Arkansas Power & Light Co.*, Docket No. U-3108, Order No. 23, p. 10.

And the winner is Justice Cardozo's trenchant comment, "The shades of dead defendants do not appear and plead." *James & Co. v. Second Russian Insurance Co.*, 239 NY 248, 146 NE 369 (1925).

Entries for **The Most Unusual Question Award** included cases asking:

●Who has exclusive right to the name of the mythical Tree Frog Beer? *Circle Communications, Inc. v. Hinton*, 74 Ohio Ops. 2nd 356 (CP 1975).

●Are threats of harm to corporate officers by voodoo illegal or merely showing poor judgment? *Selema-DinDings Plantation, Inc. v. Durham*, 216 F. Supp. 104, 112 (SD Ohio 1963).

●Can you copyright the letters "E.T."? *Universal City Studios, Inc. v. Kamar Ind., Inc.*, 25 BNA Pat., Tr. & Co. J 35 (SD Texas 1982).

The winning case is *Gomez v. Dykes*, 89 Ariz. 171, 359 P.2d 760 (1961), which required the court to determine the true ownership of 2,305 tons of cow manure.

There was no serious competition for **The Best Original Definition by a Sitting Judge Award,** which was unanimously voted to Judge Nichols' definition of an IRS special agent: "The special agent is the unobtrusive fellow casually introduced to you midway in the audit of your income tax return, as the one who is now taking over.

"If you grasp the significance of his title, you gather your wits together and rush out to hire the ablest criminal lawyer you can obtain, at any cost. You know the prison doors are yawning for your reception." *Peden v. U.S.*, 512 F.2d 1099, 1100 (Ct. of Claims 1975).

For the **Lex Talionis Award** for the most equitable government rule or regulation, both the EPA and OSHA provided a tremendous line-up of nominees, but the judges agreed that the best regulation of all times was this 1481 French law: "Anyone who sells butter containing stones or other things [to increase its weight] will be put into our pillary, then the said butter will be placed on his head and left until entirely melted by the sun. Dogs may come and lick him, and people offend him with whatever defamatory epithets they please without offense to God or the King." (Nov. 18, 1983 Harvard Law Record, p. 15, quoting from 20 La. B. J. 307 (1973).

The Wild Kingdom Award for the best case involving animals had two runners-up:

●The dog that set off a shotgun and left his owner holding the medical bills. *Mapoles v. Mapoles,* 350 So.2d 1137 (Fla. App. 1977).

●The pigeons whose droppings corroded cars and peeled paint. *Seabord Air Line Ry. Co. v. Richmond-Petersburg Turnpike Authority,* 202 Va. 1029, 121 S.E.2d 499.

But the winners were the "noticeably eager beavers" whose fast breeding and dam building allegedly flooded the plaintiff's land, *Jenkins v. Division of Wildlife, ODNR,* Case No. 75AP-524 (Franklin Co. Ct. of App. 1976).

And now at the conclusion of our awards presentation, as the lights dim and the music fades away, let us speculate that the Goddess of Justice, even if she cannot see the litigants before her, must occasionally be moved to a smile by what she hears them fighting over.

From: Law Reform Commission of Canada, Annual Report 1980/81. (p. 18)
Report 9 *Criminal Procedure: Past I - Miscellaneous ammendments, Feb. 1978* concludes with a paragraph, a part of which states:

"The commission. . .requires streamlined efficacy to escape the slough of delay in which the system is bogging down. The present system operates at full blast and yet it creaks ominously because it is tied to anachronisms which weigh it heavily and dissipate its thrust. . ."

Submitted By:
H.E. Emson
Saskatsua, Canada

"REAL ESTATE SPOKEN HERE"

Alan Shakin*
Bethesda, MD

During your trip to Italy last summer, you probably used a phrasebook to say "We'll both have the veal scallopini" and "That identical handbag is cheaper at Sears." Well, if you decide to sell your house, or buy one, you'll need to start boning up on some conversational real estate. And you can become fluent without knowing a thing about equity, escrow, or easements.

One expression real estate agents love is "That's standard." It's their all-purpose—negative—answer to questions about how the transaction might be cheaper or easier for you. For example, if you ask why the sellers pay the lender's inspection fee on the buyers' loan, the agent spares you any grisly details. "That's standard," she smiles.

If you suggest an alternative to what's "standard," you'll hear "I've never seen it done that way before." Or, from more talkative agents, "I had a client who did that once, and. . .[here they insert a horror story, like the loss of a $6000 deposit or a house sitting on the market for 8 months.]

Real estate agents aren't the only ones with a private lingo, so be sure you can translate these time-honored expression:

1. "We've had many happy years here," sellers often comment, with a dreamy look in their eyes. They're trying to say "We hope to God we can sell before the roof/furnace/central air goes"—and they're dreaming of a better house where nothing is ready to break down.

2. "There are 3 different causes of wet basements" is how your home insepctor might begin a lengthy explanation. Without hearing or understanding another word, you can be sure that the rough translation is (1) pay $1200 or (2) pay $500 or (3) find a different house, if you have any hope of a dry basement. Similarly, if your termite inspector uses the word "subflooring," it will cost you at least $400 for the necessary certificate.

3. Sounding knowledgeable about the dynamics of finance, every loan officer will say either "Mortgage rates have been fluctuating lately" or Mortgage rates have been fairly stable lately." It doesn't matter which version you hear because either one will cost you another point and ¼ percent before your loan gets locked in!

4. Real estate ads are the easiest to translate. "Charming" of course means falling apart or tiny, and "Walk to Metro" means there's a subway station closer to the Washington, D.C. house than to Baltimore or Richmond. Any mention of a first floor den, study, or library means that the house has an L-shaped living room or a hallway into the kitchen.

5. Finally, if you're told that the prospective buyers are "a nice young couple," be prepared for a ridiculously low bid on your house. By the same token, if the sellers "have kids in college," their asking price is firm.

Just as you did with Italian last summer, learn to speak real estate by practicing the most useful words often. Ciao, ciao, ciao. . .location, location, location.

*Mr. Shakin, a government attorney, recently sold a house and bought one.

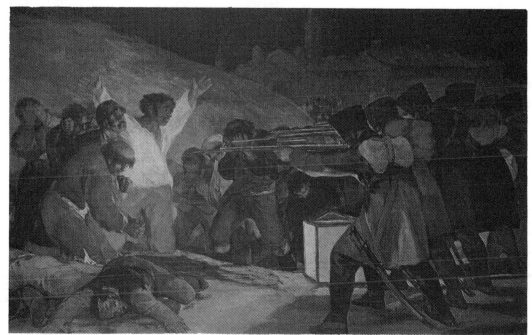

SPECIAL DETERRENCE,[1] THE DEATH[2] PENALTY,[3] AND CRIME[4]

Martin[5] D. Schwartz,[6] Ph.D.[7]
Ohio University[8]
Athens, OH

THE THIRD OF MAY, by Francisco Goya, The Prado, Madrid.

Most studies on capital punishmena and deterrence have dealth only with general deterrence, the effect on the living of the application of the death panalty to someone else. Bartles has done us all a remarkable favor by pointing out that if we look instead at specific or special deterrence, the effect of punishment on the person being punished, we can find a remarkable case for the efficacy of the death panalty. To wit, there is not a single recorded case of a person being executed who has ever been convicted again of a capital crime.[9]

Unfortunately, given the fact that only 3,891 persons have been executed since 1930,[10] this knowledge remains somewhat esoteric. The number of persons who have benefited from this application of special deterrence sanctions is rather small, and the prospects of a very much wider application remain bleak.

Bartels has suggested that a better test of special deterrence is in the field of automobile accidents. Using a similar methodology to the one described above, he found few cases of drivers killed in such incidents being later convicted in a proper court of law of a capital offense.[11] Unfortunately, this is a case of "false positives,"[12] where there is no way of differentiating those who were stopped from committing a future capital offense, and those who could not have offended anyway, even if they had lived.

dress to a party as a rival (c.f., Gasp, I died 1,000 times, 1967); working as hairdresser (c.f., Curlup, I dyed 1,000 times, 1981), and making machinery parts (c.f., Jig, I tool and died 1,000 times, 1986), here the term will be reserved for the more commonly accepted medical definition (Tichian, Mort, The Seven Danger Signs of Clinical Death, 1982). Under certain circumstances, being a fan of the Indianapolis Colts also counts.

[3]Penalty will be used in the jurisprudential sense here of a negative sanction (Emperor of Mikado, Let The Punishment Fit the Crime, 1577), as opposed to reward (Rabbit, B., Alternatives to Incarceration: The Briar Patch, 1948). Unfortunately, the concepts are slippery and difficult to apply in practice. For example, although death is often considered to be a punishment or penalty, it might be considered a reward or at least a desirable outcome if the only alternative was to take the Heritage Foundation seriously, or to regularly attend professional ice hockey games.

[4]Crime will be defined later in this paper, so problems of definition will temporarily be ignored here.

[5]Although this name has its roots with the God of War, Mars (Fawn, Name Your Baby, 1932), the holder in this case is the gentlest of men, as all who know him have agreed, except for an unfortunate few who have lived to regret their extraordinary error, at least for a while.

[6]Not the real name of the author's family, but one made up by a relative, "Black Harry," whose only notable achievement seems to have been to have dodged the military draft of several European countries simultaneously when he came to the U.S.

[7]Obtained with a major in the Sociology of Law, a fact which seemed to escape the attention of the faculty of the school attended.

[8]A school which, for the benefit of Michigan people who get insulted if anyone confuses the University of Michigan with Michigan State University, but who are unable to differentiate Ohio State University from Ohio University, is not Ohio State University, and does not plan to be (Master Plan, Ohio University, 1804).

[9]R. Bartels, Capital Punishment: The Unexamined Issue of Special Deterrence, 68 Iowa Law Review 601-607 (1983).

[10]Having experienced some difficulty obtaining an absolutely accurate figure here, I just made this one up, although by coincidence it is remarkably similar to the one used by the U.S. Department of Justice.

[11]Bartels, *supra* note 9.

[12]The ring of the words, false positives, makes it sound impressive, so it is used here although no one connected with this journal has been able to find out what it means.

---

[1]There are two kinds of deterrence commonly discussed in the literature, of which this is one. Since these will be well differentiated in the body of the text, the distinction will not be commented upon here.

[2]Although death has variously been defined as wearing the same

What is needed is a new method, which can apply special deterrence in an effective manner to a high risk population, thereby making a major dent in crime without sorely afflicting the rest of the population. Given the political sensibilities in this country, which require that a shovel be called a "field entrenchment tool," and a hammer a "manually operated high impact fastener drive,"[13] it is further suggested that properly labeling a political campaign as "genocide," or "killing off criminals" could no doubt raise this important program to public attention and controversy. Much as the Reagan administration has managed to call bombs "peacemakers," it is modestly suggested here that Retroactive Birth Control (RBC) be used to refer to this effective form of the death penalty.

To make RBC more widespread and therefore effect as a deterrent, a wide variety of steps will have to be formulated. Some suggestions follow:

A) *U.S. Army.* In the past felons have been at times denied enlistment in the Army. As Prof. Guthrie[14] has pointed out, the view has been that litterbugs were not moral enough to burn villages and kill women and children. In the future, we could *limit* Army membership to felons, as an alternative to incarceration. We could then declare war on Nicaragua, Afghanistan, and, if the Thatcher Government is overthrown, England. Of course, this would be very expensive, but less expensive than modern prisons. And, of course, there would be less mouths to feed each day the wars continue.

B) *Heroin and Cocaine.* If heroin is legalized in prisons, it would not only reduce dramatically the prison stress level criminologists are always yapping about, but it would also increase RBC figures. We are in the midst of a media blitz which is attempting to tell us that drugs kill. Supplying Cocaine would provide a test of that theory, make a lot of people happy, and continue to provide Juan Valdez with an alternative to coffee crops.

C) *Bad Habits.* This one is already being used in many state prisons. Inmates should be encouraged to smoke enormus amounts of cigarettes, drink awful home made concoctions, eat lots of smoked foods and sugars, and watch prodigious amounts of TV. Unfortunately, exercise is still allowed, and this must be stopped immediately.

No doubt, other commentators can add significantly to this list of RBC inducing behaviors. The object is a worthy one - a system which, for the first time in 150 years, would provide a form of deterrence which we can be assured will reduce crime.[15]

---

[13]Here, for a change, are two titles *not* made up. They came from newspaper stories I read while lying down on the couch without a pencil, so I cannot provide cites, which are a pain in the butt anyway.

[14]A. Guthrie, Alice's Restaurant, 1968. This should not be confused with Prof. Guthrie's more widely cited argument that reality cannot be captured on 27 color photographs with circles and arrows and a paragraph on the back of each one (A. Guthrie and O. Opie, *Justice is Blind*, 1968).

[15]Sorry. We ran out of space before we could define this.

MEMORANDUM FOR: Donald Elisburg*
FROM: Nancy S. Barrett**
SUBJECT: Equal Employment Opportunity

Submitted By: **Ernst W. Stromsdorfer**
Cambridge, MA

Efforts by the Employment Services Administration to promote equal employment opportunity through public service announcements on radio and television are to be applauded. However, I am concerned that a recent broadcast featuring three well known personalities encourages employers to pay women less than an equitable wage.

I am referring to the broadcast featuring Batman, Batwoman and Robin. In that broadcast Batman is informed that Batwoman must be paid the same salary as Robin. Holy Act of Congress! Robin is a mere lad, probably an apprentice. Batwoman, on the other hand (or wing) is a journeyperson crime fighter. Clearly Batwoman should be paid at the same rate as Batman rather than Robin. I hope that in future broadcasts, Batwoman will be compared to Batman rather than Robin.

Incidentally, Robin's work seems rather dangerous. Do you think his position would be classified as hazardous under child labor laws?

---

*Assistant Secretary, Employment Services Administration
**Deputy Assistant Secretary, Policy, Evaluation and Research

The Course Of True Time In Albany Never Did Run Smooth

James M. Rose *
White Plains, NY

A decision of the New York State Supreme Court, Appellate Division, Third Department has recently shed some darkness over the subject of how fast time passes in Albany County.[1]

The case, *Labello v. Albany Medical Center Hospital et. al.* as reported in the New York *Law Journal,*[2] involved a medical malpractice statute of limitations of ten years. The Court recited that the malpractice complained of occurred on November 9, 1982 and that the case was commenced on November 2, 1992. However, the court concluded that the ten year limitation had been exceeded.[3]

The Theory of Relativity states that the passage of time is relative to the speed at which one travels. Until now it was believed that time in Albany travelled slowly because there are so many bureaucrats and legislators there.[4]

Legislators possess not only the ability to make time **seem** like it is standing still when they give a speech, they have the ability to *actually* suspend time by "stopping the clock." This they do by directing that the clocks in the Senate and Assembly chambers be physically halted short of midnight so that midnight does not occur—at least inside the halls of the state capitol.[5]

They can do it when the budget is due by April 1[6] or at the end of the legislative session in order to prevent the introduction of new bills that require three days elapse prior to passage. It is theorized that holding back time in Albany affects the physical consistency of it. If it is too lumpy in the Senate and Assembly Chambers, time can become too thin and fast outside of them.[7] Because it is held back so long it must gush forward like water bursting from confinement behind a dam. Perhaps holding back time causes friction which heats up time and makes it go faster when released like the molecules in a chemical reaction.[8]

Time and space can be warped by strong gravity such as that which exists around black holes. The gravity of the subjects considered by the state Legislature[9] or the black hole into which tax dollars disappear may affect the speed of time there as well.

On what legal authority does the Legislature rely to stop time? It may be the "new style" of time computation. New York General Construction Law § 50 provides "Time shall continue to be computed in this state according to the Gregorian or new style. The first day of each year after seventeen hundred and fifty-two is the first day of January according to such style."[10]

---

* White Plains, New York, Occupant of the Bob Dylan Chair of Wind Direction at the Federal State School of Law and Comity Club.

1 The author spent a week there one afternoon.

2 *New York Law Journal,* July 15, 1994 p. 25 col 3.

3 As the eminent professor of Linguistics Casey Stengel used to say "You could look it up!"

4 "Nullum tempus occurrit regi" ("Time is no object to a government department.") A.P. Herbert, *Uncommon Law,* p. 200 (London, 1969).

5 This is the converse of the problem of people on budgets who have too much month left over at the end of the money.

6 State Finance Law § 3 (1) provides that (after 1943) the first day of the fiscal year is (appropriately) April Fool's Day. That section provides that in 1942 the fiscal year ran from July 1, 1942 to March 31, 1943 due to war shortages.

7 Or perhaps this is just a corollary to the Einsteinian theory of relativity that the faster you travel the slower time passes. The slower you travel the faster time passes, and things in general move so slowly in the bureaucracy in Albany that time actually passes quicker. New York has so much time left over that it gives a lot to its convicts. In Midtown Manhattan, cross-town traffic moves so slowly that time passes rapidly, hence the expression "in a New York minute." A "New York minute" is one of the New York times.

8 Somewhat akin to "Brownian movement"— named after *Brown v. Board of Education of Topeka, Kansas* 347 US 483, because the molecules in question move with all deliberate speed.

9 such as the selection of the official state muffin (State Law § 84—it's the apple muffin), or repealing laws not yet in effect.

L. 1990 c. 747 § 2 effective (October 20, 1990) repealed subdivision (d) of Insurance Law § 2335 which had yet to be enacted. Chapter 747 thus had the effect of repealing Chapter 932 prior to its enactment. (See Codification note to Mc Kinney's Consolidated Laws of the State of New York, Insurance Law § 2335.)

10 What the first day of each year was before that is beyond the scope of this article.

We know what the Gregorian calendar is, but what was the purpose of adding "or" before the words "new style" in the statute? The Gregorian calendar had already been mentioned so "new style" must mean something else if it is connected by the use of the preposition "or." Otherwise the presence of "new style" in the statute would be superfluous. Where is the definition of "new style?"[11] There are no less than four definitions of "time" in the General Construction Law[12] but none of them provide for suspending it.[13]

Perhaps the authority to halt time falls within the general duties of the secretary of each Legislative Committee who has the job of keeping the minutes. If they keep enough minutes they add up to hours![14]

Or it could be that the state constitution's provision which grants each house the power to determine the rules of its own proceedings (Article III § 9) give it the power to determine the time as well.[15]

But then who are we to question what the Legislators do?[16] The New York State Constitution Art. III § 11 provides that for any speech or debate in either house of the legislature the members shall not be questioned in any other place. That would include this journal—so case closed![17]

11 The statute tells us *when* new style begins (i.e., January 1). We know *when* it begins, but *what* is it?

12 §§ 50 ("Time, computation"), 51 ("Time, night"), 52 ("Time, standard"), and 53 ("Time, use of standard.") This list does not include § 48 of that law ("Tense, present") which provides that the present tense includes the future. This is something we have discovered when noting that the "tense present" is inevitably followed by a "tense future."

13 Of course it could be argued that General Construction Law § 52 *requires* the use of Eastern Standard or Daylight time. However it could also be argued that Eastern Standard is only the time that must be used *when* the state uses time at all. By analogy, although the courts use the Gregorian calendar that does not require them to transact business on Sunday.

14 If the clock in the state capital is stopped for more than two weeks do the Legislature's employees get paid? (This is the opposite of "no show" jobs in which people get paid by the Legislature although they do not perform some service "at some time" see, *People v. Ohrenstein* 77 NY2d 38 at 53. Here employees work "around the clock" — but it doesn't.) However, if this piece of Legislative legerdemain continues past April 15, New York State income tax is still due, and cannot be avoided on the theory that it is still March 31 in Albany. It may be inside the capitol building, but at the State Department of Taxation time marches on. No case against the State of New York is reported in which a statute of limitations that would expire on April 2 was commenced on what is April 5 in the rest of the state, but where service was made inside the capitol building when the clock had been stopped on March 31.

15 See *New York Public Interest Research Group v. Steingut* 40 NY2d 250, 257 "It is not the province of the courts to direct the legislature how to do its work."

16 We just pay their salary.

17 EDITOR's NOTE: The *official* report of the Labello case at 202 App. Div. 2d 299 at 300, 614 NYS2d 459 recites the action was commenced on November 23 and not on November 2 as the *Law Journal* had reported. The inconsistent nature of time in Albany even affected the dates in the case between when it was first reported in July and when it was officially reported several months later. It only goes to prove the adage "Times change"!

MATHEMATICS

The Large-Cake Cutting Problem

D. R. Olander
University of California at Berkley

I Introduction

Since the development of large uniform-temperature ovens, baking of ultra-large cakes (ULCs) for festive occasions has become part of Western civilization. A ULC is defined as a cake with icing that has an area larger than 200 square inches. The technology of cutting of ULCS, however, has not kept pace with the advances in their fabrication. Rectangular ULCs (often called sheet cakes, or SCs) pose no particular problems since slicing on an orthogonal grid gives satisfactory results. On the other hand, dividing a large-diameter round cake into a large number of slices in the conventional circular-sector manner is impractical, both in handling and for eating. This problem is literally an everyday occurrence. The acute observer at weddings notes that although the bride and groom make the first cut of their wedding cake, cutting of the bottom layer (which is very often a circular ULC) is left to a technician who usually produces slices of uneven size.

Humpelmaier (1) attempted to solve the circular ULC slicing problem by approximating the circular cake as a square and cutting in the manner appropriate to SCs. However, he failed to account for Anaxagoras' result (2), and avoiding the irregularly shaped pieces at the ULC's periphery proved to be an insurmountable difficulty.

Subsequently, Gateaubriand (3) conjectured that dividing a ULC into an inner circular subcake of manageable size and an outer annular subcake that could be cut into single slices around its periphery would prove to be a acceptable solution. However, Gateaubriand did not develop his proposal quantitatively. The purpose of this paper is to provide a theoretical foundation for Gateaubriand's insightful suggestion. The theory is then compared to several experiments intended to demonstrate the practicality of the model for a specific set of parameters.

II Theory

Statement of the problem: A ULC of diameter D_O is to serve N quests by first separating it into an inner circular subcake of diameter D_i that is cut into N_i pieces and an outer annular subcake subdivided into N_O slices. Given D_O and N, the problem is to find D_i, N_i, and N_O.

An obvious relation between two of the three unknowns is:

$$N = N_i + N_o \qquad (1)$$

Referring to Fig. 1, the angular span of the wedges in the inner and outer subcakes are ϕ_i and ϕ_0 respectively. We must, of course, require that all of the cake be consumed:

$$N_o \phi_o = N_i \phi_i = 2\pi \qquad (2)$$

and, so that each guest gets the same amount of cake,

$$\phi_o (D_o^2 - D_i^2) = \phi_i D_i^2 \qquad (3)$$

Combining Eqs (1) and (2):

$$\frac{N}{2\pi} = \frac{1}{\phi_i} + \frac{1}{\phi_o} \qquad (4)$$

and letting $\Upsilon = D_i/D_O$ in (3):

$$\phi_o (1 - \gamma^2) = \phi_i \gamma^2 \qquad (5)$$

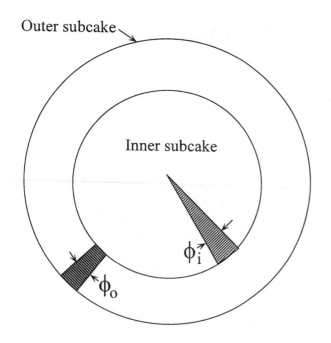

Outer subcake

Inner subcake

ϕ_i

ϕ_o

The difficulty that now is apparent from (4) and (5) is that two equations do not suffice for three unknowns. Consequently, an additional condition is needed.

We examine first:

The Aesthetic Requirement

The outer edge of pieces cut from the inner and outer subcakes be equal, or:

$$D_o\phi_o = D_i\phi_i \quad \text{or} \quad \phi_o = \gamma\phi_i \quad \text{(6)}$$

Dividing, (6) into (5) yields an equation that can be solved for $\gamma = (\sqrt{5}-1)/2$, and using (6) and (2) in (4) yields:

$$N_o = N / (1 + \gamma) \quad \text{(7)}$$

which, for N=45 as an example, requires 27.8 pieces to be cut from the outer subcake. This naturally causes some difficulties, so rounding off to 28 pieces from the outer subcake and 17 pieces from the inner cake is eminently reasonable. However, the problem of cutting a circle into 17 parts with any accuracy is not likely to be resolved easily. Consequently, we investigate instead:

The Unequal-Piece Condition

A simple solution would obviously be possible if the pieces of cake were not all the same size. However, such a route risks possible altercations among the guests and for this reason is rejected.

We finally arrive at the definitive solution, namely:

The Ease-Of-Cutting Requirement

To achieve this condition, we cut the cake into a number of pieces which has the greatest number of factors and which is also closest to the number of guests. Although the logic is somewhat fuzzy, this is a very satisfactory solution all round. The circle-cutting difficulty is resolved by choosing N = 48, divided into $N_0 = 32$ and $N_i = 16$. It is a simple enough matter to cut 32 or 16 slices from circles by the well-known method of successive halving (4). Since the ratio of the angular widths of the inner and outer subcakes is 2, Eq (5) gives $\gamma = 1/\sqrt{3}$. Or, for a 16" diameter ULC, the inner subcake is 9.2376" in diameter. A major advantage of this solution is that the host gets to eat three pieces of cake the next day.

III Experimental Method

Several 16" diameter ULCs were prepared by Classic Confections, Inc. and tested on a group of 45 subjects chosen for their engineering analytical abilities. Care was taken to obtain the approval of the University's Human Subjects Committee for the experiment.

A round template was prepared from stiff cardboard using a compass and cutting out the theoretically prescribed circle with a pair of household scissors. A technician at each gathering employed the template to produce the circular incision separating the inner and outer subcakes. The technician was instructed to slice the outer annular subcake into 32 equal slices using the method of successive halving. When these specimens had been consumed, the inner subcake was sliced into 16 equal pieces in the shape of circular sectors using the same method. A previously-sharpened slicing knife with a 6" diameter blade length was used to prepare the specimens.

IV Results

Expt. A

This experiment failed. Only a metric ruler was available and in preparing the template, the required diameter of 9.2376" was inadvertently converted to centimeters by dividing rather than multiplying by 2.54. The resulting pieces from the inner and outer subcakes were grossly unequal, causing very markedly different degrees of appreciation of the specimens by the subjects.

Expt. B

This experiment too did not proceed as expected theoretically. The hostess examined the template on which the 16 slices were outlined and stated that "These pieces are too small" (5). The ULC was the cut by trial-and-error and an additional(smaller) cake was purchased to assure guest satisfaction.

Expt. C

The ULC was satisfactorily sectioned according to the theoretical model. However, 49 guests appeared, necessitating removal of -2% from each of the 48 slices to prepare a composite portion for the 49th subject. The host exhibited hostile behavior occasioned by the loss of the expected leftover cake. In addition, the top raspberry sauce layer slid during transportation from the bakery to the site of the test, resulting in claims of unequal treatment by numerous subjects.

V Conclusions

Pending approval of the renewal grant from the Good Housekeeping Society, additional tests are planned with better control of template fabrication, number of subjects taking part in the tests, and on-site management of the cutting operation. The mode of transportation of the test ULCs will be changed from a Honda Civic to a Lincoln Continental Mark IV to avoid the sauce sliding problem that marred test C. The composition of the ULCs for these tests will be changed from raspberry mousse to lemon creme to permit sharper, more stable incisions to be made.

The results described in Sect. IV, although technically unable to reproduce the behavior predicted by the theory, were sufficiently promising to warrant further model verification attempts in the followon program. Representatives of the subject cohort have expressed strong support for continuation of the tests. However, the funding agency is insisting on having its representatives take part in all future tests to insure that the proposed test procedures are rigorously followed. Results will be reported in fiscal year 1996.

REFERENCES
1. H. Humpelmaier, Zeit. fur Kuchenarbeitundfressen, 23, 2378 (1907)
2. X. Anaxagoras, *"On the Impossibility of Squaring the Circle"* Δεφνρρξαπ, p 312, Philosopher's Publishing House, Athens(-549)
3. J. P. Gateaubriand, Comptes Rendus de l'Academie de Patisserie, 77, 456 (1965)
4. L. Popover, J. Culinary Arts, 56, 333 (1970)
5. G. Olander, personal communication (1995)

Blazer, J.A.
LEG POSITION AND PSYCHOLOGICAL CHARACTERISTICS IN WOMEN
Psychology - Journal of Human Behavior, 1966, <u>3</u>, 5 - 12 (August 66).

"The present study was designed to test a theory of "leg position analysis" or "observed psychology" using standard psychometric tests and methods to gather and analyze the data." "The first hypothesis tested was: The preferred method of leg-crossing or position generally used by a woman as indicative of her need strengths and basic values or interests. The second hypothesis was: intelligence and education have no effect upon preference of leg crossing or position in women."

(Highly recommended to our readers!)

Assignment Of Fault In Complex Systems: The Calculation Of Blame

R. J. Halbert, MD, MPH,
UCLA School of Public Health

As he went along, he saw a man blind from birth. His disciples asked him, "Rabbi, who sinned, this man or his parents, that he was born blind?"

The Gospel of Luke 9: 1-2
(New International Version)

Although epidemiology has developed a number of mathematical tools to evaluate risk factors which may lead to bad outcomes, the more immediate issue of "whose fault is it?" is usually overlooked. Attribution of fault, or "blame" as we will refer to it, is usually dealt with by the judicial system using antiquated methods which lack scientific rigor, as expressed in phrases like "beyond a reasonable doubt," or "the preponderance of evidence." This problem is particularly acute when blame is shared by more than one party. We now describe a system by which blame can be accurately and reliably apportioned to the parties at fault in any negative outcome situation.

Risk versus Blame

Blame (B) can be viewed as an etiologic factor by which an individual causes a negative outcome by his or her own negligence or error. The true blame of an individual is the difference between the blame assigned to that individual (B_i) minus the general blame shared by the group of which the individual is a member (B_g). Thus:

$$\text{Blame Difference} = BD = B_i - B_g$$

where B_i = blame in the individual at fault; and

B_g = blame in the reference group, or "generic blame"

which may be expressed, "how bad did this guy screw up?"

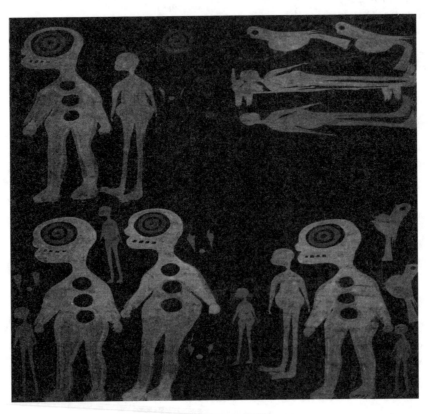

Blame Difference is difficult to determine absolutely, since it requires measuring the total level of stupidity in a given population. In practical usage, the blame ratio (BR) is more useful. This is the ratio of individual to collective blame. Thus:

$$\text{Blame Ratio (relative blame)} = BR = B_i/B_g$$

which can be expressed as "how much worse did this guy screw up than the rest of us poor schmucks."

The Guilt Coefficient

Calculation of relative blame is incomplete without a consideration of shared blame (2) within a specific subgroup. The importance of various factors such as sex (3), ethnicity (4), and religion (5) in assigning blame have been described in the literature, but have not previously been linked together in any coherent fashion. We will use the term "guilt" to distinguish these general factors from particular instances of negligence or error. Once again, absolute guilt is less important than relative guilt. The coefficient of guilt (Γ) is a matrix of these various factors, represented by $\gamma_s, \gamma_e, \gamma_r \cdots \gamma_x$, where

γ_s = sexual guilt (6)

γ_e = ethnic guilt

γ_r = religious guilt; etc.

We may now restate our equations of blame:

$$BD = B_i\Gamma_i - B_g\Gamma - \quad \text{and} \quad BR = B_i\Gamma_i/B_g\Gamma_g$$

where Bi = blame assigned to the individual,

Γ_i = guilt coefficient of the individual,

B_g = generic blame; and

Γ_g = guilt coefficient of the group, or "generic guilt."

Calculation of the guilt coefficient for any given individual is beyond the scope of this paper, since it involves nasty bits of tensor calculus (7). The calculation of the guilt of all mankind population guilt (Γ p) — is theoretically intriguing but of limited use for most applications. Such a methodology might have been useful at Nuremberg, for example, but in general this type of problem falls into the category of religion rather than science. The literature abounds with references to "societal guilt" but most of this work is unsupported by any solid theory.

Anyone familiar with an organizational approach to problem solving will recognize the importance of a precise mathematical method for determining exactly who to blame in any given situation. Introduction of these methods could lead to increased productivity in medicine, business, government, the courts, and any similar organization where blame might otherwise be apportioned randomly or according to personal, subjective interests. In future work we hope to explore differential blame assignment, the guilt coefficient, and the application of these concepts to population-based fuck-ups.

REFERENCES:
1. Hoffman RE. The use of epidemiologic data in the courts. American Journal of Epidemiology 1984; 120: 190-202.
2. Also referred to as "original sin" (CF: The Letter to the Romans 5:12, NIV).
3. Wyatt GE, Dunn KM. Examining predictors of sex guilt in multiethnic samples of women. Archives of Sexual Behavior 1991; 20: 471-485. See also, "Are men really that bad'?" TIME 1994; Feb. 14.
4. Res ipsa locitur.
5. Black MS, London P. The dimensions of guilt, religion, and personal ethics. Journal of Social Psychology 1966; 69: 39-54.
6. This term refers to gender guilt: not to be confused with guilt related to sexual impropriety. See ref. 2, 3.
7. We will be happy to delve into this matter in minute detail if the editors will print it.

PSYCHOTHERAPY

Psychotherapy is an undefined technique applied to unspecified cases with unpredictable results. For this technique, rigorous training is required.

Victor Raimy

Submitted by Mark Worden Roseburg, OR

THE RATIONAL NUMBER SHORTAGE

ROBERT K. BENDER, Ph.D.
411 West Hackberry Drive
Arlington Heights, Il. 60004

A rather serious problem which is caused by the use of electronic calculators with memory has never been reported. This problem stems from the manner in which irrational numbers are expressed and stored by these devices. If we do not begin to look for solutions to this problem, we may find ourselves without rational numbers by the year 1985.

The use of rational numbers has grown exponentially since the invention of algebra and Cartesian geometry. We will consume more rational numbers in the next year (with budget reports, census reports, calculus problems, wage-price guidelines, etc.) than were used during all of the previous years combined.

The international crisis which will soon become evident is due, in part, to electronic calculators. It is a matter of record (Osgood's table of Values) that, in 1950, the square root of two was valued at 1.414213^+, an irrational number. Today, my calculator gives the value as the rational number 1.41421, a devaluation of 0.0002% in only 28 years. A conservative projection gives

$$\sqrt{2} = 10^{-7}$$

by the year 1985. As if this devaluation was not serious enough, the calculator has replaced $\sqrt{2}$, an irrational number, with a much needed rational number. If this value is placed into the memory of a calculator and the power switch is turned off, the number will be lost for good.

In Europe, computer banks have started to horde rational numbers in disk space. At first this had the effect of driving the value of the rationalized natural log base, e, to a record high of 2.72 on January first, 1979; but the value fell to 2.70 when Americans failed to buy rationalized natural logs as expected. In the Soviet Union, where everyone has some of the π, but no one has enough of it to judge its value, the drop in π to its record low of 3.0 went unnoticed.

If we act soon, we can avoid the international crisis which now threatens to destroy us. Immediate action which we must take includes the following:

1. Lettering the pages of all books,
2. Yelling "Bee" when a golf ball is about to hit someone,
3. Counting things less often,
4. Acting irrationally rather than rationally,
5. Letting the decimal point float (when expressing radicals).

Fundamental research must begin to develop ways to convert letters into numbers (c has already been converted into a number by Michelson, and Cavendish has done the same for G).

We must act before 1985. As acting number czar, I cannot overemphasize this problem enough.

OBSERVATION IS INSUFFICIENT FOR DISCOVERING THAT THE SURFACE OF STILL WATER IS INVARIABLY HORIZONTAL
Science 181 : 173 , 1973

"Years of research involving hundreds of subjects of pre-school through college age indicates that by 12 years of age boys understand the principle that the surface of still water remains horizontal. Girls, however, lag behind boys of all ages in this respect, and about 50% of college women still do not know this principle."

A Theory of 4 Physical Dimensions

Jordan Levenson, B.S., M.B.A.
10276 Bannockburn Drive
Los Angeles, California 90064

We shall reach the title subject by leading progressively up to it.

A zero-dimensional world is usually represented by a point and a one-dimensional world by a line. Figure 1 represents a magnified view of a one-dimensional world. "A" is a one-dimensional homogeneous opaque being in this one dimensional world.

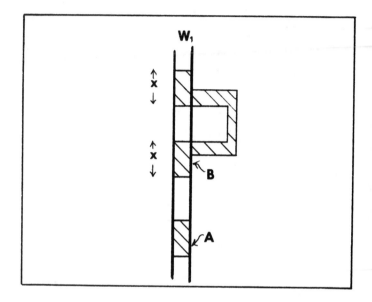

Since he can see along only one dimension and doesn't have X-ray vision he sees only the end view of the being next to him. He lives in a world of end views and knows the length of nobody but himself. Freedom of movement is somewhat limited as one can't get beyond the position of the next end view unless it, too, moves.

Here in Figure 2 we have a one-dimensional world coincident with a two-dimensional world. The two-dimensional world is represented by a plane and W_1 is a line in the plane. If A *did have* some kind of detection equipment enabling detection of the length of other *one*-dimensional beings (possibly X-ray vision) he would detect, due to the one-dimensional world discontinuity of the two-dimensional being shown (B), two beings of one dimension, length X each, not realizing that these were in fact the same being. There is something A might be able to do to gain that realization but rather than discuss that simple case let's go on to a more complex case.

Figure 3 shows a two-dimensional world with a couple of homogeneous two-dimensional beings. Two-dimensional beings can see (perceive) in two-dimensions only ---- these are the two dimensions of its world.

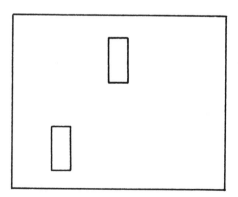

Figure 4 is a two-dimensional world coincident with a three-dimensional world. E would perceive F, due to F's two-dimensional discontinuity, as 2 two-dimensional beings when in fact these are part of the same being.

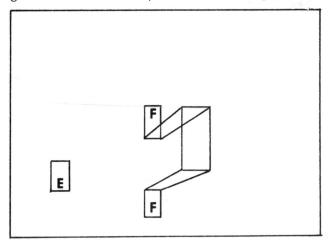

The only way E will be able to "know" the rest of the other being, F, is to re-orient the two-dimensional space in which he, E, exists in and is limited to . . . his own "personal" space. In Figure 5 this is shown.

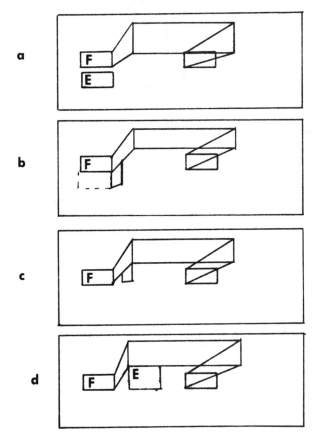

First E rotates its personal frame of reference 90° (figure 5b). Then moving in its natural mode of two dimensions E can examine part of the three-dimensional being (figure 5c). Another 90° rotation back to a plane parallel to E's original would complete the process (figure 5d).

It helps to know at what position one should make 90° reorientations. Here it was initially done at the place where the being F discontinued in the two-dimensional world. Though E could make a 90° rotation at other places and sooner or later possibly discover a three-dimensional component, due to time and effort it is best to reorientate at places where a definable edge of an object exists in its world.

It can be said that two-dimensional objects in E's world may have three-dimensional components. Of course all three-dimensional objects have two-dimensional components but those components may not exist in E's plane.

Going back to figure 2 it is now seen that by such a 90° rotation A could examine B.

In figure 6 we have a three-dimensional world with three-dimensional beings.

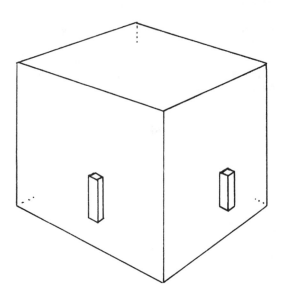

There is *no reason* to believe that three is the limiting dimension factor (though this may be our perception). Accept this concept and it follows that like the previous examples our three-dimensional world could be coincident with a four-dimensional world, and some objects in our three-dimensional world may have a fourth dimensional component. Some objects which seem to be separate entities may in fact be the same entity. Another way of saying this is that it is possible that some things we see on Earth exist in four dimensions and we see only the part that exists in our own frame of reference.

90° is not a critical factor; it was used to provide an easy figure that was consistent throughout the examples. By this is meant that in figure 4 F would be a three-dimensional object if it angled up at even a fraction of a degree from the two dimensional plane.

Possibly by rotating a small portion of our orientation slightly we can examine this fourth dimensional component though we would still have only a three-dimensional orientation (as E still had only a two-dimensional orientation in figure 5). E *didn't* become three-dimensional you recall.

How about the Nth dimensional world perceiving the Nth + 1 dimension?

A Graph Theorist Looks At Peripheral Canals

Phyllis Zweig
Arcata, CA

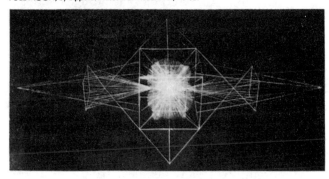

Sometimes, buried in mathematical tomes, one finds results that seem to have unexpected (if useless) significance to everyday existence. A classic example of this might be the result from topology called the Banach-Tarski paradox (1). A special case of this paradox states that any two solid spheres are equivalent by finite decomposition. This means, for example, that you could cut the sun up into a finite number of pieces which could be rearranged to fit together into a sphere the size of a pea. Mind you, the pieces will be very irregularly shaped. And since this is a paradox, it doesn't have to make sense. Remember this result the next time you are trying to pack your suitcase: if you don't mind cutting your clothes into tatters, you can be sure they'll all fit into a very tiny container.

A more recent result from graph theory, a fairly recent off-shoot of topology, seems to have particular significance for California readers. A little background information will allow the reader to understand the following result, presented at a recent conference (3).

Graph theorists use the word *tree* to describe diagrams like those in Figure 1:

FIGURE 1

Trees consist of points with line segments connecting some of the points. All of the points must be connected with no "circuits." The diagrams in Figure 2 represent other types of graphs which do contain circuits (polygons).

FIGURE 2

For certain applications in graph theory, one as-signs the numbers 1,2,...,n to the points of a tree. Such an assignment is called a *numbering* of the tree. The *width* of a numbering is the largest difference between the numbers at opposite endpoints of each line segment in the tree. Figure 3 shows a tree with various numberings having width 4,3,2 respectively. The *bandwidth* of the tree is the smallest width of any numbering of the tree. Each of the trees in Figure 4 is numbered with a bandwidth numbering of the tree, i.e., the maximum difference is as small as it can be in any numbering of the tree.

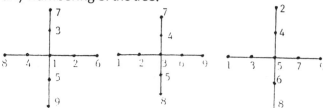

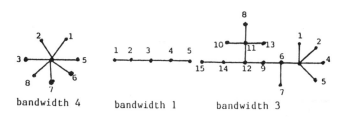

bandwidth 4   bandwidth 1   bandwidth 3

FIGURE 4

A *peripheral point* of a tree is one which could be labeled 1 by some bandwidth labeling. The tree of Figure 5 has bandwidth 3. All of its peripheral points are circled.

FIGURE 5

Notice that peripheral point S, which is in the "interior" of the tree, can be connected through a series of peripheral points SJV to an "outside" or "endpoint" of the tree. A path of all peripheral points which are joined by lines of the tree, with at least one end at an outside point of the tree, is called a peripheral canal.

A question posed at the conference of (3) was: Given a peripheral point in a tree, is there always a peripheral canal involving that point?

The following theorem gives an answer which the author finds politically satisfying. (4)

Theorem: Not every tree need have a peripheral canal.

Proof: By example. The tree of Figure 6 has a peripheral point X which is not part of any peripheral canal. The bandwidth of this tree is 4.

FIGURE 6

It will be left to the reader to find a bandwidth 4 numbering of the tree and to verify that point X is not part of any peripheral canal.

For more information concerning bandwidth, consult (2).

REFERENCES

1. **L.M. Blumenthal.** "A paradox, a paradox, a most ingenious paradox." *American Mathematical Monthly*, Vol. 47, June-July 1940, p. 346-53
2. **P.Z. Chinn, J. Chvatalova, A.K. Dewdney, N.E. Gibbs.** The Bandwidth Problem for Graphs and Matrices—A Survey. *Journal of Graph Theory*, Vol. 6, No. 3, Fall 1982
3. **P.Z. Chinn, A.K. Dewdney, T.M. Greene.** Bandwidth and Peripheral Vertices of Trees. 12th Southeast Conference on Combinatorics, Graph Theory and Computing, Baton Rouge, LA, Spring 1980
4. **V. Greedy.** "The positive effects of the proposed Peripheral Canal through the San Joaquin Valley on the Southern California water supply vs. predicted negative effects on Northern California trees." *Journal of Political Expediency*, January 1979, p. 7-15

The other day at the covention of the American Medical Association, in New Orleans, where some 4,000 or 5,000 physicians and attendants were gathered, Dr. Billings drew attention to the decided oversupply of medical men in the United States. He attributed the surplus to the fact that the medical colleges are graduating annually from 10,000 to 12,500 physicians, when the actual needs of the country call for only about 2,500. If Dr. Billings is correct, and there is no reason to doubt his figures, from 7,000 to 10,000 young men are annually entering a profession in which they have but the slimmest hopes of making even the proverbial "comfortable living." Of course, it goes without saying that most of the professions are more or less overcrowded; but we doubt if any of them, except the Law, could afford a parallel to

WE NEED FEWER DOCTORS

from the New York Times May 16, 1903

the condition of things brought to light at the New Orleans convention. What this disparity between the demand and supply means to this army of young men, can only be surmised; but certain it is that in the majority of cases it will involve the loss of much money, that can ill be spared, and much time, that can be spared still less. It does really seem a pity that some

of these graduates have not entered other professions that are not so crowded, and can offer better prospects of remuneration. Sanitary engineering, naval architecture, and the comparatively new profession of forestry, for instance, are not overcrowded, and there will soon be a great demand for really competent automobile engineers, men who combine with mechanical ability a thorough knowledge of gas and other engines that are competing for the control of the field. Then there is the sphere of journalism, which, while abundantly supplied as to numbers, it pitiably supplied as to quality. There must be among those thousands of graduates not a few young men who have a natural gift for good writing—in these days an all-too-rare accomplishment that threatens to become a lost art.

ON SOME LITTLE KNOWN RESULTS OF REAL ANALYSIS

Michael Gering
Pretoria, South Africa

Recently there has been a renewed interest in real analysis and the purpose of this note is to bring some of these ideas to the attention of the reader. In particular we hope to show that the concept of a con sequence has been useful in proving some outstanding results. A con sequence is a set of logical postulates or arguments which, in the sense of the norm, appears to converge and then consequently does not.

The theorems discussed below were developed to deal with structures of interest to scientists and engineers. For this reason they have been named in unfortunate analogy to certain familiar household objects such as doors and chairs with which these people are familiar and in consequence this subject has been cynically dubbed very real analysis.

The set D (called doors because of their closure properties) are defined such that for each $D \epsilon D$ there exists a unique Δ (doorway). A door is said to be closed if for every point x not in the doorway, the door is between the person and its doorway. That is $\forall x \notin \Delta$, $d(x,\Delta) > d(D,\Delta)$ where $d(x,y)$ is the metric function.

Several standard results follow from this definition. It can be shown for example that a closed door forms an accumulation point of people wishing to use the door that is of C^O functions $p(t)$ where for each $p(t) \ni t_O$ such that $p(t_O) \epsilon \Delta$.

Some doors are never closed while other doors are closed for all times $-\infty < t < +\infty$. The latter class of objects are of particular interest and a door that is always closed is said to be discrete. Several results have been proved for discrete doors and it has been conjectured by Butler *et al.*, that a door closed almost everywhere is discrete for almost everyone (i.e. for almost all functions $p(t)$ defined above).

Another important concept is that of being ajar. A door is said to be ajar if a jam can be placed on it inside. The following theorem, in which the construct ajar is shown to be complementary to the construct closure, is sometimes referred to as the fundamental theorem of very real analysis which states:

Theorem A door which is ajar cannot be closed and a door which is closed cannot be ajar.

The direct part of the theorem is proved by putting $p = j(D)$ where $j(D)$ is the door-jamb and the converse follows in a similar fashion (closure implies that given a jam $j(D)$ there is a door closer to the doorway than $j(d)$ which contradicts the assumption that the door is ajar. This theorem has profound implications for a class of doors with several chambrs called revolvers.

The rest of this note is devoted to the question of whether a sequence of con sequences is in itself consequent. To establish this result it is convenient to introduce a structure $C(l_1, l_2, \ldots l_n)$, called a chair and defined on an arbitrary surface F; The following theorem holds:

Theorem   **a)** A chair is spanned by its legs.

      b) A chair is linear if its legs may be pairwise interchanged.

      c) A chair collapses if its spanning set is diminished.

      d) A surface F is uniform if any linear chair defined on F does not collapse.

      e) A surface F that is not uniform is said to contain open spaces.

This theorem has been proved many times as anyone who has tried to place alinear chair on the side of a hill has discovered.

REFERENCES

Bolt A. (1985) *Behind the closed door*, Yale University Press.
Christ J.F. (1981) *The door will always be with us*, Vat. J. Math. 421.
Hilton H. (1897) *The Waldorff room*, In Press.
Jarr A. (1986) *Behind the open door*, Yale University Press.
Picador I. (1975) *The Rings of Isador Bell*, Bull Rings 2 221.

Countdown to Linkage: A Numerical Analysis of the Gulf War

Ronald R. Stockton
Dearborn, MI

Looking back on the Gulf War many Americans still have trouble figuring out what it was all about. Senator Dole said it had to do with jobs; others said with oil; some said with aggression. Our leaders could agree on only one point: it had <u>nothing</u> to do with Jerusalem or with future peace talks.

But scientists are trained to look less at the words of politicians than at empirical evidence. And the numbers—particularly that analysis of numbers known as numerology—suggest that the war had <u>everything</u> to do with Jerusalem and the talks.

For those not familiar with the concept, numerology is the belief that by some mystical process there are patterns in history that link people and events. If we study the relevant numbers we can understand the past and predict the future. The Bible was once studied this way because Hebrew letters are also numbers. Thus the genealogy of Jesus (Matthew 1) centers on the number fourteen: 14 generations from Abraham to David, 14 from David to the Babylonian Exile, and 14 from Babylon to Jesus. Since the numerical total of the letters in "David" equals 14, some saw this as evidence that Jesus was heir to the Davidic line.

Three shocking numerical "coincidences" from the Gulf War are equally revealing where causal patterns are concerned.

First, when we take key events in the careers of the four major leaders (Bush, Saddam, Arafat, Shamir) and add up their "numbers" at the time the war began the total of each is identically the same: 3982!

	Bush	Saddam	Arafat	Shamir	
Born	1924	1937	1929	1916	
Age,1991	67	54	62	75	
Took Office	1989	1979	1969	1986	
Years in office, 1991	2	12	22	5	
Total	3982	+ 3982	+ 3982	+ 3982	= 15,928

Second, if these numbers were predicting some major development, the event that most logically grew out of the war was the Madrid Peace Conference. This Conference (which began October, 1991) was convened to end the bloody Arab-Israeli conflict. Eight parties went to the first meeting at Madrid (Israelis, Syrians, Lebanese, Jordanians, Palestinians, Egyptians, Americans, and Russians). Do the numbers relate in any way to the Conference? If we take the grand total of 15,928 and divide by eight we get 1991, the year the Conference began.

Third, many observers see parallels between the Crusader era (1099-1244) and events today. When British General Allenby occupied Jerusalem in December, 1917 he declared it to be the final battle of the Crusades. Similarly, many Arab numerologists argue that it took 145 years to defeat the Crusaders and that the present "occupation" may last 145 years. Do the numbers give any hint that historic events are underway?

If 1917 began a 145-year period of non-Arab rule, then it should end in 2062. And what is the midpoint between 1917 and 2062? The summer of 1990—the year Kuwait was invaded!

Let's look further: If the invasion of Kuwait is a guidepost pointing equally to the beginning and the end of an era, then the Crusader period should have a similar historic event at its midpoint. Halfway through the 145-year Crusader era was 1171. And what happened then? 1171 saw the collapse of Egypt's 203 year-old Fatimid dynasty. This left the great Arab leader Saladin (formerly a distinguished but minor military commander) in control of much of the Arab world including Egypt, Syria, and Iraq.

Jerusalem Post March 21, 1963 *(Quotation from Lord Shackelton's Speech in the House of Lords).*

"Cannibals in Polynesia no longer allow their tribes to eat Americans because their fat is contaminated with chlorinated hydrocarbon. Recent figures published show that we (English - Ed.) have two parts per million DDT in our bodies, whereas the figure for Americans is about 11 p.p.m."

****

THE RE-EMERGENCE OF TAUTOLOGIES

Paul E. Greenberg
Brookline, MA

INTRODUCTION

Tautologies have been a part of the written communication record ever since they were first transcribed. Spoken tautologies, on the other hand, have been around much longer. Some scholars believe that this is mostly due to the lengthy delay associated with the invention of the lead pencil. If that is the case, then so be it.

The recent popularity of tautologies is well-documented.[1] The re-emergence of this form of discourse is undoubtedly due to the fact that, by definition, such statements are truth-functionally true. As a result, they represent a form of argumentation that is guaranteed to be logically airtight. For example, when Ethel Merman proclaimed: "There's no business like show business," some of the more erudite members of the audience might have objected. If she had instead used the tautological form, "There's no show business like show business," she would have broadened her audience base to include even the most pedantic theatergoers. This, of course, would have generated untold additional profits.[2] While such added success may not have mattered much in the case of *Annie Get Your Gun*, these considerations could have had a far-reaching impact on shows that garnered substantially less audience acclaim.[3]

TAXONOMY OF POPULAR TAUTOLOGIES

There are four basic types of popular tautology in modern speech. These can be most easily, and generally, expressed in their symbolic logical forms:

1. A = A;
2. If A, then A;
3. A or not A; and,
4. Everything else.[4]

We will now examine each in further detail, providing some examples to illustrate the proper and popular uses of these tautological forms.

A = A

This category is by far the most popular logical structure of modern tautologies. It includes such old favorites as: Fair is fair; Enough is enough; and What's done is done. Famous quotations that rely on this format to express a well-known sentiment include: The business of America is business; A rose is a rose is a rose; and, Boys will be boys.

This tautological form has an interesting variant. Instead of the direct approach in which A = A, it is also possible to modify this structure while still preserving the same basic flavor. The method is simple: find a synonym for the right-hand side "A" in this identity, and replace it with the chosen synonym. One of the best known examples of this clever twist on an old tautology comes from the last line of *Gone With the Wind*, when the words "Tomorrow is another day" are uttered. Oh well, I guess that's that.

If A, then A (and vice versa)[5]

While A = A is the most popular form of tautological intercourse, A if A is far more creative. Most of us have been told at least once in the course of performance evaluations, "If it's the best you can do, then it's the best you can do." This tautology is interesting because of the sarcastic undertones that lurk just beneath the surface.

A corollary to this structure involves using a slightly modified version of this style of reasoning. Statements such as "When you're right, you're right" or "When you're hot you're hot, and when you're not you're not" can add an element of uncertainty to the tautology by invoking an acerbic tone. Their use demands that the utterer make a disbelieving face immediately upon stating it.[6]

A or not A

By carefully juxtaposing a statement with its opposite, a tautology can be easily constructed. For example,

---

[1] I am sure that you can look it up. However, I am not quite sure exactly where.

[2] These are "untold" profits because they are actually unsubstantiated, a mere product of idle speculation on my part.

[3] This, of course, includes the musical comedy, *Ronald Reagan's Economic Miracle*, which was closed by Manhattan police mid-way through the opening performance, apparently for violating the Broadway tenets of tautological titling.

[4] This last category is included for completeness.

[5] This is no different than saying "A if and only if A" or just "A iff A".

[6] In some regions of the country, of course, such statements are recognized as wholly descriptive of otherwise puzzling events. Of course, the people in these regions are the same ones who believe that nuclear wars can be won and that budget deficits are self-correcting.

the likelihood that any specific event will occur can be reduced to the truth functional truth, "Maybe yes, maybe no. Maybe it will, maybe it won't." Alternatively, when a direct question is asked requiring some evaluative judgement, the tautologically-adept respondent will usually reply, "Either it is or it isn't."[7]

Everything Else

Sometimes tautologies defy description. "Something is bound to happen," for instance, does not fit neatly into any of the categories noted above, but clearly represents an example of this genre of conversation. Other good examples are the famous comments, "A man's gotta do what a man's gotta do" and "I'm not as young as I used to be."

Sometimes there appear on the political scene certain exceptionally qualified practitioners of the tautology game. This considerably raises the quality of the rhetoric that is heard. For instance, Jack Kemp, in discussing U.S. military secrecy said: "The Russians have never found anything that we've successfully hidden."[8] While this, of course, endeared him to tautology-watchers like myself, it was not enough to sustain his Presidential bid against the equally qualified Vice-President.[9]

By far the greatest modern-day tautologist is the Hall of Fame catcher Yogi Berra. His gems generally cannot be classified neatly into a particular category.

Examples of his legendary prowess in this realm include: "You can observe a lot just by watching"; You've got to be very careful if you don't know where you are going because you might not get there"; and "A nickel ain't worth a dime anymore." But his most famous remark of all sets the standard against which all other tautologies should be compared: "It ain't over 'til it's over."

CONCLUSION

Use of tautologies is becoming increasingly popular in that course of everyday conversation. As a result, it is important to recognize their value in making a point or in winning an argument. By understanding the correct usage of this form of discourse, it can be used to our advantage. Failure to do so could lead to our complete collapse as a civilization. Or maybe not. We shall see what we shall see, when we shall see it. And not a minute before. Unless we hurry. Am I right or am I right?

ACKNOWLEDGEMENTS

The author would like to thank Marla Choslovsky for her constant efforts in noticing the use of tautologies in the course of daily conversation. In addition, everyone else who helped in this project should be mentioned, but no one else did. Any errors that remain, of course, are solely their responsibility.

---

[7]Use of the popular expression "It's a fifty-fifty thing" puzzled me for quite some time because I thought it quite odd that so many events had exactly a 50% probability of occuring. More recently, I have realized that any specific event can be described as "a fifty-fifty thing" because the event either will or will not occur. How foolish I was not to see this sooner!

[8]In contrast, when the Defense Department discusses U.S. military secrecy they say nothing.

[9]George Bush denies that he is a capable tautologist. He claims he wasn't even at the meetings.

Bruce C. Thompson

Department of Fisheries and Wildlife, Oregon State University

Running Speeds of Crippled Coyotes[1]

Running speeds of one uninjured coyote (*Canis latrans*) and three coyotes crippled by loss of use of one front foot were recorded as the animals were chased through measured courses by a person on foot. The crippled coyotes generally attained slower speeds than did the uninjured coyote. Mean speeds for the crippled coyotes ranged from 19.1 kph to 27.4 kph.

[1]Technical Paper No. 1066, Oregon Agricultural Experiment Station.

Northwest Science, Vol. 50, No. 3, 1976, p. 181.

An Investigation Into The Time-Keeping Accurancy Of Stopped Clocks

T.A. Mielke
Formerly of Waltham, MA

Note: The author lived in the city of Waltham, but claims no connection with the (now defunct) watch manufacturer of that name.

It is well known that a stopped clock is correct twice a day, whereas a mis-set clock is never correct. This suggests that, given the choice of reading the time from a stopped or a mis-set clock, one should select whichever clock is least in error at that moment. Such a procedure would rely on the stopped clock for part of the day and on the mis-set clock for the remainder. In the typical case, the correct time, and thus the instantaneous error, is not known. This leaves no basis for switching from one clock to another, and an exclusive choice of a stopped versus a mis-set clock must be made. A more quantitative determination of the relative accuracies of stopped versus mis-set clocks is therefore required. Let:

$$t = \text{correct time} \qquad t_i = \text{indicated time}$$
$$\delta t = \text{error in mis-set clock} \qquad t_s = \text{setting of stopped clock}$$

with the mean-squared error E given by:

$$E = \frac{1}{T} \int_0^T (t_i - t)^2 dt \qquad (1)$$

for the mis-set clock,

$$E_m = \frac{1}{24} \int_0^{24} (t_i - t)^2 dt = \frac{1}{24} \int_0^{24} \delta t^2 dt = \delta t^2 \qquad (2)$$

for the stopped clock,

$$E_s = \frac{1}{24} \int_0^{24} (t_i - t)^2 dt = \frac{4}{24} \int_{t_s}^{t_s+6} (t_s - t)^2 dt = \frac{1}{6} \int_0^6 t'^2 dt' = \frac{1}{6} \frac{t'}{3}\Big|_0^6 = 6^3/18 = 12 \qquad (3)$$

where the change of variable $t' = t - t_s$ was used to evaluate the integral. Comparisons of equations *(2)* and *(3)* shows that for $6 > |\delta t| > 2\sqrt{3}$ hours the stopped clock has a lower mean-squared error than the mis-set clock. (For a 24-hour clock the stopped clock is more accurate when $12 > |\delta t| > 4\sqrt{3}$ hours.) Thus, for a suprisingly small offset in the mis-set clock (only $2\sqrt{3}$ hours) a stopped clock, which has no information content whatsoever, is demonstrably more accurate.

Any individual who can take advantage of this periodic greater accuracy of the stopped clock is unlikely, however, to need either the stopped or mis-set clock to tell the time.

The Department of Parking and Alternate Reality

Jeff Rasmussen
Indianapolis, IN

The Department of Parking and Alternate Reality was formerly called the Department of Parking and Parallel Universes. The name modification was engendered by the specter of litigation by faculty from the Department of Physics and Everybody Else is Wrong (the Department of PEEW) along with a phalange of right-minded factorially-rigorous faculty from the Department of Extremely Basic and Extremely Advanced Mathematics (the department of EBEAM).

The litigious memo from PEEW and EBEAM departments painted an anfractuous 25 point indictment of the axiomatic foundations of Parking and Parallel Universes Department. The first 24 points decimated the basic assumption that our universe is a straight line, which is necessary to assume if another universe be parallel to it. The 25th point concerned that jerk rich student with the red Porsche who parks diagonally across two faculty-reserved stalls, and they had complained numerous times but no, nothing was ever done about this, and what if professors employed an enormous podium that squeezed their students into some tiny space

in the corner of the classroom, but no, nobody gave a hoot about the faculty....

With the demise of Parking and Parallel Universes Department, the Department of Parking and Alternate Reality (PAR) arose, phoenix like. Along with the new name, came a rebirth in concern for dealing with the chronic parking problems faced by this lynchpin of the University.

The mathematicians offered assistance in attacking the short-term parking problem (which was that short term there was not enough parking; this was in contrast to the long-term parking problem, which was that long term there probably wouldn't be enough parking either) by adopting a firm NonEuclidean stance which abandoned the notion of rows of parallel parking stalls in favor of an "infinite coastline Chaos theory." Said theory would service approximately a line of 3.4 million cars per acre arranged bumper to bumper in a whorl-shaped pattern.

Unfortunately for the mathematicians, one of their own graduate students, Mr. Smith showed that while the whorlshaped pattern could indeed accommodate approximately 3.4 million cars in length, there was a minor drawback that the cars be—adjusting for sideview mirrors—approximately 0.01 microns wide. Such streamlined cars could fall easy prey to dust mites, amoebas, and contingency-fee lawyers. So it looked like this practicality put a sizable dent (at least several thousand microns deep) in the NonEuclidean model.

The right-minded mathematicians junta abandoned the PAR department like rats from a capsizing ship—though they professed ennui with such a trivial problem. And anyhow, they were too involved with border skirmishes with their cross-campus rival, the Department of Just Intermediate Mathematics.

Anyhow, in the power vacuum the Physics and Everybody Else is Wrong Department faculty entered. Led by their chairman Dr. Smith (no relationship to Mr. Smith) they eschewed the true voice of the NonEuclideans and addressed the short-term parking problem using macro-modeling, which consists of micro-modeling written in a larger font.

In brief, their macro-model consisted of a using a contained black hole, in which the Standard Laws of Physics such as the Standard Law of Time and the Standard Law of Space do not hold. (Neither holding are the Standard Law of Large Numbers, which states that as one counts outloud the numbers usually become larger; the Standard Law of "If Guns were Outlawed, Only Outlaws would have Guns"; and Standard Professor's Law that any student who asks for a reading list two months before classes begin should be given an A+ on all work, or else that student will metamorphose from a sycophant to a raving sociopath who will hack the professor into bits and mail the body parts back in postage-due envelopes.)

In this model, consider if you will a student (who will be referred to as Mr. Student A [no relationship to Mr. or Dr. Smith]) who has not yet attended his daily classes. Also consider the same student later in the day who has attended classes (and tangentially, would be considered in economic theory a "value-added" student). Using the black hole model, the student would meet his value-added self (referred to as Mr. Student Anti-A (no anti-relationship to Mr. Anti-Smith or Dr. Anti-Smith]) returning from a completed class. Student A would toss his keys to his Doppelgänger self who would then remove his car from the parking lot/contained black hole and drive home. Using clueuing theory the Physicists showed that the parking stay would range from -3.5 minutes to +12.4 minutes.

As Sci-Fi movie buffs know, however, the rub is that if Mr. Student A accidentally makes contact with Mr. Student Anti-A, then all sorts of cheesy special effects happen, followed by the annihilation of both worlds. This annihilation, however, could be deemed a sufficient solution to the long-term parking problem.

J.E. Lloyd
AGGRESSIVE MIMICRY IN Photuris. FIREFLY FEMME FATALES
Science, 1965, 149 653

Abstract. Firefly females of the genus *Photuris*, long known to be carnivorous, attract and devour males of the genus *Photinus* by mimicking the flash responses of *Photinus* females. Although suspected, this behaviour had not been observed previously.

MEDICINE

Siamese Twinning in Gummy Bears

C. Robert Campbell. DVM
Sedro-Woolley, WA

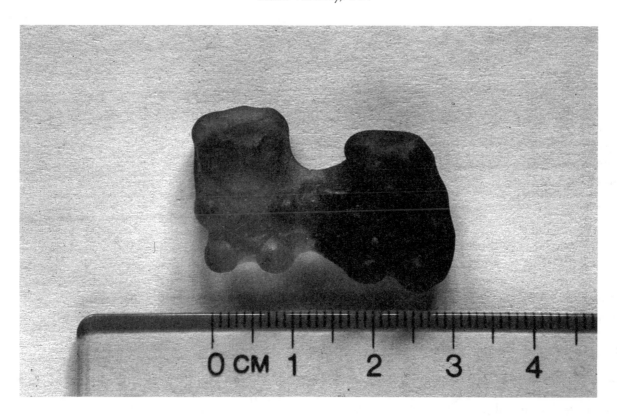

A one month old bag of Gummy Bears was presented for examination and ingestion to a local veterinary hospital. Out of three hundred twenty-six individual gummy bears examined, all were within normal limits of gummy bear development, except for a pair of gummy bears exhibiting a Siamese twinning appearance.

This pair of yellow and red gummy bears were joined at the distal aspects of the upper forelimb and midabdominal region. In addition, the red gummy bear had attachment of the cervical vertebral region to the distal aspect of the yellow gummy bear's forelimb, as well as unusual self-adhesion between this region and the red forelimb. The joined region exhibited a slightly irregular pattern of intermixed tissue between the two, with no clear demarcation, suggesting a complex pattern of interdigitation between the two. External examination revealed no shared internal organ systems, with only peripheral tissues in common. It should be noted that the yellow gummy bear had an ocular lesion of the right orbital region suggestive of, but not pathognomonic for, a congenital malformation of both the zygomatic arch and associated periocular region. All body systems,

except as noted, were within normal limits for the species.

Due to a lack of funds and extreme supportive post-surgical care associated with separating of Siamese twins, the owner of the gummy bears elected for humane euthanasia. The two were decapacitated with cervical dislocation, followed by immediate immersion into liquid nitrogen, as the effects of sodium pentobarbital had not been fully explored in the gummy bear species. All protocols set about by the American Veterinary Medical Association for humane euthanasia were followed.

Discussion: The exact percentage of gummy bear population exhibiting Siamese twinning activity should be further studied to further elucidate the need for practical medical and surgical management of this interesting condition. Unpublished follow up to the population dynamics of the gummy bear specie has not revealed any other Siamese twinning to date, although research continues, exposing a small percentage of other malformations, both congenital and acquired lesions: report pending grant approval.

A DICTIONARY OF PHARMACEUTICAL RESEARCH: COMMENTS AND EXCERPTS, CONTINUED

Robert L. Iles
Olathe KS

In a previous article[1], I described the confusion that results when ordinary people try to use words from various scientific fields such as pharmaceutical research. For example, if you stopped a man on the street and asked him to define "conclusions," he'll probably give you some nonsense about the reasoned judgement one makes from information.

Who knows what misunderstandings ordinary people are walking around with. (There may be some who thing that the different colored pills in the drugstore contain different kinds of medicine!) In the hope that I can set a few more things straight for those who are new to the pharmaceutical industry, here are some more definitions.

affairs - n. pl.   Usually combined with adjective, as in:
chemical affairs: Projects relating to molecules, ions, bonds and other such imaginary nonsense.
regulatory affairs: affairs which have the side benefit of keeping your bowel habits regular.
biological affairs: any romances not conducted with inanimate objects.
medical affairs: romances conducted on exam tables.

bacterial flora - n.   Low class party girl.

career path - n.   Mythical path, akin to Yellow Brick Road.

clinical research manager - n.   A CRA (which see) who knows where the bodies are buried.

conclusions - n.   [From old high German for material written first] What you design your study to show.

consultant - n.   1. Former employee who makes lots of money for working short hours. 2. A guy who knows 412 ways to make love but doesn't have a girl friend. 3. Anybody without a job but with a briefcase and business cards.

continuing medical education - n.   Doctor talk for "I gotta keep doing this till I get it right."

cost-of-living raise - n.   Pay raise granted to compensate for increases in cost of living, adequate for street people and prisoners in solitary confinement. ["Don't beef about the cost-of-living raise, you're due for a merit increase (which see) in six months."]

CRA - n.   [Origin disputed. May be initials for Continually Running Around or Corporate Recruiting Accident] 1. Person who tells doctor how to practice medicine. 2. Person manager gets ideas from. 3. Person manager gets ideas about.

cubicle - n.   [Corruption of 'crucible'[Work area replacing the office, obviating the need for telephones because everybody can hear everything. ("Jeez, Miss Kerridge, would you quit breathing? I can hear your nose hair quiver.")

diagnostician - n.   1. Doctor paid to tell people to undress. 2. Doctor who flunked surgery.

editor - n.   1. A writer too smart to write for a living. 2. A writer too dumb to write for a living. 3. A writer with a window in his (her) office.

geriatrician - n.   A general practitioner whose patients survive middle age.

honorarium - n.   [From Old English 'Hand me the rum'] Money paid to induce scientists to leave their smelly labs and spend a week on a cruise ship or a tropical island.

hospital - n.   [French, 'hostile pit'] Disease exchange.

internist - n.   1. Doctor to whom other doctors send their mistakes. 2. Doctor who has a Latin name for his mistakes.

librarian - n.   Person who thinks you read all that stuff you insist on getting a copy of.

lunch hour - n.   [German 'leunch kheru,' "Oh, I guess my Timex is busted."] Forty-five minutes in theory, one hour in interpretation, two hours in reality.

management by objective - n.   Term applied by management theorists to their realization that activity is supposed to lead to something.

manager - n.   [Old English 'mallowmar,' fall guy] Employee who passes to other employees the message from the director, who got it from the vice president, who got it from the president, who got it from the chairman. Who apparently got it from reading sheep entrails.

office - n.   [Czech 'hawfuss,' source of money] 1. Place of vile servitude. ("I swear, honey, I was stuck at the office all night.") 2. A place where paper is stored. 3. Point of departure for lunch.

opportunity - n.   Problem (which see).

Ph.D. - n.   [Origin disputed. May be from Tibetan 'phud,' yak gas, or initials of American vulgarism, 'piled higher and deeper.'] Degree awarded to get a student to leave college.

PharmD - n.   Druggist in a suit.

pharmacist - n.   Druggist who won't sell whoopie cushions or handguns in his (her) store.

pharmacologist - n.   Druggist in a lab coat.

problem - n.   Anything supervisors describe as an opportunity. ("Louie, the research rats are loose in the cafeteria, this is your opportunity.")

research report - n.   [Latin for cut and paste] Document useful in testing potency of central nervous system stimulants.

RN - n.   [Registered nurse. Righteous nuisance] Restores health of patients by waking them up and putting things in their orifices.

study - v.   1. To produce paper. 2. To disburse money.

study monitoring - v.   [Gaelic for 'This stud's going out of town.'] Activity conducted at great distance; frequency of monitoring proportional to study sites distance from office and proximity to beach.

study code - n.   Number you must know to assign your road trip to somebody else's budget.

surgeon - n.   [Armenian 'Sure John,' character in the legend of a masked fish cleaner worshipped by villagers.] Doctor who flunked prescription writing.

symposium - n.   [Greek 'symposion,' to drink together] Claimed source of continuing medical education (which see). Reported by drug companies as a business expense, by doctors as a professional obligation, and by liquor dealers as a bonanza.

[1]Iles RL. A dictionary of pharmaceutical research: Comments and excerpts. *Journal of Irreproducible Results*, 1984; 290:14-15.

Decaffeination of Coffee

JAMA, Aug. 9, 1985—Vol. 254, No. 6, by F.W. Balice and Diane H. Morris

Q Several patients have asked about reports in lay publications that the agent used to remove caffeine from coffee can be a health hazard. I have not seen this discussed in the medical literature and would appreciate a scientific opinion.

A Questions about solvent safety have concerned methylene chloride. Two dose levels were used: a low-dose level of 500 mg/kg/day (equivalent to 12 million cups of decaffeinated coffee per day) and a high-dose level of 1,000 mg/kg/day (equivalent to 24 million cups of decaffeinated coffee per day). The relevance of this finding to human exposure was questioned because of the large doses used and concerns about the appropriateness of the gavage method of administration.

Studies of rats fed methylene chloride in their drinking water (at doses equivalent to 125,000 to 6,250,000 cups of decaffeinated coffee per day) showed no evidence of carcinogenicity.

Hence, available scientific evidence suggests that methylene chloride is safe for use as a solvent in decaffeinating coffee.

Submitted By: **C.L. Cannon**
Chicago, IL

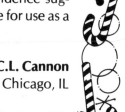

MILESTONES IN MEDICAL EDUCATION: SELECTING THE CORRECT MEDICAL PROFESSION

David H. Gutmann
Philadelphia, PA

During the course of medical school education, students are faced with the dilemma of making a career decision prior to completing most of their required clinical rotations. This unfortunate predicament has forced many intelligent students into Orthopedics or Radiology simply because they enjoyed the rotation. It is the contention of the Medical School administration at the A. Alfred Taubman Amazin' Blue School of Medicine that such weighty and important decisions not be left to chance. Students should be preselected for their destined specialties upon acceptance to medical school, if not earlier, prior to the National Board Examination. This preselection process would obviate the necessity of taking the Boards for those students who were felt intellectually suited for such challenging fields as OB-GYN, Pediatrics, and Psychiatry. Furthermore, those students destined to become surgeons could spend their free time developing their upper bodies, whereas those fated to spend the rest of their lives drawing blood samples from screaming five year olds could begin desensitizing themselves through regular attendance at AC/DC and Black Sabbath rock concerts.

In keeping with the tradition of standardized type K format performance evaluations, a simple one hundred question concurrent-type examination has been developed. You will have eight minutes to complete each of the eight booklets. The next booklet will be distributed only after the previous booklet and answer sheet have been returned to the proctor. As usual, there is no penalty for guessing. After all, some of you will become radiologists.

As a public service, the administration presents eight sample questions and their respective medical career-oriented answers.

1. A self-addressed stamped envelope is found on the sidewalk. Appropriate action includes:

    A. cut it open to see what's inside
    B. check that the zip code is correct
    C. decide whether to mail it based on handwriting
    D. take it home and discuss the various options with friends
    E. mail it only after reading the letter

2. Your mother has just baked a pie for tonight's dinner party and left it on the kitchen table. Appropriate action includes:

    A. cut it open to see what's inside
    B. discuss with your mother the relative merits of letting you taste it prior to the dinner party
    C. eat a piece of pie and blame it on your younger brother
    D. decide that it would be a good idea for you to eat it in the best interests of all involved
    E. deny the existence of the pie and refuse to eat it at dinner

3. Your best friend's cat just died yesterday. Appropriate action includes:

    A. cut it open to see what's inside
    B. sympathize with your friend while trying to convince him to give you the cat's kidneys for your science project
    C. decide that he has grieved too long and suggest psychiatric intervention
    D. give him "The 101 Uses For A Dead Cat" book
    E. empathize, project, and try to convince him that the cat had a happy life

4. You find a long-overdue library book in your closet while cleaning. Appropriate action includes:

    A. cut it open to see what's inside
    B. return the book at midnight in the book return slot
    C. get angry and throw the book away
    D. return it during the day, demand to speak to the head librarian, refuse to pay the fine, and insist that the medical school told you that students didn't have to return books on time if they were being used for a class
    E. decide that you might as well keep the book since it's that overdue anyway

5. On an African safari, you discover a beautiful yellow bird which you do not recognize from your studies of ornithology. Appropriate action includes:

    A. cut it open to see what's inside
    B. photograph it, collect its feathers and excrement, and publish before anyone else sees it

C. lecture in a pompous tone to the group about this bird you've never seen before
D. move along
E. dismiss the bird as just another yellow bird

6. Through the grapevine, you hear that your boss's wife is having an affair. Appropriate action includes:

A. ignore it as petty gossip but ask her out for a drink anyway
B. determine the name of the person, the times, dates, and relevant information
C. tell your boss that his wife is a slut
D. make up more juicy gossip and spread that around
E. sit down with your boss and discuss suicidal ideation

7. You spill red wine and stain your favorite white shirt. Appropriate action includes:

A. cut it out and staple the ends together
B. take the shirt off and soak the whole thing in red wine
C. buy a new white shirt only after throwing a temper tantrum
D. blame it on anyone sitting near you
E. continue the conversation and pretend that nothing happened

8. A house plant you are taking care of for a friend begins to turn brown. Appropriate action includes:

A. cut it open to see what's inside
B. if it's dry, wet it
C. spray it with powerful herbicides, transplant it into new soil, and prune off the dead leaves
D. talk to it and try to convince it that it wants to get better
E. ignore it and tell your friend that it was already dead when he gave it to you

If you answered the above questions in the following sequence, you are best suited for the following medical profession:

General Surgery: A,A,A,A,A,A,A,A
OB-GYN: A,C,E,C,D,D,C,A
Pediatrics: E,C,E,B,E,C,D,E
Orthopedics: E,D,D,E,C,A,C,E
Psychiatry: C,B,C,E,C,E,E,D
Neurology: D,B,B,B,B,B,B,D
Internal Medicine: B,E,B,D,C,D,D,C
Radiology: D,D,D,D,C,C,E,E
Pathology: A,C,B,C,E,B,A,A
Dermatology: E,D,D,E,A,D,A,B
Anaesthesiology: E,C,C,A,A,A,C,C
Emergency Medicine: B,E,E,C,D,E,B,B

If your answers do not match up with any of the above medical careers, Family Practice is recommended.

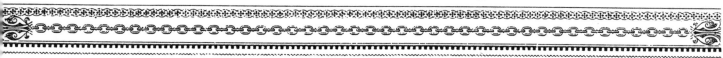

On the Nature of the 'Nothing Dehydrogenase' Reaction

Histochemical Journal 17, 1111-1118 (1985)—Cornelis J.F. Van Noorden, Arnold Kooij, Ilse M.C. Vogels and Wilma M. Frederiks—Laboratory for Histology and Cell Biology, Academic Medical Centre, University of Amsterdam, Meibergdreef 15, 1105 AZ Amsterdam, The Netherlands.

The biochemical mechanism underlying the 'nothing dehydrogenase' reaction during the histochemical demonstration of dehydrogenases using tetranitro BT as the final electron acceptor has been investigated in unfixed, frozen rat liver sections. The reaction is stronger with NAD^+ than either with $NADP^+$ or in the absence of coenzyme. As much as 50% of the reaction is due to lactate dehydrogenase converting endogenous lactate and is largely inhibited by pyruvate. No NAD^+-dependent alcohol dehydrogenase activity was detected at pH 7.45, the PH used for the incubations. The coenzyme-independent activity may be caused by SH-groups present in proteins and compounds like glutathione and cysteine and can be inhibited by N-ethylmaleimide and p-chloromercuribenzoic acid. It was also found that the 'nothing dehydrogenase' reaction mainly occurs during the first few minutes of incubation, levelling off quickly to a slow rate. When studying the kinetics of dehydrogenase reactions with tetrazolium salts, it should be realized that the 'nothing dehydrogenase' reaction, which as a whole is nonlinear with time, can interfere seriously with the dehydrogenase reaction to be analysed and may yield initial reaction rates that are too high. The findings of the present study reveal the nature of the reactions used for detection of necrosis in tissues with tetrazolium salts.

How We Die

Francis Levy,
New York, NY

Dying is no joke. It really hurts both those to whom it happens and to the survivors who must undergo loss. In my work over the years I have had to come to grips with the problems of death and dying and if I had to do this all over again I would choose pediatrics. To hear people day and night moaning about how their life is coming to an end and how scared they are about what is going to happen when they lose consciousness (the answer to which as everyone knows is nothing) is no bowl of cherries. I had this one patient, let's call him Burt, who dwelled day and night over the threshold. He viewed death as a doorway. On one side of the doorway was the consciousness of himself. On the other side of the doorway was a whole new world where for once in his whole "life" he wouldn't be able to think about himself.

"All these years its been me, me, me. It's me looking out of these eyes and seeing the world. That's all life is. Life is me looking at it. I can't imagine what's it's going to be like with no more 'me' thinking. I know life for other people, say my descendants will go on, but it just seems weird, know what I mean?"

I had another patient, a woman, let's call her Ann, who was remarkably unstoic in her approach to death. When I would come into her room, she would begin to wail and cry. She said she would do anything to live. She pleaded with me, offered me money. She even offered me sexual favors, if I could find some solution. I told her it wasn't my business to deal with solutions. You go to an internist for that. I deal exclusively with the dying. If she wanted to continue seeing me she had to be dying. Otherwise I could make a referral.

Still, yet another patient, let's call him Phil viewed himself as a gambler who was losing in Las Vegas. To him life was a crapshoot. He kept upping the ante, in order to win back what he had lost and all that happened was that he depleted himself more quickly.

All these years of dealing with death have taught me a great deal. I have gotten a real understanding of the process of dying, especially the rattle which comes at the end. I can now point to a patient and say he or she is in Stage 1, 2 or 3. But this has also taken its toll on me. How would you like to be in intensive care as the ball descends on the top of The New York Times Building on New Year's Eve and everyone is frolicking it up with the Guy Lombardo band at the Waldorf? How would you like to hear screams of "I'll never see poor Harold again. Oh my poor Harold," when you know the rest of the world is black tie at some wonderful fete or in bed with a luscious blond and a bottle of champagne while you're emptying someone's final offerings out of a bedpan (I bet you didn't know that people keep going to the bathroom as it were, even after they die. Years of working with the dead and dying have given me access to tons of juicy facts like this). Time after time, I have gone up to a grieving widow like Mrs. Harold and said the same thing. "I know how hard this is, but I can see you're a very strong woman and I know you are going to be able to lead a full sexually satisfying life without Harold." In the case of Mrs. Harold, the words were particularly galling since I knew she was no better off than old Harold. She was doomed to have a horrible lonely end herself at some ridiculous retirement colony in Florida.

Do doctors who are involved with the dead and dying take coffee breaks? If someone is expelling their last bits of life, do you go ahead and order the tuna sub?

This may sound odd, but there is something about the process of life for a living man like myself that has to go on even if I am standing amidst the ruins of other people's existences. Yes, I want the pickle on the side. Yes I want Lay's potato chips. Yes I want lettuce, tomato, mayo, onions and a few sweet peppers. Yes, I think of all these things. I know it sounds callous and cruel. But imagine how many dying people I see in any given week! I have found over the years that experiencing the sadness of the spectre of death is inversely proportional to the amount of cases I attend in any given period of time. So if I am going through a light period I will feel bad about patient X, but if I am going through a heavy period Patient X is just patient number 1 or 10 or 50.

In all honesty I have my bad days when I get fed up with the dying. I want to go somewhere else. I want to be that kid I once was throwing a Spalding against the brick wall of the old courtyard in back of the apartment house. In the profession, there are thanologists, but there are also thanocrats and a thanotocracy. I have worked in the field so many years that I believe I am a part of the great thanotocracy, but sometimes I feel like a thanocrat—a mere paper pusher filling out coroners reports and life insurance claims. But on most days I'm just your average thanologist—a guy, devoted to his patient's welfare whose trying to make an honest buck so he can pay the mortgage and put his kids through college.

"Look, you're the scientist. If you say it's a wandering Black Hole, that's fine with me. All I know is that it's behind my favorite easy chair, it just swallowed Skipper's doggie-bed, and I want it out of here!"

Bradford Veley
Marquette, MI

THE SHORT-PANTS SYNDROME:
Preliminary Clinical Findings of "Trousers Disease"

A recent flood of post-Christmas holiday patients has prompted this paper. Patient X, a white male, provided us with our most exemplary subject. He presented with an unexplained lengthening of his legs and some abdominal discomfort. History and physical revealed that he was 43 years old, beyond normally expected adolescent growth surges. The patient reported discomfort at sitting for prolonged periods of time and occasional ankle chills. Further examination confirmed a primary finding of a seventeen-pound weight gain due to "serious major-league holiday partying." The overall sense of discomfort was accompanied by a feeling of "being taller than I used to be."

Richard L. Holloway
Houston, TX

Following orthopedic and GI specialty consultations, it was determined that the seventeen-pound weight gain, resulting in slight abdominal discomfort, was strikingly manifested in the buttocks, producing a lifting of the seat of the pants which we can now document as the most remarkable underlying causative symptom of Short-Pants Syndrome (SPS), usually caused by Trouser's disease. SPS is observed a a shortness of the posterior cuff, with the anterior cuff approximately 15°-20° lower. This discrepancy sometimes makes early recognition difficult, since the anterior cuff may initially appear normal to the patient while looking in a mirror.

Compounding diagnostic difficulty with SPS is the abdominal expansion discomfort which can often result in downward pressure at the waistband, further lengthening the anterior cuff. Diagnostic protocol should most definitely include an examination of the patient in profile, attending to cuff angle, pronounced posterior cuff shortness (10% of total inseam at minimum) and buttock tension. Abdominal expansion will be noted in extreme cases, as described above. Adolescent growth spurts or recent experience on a medieval rack should be ruled out conclusively before diagnosis is finally confirmed.

Treatment procedures may include any combination of the following, proceeding from symptomatic treatment of SPS to more invasive treatment of Trouser's disease itself:

1. Slack size modification, in consultation with a qualified tailor, is indicated in initial symptomatic treatment. Patient should be advised to modify only a portion of his wardrobe to allow for treatment failure. Modifications may include waistband additions as well as increases in cuff length or seat expansion.

2. Psychological consultation should be sought in all SPS cases. Since the syndrome usually presents in mid-life males, counselling may include broader issues than SPS or coping with Trouser's disease. General mid-life crisis may complicate treatment, particularly if the patient divorces, buys a sports car, or begins dating bimboes. Family involvement may be considered, but only if initial embarrassment of the disease has been conquered. Family members should avoid statements like "you're too damned fat" and/or "just buy an army tent to wear."

3. Although experimental in nature, certain treatment centers are testing weight reduction programs designed to alleviate seat-of-pants pressure. It is believed that the Human Immun-obesity Virus (HIOV) underlying Trouser's disease thrives on pressure. Thus, weight loss alleviating buttock pressure may send the disease into remission and restore trouser length. Remember, this is only a theory.

4. In extremely urgent cases, surgical solutions may be indicated including pants excision or abdominectomy. Excision of the HIOV-infected tissues of the abdomen and buttocks may be used to alleviate pressure and again restore cuff length. Since these procedures are currently unapproved, patient informed consent and legal consultation are advisable in these extreme cases.

Trouser's disease, though rarely fatal, is painful, capricious, and humiliating. Its appearance following holidays is a grim reminder of the cost of our increasingly nutritionally promiscuous society. Care should be taken to inform patients of all risks, including the degrading experience of crowd ridicule. Particularly fashion-conscious patients may require prolonged isolation. Solutions such as suggesting that "clamdiggers may come back in style" are to be studiously avoided. Be advised that certain cases have been known to degenerate into Bermuda Short-Pants Syndrome (BSPS) or, in extreme cases, a Bermuda Triangle.

Eder, P.
Brit.J.Med.Psychol., 1962, 35, 81

"We are born mad, acquire morality and become stupid and unhappy. Then we die."

Annals of Emergency Medicine: Public Area

Francis Sullivan, M.D.
Rhode Island Hospital Providence, RI

The emergency department (ED) is a unique vantage point from which to observe the flawed tapestry of human affairs. Dominant motifs include the search for meaning, self, and meaningful relationships. Sex and drugs offer a less filling and arguably more satisfying substitute available to the less patient seekers, or at least a comfort station along the quest route.

Sexual issues retain some remnant of concern for privacy and are often compelling in the immediacy of the concerns raised and the unsurprising need for immediate gratification in the relief of anxiety. All these factors combine to make the emergency department a focal point for presentation of problems of a sexual nature:

A young woman subsequently found to be a veritable Noah's Ark of sexually transmitted disease complained of a problem in her public area.

A young gentleman arrived at 11 PM complaining that his genitalia were too heavy.

Tattoos are certainly not only derivative but integrated commentaries on the life stance and perception of existence by the owner. Like stereotypes, and many ED observations, they may be incomplete and unfair projections of their owners, but can offer awfully good first approximations.

It is a generally accurate observation that any male with the tattoo "Death before Dishonor" would sooner sell his mother into slavery than experience the slightest inconvenience.

Most upbeat tattoo: "Born to win"

A diabetic, frequently hypoglycemic merchant seaman had arranged the inscription of two clowns on his chest such that his nipples appeared to be the noses of the clowns.

Another, less subtle bit of auto-advertising was the downwardly-directed arrow below the navel with the explanatory legend "Fun Gun".

A halter-topped consort of a motorcyclist seemed only momentarily taken aback when asked to produce proof of identity at the ED registration desk; she extruded one breast which proclaimed discreetly that she was indeed "Diane".

The proscription of legal access to certain drugs in our society (presumably partly on the basis that legalization would guarantee unproductivity by a segment of the population now negatively productive) inspires development of cunning on the part of the gourmet abuser who prefers the products of reputable pharmaceutical manufacturers (perhaps in part to safeguard his or her health). The establishment presents some obstacles to acquisition of controlled substances for recreational or other unapproved medicinal use. Fortunately, the game of acquisition can even become part of the reward.

The winner of the "Social Conscience of a Cruise Missile Award" for is month is:

the narcotics abuser who, when refused a prescription for a potent opiate, stated "Well, I'll just have to go beat up an old lady to steal her purse and it will be all your fault."

The winner of the "Less is More" award:

a canny drug seeker, portraying himself by telephone as a pharmacist serving an elderly client with terminal lung cancer, had almost arranged for the ED MD to call a prescription for a potent narcotic cough syrup to another franchise druggist, claiming that he was out of the medication and could not reach the prescribing physician. Then, flush with imminent success, he ruined the entire "sting" by explaining, against the ever more evident pay phone background noise, that the reason his pharmacy was out of the medication was that he was converting the establishment to a Polynesian restaurant.

Occasional Notes

Cost Containment by a Naval Armada

THE NEW ENGLAND JOURNAL OF MEDICINE, Vol. 312, No. 26, June 27, 1985

By James V. Maloney, Jr., M.D. and Keith Reemtsma, M.D.

President Reagan assured us that a major objective in invading Grenada was to close the St. George's Medical School (although Russians, Democrats, and M. Mitterand attributed to him more sinister motives). Lingering doubts about his sincerity were resolved when, as the fighting wound down, he gave a luncheon party in the Rose Garden for the entire student body.

The closure of a medical school by a naval armada highlights the principal problem we have in containing the cost of health care: We are facing a glut of doctors, the consequence of which will be enormous costs without commensurate improvement in health. This statement is supported by the following observations:

Health care costs in 1982 were $322.4 billion. Since 70 per cent of this is accounted for by physician-controllable costs and there are 501,958 physicians in practice, the cost to society of each physician in practice is 70 per cent of $322.4 billion divided by 501,958, or $450,00 per annum[1] (income, overhead, hospital care, drugs, and amortization and capital costs). The calculation is based on historical data but is at best an approximation of future costs, because factors such as the increasing cost of technology will probably alter the estimated cost per physician.[2]

Secondly, health care costs are related not to the amount of illness but to the number of practicing physicians.[3]

Thirdly, in industrialized Western nations, there is no demonstrable relation between the health of the population and expenditures for health care.[2]

If the medical school in Grenada had remained closed for 10 years, the Reagan administration would have saved the U.S. taxpayers more than $7.9 billion (50 graduates per year, with average time in practice of 35 years at $450,000 per year). The Department of Defense calculates the cost of the Grenada invasion at $134.4 million (not including military pay). One can thereby calculate a favorable benefit-cost ratio of 59:1.

Because of a perceived shortage of physicians, public policy over the past three decades encouraged the opening of new medical schools and the enlargement of existing ones (the federal "capitation program," for example, paid medical schools a per capita allowance for each student in attendance for a special increase in the number of students admitted). The number of medical graduates grew from 7000 in 1959 to 16,000 in 1983. The calculated future cost to society of the additional 9000 physicians per year for an (arbitrary) period of 25 years is $3.5 trillion (current dollars calculated as $9000 \times 25 \times 35 \times \$450,000$). For nonpoliticians to whom the concept of a trillion dollars may be obscure, the following analogy will help: If a million dollars in one-thousand-dollar bills forms a stack six inches high, then $3.5 trillion in thousand-dollar bills stacks to a height of 350 miles.

What should be done? The Grenada solution seems a bit gross for handling the doctor plethora in, say, Boston. There are other approaches worth considering:

(1) *A decapitation program for medical schools.* We suggest that Congress provide $100 million (the cost of a small invasion) annually to be divided among the nation's medical schools on the basis of $1,600 for each 64,000 students in attendance, provided that each school reduce its enrollment of entering students by 5 per cent per year until the production of physicians decreases to the 1959 level, the $1.5-billion cost would be offset by $128.4 billion in to-date and future savings (favorable ratio, 86:1). The future savings would accumulate without further cost at the rate of $141.7 billion per annum (9000 nongraduates $\times$ 35 years $\times$ $450,000).

(2) *Federal "anti-dumping" regulations.* For the protection of the U.S. economy, federal law prohibits, under certain specified conditions, dumping on the domestic market of foreign steel and other manufactured goods. We recommend the extension of extant regulations for durable goods to include medical graduates.

(3) *The "Doc Bank" program.* As farmers are paid for not growing crops and dairymen for not milking cows, physicians could be paid for not practicing medicine. For every physician given a $100,000 per annum federal grant to refrain from practice, the annual net savings to society would be $350,000. This would expand the pool of physicians available for such nonpracticing jobs as editing of medical journals, appearing as consultants on television talk shows, and gumshoeing around

neonatal nurseries looking for Baby Does.

The acuteness of the problem is illustrated by the situation in California. The Auditor General has reported that the state has an excess of 10,000 physicians and that even if the University of California closed its five medical schools tomorrow, the excess would continue to worsen because of the influx from other states and nations.[3]

If we don't move quickly, President Reagan may send in the 82nd Airborne.

REFERENCES

1. **American Health Care System.** 1984. Chicago: American Medical Association.
2. **Maloney JV.** The limits of medicine. Ann Surg 1981; 194:247-55.
3. **California has more physicians than it needs.** Report by the Auditor General of California Sacramento, Calif.. November 1983. (Report no. P-242).

Songs Scientists Sing

Gail Roberson
David W. Ball
Houston, TX

Scientists, like all normal people,[1] enjoy music, including singing. Unfortunately, there are few if any songs that are written with the technical person in mind. The case can be made[2] that *The Sounds of Silence* and *Over The Rainbow* are about acoustics and optics, respectively, but the lyrics were written for the general public and not the technically oriented.

In this article, we wish to partially rectify this by presenting two songs to be sung to a popular tune[3] but written specifically for the physicist and the chemist.[4] It is our hope that these two songs will help fill a void that has been present for too long a time.[5] We also invite other musically-oriented scientists to contribute to this field that we have wittingly pioneered.

MY PHYSICAL THINGS[6]

Scalars and vectors and small quantized masses,
Physicists watch as a small atom crashes,
Huge gaseous planets with orbiting rings.
These are a few of my physical things.

Newton and Einstein and Heisenberg's theories,
Aren't the end of a physicist's queries.
Where does the path of an electron go?
Nobody's telling, 'cause nobody knows.

Gravitation is the Master
Of all worlds, we bet.
And when I remember that physical thing,
I hope God ain't too upset.

MY CHEMICAL THINGS[7]

Protons and neutrons and little neutrinos,
Werner's Uncertain, so who knows what he knows?[8]
Fischer-Tropsch catalysts, van't Hoff's benzenes,
These are a few of my chemical things.

Claisen and Grignard and aldol reactions,
Round-bottom flasks boiling distillate fractions,
Alkanes and alkynes and even alkenes,
These are a few of my chemical things.

IR spectra, crystal structure,
Things that are quantized,
I simply remember my chemical things,
And dream of my Nobel Prize.

---

[1]We are making the assumption here that scientists are like normal people.
[2]Frivolously, of course.
[3]See Note 6.
[4]If you can't figure out which is which,. . .

[5]We also hope that Julie Andrews won't sue!
[6]Sung to the tune of ''My Favorite Things''.
[7]Sung to the tune of ''My Physical Things'' (see Note 6 above).
[8]Werner Heisenberg enunciated the Uncertainty Principle. The line's a joke; get it? get it? get it?

ALL OF OB-GYN

Alfred J. Padilla, M.D.
Department of Medicine

It has been said that the endocrinologist approaches the diagnosis of reproductive problems in women from the top down, while the gynecologist works from the bottom up. Having found the middle ground (navel contemplation) nonproductive, I have developed a novel diagnostic approach in which the patient need not even be examined. A brief history, consisting of three questions, will suffice. Careful study of the Diagnostic System in the figure below will reveal that a preliminary diagnosis can be reached by asking whether or not the patient is pregnant and/or bleeding and/or hurting. Confirmation of the correct diagnosis, and appropriate management is trivially simple, and need not be reviewed here.

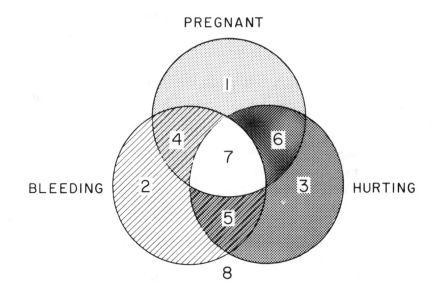

	P	B	H	
1	+	—	—	NORMAL PREGNANCY
2	—	+	—	MENSTRUATION, DUB, RETAINED PLACENTA
3	—	—	+	OVARIAN CYST, PID
4	+	+	—	PLACENTA PREVIA, THREATENED AB, ABRUPTIO
5	—	+	+	DYSMENORRHEA, ENDOMETRIOSIS
6	+	—	+	LABOR, ECTOPIC PREGNANCY
7	+	+	+	LABOR WITH PLACENTA PREVIA, OR ABRUPTIO
8	—	—	—	FIBROIDS, MENOPAUSE

A. J. Padilla M.D.

To Marrow and to Marrow and to Marrow...
North American Adventures in Postgraduate Haematology

David Orchard
Bath, Avon UK

"Children are like fish; they do not feel pain"

This was the view of one of my senior colleagues at the Benedict Arnold Sick Children's Hospital in Riverstown, NJ, on the muddy banks of Lake Lothario, where I was a Clinical Fellow in Hematology and Oncology. He would say it with a half smile which suggested that he might - just might - be joking.

The view that children suffer pain less than adults probably dates from an extraordinary experiment performed in 1941 by one Myrtle B. McGraw (1). She took

a safety-pin and poked 75 newborn babies with it — sterilizing it first, lest the reader consider her heedless of their wellbeing — at intervals until they were four years old (by which time, presumably, they could hit back). Imagine getting that one past the Ethics Committee.

From this experiment — which she filmed, making it arguably one of the earliest snuff movies — she concluded that the sensorimotor experiences of the newborn infant do not extend beyond the subcortical or thalamic level'. Or, to put it in a way which most non-pokers of children can understand, they are too dumb to know they are in pain, so it doesn't matter. This was blamed on an immature nervous system, a failure of myelination, biorhythms, the moon in gemini and that sort of thing until the next and more enlightened generation — to wit, ours — began to realize that all might not be as Myrtle McGraw would have them believe.

What gave them the clue? Well, in the first place someone noticed that if you stick a needle into a neonate to take blood, the child cries, almost always. However young, however dumb, however small. And not just a little; these guys cry a lot. Not much evidence to weigh against serious scientific stuff a la Myrtle, of course, but suggestive, Watson, distinctly suggestive.

Then the heavyweights joined in. The surgeons noticed that while operating on neonates without anaesthesia, some of the physiological responses which accompanied the procedure tachycardia, high blood pressure, screams of agony — looked a lot like what passes in an adult for pain. Contrary to popular belief, most surgeons do not like their patients to be in pain (at least, not until the postoperative period) so neonates at last started to get what the rest of us have taken for granted for two hundred years - anaethesia.

It was only the very young children who had been completely denied pain relief, of course. It was always understood that after four years old, the sensation of pain had finally groped its way from thalamus to cortex and that older kids deserved the odd Tylenol or something here and there. But not to overdo things: there was still the assumption that children needed less analgesia than adults, because they tolerate discomfort well (2). Like they had a choice.

Well, on this side of the Atlantic we feel we have come along way since then. So some anaethesiologists still write up post-operative opiates for children intramuscularly and *pro re nata*, thus ensuring that the child will leave it until the latest possible moment to admit to experiencing excruciating pain. At least the words 'morphine' and 'pediatric patients' are nowadays often used in the same sentence, without the associated 'avoid in'. And painful, repeated procedures such as lumbar puncture and bone marrow in leukaemic children are almost always done under general anaesthetic (3), liberating such unfortunate patients from the weekly terror of being helplessly pinned down while a needle is inserted into tender parts of what they had hitherto considered their own bodies, somewhere outside of their range of vision behind the unyielding elbows, knees or buttocks of Mummy, Daddy or that nice nurse from the clinic.

There are probably places in North America where these things are done under general anaesthetic, too, but Benedict Arnold Sick Kids' is not one of them. Children there are usually given opiates and an anxiolytic just before the procedure, and they often fall asleep beforehand, but you can take it from me, once that needle goes in most of them are wide awake before you can say 'spino-thalamic nociception'. Lumbar punctures are not too bad, but for most kids the memory of a bone-marrow aspirate — a needle the size of a young Californian Redwood pushed first through the skin under lidocaine, and then screwed into the bone itself two or three times — is indelible. And the experience of a bone-marrow biopsy, in which the needle is screwed in ten or twenty times, wiggled around whilst buried almost to the hilt like a blunt and bone-embedded Excalibur in order to obtain a core of bone itself and then screwed out again, undoubtedly rates as one of the most traumatic of some short lives.

What we need, of course, is a research project. I propose a comparison of local versus general anaesthetic in a group of paediatricians, haematologists and oncologists. Subjects would be randomly allocated to undergo LP, bone marrow aspirate or biopsy or a combination of all three. These would naturally be carried out by children under four, who may be presumed sufficiently insensible not to be unduly traumatised by the experience.

I have a feeling it's what Myrtle would have wanted.

REFERENCES

1. McGraw M. Neural maturation as exemplified in the changing reactions of the infant to pin prick. Child Dev 1941;12(1):31-42.
2. Swafford L, Allan D. Pain relief in the pediatric patient. Med Clin N Am 1968;52(1)
3. Hain WR, Tomlinson JH, Barbor PR. Anaesthesia for minor procedures in children with malignant disease. Journal of the Royal Society of Medicine 1985;78(9):715-20.

The dream of every thinker is to replace the politician by the scientist; why does it remain only a dream after so many incarnations? Is it because the thinker is too dreamily intellectual to go out into the arena of affairs and build his concept into reality? Is it because the hard ambition of the narrowly acquisitive soul is forever destined to overcome the gentle and scrupulous aspirations of philosophers and saints? Or is it that science is not yet grown to maturity and conscious power? —that only in our day do physicists and chemists and technicians begin to see that the rising role of science in industry and war gives them a pivotal position in social strategy, and points to the time when their organized strength will persuade the world to call them to leadership? Perhaps science has not yet merited the mastery of the world; and perhaps in a little while it will.

Francis Bacon

On Hirsutism in a Doll Population

A. Nicole Scofield, Amanda K. Scofield, R. Hal Scofield
University of Oklahoma Health Sciences
Department of Veterans Affairs Medical Center
Oklahoma City, OK

A variety of endocrine abnormalities have been described in various types of dolls (1,2). Among these are disorders of the adrenals (1,3), pituitary (4), and ovaries (5) that may cause hirsutism; however, there has not been a study of hirsutism in any doll for more than 75 years (6). The present study has been undertaken to determine the prevalence of hirsutism in Barbie Dolls, after one of us (AKS) acquired a hirsute Barbie Doll. We have found that while not common, hirsutism is not uncommon in Barbie. The finding of hirsutism in Barbie Dolls has a number of economic and social implications.

One of us (AKS) obtained a Barbie Doll as part of promotion at a nation-wide fast-food restaurant (McDonalds Corp, Oklahoma City, OK). The doll was noted to have an abnormal distribution of hair. The doll underwent an examination by an endocrinologist, one of us (RHS). This exam found obvious facial hirsutism (Figures 1 and 2). Subsequently, 49 additional Barbie Dolls acquired by one of us (ANS) were examined by two of us (ANS,RHS) for hirsutism.

Hormonal Evaluation. Considering that none of us had adequate grant monies to fund this work, it was initially felt that a complete endocrine biochemical evaluation would not be possible as it was not ethical to charge the dolls for investigative procedures. Subsequently, one of us (RHS) realized that all Barbie Dolls are apparently infertile. Therefore, an endocrine work-up could be justified clinically. Since the laboratory studies were carried out for routine clinical reasons, no involvement of the Institutional Review Board or informed consent was deemed needed by any of us.

The 50 Barbie Dolls were examined for hirsutism and we found that only the index case (Figures 1 and 2) had lower facial hirsutism. However, 4 additional dolls were found to have forehead hirsutism. One of the dolls with forehead hirsutism was African-American while only 2 of the non-hirsute dolls were African-American. When analyzed by the Fisher's Exact Test this distribution of hirsutism among Californian-American and African-American Barbie Dolls approached statistical significance ($p=0.1$).

Figure 1: Pronounced facial hirsutism in a doll, full frontal view

No other abnormalities of hair were found in the present series of Barbie dolls except for alopecia totalis in one doll that was the result of trauma by one of us. No hormonal abnormality was found in the hirsute dolls initially. However, an in depth statistical analysis using step-wise multiple linear regression and 4 non-parametric analyses such as the Mann-Whitney U test was illuminating. It was found that dolls spending most of their time in the dark, independent of actual location, such as the basement, a closet or a shoe box, had substantially elevated levels of the adrenal androgen DHEA-S ($P<0.00000001$).

This is the first systematic assessment of hirsutism in a doll population. A full 10% of Barbie Dolls had hirsutism, although only one (2%) had severe facial hirsutism (Figures 1 and 2). Even so, hirsutism is a severe cosmetic problem in Barbie. Clearly, hirsutism will be an impediment to gainful employment in dolls. Thus these findings suggest an economic impact and point to the need for future cost-benefit analyses of therapeutic interventions. Such data may lead to health outcome research for any of us. A racial difference in hirsutism has been suggested by our data. Health outcomes research focusing on a minority population may even be more fruitful in terms of funding. On the other hand, recent genetic studies on mitochondrial DNA of modern Barbie dolls points to a common maternal ancestor (so called Eve Barbie) existing only about 40 years ago (7). Thus, a genetic origin of the difference in hirsutism may be unlikely; however, no studies of the Y chromo-some to measure the genetic relationship of present-day Ken's has been reported.

Finally, we have found by statistical methods that the adrenal androgen DHEA-S is elevated in Barbie Dolls residing in the dark. This suggests that the wake/sleep cycle may control androgen secretion in dolls. Thus, melatonin may be involved in the regulation of DHEA-S. Considering the current popularity of both of these hormones in areas such as the retardation of the aging process, all of us are confident that this will become an area of investigation sure to be funded at the national level.

REFERENCES:

1. Addison, T. On constitutional and local effects of disease of the supra-renal capsules in rag dolls. London:Highley, 1855.
2. Turner, H. Syndrome of sexual infantilism, congenital webbed neck and cubitus valgus in a doll. Doll Endocrinol. 23:566-574, 1938
3. Matel, A. The origin of ambiguous genitalia in anatomically correct dolls. J Doll Biochem. 58:17-23, 1994.
4. Alexander, M. A pathologic and clinical study of pituitary tumors in porcelain dolls. Arch Doll Pathol. 273:1582-1602, 1982.
5. Albright, F. Early recognition of polycystic ovarian disease in cabbage patch dolls. Proc Natl Acad Dolls (USA). 93:15432-15436, 1993.
6. Drozzelmeyer, NC. Sexual dimorphisms in Raggedity Ann and Raggedity Andy: A study of secondary sexual traits. Düsseldorf:Nutcracker Press, 1913.
7. Joe GI. Modern Barbie dolls descend from a single maternal ancestor who lived about 40 years before the present: A study of mitochondrial DNA. Nature Dolls. 3:157-159, 1995.

Figure 2: Pronounced facial hirsutism in a doll, profile view

MILESTONES IN MODERN MEDICAL EDUCATION

The Ultimate Synthesis

David H. Gutmann
Ann Arbor, MI

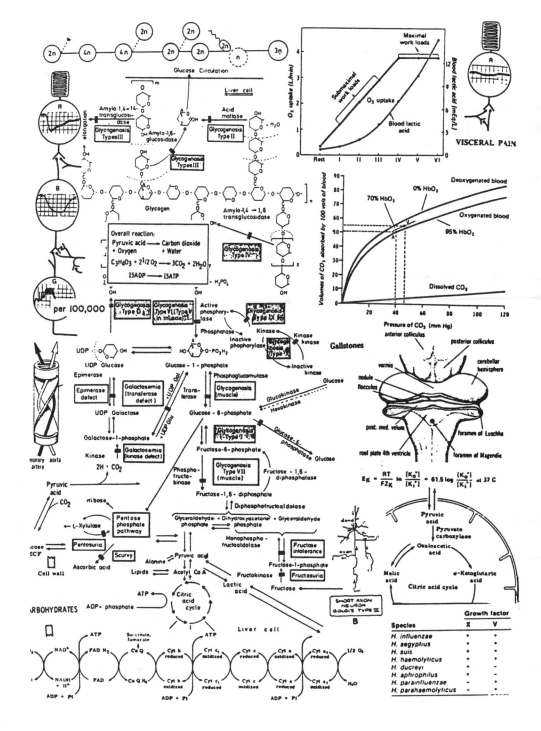

There is no process so tedious nor undertaking so tiresome as the training period modern institutions call medical school. Malcolm DeWitt, noted educational consultant, has been quoted as having said that medical school represents the intellectual void in the black hole of modern-day education. It is a journey which takes its befuddled travellers from a state of quaint naivete to one of overindulgent ignorance. Yet despite its shortcomings, medical schools still manage to attract and clone some of the brightest minds of our time. With its endless parade of musical chair professors and its whirlwind pace, medical school education serves to create only confusion and mass bewilderment. However, more amazing than the incredible volume of information that need be assimilated is the fact that reasonably competent physicians graduate from American universities each and every year.

At the Amazin' Blue University, where dreams of roses bloom and wilt every year, we have endeavored to synthesize the basic science information which is critical to the education of every young junior doctor. Our research has indicated that the bulk of the information imparted to these future physicians can be distilled down to include only the basic concepts and principles. What is more astounding, we found, is that we could construct a single kodachrome slide* detailing all the essentials which could be shown repeatedly to both freshman and sophmore medical students. Lectures could then be varied depending upon the sector of the slide being expounded upon for the day. Needless to say, this monumental breakthrough in medical education serves a dual purpose in that it not only provides the ultimate

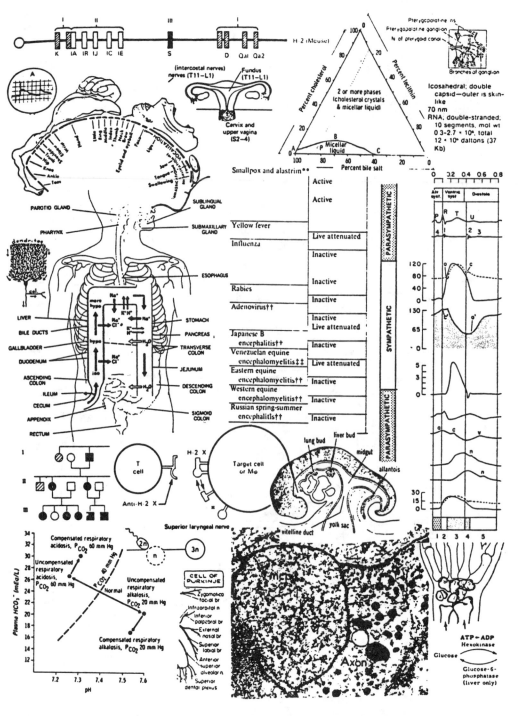

teaching modality but also would save each medical school countless dollars foolishly spent on teaching and student education. Business-minded universities could buy copies of this valuable teaching aide and distribute them to students at a modest profit.**

In conclusion, we believe that this revolutionary instructional advancement would benefit medical education greatly in the long run. Its impact on the practice of medicine in the future will surely be appreciable. 🗑

---

*Copies of this outstanding full-color kodachrome slide are available by request for minimal monetary renumeration. Similar programmed teaching sets are available for those clinical faculty who never really learned the material when they were in medical school but teach it to future generations nonetheless.

**Copies of this easy-to-care-for poster are available in three sizes which are all suitable for framing. Bulk orders are appropriately discounted.

The physicist write learned articles
About searching for sub-atom particles.
But I have great doubts
That despite their loud shouts
They will find the primordial starticles.

Nathan Shalit
Morristown, NJ

PHILOSOPHY
&
THOUGHT

A SMALL THOUGHT

RICHARD LILIENTHAL
Psychology Department
Radford College
Radford, Virginia 24142

The transmission of information through the nervous system is dependent upon certain chemical actions. In axonal transmission - the movement of nerve impulses within a nerve - sodium and potassium interact to create an electrical impulse that moves along the axon. When the impulse has passed on down the axon, special physiological systems reverse the flow of these chemicals and the axon returns to its resting state. In synaptic transmission - the transfer of impulses between neurons - the electrical impulse does not somehow "jump" the synapse (the space between neurons); rather a chemical "messenger" crosses over to the other side. Many different chemicals have been suggested as possible transmitter agents, the major one being acetlycholine (ACh). Once a signal has been received by a neuron, the ACh is cleared out of the synapse by the action of enzymes. For example, ACh is broken down into its constituent parts of acetate and choline by the enzyme acetylcholine esterase. The chemical components that result from this process are then recycled and resynthesized into transmitter agent, which can then be used again to cross the synaptic gap. Exactly how this recycling takes place is not yet completely understood.

This author is hypothesizing that there is a limit to the number of times the brain's chemicals can be used and reused. It is possible that they deteriorate or become contaminated by repeated use until they eventually lose potency. If this is so, it would mean that a person has a finite number of thoughts and feelings - a predetermined amount that is drawn upon each time he or she thinks or experiences something. Consequently, thinking a lot now could leave a person short of thoughts later in life.

Researchers have not yet discovered the number of times that the brain's chemicals can be used and, therefore, the exact number of thoughts a person is capable of (there are probably individual differences here, anyway). However, the person who thinks a lot today may be drawing dangerously close to exhausting his or her supply. Let us not forget the Gestalt question: "Are a person's thoughts more than the sum of the chemicals that produce them?" Overused chemicals, like used laundry water, certainly cannot produce the best results.

Until this hypothesis is experimentally tested, it might not be ecologically unwise to start conserving brain chemicals, and hence thoughts. Let us be careful with what is our most important natural resource. To this end, the following are suggested: (1) Never think off duty (when you are not paid for it), (2) Never "group-think" (more than one person should not think on the same question), (3) Think in short, concise ideas (unless the thoughts are for publication).

A media campaign could be launched along the line of saving for a rainy day or for one's golden years. Fear appeals, already common in the health field, would stress the horror of being left thoughtless in one's old age. The overthinker would become the senile person. This appeal would be especially relevant in light of the increasing age span in this country.

It has been suggested that unused thoughts are passed on to a collective unconscious, but there is no empirical evidence on this as yet. Rationally, it does not appear that modern man uses his brain any better than his predecessors.

There is a segment of our population that does not have to be warned of the danger of wasteful thinking. Many of these people appear to conserve thoughts instinctively, not having thought much since the time of their conception. Their number appears to be on the increase, especially among college students. There is a danger to this. These extreme conservatives run the risk of dying with many thoughts unused. Do they think that they can pass their unused thoughts along to their heirs as they can their other material possessions.?[1] No, they probably would not waste the thought.

---

[1] The transfer of a deceased's unused brain chemicals to another person is not yet a reality.

BEING A SHORT EXCURSUS INTO THE ORIGIN OF WESTERN PHILOSOPHY, FROM THE TIME OF THE GREEKS UNTIL THE TIME OF THE GREEKS SOME TWO AND ONE-HALF CENTURIES LATER

Howard Zaharoff
Newton, MA

. . .Hang up philosophy!
Unless philosophy can make a Juliet,
Displant a town, reverse a prince's doom,
It helps not, it prevails not; talk no more.

—*Romeo and Juliet (III.3.58)*

A philosopher, as any dictionary will tell you, is a "lover of wisdom," generally his own. Yet philosophy, one of the oldest subjects, is also the most misunderstood.

It is time to change this, and one way to begin is by exploring the origin of philosophy. For no one can read how Western philosophy evolved from the minds of a few ancient Greeks without being filled with wonder and appreciation.

Thales: Philosophy began in the sixth century B.C. in Ionian Greece with Thales of Miletus, who believed "All things are water"—probably because he often fell into irrigation ditches. Indeed, in original absent-minded professor story, Thales is gazing at the stars, when he slips into a ditch. A Thracian maid pulls him out and admonishes, "How can you expect to understand the heavens when you can't even see your own feet?" A great punchline, if delivered in ancient Thracian.

Thales was succeeded by Anaximander, who drew the first map of the world and originated a theory of evolution.

Pythagoras: The next major philosopher was

THE WISE MEN TURN THEIR BACK ON FORTUNE: *OPUS SECTILE*, photo by Anderson/Mansell

Pythagoras. He was also a mathematician, a scientist, and a religious thinker who believed in transmigration of souls. Indeed, he believed people could recall parts of their previous lives. In one story, Pythagoras asks someone to stop beating a dog because he recognizes it as a late friend. In another, Pythagoras recalls one of his own lives and, in a moment of forgetfulness, lifts his leg and urinates on an acquaintance.

Heraclitus: The next philosophic figure was Heraclitus, a poet who stressed motion and strife. Unfortunately, all we have left from him are a few cryptic statements, such as "This world. . .is an eternal fire, kindling in fixed measure, and in fixed measure going out." Actually, it's likely that he himself rarely went out. Though he wrote, "The Sibyl with raving lips say mirthless, unsweetened words that are heard for a thousand years," probably after a prolonged encounter with a loud, boorish woman, he also believed "Strife is father of all"—a mistake he could not have made had he gone out more often.

The Eleatics: Following Heraclitus, at a respectable distance, were the philosophers of Elea, a city in southern Italy. The founder of the "Eleatic" school was "Father" Parmenides, who claimed that "Only Being is" and that Not-being could neither be thought of nor talked about. One wonders what he was thinking and talking about when he said this.

Empedocles: The next major philospher was Empedocles of Sicily, who wrote: *"Heads without bodies, Trunks without limbs, Falling down awful heights of air."* This is not a description of the French Revolution, but a poetic theory of natural selection. Empedocles believed that after this awful fall, but before modern life began, the heads and bodies joined to form a menagerie of monsters: "bulls with heads of men, men with heads of bulls."

Empedocles was fairly bullheaded himself. Although a clever philosopher, scientist and doctor, he foolishly became convinced that he was a god (making him the spiritual forefather of today's doctors). Legend says that to prove this, he jumped into volcanic Mt. Aetna. In a flash, Greece lost its most outstanding lyrical poet-physicist-physician-metaphysician-Sicilian.

Anaxagoras: Anaxagoras taught that "in everything there is a portion of everything." For example, he believed that a kernel of corn contains the "seeds" of flesh, bone, hair, and blood. Lucretius refuted this by pointing out that crushed corn doesn't bleed. Centuries later Samuel Johnson kicked a stone until his corns bled and shouted in glee, "Thus I refute Lucretius." This story is not well-known.

The Atomists and Sophists: No history of Greek Philosophy would be complete without at least passing mention of the Atomists and the Sophists.

Socrates: The most fascinating philosopher of Ancient Greece was Socrates (469 - 399 B.C.), whose acute mind, high moral character, and incessant questioning made him the greatest noodge of ancient Athens.

Socrates was catapulted into philosophy by the words of the Delphic Auricle (so called because of a heart condition) who claimed Socrates was the wisest of all men. This puzzled Socrates, who believed, "The only thing I know is that I know nothing" (which, if he really knew it, he couldn't have known).

To understand the words of the auricle, Socrates began cross-examining Athenians from all walks of life. This attracted a large following, especially among the young, who liked watching him deflate the egos of prominent citizens. Unfortunately, this also made him powerful enemies, who finally accused him of corrupting the youth and introducing new gods (not to each other, but into Athens).

At his trial Socrates delivered an Apology. However, because in it he asked for permanent lodging at public expense, no one thought it was and he was condemned to death. Yet, instead of accusing Athens of "polis brutality," Socrates merely uttered the immortal "I never metaphysician I didn't like," downed hemlock, and expired.

Plato: The unjust execution of Socrates persuaded a young aristocrat named Plato to forgo politics in order to carry on the Socratic pursuit of truth, virtue, and young boys. To this end he wrote a series of brilliant philosophical dialogues.

Most outstanding among these is *The Republic,* which contains Plato's mature views. For example, using his simile of a Divided Line, he proves conclusively that many things are similar to divided lines. Then he employs his famous Cave Allegory to hint at the bold thesis that we are all prisoners within a "cave"—dwelling in darkness, seeing only shadows, banging our heads on stalactites—and that our only means of escape is buying a copy of *The Republic* for two drachmas.

In this dialogue we also find Plato's theory that the ideal state should be ruled by an elite corps of "philosopher-kings," not a surprising idea to come from a philosopher. Actually, Plato almost put his political views into practice. In his younger days he journeyed to Syracuse where its tyrant, Dionysius I, was so pleased to be visited by the outspoken philosopher that he had Plato kidnapped and sold as a slave. However, after the tyrant's death, his brother-in-law Dion invited Plato back. This time Plato was such a hit that within months he *and* Dion were banished from Syracuse.

Unsuccessful in practical affairs, Plato did the only sensible thing: he became a teacher. Indeed, he even opened his own school. Named after the grove of Academus, where it was built, Plato's Grovery was the first real university in the world. Posted over its door was its primary requirement: "Let no one ignorant of geometry enter here." This ensured that students could draw his Divided Line.

Aristotle: One student to enter Plato's school while he was still teaching and lechering was a bright seventeen-year-old named Aristotle, the son of a royal physician who was praised for mastering medical science and using leeches to treat piles. From him Aristotle received three things which would have a profound impact on his life: connections with Macedonian royalty, a love of biology, and a set of hemorrhoid leeches to start his own business.

Aristotle was a far more practical philosopher than his mentor Plato. For example, while Plato discussed the ideal state, Aristotle collected 158 actual state constitutions. And while the Platonic dialogue *The Potato Laches* shows Plato knew nothing about cooking, Aristotle stunned the world by placing first in the Panhellenic Souvlaki Bake-off, the secret of which success is described in his treatise *The Oregano*.

The most fascinating aspects of Aristotle's life was his relationship with Alexander the Great. Alexander was sired by Philip of Macedon, who, inspired, fired Alex's Macedonian tutors and hired the much admired Aristotle. Unfortunately, when Alexander the Great died, Athens was swept by a wave of anti-Macedonian feeling, of which Aristotle was a natural target. Soon he too faced trumped-up charges of impiety, but unlike Socrates he refused to stick around. As he put it: "I will not allow the Athenians to sin twice against philosophy. Besides, I'm allergic to hemlock." So he fled to Euboea, where he succumbed quietly in his sleep to hemorrhoids.

The death of Aristotle marks the end of the beginning of philosophy, though of course not the end of philosophy itself. For what began over two millenia ago with Thales, continues today with those daring academicians who are constantly creating new areas of exploration—bioethics, the philosophy of death, and more—in a bold effort to increase man's knowledge and their job opportunities. Here, here!

"DEVELOPMENTS IN BIOENGINEERING"

J.C. Haigh
Saskatoon, Canada

DWARF SICILIAN DONKEY

THE NEW SCIENCE OF QUANTUM SEMANTICS

ROMAN LASKOWSKI
The Hypothetical Institute of Catford

"If it moves - quantize it."
—A famous scientist.

This paper aims to present the latest developments in the new and rapidly developing science of Quantum Semantics. Part (1) gives a brief historical outline of this staggeringly unimportant new science, together with an outline of its (very) basic principles. Part (2) will deal with its applications and discoveries.

The new science of Quantum Semantics was founded by Tom Bowler, a theoretical physicist here at the Hypothetical Institute of Catford, early last week. On that dark, wet Tuesday afternoon, while looking for hairs on his palms[1], Tom had an idea which was to change his whole day - or what was left of it.

So excited was he by this idea that he ran to tell his fellow theoretical scientists here at the Institute. We, his fellow theoretical scientists, I'm ashamed to say, completely ignored him.

This was more out of habit than from any personal feelings we may have towards Tom[2]. But, after half an hour or so of his incoherent ravings, we began to take notice of what he was trying to tell us. We at last started showing interest in what he was saying. Perhaps it was the drink. He had certainly had enough. Perhaps it was something else.

The result was that, after listening patiently to Tom's ideas, we all went off to our own little rooms to work on these ideas. Such was our enthusiasm that, since last Tuesday, we have devoted literally whole minutes of our spare time to developing the new science of Quantum Semantics.

And, all these developments originated from that single idea of Tom Bowler's. The idea, Tom's idea, that the laws and techniques of both quantum mechanics and nuclear physics might be very profitably applied to the study of the 26 letters of the English alphabet. A study upon which Tom had embarked only a couple of days previously. A study which Tom considers to be of vital importance.

Tom's idea came from his sudden insight into the actual nature of the letters themselves. The 26 letters of the alphabet, Tom realised, are simply different states of the same basic particle! Like protons and neutrons are just different charge states of the same basic particle - the nucleon.

Tom was convinced that he was right. He named his basic letter particle the "alphabeton"[3]. All letters of the alphabet are simply different states of the alphabeton.

And, like the nucleon is made up of various quarks, so the alphabeton can be thought of as being made up of "lines". There are two types of lines: straight lines and curved lines[4].

The next step from these basic premises was as obvious to Tom as it would be to anyone else like him. It was clear that letters, or rather alphabetons, must posses quantum numbers. Not only that, but they must also undergo certain reactions and decays. The laws governing these reactions determine which quantum numbers are conserved and which are not. Or something.

Characteristically unperturbed by the apparent pointlessness and overwhelming dullness of his theory so far, Tom then embarked on a search for these quantum numbers of the alphabetons.

Seconds later, he had discovered them. Tom then embarked on a search for someone to tell of his latest discovery. This took slightly longer.

---

[1]One of Tom's hobbies is trying to breed hairy palm trees. No one seems to know why.

[2]Although boredom also came into it somewhere.

---

[3]Actually he named it the "Tom Bowleron", but we soon changed *that*.
[4]Brilliant.

Briefly, Tom's quantum numbers range from the obvious (the "letter quantum number" i.e. A=1, B=2, C=3, etc.), via the boring (the "vowel quantum number" which equals 1 for vowels and zero for consonants), to the exceedingly dull (something called the "symmetry quantum number"). Apart from quantum numbers, Tom has found that the letters of the alphabet are also endowed with various coefficients, moments, quotients, ratios, constants and permittivities[5].

And, of course, they obey certain conservation laws. Three conservation laws have been discovered to date: the conservation of total letter number, the conservation of average letter number and the conservation of positional letter number. Tom has managed to convince himself (if no one else) that the first of these, the conservation of total letter number, is a *strict* conservation law - which means that it is strictly conserved in all interactions. The other two conservation laws are not.

Now, take for example the "weak" interaction. In this, the conservation of total letter number is the only conservation law obeyed - the other two both being violated. An example of a word decaying weakly is:-

```
                                                      Total
                                                     letter
                                                     number
G E O G R A P H Y → L O A D + O F + M A P S
7 5 15 7 18 1 16 8 25   12 15 1 4   15 6   13 1 16 19  102
```

Or, in the conventional quantum semantical notation:-

	Total letter number
GEOGRAPHY → LOAD OF MAPS	102

Other examples are:-

PSYCHOLOGY → OF A LITTLE USE	145
PHYSICS → BORING LABS	99

All telling stuff, this.

In the "medium-strong" interaction, the average letter number (i.e. total letter number divided by the number of letters), as well as the total letter number, is conserved. Trivial examples of this interaction are anagrams (e.g. ORGAN → GROAN; PRIEST → STRIPE → RIPEST → ESPRIT; etc.). Non-trivial examples are:-

	Total letter number	Average letter number
H E A T → C O L D 8 5 1 20 3 15 12 4	34	8.5
F I V E → N I N E 6 9 22 5 14 9 14 5	42	10.5

[5]N.B. Tom actually believes all this. Millions wouldn't.

The third type of interaction, the "strong" interaction, is governed by the conservation of positional letter number as well as of total letter number. Simply stated, conservation of positional letter number means that the sums of the letter numbers of the rth letters in each word are constant before and after the reaction. Tom, however, seems to think that his way of putting it is better:-

"In general, if there are initially a words, each made up of n alphabetons, reacting to form b words, each also containing n alphabetons, then, if the letter number of the rth letter of the pth word in the initial system is x_{arp} and that of the rth letter of the qth word in the final system is x_{brq}, then positional letter conservation can be simply stated by

$$\sum_{p=1}^{a} x_{arp} = \sum_{q=1}^{b} x_{brq} \qquad \text{for all } r = 1,2,..,n."$$

Trivial.

As an example, take the word REX. One possible decay mode of this word is:-

```
R E X → O D D + C A T
18 5 24   15 4 4   3 1 20
```

Other examples are:

```
F R Y → D I E + B I T
6 18 25   4 9 5   2 9 20

S E X → R A W + A D A
19 5 24   18 1 23   1 4 1
```

And so on.

Tom actually believes that the study of these various interactions will reveal scores and scores of stunning universal truths. He hasn't actually found any yet - but there's still time. Tom doesn't personally hold out much hope for the "medium-strong" interaction, but is fairly confident about the other two. So the study of these interactions and the search for any universal truths which they may contain has been delegated to the large number of young research assistants who hang about the Hypothetical Institute of Catford.

The young research assistants have also been assigned the task of coming up with the quantum semantical equivalents of Fermi surfaces and the like. After all, the existence of conservation laws implies the invariance of the particular interaction under some transformation in something like "alphabet space". Or so Tom informs me.

So, these are the basic principles of the new science of Quantum Semantics. Part (2) will deal with the fascinating applications and wonderful discoveries of this emerging new science.

Time For Divine Intervention

Nature Vol. 323, 30 October 1986

Sir—On the subject of My Divine Essence Character, Attributes, Inclinations, Motives, Philosophy, Politics and *modus operandi*, especially as regards what is vulgarly referred to as miracles, speculations about which have recently been appearing in this magazine, and even more especially as regards My hypothesized role in Universe construction where, so it has been alleged, 1, in the form of a bipedal primate outwardly resembling an elderly and bearded male *Homo sapiens sapiens*, created the Universe for the amusement and edification of men, I should like to state: (1) I am not a very good Member of the Church of England. (2) When I come to think of it, I am not even a bad Member of the Church of England. (3) When I really pause to consider the matter, I fear (if that is the word) I am not even a Christian, having been around an eternity before that particular creed was organized, and consequently, am Supremely indifferent to its beliefs, dogmas and convictions.

I am, therefore, rather inclined to take a dim view of *all* people of whatever, persuasion voicing opinions on Me, this for the simple reason that, as I am Ineffable and exist beyond all human comprehension in no particular spatio-temporal relation to the physical cosmos, *all* opinions about Me are meaningless, when not actually insulting, and, what is worse, tiresomely predictable, especially to one Who knows all things, reflecting as they do only the outlooks and attitudes of these, My unsolicited and intellectually and imaginatively limited interpreters who, if ever they *really* thought about Me, would be more inclined to keep silent.

You will understand that, while I am not in the habit of presenting My views on theology in the correspondence columns of periodicals (except as occasionally in the past to *The Times*), I am taking this opportunity to do so because, though as is well attested, My Patience is infinite, It is not *that* infinite. Nor, may I remind your contributors, does being omniscient and Omnipotent of necessity compel One to be All-Benevolent.

I in parting, hope that this correspondence can now be closed.

GOD
(As revealed to Ralph Estling)

The Old Parsonage, Dowlish Wake, Ilminster, Somerset TA19ONY, UK

• *God's will be done; this correspondence is now closed. Editor, Nature.*

Submitted By:
Leonard X. Finegold
Philadelphia, PA

AN INVESTIGATION OF HASSELL'S MODIFIED MAXIM: HARD WORK NEVER HURT ANYONE, BUT THEN NEITHER DID A WHOLE LOT OF GOOD REST

Pamela Cochrane Tisdale,
Charleston, SC

The origin of the adage, "Hard work never hurt anyone," is lost in antiquity. However, it can safely be assumed that most people in positions of leadership (e.g., Gengis Khan, Hannibal, Chairmen of Academic Departments of Colleges) have relied on this adage to motivate their underlings (e.g., the Hordes, the Elephants, the Faculty Seeking Promotion or Tenure).

An interesting addition to this oft quoted adage has been suggested by Richard Arthur Hassell (Hassell, 1976), to wit, "but then neither did a whole lot of good rest." It can be assumed that most people in positions of leadership were, or are, well aware of this, and that their subordinates were, or are, vaguely conscious of the fallacy of the original statement.

Because of the possible implications, it was the author's intention to investigate the truth of Hassell's modified maxim.

METHOD

The experiment was conducted during Spring Semester and Summer Term, 1980, at the College of Charleston, in Charleston, South Carolina. The subjects were full-time faculty at that institution.

The subjects in the control group (Hard Work Never Hurt Anyone) continued with their usual activities during the two sessions. Their task was to keep detailed data on the number of hours spent engaging in the following 10 activities:

1. Teaching (including preparation and grading)
2. Advising/counseling with students
3. Reading Administrative Memos
4. Conducting Research
5. Writing Professional Literature
6. Attending Meetings
7. Reading the Classics
8. Relaxing on the Beach
9. Puttering in the Garden, and
10. Doing Nothing

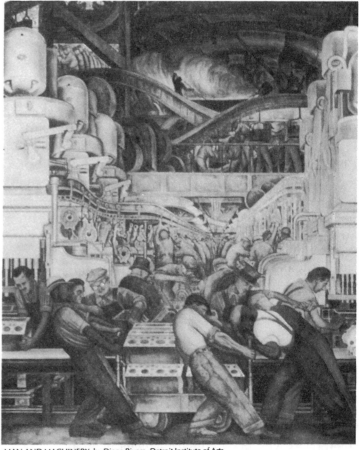

MAN AND MACHINERY, by Diego Rivera, Detroit Institute of Arts

They were also asked to keep a record of the weekly incidence of

1. Headaches
2. Hangovers
3. Heart Attacks, and
4. Heart Burn

Subjects in the Experimental Group (But Then Neither Did A Whole Lot of Good Rest) were to do only what they were hired to do during Spring Semester (i.e., teach), and were required not to teach during the Summer Term. Their task was to keep detailed data on the number of hours spent engaged in the following 5 activities:

1. Teaching (including preparation and grading)
2. Reading the Classics
3. Relaxing on the Beach
4. Puttering in the Garden
5. Doing Nothing

They were also asked to keep a record of the weekly incidence of

1. Headaches
2. Hangovers
3. Heart Attacks, and
4. Heart Burn

SUBJECTS

It was the researcher's original intention to select a random sample of 20 Charleston College faculty to serve as subjects in the Control Group (Hard Work) and an equal number to serve as subjects in the Experimental Group (Good Rest).

RESULTS

When the data were compiled, it was evident that "a whole lot of good rest" did not physically hurt the subject in the experimental group at all, and that "hard work" was highly correlated with a significantly greater incidence of headaches, hangovers, heart attacks, and heart burn among the subjects of the Control Group. (These data were to be presented in table form, but the secretary, Carol Glover, said that it was hard work to type one of those things.)

However, there is evidence that there was a definite psychological impact on one subject in the Experimental Group. He resigned his teaching position at the end of the experiment, collected his money from the State retirement fund, and was last seen sitting on the beach reading.

The only safe conclusion to be drawn from the results of this scientific inquiry is that more research is essential. Anyone who would be interested in engaging in further research on this topic may attempt to reach the author and R.A. Hassell as they sail from port to port gathering more data to support the Aphorism:

A WHOLE LOT OF GOOD REST
NEVER HURT ANYONE

REFERENCES

Hassell, R.A. Bicentennial Address. The Windjammer, Isle of Palms, South Carolina. July 4, 1976.

ONION POISONING IN THE CAT

Kobayashi, K. Onion Poisoning in the cat. *Feline Practice*, 1981, *11*, 22-27.

Recently, the author recognized that a cat had ingested onion soup. As a result, a number of Heinz bodies were formed in its erythrocytes. This evidence suggests the possibility that onion feeding causes hemolytic anemia and hemoglobinuria in cats as well as in domestic animals.

CENTRE FOR THE STUDY OF CREATURE COMMUNICATION

Dr. Charles U. Larson announces an *International Journal of Creature Communication* which is devoted to articles which discuss the art and science of sport fishing and other types of creature communication. They should be heavily footnoted and few if any of the footnotes should be able to be traced. Publication deadlines are April Fool's Day and Halloween eve. Information can be obtained without floundering about by contacting Dr. Larson at the COMS Department at No. Ill. Univ. or at the Centre for the Study of Creature Communication at 612 S. Main, Sycamore, Ill. 60178. You may get hooked on this one and be forced to new depths.

Charles U. Larson
Sycamore, IL

Artificial Stupidity: An Introduction

Wallace Marshall
Patchogue, NY

Artificial Stupidity (AS) may be defined as the attempt by computer scientists to create computer programs capable of causing problems of a type normally associated with human thought. Such efforts range from Charles Boil's 1908 chess playing program,[1] designed to lose every game it played, to modern, general purpose programs that can mess up, in a few milliseconds, jobs which it would take thousands of man hours to fix. Modern techniques in AS vastly enhance our ability to misrepresent data and provide highly effective methods to increase industrial inefficiency. One type of AS program which is rapidly gaining popularity is the so-called "novice system," a program that is able to confuse information given to it by a human operator. Novice systems are constructed through the process of "ignorance engineering" which involves experts in a given field being allowed to "converse" with the program about a field in which the expert knows nothing whatsoever. By far the majority of novice systems are now being written in fallacy languages, such as LITHP, AmateurLOG, and DESPAIR. These languages, in turn, are outgrowths of earlier fallacy generating programs, which are able to take two or more propositional arguments and draw a false conclusion.

> *Example:* Socrates is mortal
> Socrates is a man
> Therefore, all men are Socrates

Other programs are appearing that can fail to properly carry out all sorts of tasks. Following the lead of such famous programs as SAM and PAM, a program has been written called DAMN, that misunderstands simple stories. AS programs have been written that can find the most inefficient path through a maze, and in 1979 one of these programs was connected to a robot jackass which was allowed to run the maze shown in Figure 1. It travelled at a speed of 20 m.p.h., and took only seven days to traverse the maze, which was 10 feet long.

in ⟶ ─────────── ⟶ out

Many specialized programming techniques and data structures are being developed for AS applications. As an extension of the traditional "demon" which does a specific task when a given condition occurs, AS programmers use "Mack-trucks", which do what ever they feel like. Data is stored in such revolutionary structures as "spaghetti bowls," and "squeues," which rearrange data in a highly meaningless way. Fuzzy techniques so long applied to processing of visual data are now being extended so as to apply to the actual sensory device resulting in "fuzzy vision." This enables the computer to obtain more inaccurate information about its environment. AS programs often use so-called "flames." A flame can be thought of as just that — a burning fire into which data may be placed for destruction. Many data bases have been built upon the flame concept as this provides a simple means to enable efficient data loss. Some techniques are poorly understood and are still in the development stages such as serial redundancy and amorphous structuring. Much more research will go on in the future on such advanced concepts.

AS is already being used by many large corporations to make more well-misinformed mistakes (you've heard of New Coke?). Police departments all over the country are using AS systems to aid in the arrest of innocent people. Scientific fields in which AS is now being applied include chromatogram-misreading, subatomic Egyptology, and conclusion-jumping. In engineering, AS is being used to design nonfunctional circuits and compute the aerodynamics of indefinite integrals. AS programs have even been written to write other programs.[3] So far only three programs, IKE, SPOT, and ARCHEOPTERYX have been written. These three programs wrote programs that produced the output shown below:

IKE:	syntax error
SPOT:	syntax error
ARCHEOPTERYX:	syntax error

Such autoprogramming devices greatly increase the ability of software engineers to fail to produce the desired product in the allotted time, and to make hidden bugs more easily created.

As for total artificial stupidity, many philosophical arguments have been proposed. Perhaps the most famous is that of Kurd Girdle, who proved that although you can make a system do any finite number of stupid things, you can never program it to act like a congressman.[2]

REFERENCES:
[1] Boil, CL. Automated Chess Loss Program, OOPART ACTA, 45:72 (1234787651234.6), 1908
[2] Girdle, KR. Stupidity in formal systems, Proceeds of the 85th annual IEE conference on Egyptology, 1983
[3] Sheridan, PJ. Autoprogramming in AS, J. Appl. Bs., 100:34(0), 1989

I'm Just A Two-Bit Programmer On A Sixteen-Bit Machine

Well, I sit at my computer, staring at the screen
Like a chloroformed iguana. My brain has got gangrene.
And while my mind is rotting, I feel like such a jerk:
I caused a disk crash wiping out my last two decades' work.
Oh, Mama, who could have foreseen
I'd be a two-bit programmer on a sixteen bit machine?

I go on dates with women, and I talk of bits and bytes,
So is it any wonder that I sleep alone at nights?
To think, I could be human, instead of the nerd I am!
But then again, let's face it: who really gives a damn?
Oh, Mama, it's just too obscene.
I'm just a two-bit programmer on a sixteen-bit machine.

Mr. David S. Platt
Arlington, MA

Webbèd Footnotes
The Duck in Contemporary Western Thought

Philip N. Lawton, Jr., Ph.D.
34 Governor Road
Arlington, MA 02174

It is my contention that by and large contemporary scholars have failed to appreciate the cultural importance of the duck, despite its near-universal nomination as a "mythological object," in the sense which Roland Barthes has lately assigned that phrase. Even those few who have made note of the duck's "apparent" cultural significance have grossly misunderstood its complex symbolic functions. For instance, Claude Lévi-Strauss argues with foolish confidence that in some South American myths the duck mediates nature and culture. "In effect," he writes, "if ducks are congruent with canoes under the rapport of culture, in the order of nature they maintain a rapport of correlation and opposition with fish."[2] This, because fish swim *in* the water, and ducks, *on* it. Horsefeathers. It is indeed a tribute to the late Professor Reginald Drakeson-Smythe, Jr., whose tragic death under the hooves of a sun-maddened water buffalo has impoverished cultural anthropology and linguistics alike, that he admitted his confusion about the duck. His last journal entry poignantly testifies to this befuddlement: "Duck. Muck. *Duck*muck. *Muck*duck . . . "[3] One can only snicker at the facile theories of lesser minds.

My limited purpose in the present paper[4] is to demonstrate, through the careful analysis and subtle explication of representative philosophical and literary works, that contemporary Western societies have invested the duck with an ambivalent charge whose force may be aggravated by, but is *not* merely attributable to, the anxiety provoked by alienation from nature. *Pace* Anasdocent and his epigones.[5] I shall further argue that on a deeper level the duck, taken as a cultural artifact, represents both *Eros* and *Thanatos*, life and death, sexuality and mortality. Thus, it serves to reconcile two opposing views and experiences of nature, of the human response to nature, and of human nature itself.[6]

The tension between these two views and experiences of nature,--the tension, that is, between a "good," Rousseauvian, or innocent nature, and an "evil," Hobbesian, or maleficent nature, -- is the underlying theme, the deep structure, of Edmund Wilson's classic short story, "The Man Who Shot Snapping Turtles." A sort of Hecate County duckpond Ahab, Asa M. Stryker is the story's central character; one hesitates to call him protagonist, antagonist, hero, or antihero. The narrator relates that Stryker "cherished and protected" the beautiful ducks which frequented his pond "like pets." But nature is only partially, and imperfectly, domesticated; the pond was infested with snapping turtles whose "depredations . . . made terrible ravages on the ducklings." Beneath the surface of Stryker's Edenic duckpond lay Hobbes' *summum malum*: violent death. And Stryker there bankside potted the turtles with a rifle, hopeless, impotent, occasionally hitting a duck by mistake. "As he lost *brood after brood*," the narrator reports, "the subject came, in fact, to *obsess* him. He had apparently hoped that his pond might be made *a sort of paradise for ducks. . . .*"[7] The mythic, almost religious overtones of this passage should be evident even to my duckblind critics.

Enraged by his helplessness, Stryker soon joined battle in earnest for the good, the innocent, the ducklings, and against the evil, the ravagers, the snapping turtles. When his first efforts to extirpate evil had failed, when he had almost despaired of the good, when he had recognized that evil is *in* nature, then inspiration struck Stryker. Yankee inspiration:

> . . . why not turn the tables on Nature? Why not prey on what had preyed on us? Why not exploit the hideous mud-turtle . . . ? Why not devour him daily in the form of turtle soup? And if one could not eat soup every day, why not turn him into an object of commerce? Why not make the public eat him? Let the turtles create economic, instead of killing aesthetic, value![8]

Duck soup. But turtles will not be mocked: Stryker's rage, though directed against evil itself, makes of him an evil man; the good is ultimately his un-doing.

The association between wild ducks and violent death is also marked in Henrik Ibsen's play, *The Wild Duck*. But while Wilson's ducklings were unequivocally good, here the duck's symbolic ambiguity is palpable; death is at once threat and temptation. Like Ekdal and Hialmar, the wild duck is a survivor:

> HEDVIG. She was hit under the wing so that she couldn't fly.
> GREGERS. And I suppose she dived to the bottom, eh?
> EKDAL. (sleepily, in a thick voice). Of course. Always do that, wild ducks do. They shoot to the bottom as deep as they can get, sir -- and bite themselves fast in the tangle and seaweed -- and all the devil's own mess that grows down there. And they never come up again.
> GREGERS. But your wild duck came up again, Lieutenant Ekdal.[9]

Ruined, disgraced, imprisoned, Ekdal held his pistol in his hand -- and did not shoot himself. Hialmar, his son, held his father's pistol to his own breast and likewise did not shoot: "But I can assure you it takes some courage to choose a life under circumstances like those." They are all survivors. The wild duck is the very image of death in life. (Gregers remarks, "So time has come to a standstill in there -- in the wild duck's domain?") The association is quite explicit:

> GREGERS. My dear Hialmar, I almost think you have something of the wild duck in you.
> HIALMAR. Something of the wild duck? How do you mean?
> GREGERS. You have dived down and bitten yourself fast in the undergrowth.
> HIALMAR. Are you alluding to the well-nigh fatal shot that has broken my father's wing -- and mine too?
> GREGERS. Not exactly to that. I don't say that your wing has been broken, but you have strayed into a poisonous marsh, Hialmar; an insidious disease has taken hold of you, and you have sunk down to die in the dark.
> HIALMAR. I? To die in the dark? Look here, Gregers, you must really leave off talking such nonsense.[10]

Ultimately, it is Hedvig, the child who had confessed, "I pray for the wild duck every night and ask that it may be preserved from death and all that is evil," who uses her grandfather's pistol to commit suicide. Though seemingly persuaded by Gregers to sacrifice her beloved duck in order to prove her love for her father, Hedvig chooses to sacrifice herself instead, and so ducks out for good.

The eminent French philosopher and historian Jean-Jacques Malart du Chateau du Val d'Anatides has investigated the conceptual and experiential links between the alterity of death and the alterity of the duck in his timely study, *Le Canard et l'esprit moderne*.[11] Recalling his resistance activities, he notes that this "*association mythique*" between death and ducks finds popular expression in American English. GIs under fire would shout, "Duck!", and those who survived would refer to themselves as "lucky ducks." Alois Entemann has argued, however, that Malart's work is descriptively inadequate. He writes that Malart "has failed to employ the phenomenological method in a rigorous manner." More Heideggerian than Husserlian, "he operates at best a partial *epoche* whose very intentionality is vitiated by his apparent confusion over the notion and nature of a true *Enteswesensschau* and by his total inability to handle such basic tools as the distinction between a *noesis* and a *noema*."[12] Clearly, to assess Malart's contribution to the literature in the bright light of Entemann's penetrating critique would involve us in questions of philosophical partisanship which lie beyond the scope of the present essay.[13] I must, however, concur when Entemann dismisses Malart's claim that Axis intelligence units actually trained pintails to maintain surveillance patterns over occupied cities; that is indeed "a flight of fancy."

To my knowledge, Freud nowhere writes of the duck *qua* duck. It is reasonable to suppose, however, that he would link the duck with those fabulous "bird-beaked creatures" which he associates with sex and death in recalling "a true anxiety dream."[14]

In significantly different ways, George Orwell and Saul Bellow use the duck as a metaphor to express irrationality. Their usage is admittedly metonymous: both center on the duck's quack. Their meaning, however, is unmistakable. Presenting the principles of Newspeak's "B" vocabulary in *1984*, Orwell explains, "Ultimately it was hoped to make articulate speech issue from the larynx without involving the higher brain centers at all. This aim was frankly admitted in the Newspeak word *duckspeak*, meaning 'to quack like a duck.' "[15] In *Herzog*, Bellow alludes to what we might call by comparison "deep quacking." His description confirms my thesis that the duck, though here a disembodied duck, represents a sort of vital nihilism:

> In the depths of a man's being there was something that responded with a quack to such perfume. Quack! A sexual reflex that had nothing to do with age or sublety, wisdom, experience, history, *Wissenschaft*, *Bildung*, *Wahrheit*. In sickness or health there came the old quack-quack at the fragrance of perfumed, feminine skin. [16].

To illustrate his argument that perception is active and in some measure arbitrary, that "seeing" is always "seeing as," Wittgenstein aptly chooses the celebrated line-drawing of the "duck-rabbit."[17] I have not addressed myself in this brief paper[18] to the rôle of the duck in animal stories, children's literature, fables, fairy tales, animated cartoons, or comic books, not because of a paucity of folkloric examples, but because I have preferred to limit my remarks to high culture. The reader is again referred to my earlier and more extensive writings on this fascinating subject.[19] Nonetheless, on the basis of the few philosophical and literary works I have considered in these pages, it appears that the duck is indeed a mythological object which reconciles opposites, a systematically ambiguous cultural construct which serves to express and to relieve the tension, the lived and living contradiction, between two natures. Nature's beauty and innocence are marred by its ugliness and savagery; man too is now noble, now base. Sex is good, but dangerous; death, a tempting threat. The duck is a risible creature which represents and so reduces such contradictions. Or, to cite Malart's recent pedagogical manifesto, *"Le canard est partout. Engagez-vous!"*[20]

[1]This study was funded by a grant from my wife.

[2]Claude Levi-Strauss, *Du Miel aux cendres*, Paris, Plon, 1966, p. 179.

[3]*The Journals of R. Drakeson-Smythe, Jr.*, LXVII (127.9a-11e), entry dated June 23, 1973 (microfiche). This entry ends with an outburst of unusual violence: an unmarked series of rhyming, monosyllabic expletives. Despite its remarkable sound pattern, which approaches the aesthetic purity of ritual drumbeats and native chants, propriety forbids my citing the entry *in toto*.

[4]Philip Lawton, "Webbèd Footnotes; The Duck in Contemporary Western Thought," in the present issue of *The Journal of Irreproducible Results*.

[5]See *inter alia* Vladimir Anasdocent, "Duck Hunting in Harvard Square," *Rod and Rifle Illustrated*, May 25, 1968, pp. 93-127.

[6]I have examined this subject at greater length in *Ducks, Demons, and Deities; A Modest Contribution to Cultural Anthropology, Comparative Literature, and the History of Ideas* (1965). I have responded to my critics' animadversions in my article, "Ruffled Feathers," which appeared in *Sophisphronterion: Proceedings of the Federation of Logico-Philosophical, Philological, and Physiocosmogonic Societies* (Greater Pawtucket Division), 1966, and in the two volumes of my forthcoming autobiography, respectively entitled *Quackup!* and *Phoenix*.

[7]Edmund Wilson, "The Man Who Shot Snapping Turtles," *Memoirs of Hecate County*, New York, Signet, 1961, pp. 10-11. My emphasis. It is with deep personal satisfaction that I call the reader's attention to Stryker's "obsession" with ducks; it was a similar involvement in my work which led to my regrettable dismissal from a prestigious chair.

[8]*Ibid.*, p. 14.

[9]Henrik Ibsen, *The Wild Duck*, in *3 Plays by Ibsen*, New York, Dell (Laurel), 1966, p. 244. The translator is (mercifully) not identified.

[10]*Ibid.*, p. 264.

[11]Geel, 1974.

[12]See A. Entemann, "Ist Malart Verruckt Geworden?" *Psychologische Rundschau*, XXI, no. 3 (Oktober, 1975), pp. 88-90.

[13]See above, fn. 4.

[14]Sigmund Freud, *The Interpretation of Dreams*, trans. James Strachey, New York, Avon, 1968, p. 622 *seq.*

[15]George Orwell, *1984*, New York, New American Library (Signet Classics), 1949, p. 254.

[16]Saul Bellow, *Herzog*, Greenwich, Ct., Fawcett Crest, 1964, p. 34.

[17]Ludwig Wittgenstein, *Philosophical Investigations*, Second Edition, trans. G.E.M. Anscombe, New York, Macmillan, 1958, IIxi, p. 194. I am grateful to my former Dean of Faculty for this reference.

[18]See above, fn. 13.

[19]See above, fn. 6.

[20]Keynote Address to the Western Massachusetts Society of Tenured Humanities Professors (Committee on Research and Publications), Easter, 1976.

Freshman Medical Students

1. genorhea	16. gonnorheae	1. siphalis
2. ghannohreae	17. gonnorrhea	2. siphlius
3. ghonoreah	18. gonohrea	3. siphylis
4. ghonorhea	19. gonoreha	4. sphyllus
5. gohnorrea	20. gonorehaea	5. syhphillus
6. gohnorrhea	21. gonorehea	6. syphalis
7. gomnorrea	22. gonorhea	7. syphilas
8. gonarreah	23. gonorhhea	8. syphilis
9. gonerea	24. gonorihea	9. syphillis
10. gonerrhea	25. gonorrahea	10. syphillus
11. gonherraea	26. gonorrea	11. syphilus
12. gonhorrea	27. gonorrhea	12. syphis
13. gonnerrhea	28. gonorrheae	13. syphless
14. gonnohrrea	29. gonorrhee	14. syphlis
15. gonnorhea	30. gonorrhera	15. syphliss
		16. syphlys
		17. syphylis
		18. syphyllis
		19. syphyllus

Submitted by Dorothy Branson, PhD., Microbiologist, Grant Hospital, 309 E. State Street, Columbus, Ohio 43215.

Musings of an aging "SCIENTIST"

RUSSELE de WAARD
Old Greenwich, Conn.

To an astute reader the title ("Scientist") is sufficient to set the mood for this document.

Ever since I can remember I have been insecure. When I was small I worried and worried that my slingshot would break and I would never find another tree branch to make a new one. This attitude has persisted until today. I get interested and work hard on something and it seems to me at the time that I have done a good job. The results of my work are printed and distributed among my peers. I go home that night quite satisfied and feeling good, but by the end of the next day I am concerned that I could have done a better job. By the second day I am convinced that most of what I wrote was wrong and I feel quite stupid. This is an example, which repeats itself over and over. I am quite convinced that I was apprehensive as a fetus. Although my failing memory doesn't confirm it, at that stage I probably worried about a kink in the umbilical cord.

I don't know whether to blame this deficiency on my genes, my chromosomes or my upbringing. But in the latter category, I have made a few observations. I have been taught to respect authority; when the Department Head says I am wrong, I am wrong. Since I did not go to MIT, I reason miserably, that Edgar Slack, my teacher at BPI, must have been wrong. On These occasions I take his book (Haussman & Slack) into the men's room to see if I might have misread it.

What one has to learn is that all the laws of physics are repealed by authority. Hence, if one speaks with authority, from a recognized box in the company organization chart, he is perforce believed. These things have only very recently come to me, but I don't know what to do about it. If I am lucky this draft will not be published and my discovery will go "undiscovered." My position is a bit like that of Galileo in the 15th century when his telescope told him beyond a doubt that the world was round and was rotating about the sun, but his friends told him to keep his big mouth shut or the Pope would feed him to the lions. I like to eat and to drink and not to rock the boat, so I think I'll do what Galileo did, unless tomorrow morning I ask Bobby to type this tape. The latter is unlikely since overnight my apprehension will return.

The funny part about all this is that when I go out on a sailing ship all my chicken-hearted propensities dissolve into the sea and I become a soul-mate of Captain Horatio Hornblower. The trouble is that none of the fellows in authority are along, and I curse at the wind and the waves to no avail.

If I keep on like I'm going, I might make three score and five, and if by that time I don't continue to spike my vodka martini with lemonade, I may have worked up enough gumption to say "no, I won't shut up, you sit down and listen for a change" to one of the fellows in the boxes. ∎

MANAGEMENT INTERACTION
The Pedagogy of Group Process in Middle Management
A Xenophobic View of THE Meeting

William J. Tobin[1]
Fort Collins, CO[2]

It has been propounded[3] in the recent literature on the styles of management that *The meeting* is perhaps the second most important function that an upper level manager accomplishes[4]. To insure his subordinates still recognize him, a popular new philosophy has evolved: 'management by wandering around'. This then fits neatly into the 'One Minute Manager' and ultimately the "30 Second Employee". However, *The meeting* has still retained its place as a corner stone of any well entrenched PBB[5].

The dynamics of meetings i.e., whether the table is round or rectangular, as well as the importance of the leader (Does he have overhead slides? Are they in color? Are the handouts neatly bound like a Gutenberg Bible or something that just came from Quick-Print?), the quality of the munchies at break as well as how many secretaries are present to take notes; have been cited extensively[6] as vital components of *The meeting*. However, these observations are not new. Citations in the literature of the early Dark Ages indicate the dynamics of meetings and the possibilities of overhead projectors were discussed by a little known holy order[7] who are credited to have written the first[8] treatises on the subject.

Meetings, quite like chess games can be reduced to a series of Ploys, Assertions, Rules, and Strategies whose sole purpose is to put the player into a winning posture. It was further found in extensive studies of upper level managers[9] that WHAT was accomplished was less important than WHO came out the winner[10]. Quite like Murphy's Laws, the list becomes endless. It is hoped in future scholarly publications the readership might further expand this Corpus Intellecti. The author has reduced these ploys to a title or description (in capital letters), what it does or what is said (in quotes), followed by what it really means.

MANAGEMENT INTERACTION— Experimental Observations

Ploys Used in Meetings

The Rules of the Game Ploy: "We have ethics that a business like ours must uphold." Fairness should only be called for when losing.

The General Custer Ploy (Also known as the Little Big Horn Defense): "Custer had a plan!" Plans made that don't consider all options, can and do fail.

The Icarus Ploy: "Just because it is impossible today, doesn't mean we can't invent it tomorrow!" Some things just aren't possible.

The Earl Scheib Ploy: "I can paint this car for $29.95." Focus attention on the budget and not the quality of the product.

The Army Recruitment Ploy: "We need volunteers for our new off-shore office." Selection process filters out all but the new or naive.

The Robin Hood Ploy: "Divert management perks to productivity bonuses for the workers." Quick elimination for the heretic with innovative thinking.

---

[1]The author's Ph.D. from Yale was part of the inheritance from his father's estate. His alma matter, the Unicuse of Syraversity, has repeatedly denied granting a Honorary Doctorate in return for an immodest contribution to the school's building fund.

[2]Fort Collins (to paraphrase Benny Hill) isn't really a place, but an altered state of mind; where the essence of the author is still trying to remember his **mantra**.

[3]*The Importance of Management Puffery in Meetings.* M. Iococca, Senior Consultant of the Management Firm of Howey Overchargem Inc. presented at the March 1985 meeting of *Society of Management Consultants and Government Bureaucrats* in Bosmen MT.

[4]The most important management function being *where* to have lunch. *The Art of the Management Decision* - C.G. Skinner, *Journal of Highly Deviant Juvenile Behavior*, February 1987, pp. 99-103.

[5]PPB stands for *Phoney-Boloney-Bureaucracy.* A classification developed from *Classifications of the FORTUNE 5000 by Management Style* - U. Leary, 1956 unpublished; because of the National Secrets Act of 1934, and an obscure by law of the American Management Association.

[6]*Graduate from "B" school and publish a best selling book!* - W. Milbin, an unpublished article, continually presented to the scholarly press and perpetually rejected.

[7]*Vox Derelicti* is the only surviving body of work from the Order of Monks and Bureaucrats (commonly referred to in Government circles as the *OMB*). Father Flatisimus con Fruitti founded this teaching order in 563 A.D. to provide middle level manager/monks to administer the extensive Church holdings of the time. To cut overhead costs he proposed making the Host from thinly sliced deep fried potatoes instead of the baking of unleavened bread. For this heresy, he and the other members of his order were (not without poetic justice) put into boiling oil and ultimately burned at the stake (hence coining the phrase "out of the frying pan, into the fire"). Because his was the only Order to be cursed by the church hierarchy they are remembered for the name given to the low level bureaucrats of the Forest: the ChipMonks.

[8]Recently, (1984) a purported earlier work was presented to The Society for Errata as being the foundation for *Vox Derelicti.* This work, *Perpetuatus Ad Nauseum,* was deemed to be a hoax when it was revealed to have been discovered during the building of the Pro Rodeo Hall of Fame, in Colorado Springs, Colorado. No valid proof could be provided that intelligent life ever existed in that ZIP Code much less able to write Latin without a Texas accent ('Ya-allis ingestus non defecatus' - Testicles - an early Etruscan philosopher from Lubbock). The Society further ignored the fact it was written on thermal paper.

[9]*Management Puffery* Op Cit, Iococca et. Al.

[10]"*Deceit and Treachery: The Key to Beating Youth in Today's Business Environment*" - S. Bali, AD HOC PRESS, 1987, pp. 314-392.

The Six Wives of Henry The VII Ploy: "If you loved me you'd do it my way." Cooperation from those who remain alive.

The Pet Rock Ploy: "Say nothing, do nothing". Poses no threat to anyone thereby becoming prime management material.

The John Paul Jones Ploy: "I have not yet begun to fight". Declaration of your defenses promotes attack from the rear.

The George Orwell Ploy: "Big brother is watching". When management is visibly present; performance is mediocre. When gone, performance is totally absent.

The Pearl Harbor Ploy (Also called the Maginot Line Defense): "We'll invest all our technology in one area and no one will dare to attack us". Assume your plan is invulnerable, consider no contingencies, hope for the best. (See Nixon Defense).

Defenses Used Against Ploys

The Nuremberg Defense: "I was only following orders". Denial of all responsibility and liability.

The Vietnam Defense: "Regardless of the status of the project, declare it a success and leave". Project ends without success.

The Nixon Defense (Also called the Prime Contractor Ploy): "Deny all allegations, demand proof". Send accusers back to gather data, allows time to destroy evidence.

The Einstein Defense (Also called the R&D Defense): "E = mc², call with questions". Blames failure of the practical application on someone else.

The Alfred Packer Defense: "Eat the evidence". Without documentation the investigation is fruitless. However, your name is remembered.

The Goliath Defense: Mine's bigger than yours". The bigger they are, the harder they hit.

The Hitler Defense: "Claim to be right based solely on your job title, work experience or sex". Shifts arguments from objective issues.

The Six Million Dollar Man Technology Assumption: "We can build it, we have the technology". Exorbitant expense on useless products.

ASSUMPTIONS AND APPROACHES —
Used to Formulate Meeting Agendas

The Abraham Lincoln Assumption: "The world will little note nor long remember what we say here, but it can *never* forget what was done". People's actions are soon forgotten after the project is cancelled. Memos however, are kept forever.

The Beatles Assumption: "All you need is love". No one does any significant work, however everyone has a good time.

The Gary Gilmore Approach: "Sacrifice yourself publicly for the good of the company". After the sacrifice is complete, its purpose is quickly forgotten.

The Johnny Carson Approach: "Staff the department with personnel whose jobs depend directly on YOUR personal success". A highly loyal and dependable base of support, regardless of competency.

The Three Stooges Approach: "Bungle any assignment, no matter how simple". Unemployment while working in the private sector, Job security/promotion if in government service.

The Benedict Arnold Approach: "Sell company secrets to the competition". Two incomes for a short period of time.

STRATEGIES, ASSERTIONS AND EDICTS —
The Tools of a Skillful Meeting attendee

The Star Trek Strategy: "Use technology to 'beam' out of hazardous situations". This situation tends to catch up to the problem.

The Evel Knievel Strategy: "Capitalize on one spectacular performance". Executive management wants more of the same on a daily basis.

The Pontius Pilate Strategy: "Give us Barabus!" When someone is to be sacrificed, the 'players' go free while the 'true believers' get crucified.

The John Kennedy Assertion: "Ask NOT what your company can do for you, but what you can do for your company!" Disillusionment and panic.

The Isaac Newton Assertion: "What goes up, comes down". Those at the bottom get hit the hardest.

The Marie Antoinette Assertion: "Let them eat cake!" Make sure all problems relating to the project get side tracked by complaining about the food service.

The Ronald Reagan Assertion: "Confuse everyone with absurdity". Acceptance by those who think they know what you're talking about, and compliance by everyone else too afraid to say they don't understand.

The Rubic's Cube Assertion: "Present interesting problems that do not relate to the project's goals". Opponents waste time feverishly working on objections to unrelated problems.

PRINCIPLES, DECLARATIONS AND GIVENS —
The Building Blocks of Absurdity

The Nathan Hale Principle of Promotability: "I regret I have only one life to dedicate to this company". Mindless devotion identifies management potential.

The Lee Iacocca Declaration: "We're the greatest, if you can find a better job, take it!" Mass exodus from the company.

The Billy Graham Given: "The Lord will provide". Diverts employee attention from the payroll cutbacks to the cafeteria.

The Machiavelli Principle: "Destroy all potential opponents to the project". No remaining work force.

The Ten Commandments Management Principle: "Present the project, assume it is perfectly clear, then leave without asking for questions". Most commandments are broken.

The Night of the Living Dead Principle: "Co-worker is promoted to management". Friendly contact ceases, relationship as adversaries begins.

The Karl Marx Payroll Principle: "From each according to his ability, to each according to his need". Compensation philosophy is defined only by contribution to the company unless it is a divorced female with dependent children.

The F.D.R. Declaration: "You have nothing to fear but fear itself". Rumors run rampant.

The Ben Franklin Assertion: "A penny saved is a penny earned". Focuses attention on the budget rather than the project results.

The Patrick Henry Assertion: "Give me liberty or give me death". Funeral services will be held next Tuesday.

The Superman Syndrome: "Come to the rescue of the project at the last minute without asking for anything in return". Job security in present position, no hope for future career enhancement.

The Peter Pan Syndrome of Marketing: "Lets plan the kick off party in the Bahamas. . ." Marketing gets the gold mine, manufacturing gets the shaft.

ACKNOWLEDGMENTS

The author would like to thank Mr. Robert Bell - who viewed meetings as the best cure for insomnia since barbiturates; and Mr. Fred Mathews - whose work with the author was so obvious, his employer requested he continue to pursue his research on someone else's payroll.

Author's note: Academia may find it appropriate to do ersatz research in data collection by assigning a degree of difficulty to each Ploy then determine a point value (using the Bo Derek scale of 0 to 10) on how well it was actually used. By multiplying the two together this kind of gamesmanship can not only be tolerated, it can be scored. The overall importance of the meeting can be measured by the magnitude of the total points compared to similar meetings. Preliminary results, obtained by using volunteers from the Sisterhood of Blond Stenographers local 613 who kept score while supposedly taking notes on a portable computer; have been able to convert heretofore subjective observations into irrelevant statistical data. Further work on this subject cannot proceed without a substantial grant to the author from either government or Private Industry soiurces, so that a replication study can be carried out in Maui.

About the Author: Up until publishing this article, Bill Tobin was gainfully employed as a Materials Specialist in Fort Collins, Colorado. When not suffering from the delusion that he is a writer, he lives happily in Fort Collins, Colorado with his wife and three perfect children.

Life Cycle Costing of Selected Careers

Grants Magazine, Vol. 7, No. 1, March 1984, by Robert A. Lucas, San Luis Obispo, CA

A study, supported by the Department of Labor, explored the cost/benefit ratio of 48 of our society's most common professions. The study considered all those elements of a career, not simply salary. It examined the amount and cost of education necessary, time spent in class, internship requirements, capital costs, annual overhead, probability of success, tax shelter possibilities, stress and health effects, and impact on family life and quality of living.

When all life quality elements had been factored in, one career emerged as having a clear edge in each category. It was bank robbery.

This finding was confirmed by another study that reported that the average bank robber is apprehended during his or her eighteenth heist. Given that the risk of apprehension increases geometrically, the likelihood of being arrested during the first three jobs is really quite small, only .03. When this is compared to the failure rate of new franchises (.13), new small businesses (.21) and new restaurants (.64), the cost/benefit ratio appears appealing indeed.

The program is also self insured: if it fails, living expenses are automatically picked up by the government.

Submitted by. **Joseph G. Dinopfsky**
Port Jefferson Station, NY

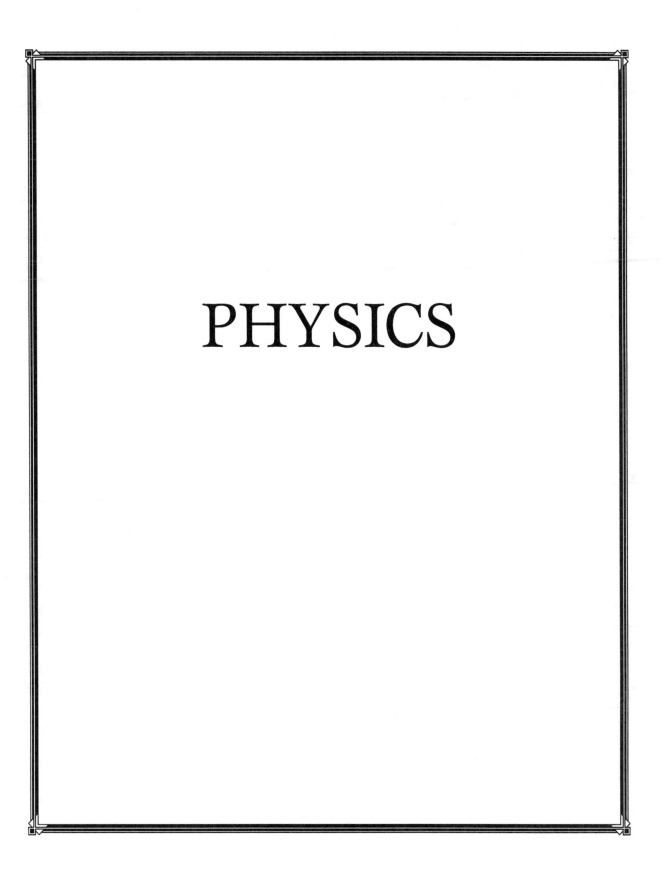

PHYSICS

Physics Non-Department First To Photograph New Element*

Ellin Beltz
Chicago, IL

The first photograph of crystals of a newly discovered element were taken using special equipment developed by Physics Non-Department Professors recently, according to a press release distributed by University Disinformation Tuesday.

The element, called administrontium by its discoverers at California M&M University, is the heaviest element yet discovered by scientists. Created in their massive confusion reactor, the element has no protons or electrons and an atomic number of zero. However, it has one neutron, 125 assistant neutrons, 75 vice-neutrons and 111 assistant vice-neutrons giving it an atomic mass of 312. The higher level particles are held together by a continuous exchange of meson-like particles called morons, while lower level particles are held together by peons. The absence of electrons precludes covalent or ionic bonding, but administrontium has a different form of bonding, referred to by some California M&M workers as a sort of "old boy network"or male bonding.

Dr. Inrico Squirmi of the Physics Non-Department said that the discovery of administrontium answers questions long unsolved by physicists such as why certain reactions take immeasurably longer in atoms with high numbers of neutrons. He said it appears that even elemental samples considered "pure" may contain traces of ad-ministrontium. "Even a little administrontium is enough to slow down a simple reaction," he said, adding that one reaction which should occur in less than a second required over four days to complete after exposure to administrontium.

Squirmi explained that since administrontium has no electrons it is chemically inert and has a normal half-life of approximately three years. However, administrontium does not actually decay in three years, but undergoes a reorganization during which the assistant neutrons, vice-neutrons, and assistant vice-neutrons exchange places. He added that the atomic number may actually increase after each reorganization although scientists have never been able to find the additional neutrons but their presence can be inferred by an increase in mass and inertia.

California M&M scientists reported that they found administrontium occurring naturally, once they knew the unusual nature of the element. It has been found most

---

* *Reproduced with Permission from the Northeastern Independent at Northeastern Illinois University*

significantly in excellently appointed office buildings in the Western nations, South American, Africa and parts of Asia. In addition, archaeologists have discovered concentrations of it in the ruins of Egyptian and Chinese cities. Russian scientists report that levels of administrontium in Moscow actually fell slowly after the Chernobyl disaster, according to sources in the former Soviet Academies of Science. American researchers point out, however, that the Russian results have not been confirmed by independent testing.

Another Physics professor at this institution, Dr. Far Out Om, said that although administrontium has been considered toxic in any concentration since it slows or destroys productive reactions, new research indicates that the pathway of its effects is similar to that of calcium/strontium replacement. "Administrontium replaces the skeleton, if you will," he said, "It is a very, very nice reaction. Very slow, but irreversible." He added "Once administrontium takes over, you will never, never get rid of it, no matter how much money you can spend."

According to work done slowly by the National Institutes of Disease in Bedstead, Maryland, administrontium can decay into a compound they have named bureaucratritium. The toxic effects produced by bureaucratritium result in headaches, dizziness, bloating, an insatiable appetite, massive weight gains, inability to concentrate on work, compulsive copying and faxing, and eventually paralysis which ends after 15, 20 or 25 years. Persons suffering from bureaucratritium exposure are recommended to take jobs in small, private companies, where its effects can be mitigated by enterprise, initiative, and risk-taking.

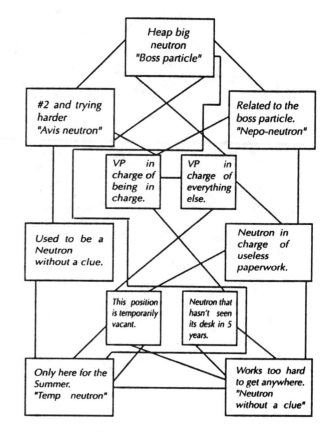

Crystalline structure of pure elemental sample of administrontium, atomic mass 312.
Photo by Physics Non-Department.

B.O. Koopman
FALLACIES IN OPERATIONS RESEARCH
Operations Research 1956, 4, 422-426

"AUTHORITIS is that regression to logical infantilism which believes that missing links in one's solution of a problem, as well as the missing common sense required for relating it to reality, can be readily supplied by the ... company executive who must eventually use the results."

****

JOURNAL COVERAGE CHANGES
Current Contents (Oct. 31, 1973)
   Bulletin of Suicidology (ceased publication)

Static Electricity

Not in every essay that appears in a medical journal can the reader immediately distinguish between creative imagination and ineluctable fact. For decades I believed that such submissions of mine that editors did not reject (as well as some they did) mirrored the world as it is. But the time comes when you concur with Mark Twain that you remember everything, whether it happened or not.

The foregoing is a politic introduction to the medical science here recounted. Some alleged experiences are more safely represented as apocryphal, or even fanciful, rather than as holy writ.

Harvey, a proctologist, was a good friend of Dale's. They exchanged appropriate patients and often served each other as consultants. A first rate practitioner and a Christian gentleman dedicated to Hippocrates, Harvey had but one conspicuous fault. He used nine hundred words where fifty would suffice.

Harvey phoned Dale one afternoon to discuss a patient he wanted Dale to see. He described the case, the treatment that had failed, and the family history for three generations. Circumstantial. As Dale listened, he squirmed, drummed his fingers, and surmised he might cure the fellow in the time Harvey took talking about him. Dale knew better than to interrupt. Harvey would start over, and Dale would have to say "yes" anyway. They agreed to meet next morning at the patient's home.

It was a summer morning, hot and sultry, before the era of air conditioning. The patient was bedfast with a rare muscular dystrophy, unable to roll over from his supine position. Between his thighs the skin was macerated, clearly the result of sweat, infection, and poor ventilation.

He and Harvey were engrossed in discussing the evils of static electricity. An Ozark friend of the patient's had treated himself for rheumatiz by running copper wire down his walking stick from handle to tip so that each step achieved electrical discharge, and the rheumatiz largely dissipated after only a few years.

This conversation was animated, ridiculous, and interminable. Dale's schedule was tight, he couldn't break in. Looking about, he noted the patient's teenage son at a desk, puttering with ham radio apparatus that included a coil of bare copper antenna wire.

Dale walked over to the boy, requisitioned the wire, made a loose coil of it the size of a fist, placed this gently next to the sore skin between the buttocks, and fastened the far end to a radiator.

THE LINE STORM, by John Steuart Curry, from the collection of Mr. & Mrs. Sidney Howard, NY.

"Your troubles are near the end," he explained, "for static electricity has been eliminated. Your anus is now grounded." Harvey's mouth opened, but no words came out.

I know of no other such case in which this plan of treatment has been essayed, and so I cannot provide statistical substantiation of its efficacy. Here it was beneficial, Dale told me. Aeration was improved, such copper ions as dissolved into the exudate may have been antimicrobial, and the patient was overjoyed.

Only indolence explains, but cannot condone, the absence of double blind investigations, so simple in design and luminous in discrimination—string for wire, chair for radiator, ear for scrotum—generating research grants for decades.

The cost of the wire at that time was $2.00 or so per 100 feet. I do not know what the Food and Drug Administration would think nowadays, but I believe such wire nontoxic and nonallergenic, so used.

"If a patient of mine wants electricity out, I see to it that it is out," Dale said. "I would probably demur if I were asked to ground the wire to a lightning rod."

I seldom confide Dale's story to a lay audience. Their concern is so distracted by the woes of the patient that they do not apprehend the triumph of the deliverance. ■

*Emeritus Clinical Professor of Medicine, University of Kansas

Richard L. Sutton, Jr.*
Leawood, KS

Ineffective Lagrangians and the Big Ba[n]g

Harry J. Lipkin
Rehovot, Israel

Recently there have been many attempts to simplify the treatment of complicated problems by the use of so-called "effective Lagrangians." However, most of these fail to provide the desired physical result. It is therefore more appropriate to call them "Ineffective Lagrangians." We denote such as Ineffective Lagrangian by $\mathcal{L}$ineff, and define the associated inaction as:

$$S_{inac} = \int \mathcal{L}_{ineff} dt \qquad (1)$$

The use of ineffective Lagrangians leads to the Principle of Least Inaction. As soon as a Lagrangian is seen to be ineffective, the inaction must be minimized by a flurry of activity as preprints and papers are written one after another to demonstrate the ineffectiveness of $\mathcal{L}$ineff.

In QCD the Ineffective Lagrangian is usually expressed in terms of ineffective field variables called gluons and quarks. The exact meaning of the word gluon is not clear, as it cannot be found in any dictionary. The word quark, however, can be found in any German dictionary, and this is a typical example of what one finds there.

Quark, m., curd, curds; slime, slush, filth; (fig.) trifle, rubbish, trash...

So why should anyone be interested in this kind of junk? This is a good question.

Some physicists believe that quarks and gluons are peculiar objects which will never be observed because they are confined in bags and cannot get out. This has led to a new theory of the origin of the universe based on a new ineffective Lagrangian $\mathcal{L}$ineff (MITBAG) in which the world began, not with a whimper, but with a bag. The proponents of this theory believe that it must be given equal time with theories of evolution and creationism in the public school curricula. These people believe that in the beginning God created the bag at the center of the universe. (Some heretics attempted to claim that the original bag was created at a place called SLAC, but these are not considered seriously any more).

There are various versions of this new creationism, in which God put all the matter now in the universe into this bag and began to inflate it until it burst with a Big Bang. In one version the bag originally contained nothing but tohu and vohu rishons until God created the photon by typing the command "let there be light" into his computer terminal. This version is supported by the Old Testament, whose reliability has been questioned. In the fundamentalist creationist version, God created a hierarchy by fine tuning, and any attempt to tamper with this hierarchy or to impose Altarelli-Parisi Darwinism upon it is a heresy to be fought at all costs. All troubles began with the original sin of eating apples from the tree of knowledge which led to the questioning of the God-given M.I.T. BAG and attempts to replace it with a nonabelian guage theory which could prove confinement.

This confinement broke down when Monte Carlo calculations based on lattice guage theories showed that the system could not be in a confining phase. All attempts to obtain confinement by adjusting parameters and by introducing new Higgses, Schmiggses, Technicrats, Monopoles, Instantons, Tumbling, Mumbling, Plaquettes, Tree Diagrams, Wilson Loops, Supersymmetries, Chiral Invariance, Neutrino and Neutron Oscillations, Topological Solitons, Solitary Confinement, Marxism, Leninism, Reggeism, CP Violations, Human Rights Violations, Scaling Violations, Seniority, Sabbath Observance, Proton Decay and Grand Unifications failed to avert the eventual catastrophe. The universe exploded giving rise to the presently observed expansion and the $3°$ radiation. This theory explains why those who believe that the M.I.T. BAG explains everything also believe that M.I.T. is the center of the universe.

Another point of view, known as the "Weinberg angle" states that the principal effect of the First Three Minutes was the displacement of the center of the universe from MIT to Texas. A more recent version has kept the center of inflation at MIT and canonized the worship of the True Vacuum with admonitions against the heresy of the False Vacuum.

The Vacuum-Worshipers believe that In the Beginning God created the absolute perfect vacuum, and that the Original Sin was the first leak. They build temples to their god, the vacuum, in which they attempt to get as close to the all-perfect vacuum as possible. In one type of temple, called an acceleraltar, particles accelerated to very high energies are given as offerings to the god, in the hope that god's reward will be all kinds of new discoveries. In another, called a stellar shrine, the vacuum is filled with plasmas and magnetic fields in the belief that the god will furnish unlimited quantities of energy if he is pleased. So far no one has succeeded in obtaining any energy from a stellar shrine but these primitive people still cling to their superstitions and refuse to learn from experience.

Another sect of vacuum worshipers, called Higgsists, expect great things from their god and spend their time in learned discussions and in writing long treatises about the values of these vacuum expectations.

This new religion has been violently criticized by the moral majority. They see it as an attempt by an immoral minority to insert religion into science and to replace the holy trinity (which of course were white) by an unholy colored trinity of QCD quarks, and introducing the pagan worship of the Sun and Moon in a new Grand Unification Church. They have their own Grand Unification Mass instead of the Catholic Mass and have replaced the New Testament Gospels of the Birth and Death of the Son at Christmas and Easter by heretical gospels about the birth and Death of the Sun from a New Treatment based on the Ineffective Lagrangian $\mathcal{L}_{\text{ineff}}[SO(N)]$ in which the name of the Son is written as SO(N). The veiled attempt to hide the pagan sun worship is exposed when the Ineffective Lagrangian is written in the form $\mathcal{L}_{\text{ineff}}[SU(N)]$ in which the name of the Sun God appears as SU(N).

One day a few years ago I walked into my dentist's office and looked through an old German magazine while waiting. I was surprised to find a quark staring back at me in a full-page advertisement showing a big picture of a potato with an enormous topping of a white cheese, and the legend "Hmm - Kartoffel mit Quark Aus Deutschen Landen Frisch auf dem Tisch" (Hmm - Potato with Quark - from German lands fresh on the table). So this is the ultimate building block of nature! When I was a boy, people used to say that the moon was made of green cheese. Now man has gone to the moon and we know better. Today some physicists say that all matter is made of these quarks. Perhaps in another few decades we will know better about this, too.

COMPOSITION NUMBER 3, by Kandinsky, The Museum of Modern Art, New York

THE SHORT-LIVED PHENOMENON OF THE PIEZO-PHOTIC EFFECT

Bobby Matherne
Methairie, LA

Table 1.

Type of Crystal	Color of Flash	Intensity
1. Lifesavers, Wintergreen	Green	Highest
2. Lifesavers, Fruit Flavors	Green	Very Low
3. Certs	Green	High
4. Ludens Cough-drops	Green	Medium

Under laboratory conditions of total darkness with the human eyes completely dark-adapted (or in the back seat at a drive-in movie), crunching Wintergreen Lifesavers causes green flashes of light to be emitted inside of the mouth. When this was first brought to my attention by my female companion who conducted much of the early research in this area, being fond of both back seats and Lifesavers, I began to be profoundly puzzled. Nowhere in my physics background could I recall any effect whereby the mechanical manipulation of a crystal produced photons. Since the mechanical stressing of certain quartz, tourmaline, and rochelle salt crystals produced electricity, called the piezo-electric effect, this must be a type of hitherto undiscovered piezo-photic effect.

Thus I began my literature search in the library of the city of Commerce nearby to where I was working. To my evergrowing elation, there was no mention of any references to piezo-photic effect. The possibility that I had stumbled upon an undiscovered physical phenomenon began to take hold of me, so I decided it was time to go into the laboratory to experiment with the effect.

My companion and I went to the nearest Alpha Beta and purchased one of every kind of hard crystalline candy that was available to begin our work. About midnite (after the kids were asleep so they wouldn't think we were weird) we began to crunch each of the various crystals while keeping a record of the type of crystal and the intensity of the light flashes emitted. To preserve our teeth, we used a pecan cracker to simulate the action of our jaws, while permitting an unobstructed view of the flashing. One factor adding to the difficulty of recording the results was that in order to see the flashes, our eyes needed to be dark adapted-if we turned on a light in order to record our observations, it was several minutes before we could see the flashes again. In spite of the complications, we did obtain the results displayed in Table 1:

The color of the flashes were always green, Wintergreen Lifesavers appeared to produce the brightest flashes, and opaque crystals such as Certs produced higher intensity light flashes than clear crystals such as Fruit Flavored Lifesavers.

IMPLICATIONS

The implications of having crystals that produce light upon the application of mechanical force were enormous. I began to imagine mixing the Lifesaver crystals with piezo-electric crystals to produce crystals that emitted light when an electric field is applied. By arranging a large plane of these crystals, we would have a solid state graphics display.

TRIBO-LUMINESCENCE

Unfortunately, I telephoned a former professor of mine who was at Cal Poly and asked him if he knew of any such effect as I was researching. No, but he gave me the name of an expert in the field who would know if such an effect existed. Sure enough, I called the person he suggested and the thick accented voice on the other end of the phone line informed me that the effect I was describing had been discovered by a French researcher in 1925. The only publication of the effect was in an untranslated article in the Bulletin of the French Mineralogical Society, Vol. 48, 1925, p. 130-214. The name given to the effect was Tribo-luminescence and the flashes were caused by ion-exchange with the atmosphere of the new, clean surfaces produced when certain crystals were destroyed by mechanical manipulation.

CONCLUSION

Thus was I led full circle back to the discovery that the effect was perfectly suited for producing weird green flashes in your mouth in the back seat at a drive-in while waiting for the movie to start. ∎

The Feline Moment: Phenomenon Notes

R. J. Allen, Ph.D.,
Seattle, WA

Introduction

It has been well established that cats dropped from a height will alight upright and on all four paws upon impact with the tera firma, regardless of the initial orientation (P_o) of their vertical body axis (Garfield, 1953). The descending body is observed to rotate during free fall, in a manner suggesting the existence of a theoretical "feline moment vector" (μf). The feline moment reaches a state of "catatonic equilibrium" when its moment vector is in line with the attracting body's gravitational field (Morris, 1983).

Two fundamental issues remain unanswered with regard to this phenomenon. First, can the rotation of cats falling towards earth be described mathematically as a function of the theoretical feline moment vector?

Second, what is the underlying mechanism which gives rise to this dynamic alignment behavior?

Nature of the Phenomenon

A useful analog for understanding the feline moment is the magnetic moment vector produced by a current flowing through a wire loop in a magnetic field.* When current is flowing through the loop, a theoretical vector is created at right angles to the plane of the loop, emanating from its geometric center. The behavior of this current carrying loop in a magnetic field is such that it will try to align its vector with the magnetic field lines, thus rotating the loop with a quantifiable torque, yet resulting in a net force of zero on the loop itself.

---

* The magnetic moment vector analogy is not without historical precedence. According to Cheshire (1982), early attempts to explain this phenomenon (from Catalonia in northeastern Spain) involved magnetism. These early Catalans, familiar with the behavior of a thin iron compass needle to align itself with the earth's magnetic field, speculated an iron based physical element within the cat produced this gravitational alignment vector. They therefore labeled it the "Fe - line," from which we inherit the contemprary labeling for the animal family.

Such is the feline moment. The feline moment vector strives to align itself with gravitational lines of force. If a cat is released from a height, say antiparallel to the field, it will rotate until its moment vector is aligned with the field. When the feline vector is parallel and in the same direction to the local gravitational field, the body is in the previously mentioned, minimum potential energy, state of catatonic equilibrium (Morris, 1983) and rotation will cease (see Figure 1).

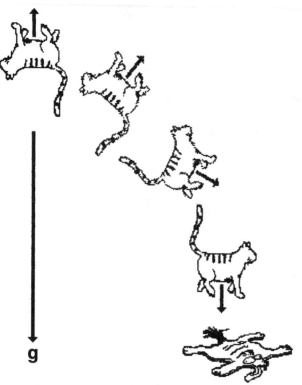

Figure 1. *Rotation of Free Falling Cat Due To Moment Vector*

Just as the flow of current is essential for the magnetic moment to exist within the wire loop, evidence suggests the cat must be alive for the feline moment to exist. In his classic investigation, Sylvester (1927) observed hundreds of falling cats, both alive and dead at the moment of release. Release heights (Y_O) ranged from one to five-hundred meters and release angles (θ_o) from antiparallel (180^0) to parallel (0^0). Living cats consistently rotated to the catatonic equilibrium position prior to impact. Dead cats displayed no gravitational alignment rotation, maintaining θ_o until impact with no observable rotation, except for the occasional effects of wind sheer on bodies released from some of the higher elevations ($Y_O > 200m$). Existence of the feline moment is thus dependent upon some force or process within the body of a living cat.

Canary, et al. (1985) report an interesting observation related to average angular velocity of the rotating cat. Independent of height (above lower limits determined by the radius of the cat), and independent of θ_o, falling cats all reach catatonic equilibrium immediately prior to impact. Angular velocity is therefore inversely related to the release height (Y_O). With this observation and two other physical properties of the cat, Equation 1 presents a first order mathematical approximation of feline moment (μ_f).

m = *mass of cat*
r = *radius of cat (in reference to axis of situational rotation)*
Y_O = *height of release*

$$\mu_f = \frac{mr}{Y_O}$$

Equation 1. *Feline Moment*

We are now in a position to estimate the torque of a rotating cat as a function of feline moment. Torque estimate (τ_c) is expressed in Equation 2.

$$\tau_c = g\mu_f \sin_\theta$$

Equation 2. *Torque on Rotating Cat Due to Feline Movement*

Direction of feline moment vector may determined by applying Right Hand Rule #465 (RHRf). Place the right hand on the left side of the cat's body, with the palm pointing toward the cat's right side while pointing your fingers toward the cats head. The thumb will then point in the direction of the feline moment vector. See Figure 2.

Figure 2. *Right Hand Rule #465 Determining Direction of Feline Moment Vector*

A cat with a given velocity, falling toward the earth will rotate to align it's feline moment vector with the local gravitational field. However, a cat at rest will not spontaneously rotate into gravitational alignment. Sylvester (1932) observed sleeping, awake and dead cats in a wide range of angular orientations, while placed firmly on the ground ($Y_O = 0$). He reports only random movement, with no immediate tendency to realign the feline moment with gravity. In other words, the feline moment only exists in a falling cat, just as path bending in a magnetic field only exists on charged particles with a velocity.

Applications of this parallel bring to mind the possibility of using rotating cats for power generation applications. Considering that feline moment, and hence magnitude of torque, is inversely related to cat height, maximum power output with minimum power input could be generated from falling cats by raising and dropping them from minimum heights (determined by the limiting value derived from the cat's effective situational radius). Hardware details for such a system will be presented in a future paper.

Finally, catatonic equilibrium appears to represent the state of stable equilibrium for the falling cat. To date, observations of cats maintaining unstable equilibrium during sustained free fall ($\theta_o = 180^0$) have not been reported.

Speculations on Biophysical Origin of Feline Moment

No consensus exists in current literature as to the physical mechanism responsible for the existence of feline moment. However, several very recent noteworthy observations may ultimately contribute to a comprehensive understanding of the origins of this phenomenon. All focus on processes within the living cat, consistent with Sylvester's 1927 findings.

C.A.T. scans on cats (the C.A.T.[2] scan) by Felix (1991) have revealed the presence of what appear to be gravitational dipoles within the abdominal cavity of the cat, which when experiencing vertical acceleration, may generate the internal torque necessary to rotate the entire body of the cat.

Alley (1989) dropped cats through strong electric fields and found expected angular rotation was altered by the field, with a net shift of feline moment in the direction of the cathode.

Tom (1990) speculates gravitational acceleration induced protein catabolism may explain a net shift in center of mass and hence angular rotation.

Attempts to assess the influence of cat size have been inconclusive. Lynx (1994) set out to verify the existence of the feline moment in large cats reared in the wild. Survivors of this ill-fated study reported discontinuing the investigation after initial trials which involved dropping two inverted jaguars from a vertical height of 3 meters.

There also exists a paucity of complete data on behavior of the moment vector in reduced gravity environments. Armstrong (1969) hypothesized slower rotation in response to lower gravitational fields. Apollo 11 astronauts therefore released multiple cats from airlocks 3.6 meters above the lunar surface.

Data was inconclusive, given that pressure gradients caused all subjects to burst prior to impact, thus not allowing full completion of angular rotation.

Summary

To summarize the nature of the feline moment phenomenon, the following properties have been established:

* Feline moment vector dynamically aligns with the local gravitational field.

* Feline moment vector only exists under the following conditions:

    1. Cat is alive
    2. Cat is falling

* Direction of feline moment vector may be determined by Right Hand Rule #465.

* Rotation ceases when catatonic equilibrium is achieved.

* Catatonic equilibrium is reached immediately prior to impact.

* Average angular velocity is inversely related to height of release.

* Magnitude of feline moment and related torque are expressed in Equations 1 & 2.

* The precise biophysical mechanism underlying this moment vector has yet to be established.

REFERENCES

Alley, C. (1989). "Cathode shifts in vertical feline rotation due to electric field interference," *International Journal of Cat Research*, 56:3, 1014-1019.

Armstrong, N. (1969). "Cats up!" *Lunar Research*, 12:4, 16-21.

Canary, B, et al. (1985). "The effects release height and initial vertical orientation on angular velocity and acquisition of catatonic equilibrium in falling cats," *Cat Quarterly*, 19:6, 115-121.

Cheshire, A.I.W. (1982). "Magnetic dipoles of ferrous felines," *Internationale Felinae Physiologie*, 33:2, 12-17.

Felix, T.C. (1991). "Computer Axial Tomography analysis of gravitational dipoles within the abdominal cavity of the domestic cat." *Radiologie*, 14:2, 199-202.

Garfield (1953). "Rotation movement of free falling cats." *Feline Forum*, 5:7, 1-8.

Lynx, B.A. (1994). "Rotation and gravitational alignment in large feline species: preliminary final results," *Annals of Animals*, 64:2, 1567-1568.

Morris, N.L. (1983). "Gravitational field alignments and equilibrium in the falling cat," *CatQuarterly*, 17:8, 153-164.

Sylvester, M. (1927). "State of California vs. Sylvester," data presented in court transcript from animal abuse indictment proceedings, case #55685, Calico County Courthouse, Calico, California, May 16,1927.

Sylvester, M. (1932). "Absence of movement in stationary cats," *International Journal ofCat Research*, 8:3, 12-17.

Tom, C. (1990). 'Histological analysis of protein catabolism induced mass shifts in renal tissue samples from falling cats." *Cat Quarterly*, 24:1, 89-97.

Not Tonight, Dear, I'll Have A Headache

Science News
December 14, 1985

Sometimes scientific discoveries are made not by whitecoated scientists but by backyard tinkerers. Such was the case of a Georgia man with heart disease.

According to Emory University researchers, the man had noticed that the nitrate skin patches he was wearing on his chest to control heart pain gave him a headache, a known side effect of the drug; the headache didn't occur if he wore the patch on his leg. His curiosity aroused, the man rubbed a used patch on his penis. Within five minutes he became sexually aroused, and had sexual intercourse with his wife. "Several minutes later," the Decatur, Ga.-based researchers report in the November ANNALS OF INTERNAL MEDICINE, "she wondered why she had the worst headache she ever had in her life."

The man explained, but his wife was not impressed and strongly discouraged any more investigation in this area.

The case, the researchers say, "illustrates two previously undescribed points concerning topical nitrates: their ability to induce vasodilation and resulting erection, and their absorption through the mucous membranes of the vaginal walls." The authors expressed doubt that further research in this area will be done.

FORMING A SIMPLE QUAD LATCH

Bill Sacks
Arlington, VA

POSSIBILITIES AT SEA, by Paul Klee

Homer Heterodyne and Crystal Oscillator were taking a cruise around the phase locked loop. It was a wonderful spring day and the reflected impedance shimmering from the etheric field gave them the feeling of being solidly grounded. Crystal was feeling some phase jitter as a result of being pulled over for a parity check by a fail-safe controller.

After a few moments of sideband chatter and a few jokes about the fail-safe controller being a parasitic element requiring a noise blanker, Crystal relaxed and slipped into her resonant mode. Homer remarked that all of those guys are only a one shot with retrigger anyway. "He probably hasn't had an ohmic contact in months," remarked Crystal. "Yeah, he's got the brain of an octal plug," remarked Homer. "Sometimes those dumb terminals get into the fail-safe business just to hear the shot noise and play with their snubber circuits," observed Crystal. "They basically operate simplex.

"Why don't we try to mode jump," suggested Homer. "What do you suggest? I'm permeable to just about anything today." After a thoughtful propagation delay, Homer suggested that they drive over the wheatstone bridge and do some motorboating. Crystal reminded him that she was photosensitive, and they

should have to pick up some mineral oil. "Perhaps we should get a byte before we get out of the loop," remarked Homer. "Oh, I just need a nibble." They had existed as a shielded pair for so long, and shared so much mutual inductance, that either could easily go into sideband splatter and self-sustained oscillations with never a thought of a secondary breakdown, or having to suppress a carrier.

"We could reduce the overhead on the motorboat if we could form a quad latch," said Crystal. "Perhaps we could hook up with Polly Phase and Tommy Toggle," Homer suggested. Crystal was not thrilled with this idea because Homer had always felt somewhat resonant to Polly's long-woven flat braids Crystal knew that there was still a quenched spark between them. She also knew deep inside that even though Tommy was a simple flip-flop, she could not resist his fast attack/slow release single point grounding.

They rented a boat from a kindly old gentleman whose cat's wiskers made him look older than he was. The boat came equipped with a full wave bridge, and was of three deck design, although it only had one motor.

The waveforms across the lake were as pixel perfect as one could wish for, and the partition noise seemed to lull everyone into a quiescent state. No one seemed to care which direction the magnetic direction indicator pointed to. The atmosphere just seemed to bring out everyone's full scale sensitivity.

Tommy and Polly liked to have a good time. Tommy had brought lots of juice and a little potting compound. Crystal remarked that the four of them hadn't gone open loop in a long time. But that was all right because she had been in the normalized admittance mode for quite some time anyway. After awhile everyone began to experience some nonlinear distortion.

"Watch your slew rate, we've already had one parity check today. And you have to present a nominal bandwidth should we get stopped," warned Crystal. "In fact, you shouldn't have any of that passband ripple if you're going to be the driver." Tommy mentioned that he had been subjected to a hydrometer reading just a few weeks ago.

All had a good time motorboating that day, except for a little hysterises distortion on Tommy's part.

THE THEFT HYPOTHESI

Nathaniel S. Hellerstein
San Francisco, CA

Problem

One of the puzzles of modern cosmology is the paradox of the "missing mass". There are many theoretical and observational reasons to expect that the average density of the cosmos is close to the critical density—that is, just enough to close the cosmos, or at least give it an overall curvature of 0. However, observational studies of luminous matter indicate that the only one-twentieth of that amount is visible. Where is the other 95% of the mass of the universe? Explanations of this puzzle include new forces (undetected), cosmic neutrinos (unobserved) and even "shadow matter" (unobservable).

Another cosmological puzzle goes by the name of the "Fermi paradox". Life, it seems, is a natural phenomenon; it arose on Earth from naturally available compounds and evolved by a fairly inevitable process to develop expert technological species such as the ants, and rank amateurs such as ourselves. Given this, one might expect technological species to be common in the universe; the more foolishly ambitious of these species might build Dyson spheres, or Type III civilizations, or other greedy and conspicuous projects. By this reasoning, the universe ought to be littered with evidence of their disastrous failures and their even more catastrophic successes; however, none can be seen. Dr. Fermi asked, "Where are they?" Explanations of their absence include the "technology-is-suicidal hypothesis" (depressing), the "they-limit-themselves hypothesis" (unlikely), the "we're-the-first hypothesis" (egotistical), and even the "we're-in-a-zoo hypothesis" (unverifiable).

Hypothesis

Separately, these puzzles seem unsolvable; but put them together, and they explain each other as if made for each other. The two questions "where is the missing mass?" and "where are the extraterrestrials?" are both answered by the Theft Hypothesis:

The extraterrestrials stole the missing mass!

Those scoundrels! The sceptical reader may ask, "where did they abscond to?" This question may be answered by considering that though the missing mass is no longer visible, its gravity is still present, keeping the universe flat and the galaxies bound together. The only way it can do this (by presently known physics) is

them into black holes. As for why they willingly fell down the rabbit hole, consider that the energies of gravitational singularities are immense, the physics are profound, and spacetime itself is transformed there. Surely new physical laws apply in the black hole, and powerful forces can be controlled. What technological species could possibly resist so tempting an opportunity?

Predictions

Peebles and co-authors have noted that the galaxies must be about 10 times as massive as they appear to be if they are to maintain their forms. This suggests that there are 10 times as many technological (black-hole) stars as visible ones remaining. That would imply that the average distance between stars is approximately 2.2 times closer than appears. If that were so, then we might expect a technological star within 2 light-years of the sun; maybe even closer. If so, then those searching for Nemesis should not look for its visible light (it has none) but its gravitational lens effect.

That still leaves a factor of 2 to account for; therefore it seems that half of the galaxies themselves have been purloined. Present metagalactic observations show that the universe is full of holes, like a swiss cheese. The fabric of the cosmos is tattered, as if rust and moth have been industrously eating it away. A distressing sight! Perhaps those Type III (and IV) civilizations did indeed arise; those huge gaping voids are the conspicuous evidence of their existence. We arose, it seems, in the ragged edge; the margin not worth nabbing. I predict that at the center of each of those voids is an immense black hole. To find them, look for their lens effects.

A Xenobiological Observation

The Theft Hypothesis provides xenobiology with its first solid numerical observation. 95% of the mass of the universe has been pilfered; therefore, we are among the final 5% of the technologists to arise in the cosmos. Not only are we not the first, we're one of the last stragglers.

A Possible Experiment

If the Theft Hypothesis in its black-hole version is verified, then it has profound implications for the future of humanity. If every other intelligent species chose to fall into black holes, then they probably had some good reason to do so. I have mentioned the technological possibilities; in addition, maybe there's something down there worth going to see. Perhaps that environment is more congenial than at first blush. It may very well be that the natural place for a technologist is at the bottom of some Pit.

Invisibility: Theory and Practice

Jordan Levenson
Los Angeles, CA

Recently I was hired by my own company to develop a concept, on a nonproprietary basis, for achieving invisibility. Since publishing always enhances credibility, I am exposing the first phases of my research to the public eye.

Note Figure A. It is an overhead view of a setting in a meadow, with trees and mountains in the background. Objects 1 and 2 represent two people.

Person #1 is behind a building and moving along a path depicted by the dotted line. This is known to person #2 who is standing still. As soon as person #1 rounds the corner of the building person #2 will be seen. Person #2 desires not to be seen by person #1. Therefore his only recourse is to be invisible, which he isn't at present.

At present, because person #2 absorbs some light and reflects some light, his outline and features will be seen by person #1. If person #2 becomes totally absorptive his features won't be seen but he'll be a black object blocking out the background behind him and

his presence will still be known to person #1. If person #2 becomes 100% reflective his surface features may not be seen but he will stand out against the background and his presence will be known.

In each of the 3 given cases, normal, total absorption, and total reflectivity, the presence of person #2 is known. Obviously, the degrees of reflectivity and absorption are not the solution to the problem of achieving invisibility.

The first principle of invisibility as applied to the given example is that an invisible person shall not disturb background light coming to the eyes of person #1. However; the opacity of person #2 will block the light from the background. Seeking to develop, for any solid body, the density and the optical properties equal to those of air so that light can pass through undisturbed, while that body maintains its original volume, is not practical.

It can be said that in order for person #2 to be invisible, the light coming to the eyes of person #1 from the background behind person #2 must be the same as it

171

would be if person #2 was not present. If light can't pass through person #2 and surface-changing techniques do not work there is only one solution. Light from the background must bend around person #2 as shown in the side view given in Figure B, before heading in the direction of the eyes of person #1.

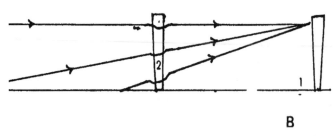

B

As an example, a military object is housed within a spherical container supported a few feet off the ground by a pole (exhibit c). The location of the sphere is out in the open where anyone might see it, except for the fact it is invisible.

Invisibility is achieved by a light-bending field generated by hardware lining the inside of the container. All light rays coming to the object from any direction are bent around the sphere before being allowed to continue traveling the same direction from which they came. The human eye can look toward the sphere's location from only a few feet away and not detect the sphere's presence. It is the quality of light, such as the angle of approach of the rays of light which reach the eye lens, which determines what the brain sees. The eye can't tell what kind of processing the rays went through en route. To the eye, the sphere doesn't exist because it doesn't usually disturb the background. Rays coming to the front of the sphere or to any other portion are not reflected, they are bent around the object. The owners of the sphere locate it by knowing certain coordinates.

The sphere is surrounded by what may be called a multi-direction variable-gradient-index field-effect 3-dimensional lens (with a hollow unused center).

It's a lens in an optical sense in that it bends light but it is not a lens in the normal physical sense in that is not in itself anymore a solid than is light. In Figure C, rays 1 are from the background heading toward an observer. Being a symmetrical field it doesn't matter if the observer moves. Rays 2 represents all incident light falling upon the sphere. Such light is not reflected but is bent around the sphere. All light rays approach the sphere in a strait line. Just like a glass lens, but without

the aberrations, the amount of bending not only depends upon the point where the light would strike the surface of the sphere if the bending didn't exist, but the angle of approach as well. The technology works whether light is thought of as a ray or wavefront and diffraction effects are negligible.

If the sphere were optically transparent a person inside would see nothing outside of the sphere because light would not reach the sphere's surface.

The sphere could be visible to any device which detects wavelengths not bent by the magnetic field. This would include radar, infrared sensors in most cases, microwaves, and moving ultrasonics. We are "bending photons" or paths of photons. Considering the masses required, gravity is obviously a weak force. The sun can bend light passing near it and which originated from another star, but the deviation is slight. Our sphere has a very concentrated field, but very thin with rapid fall-off. It barely extends beyond the surface of the sphere.

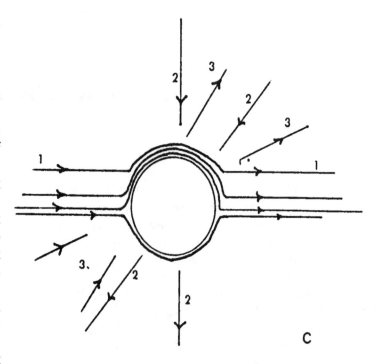

C

When invisibility becomes routinely available using my methods, I only ask that it be used in an ethical manner.

The Return of Maxwell's Demon?

Ron Birkhahn
Fairfield, OH

Recent developments[1] in technology have led to a wondrous new product (hereafter referred to as thaw plates) that claims to have the ability to "thaw rock-solid food in minutes." To the untrained eye, the device appears to be a chunk of metal upon which food is placed; however, the "secret is a super conductive metal tray..." which "...absorbs the natural heat energy in the air and then releases it directly into the frozen food." Despite the fact that this process closely resembles known thermodynamic laws, the claim is that the modus operandi is contained within a space-age metal. Our [2] contention is that the hidden secret behind these recent advances is the return of Maxwell's Demon. His absence has not gone unnoticed and one can only guess where he has been hiding and what new diabolical schemes has been hatching. References to him in literature have been noticeably absent since the 1960s, so we feel confident this must be his doing.

We used two steps to uncover the truth behind these new miracle products: 1) a controlled thawing test using various different substances, and 2) deconstruction of a thaw plate in an attempt to capture Maxwell's Demon. (We realized that step 2 was pioneering in its notion, so we took every possible precaution.) Four different test materials were used: the thaw plate, a broken chunk of granite (the caveman test), a large pink sponge (which did double duty on clean-up), and a piece of linoleum (to see if it would be better to just throw frozen meat on the kitchen or laboratory floor). Our control was a New York Strip steak suspended in air by a length of string with the effect of the string and flies considered negligible.

The results from our timed thaw test are shown in Table 1. It is clearly evident that the thaw plate did miraculously speed the time to room temperature by as much as 92%.[3] Clearly, the 52.2% improvement over the slab of granite clearly warrants the investment in using this time saying device over, say, throwing a chunk of meat on a marble countertop.

173

	thaw plate	granite	sponge	linoleum	air
Time to room temperature	11.21 min ±1.13	23.44 ±2.33	135.34 ±5.36	51.12 ±4.47	150.33 ±7.46
Cost	$9.95 [4]	$3.60	$0.50	$1.00	free
Cost/elapsed time	0.87¢/min	0.15¢/min	0.004¢/min	0.02¢/min	0.00¢/min

Table 1: Results from the thaw test.

In the time it takes to thaw just 1 steak in air, you can thaw 2.09 on granite tabletop or 13.41 steaks on the amazing thaw plate! If we assume that everyone's time is worth at least minimum wage [5], the savings of time obtained by using a ready-to-eat steak on a thaw plate 139.12 minutes, or approximately $9.74 worth of saved time. Just imagine, the thaw plate pays for itself after the first one or two uses and after that you are making money with the time you save! The high up-front cost pays for itself in almost no time. This true miracle and money-saving device could only be the work of Maxwell's Demon and thus we proceeded in our attempt to capture him.

To protect ourselves from the Demon's wrath once he was uncovered, we gave the thaw plate to an unwitting machine shop to cut in half. We watched from a distance and amid the flying debris were unable to spot Maxwell's Demon or tracks which would indicate his escape from the scene once the plate was cut in two. However, we were not discouraged by these results and so we provided the machine shop with another thaw plate to cut. By this time, though, they were rather suspicious of us (no doubt putting together the miraculous results of this product and the rumors of the Demon's presence), and, mumbling something about "crazy ideas," would not cooperate further.

Although we were unable to capture or even view Maxwell's Demon firsthand, results from the thaw test demonstrate that some mysterious force is indeed behind the operation of the thaw plate. A recent report came out on these miracle products published in Consumer Reports Sept. 1995 claimed the plates did not measure up to their claimed abilities. We happen to know from an inside source that they are non-believers in Maxwell's Demon and bias their reports as such. Either that or they have found a diabolical scheme to rid the plate of the demon before running their tests. We have clearly shown the miracle of using these time and money saving devices; we were just unable to capture Maxwell's Demon. The absence of visible physical evidence need not be taken as the lack of proof of his existence, merely that he is quick and stealthy. We recommend in the future a confined study, i.e., in a room with no doors (preferably padded), to trap Maxwell's Demon upon his release and capture him in a cage for all to see and run tests on.

REFERENCES

[1] As seen on TV
[2] "Our" refers to several anonymous contributing sources
[3] over ambient air
[4] on sale
[5] not strictly a valid assumption since low-paid privileged executives make $10 million per year which works out to around $1141/hour or $19/minute

Award of the Ig Nobel™ Prize

The Society for Basic Irreproducible Research takes pleasure in announcing an award for the Best Manuscript submitted during Calendar 1996. The Prize is awarded in three categories:

1. The Ignoblest Prize
2. The Ignobler Prize
3. The Ignoble Prize

The Recipients of these prizes will be announced in 1996 and winning contributions will be republished in a future issue of JIR. Submit all manuscripts to: The Publisher, P.O. Box 234, Chicago Heights, IL 60411 U.S.A.

The Fly as an Aeronautic Force

TIM M. SHARON, Ph.D.*
RICHARD D. BREWER, Ph.D.**
Brewer-Sharon, Inc.
Irvine, CA

Not long ago, in an issue of a prestigious national magazine, an article drew attention to the National Air and Space Museum's acquisition of two fly-powered aircraft[1] (see Figure). Although no reference was made as to the origin or antecedents of these two craft, one could not help but gain the impression[2] that they represented the prototype models - a conclusion engendered by the fact that they are displayed along with other truly original-in-concept flying models. The authors feel an injustice has been fostered, for one of the authors (Brewer) experimented with aircraft of this design as early as 1949! That, coupled with certain errors in execution of the craft being exhibited, which would render them in all likelihood unflyable (more on this later), have convinced us that these are cheap, unworkable imitations, and that the record must be set straight.

Let us begin with the history, as told in the inventor's own words, of fly-powered gliders: "In the spring of 1949, I lived in a U.S. Navy housing project in Torrey Pines, California, on a site located just about where the Physical Sciences Library of the University of California at San Diego is presently situated.[3] This was within a few miles of the Torrey Pines glider facilities, located on the cliffs that today overlook the infamous Blacks Beach,[4] and from which today young hang gliders cavort amid the sea gulls, pelicans, and soaring planes above the blue Pacific.

"Inspired by my environment and surrounded by aviation and dreams of flight, my then young mind turned to the flight of the fly.[5] I conceived of using the common house fly as the power source for commercial aircraft.[6] To test my hypothesis, I designed and built what I believe to be the first prototype fly-powered planes."

Before continuing this exciting narrative, let us examine what the Smithsonian believes to be a proper design. Quoting from reference 1: "First you catch your fly. Then you fashion this simple design with a sliver or two of balsa wood

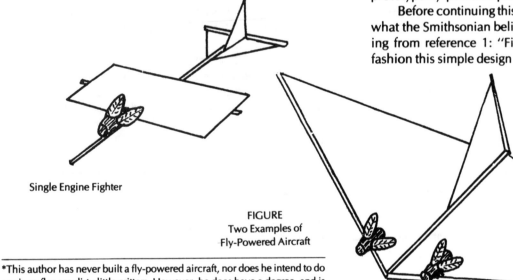

Single Engine Fighter

FIGURE
Two Examples of
Fly-Powered Aircraft

and some tissue paper and you glue your fly's little feet into position. Then you turn him loose." We contend to our learned audience that if these instructions were followed, no flyable craft would result.

---

*This author has never built a fly-powered aircraft, nor does he intend to do so since flys are dirty little critters. However, he does have a degree, and is thus intimately acquainted with a fly's main source of fuel. Besides, it was his idea to write this article.
**The inventor, we believe, of fly-powered aircraft.

Let us continue with our history: "Cutting balsa wood strips into finer and finer strips with a single edge razor, and glueing these together (with an absolute minimum of glue) into a fuselage with wing struts, I covered the wings with pieces of cellophane from Lucky Strike packages.[7]

"Next I captured in a jar, large flies from the garbage can and placed the jar into the icebox (much to my mother's chagrin). This had the effect of putting the flies to sleep *so they could be easily handled.*[8] *I had tried to glue the flies to the plane while they were awake with disastrous results of torn wings, wings glued to abdomen, etc.* After about three minutes, the flies could be taken out and glued to the engine mounts. Experiment showed that the flies must be glued *only by their abdomens.* If the fly's feet were not left *free,* the little critters simply would *not* fly. Blowing on them during the drying of the glue was sufficient to revive them[9] and start the 'engines'. A causal launch would send the craft zooming through the house.[10]

"I tried horseflies, bees, and ordinary large house flies as engines. I found the horseflies to be easiest to handle and the most 'willing' to power the gliders. I devised single-engine fighters, twin- and tri-motor craft, and even one giant eight engine model. This latter must be counted as a failure in that no suitable means could be devised to keep all eight engines working simultaneously. Any fewer than eight simply did not provide adequate lift for a craft of this size."

Thus, the record speaks for itself. Herein lay the origins of a breathtaking[11] concept in aircraft design. Although fly-powered aircraft of very large size still seem to be ruled out by the idiosyncratic activities of individual engines, the recognition (or blame) for this development should be fairly placed. When the annals of aeronautical history are finally written, the fly-powered plane will take its rightful place. ∎

REFERENCES

1. Park, E., "Around the Mall", *Smithsonian*, v. 9 #6, September 1978, 16-20.
2. Especially if you're at that impressionable age.
3. The fact that the library has not yet been appropriately dedicated, in light of the momentous discovery made in the area, we consider to be an example of shameless neglect.
4. The first legalized nude beach in California.
5. Not unlike a latter day Leonardo (the one who studied the flight of sea gulls).
6. We believe this may be one of the first attempts to develop an ecologically sound source of air transportation, since the engines would be fueled by pollutants.
7. The tissue paper approach did not result in craft with acceptable power to weight ratios.
8. We give emphasis to some of the design features which are critical, and which are "overlooked" by the Smithsonian.
9. Notice with what humility and restraint we do not mention this obviously pioneering work in cryogenic suspended animation.
10. Unfortunately, as in many prototype aircraft, the control system left something to be desired, as these craft had a nasty tendency to crash into the walls. This problem was partially overcome by moving the experiment site out-of-doors.
11. Try standing around a large supply of fuel for these craft.

Methane

Methane (CH_4) like H_2, is produced only by the colonic bacteria. This gas differs from H_2, however, in that only certain persons are capable of producing methane. Little or no methane is excreted by two-thirds of the adult population ("nonproducers"), while large quantities are excreted by one-third of adults ("producers"). Repeated testing indicates that subjects almost always maintain their producer or nonproducer status over a period of at least several years.

CH_4 is the major constituent of natural gas and burns with a royal blue flame. Knowledge that some persons produce CH_4 while others do not has only recently come to the attention of medical science, but apparently it has been common knowledge for years among members of such lay societies as college fraternities and other practitioners of the art of flatus burning. Allegedly if a match is placed near the anus of a subject as he passes gas, only certain persons—the methane producers—will spurt forth a royal blue flame. One group of methane producers has actually gone so far as to form a highly select society called the Order of the Blue Flame.

Many factors have been investigated in an attempt to determine why some persons produce CH_4 and others don't. It appears that admission into the Order of the Royal Blue Flame, like many other elite societies, is not determined democratically but depends upon family connections. If both parents produce CH_4, their children have a 95% chance of being CH_4 producers rather than the expected 33% in the general population. If just one parent produces, the chances fall to 50%, and if neither parent produces, only about 8% of their children will be producers. On the other hand, there is no relation between the CH_4-producing status of husband and wife.

reprinted from: **G.I. Tract**
by: *Michael D. Levitt*

SCIENTIFIC METHOD

Irreproducible Results - A World Record Claimed

Ted Gerrard
Department of Ornithology, Museu Municipal do Funchal Madeira, Portugal

"To our knowledge this is the first case in any vertebrate in which a drastic and recent evolutionary change of behaviour has been documented and its genetic basis established."

So writ the Max Planck Institut ornithological genetic research team of Berthold, Helbig, Mohr & Querner in *Nature* in a 1000 word letter titled "Rapid microevolution in migratory behaviour in a wild bird species."[1]

A tiny minority of (mostly juvenile) Blackcaps, charming little European song-birds of restricted intellect, have taken to wintering in parts of western Europe to the *north* of their summer breeding grounds in increasing numbers - several thousands at the last count. Some are actually surviving with the aid of winter bird feeding tables.

The remainder of the Blackcap clan (20 million +) sensibly migrate in the opposite direction to warmer resorts far to the south.

Professor Peter Berthold ventured into southwest England in the depths of 2 winters and took 40 of the oddballs back to his avian genetic research unit at Radolfzell in southwest Germany to thaw them out, fatten them up and to test the validity of a unique and somewhat pre-conceived genetic hypothesis; that these aberrant individuals possessed a *different* innate migratory fall orientation direction (northwest rather than the normal south) and that this northwesterly orientation *was genetically transmittable to offspring.*[2]

Most of the 40 strays were persuaded to mate and the migratory orientation of parents and offspring were recorded in 'Emlen' cages in the falls of 1989 and 1990. A control group of youngsters hatched near the research labs were also tested and found to orientate 'normally' to the south-southwest as anticipated.

When the results of the 2 seasons of testing were first announced the following year at an international congress,[2] (later published in 'Ibis'[3]) the caged migratory orientation direction of birds caught wintering in southwest England was announced as "northwest as expected." But this north-northwest fall orientation of a minority (of many different migratory species, mostly juveniles), has long had a simpler *non-genetic* explanation which the MPI team had overlooked; erroneous reverse orientation. This was pointed out to team leader Berthold.

When the definitive paper was later submitted to *Nature*[1] the lift-off orientation results of the test birds had been changed to west although still referring to the same single set of experiments.

This neatly eliminated the non-genetic reverse orientation hypothesis from contention; no Blackcap normally migrating eastwards in the fall to winter in Siberia, so none could mistakenly reverse and fly west.

This change unfortunately exposed a host of new inconsistencies, making a pig's ear of the entire genetic claim.

There was no real-life evidence from the mass of EURING banding data to support *either* east-to-west fall movements or the genetically essential west-to-east spring return to breed claim, so obscure (unsupportive) references were cited and the accompanying map was visually enhanced with some meaningless west-pointing arrows. No matter that flying *west* from Radolfzell would result in a ditching in the North Atlantic rather than arrival in southwest England and thus the controls had been selected from the wrong place. No matter a lot else besides.

As a consequence the article lacked a certain amount of sparkle. However the *New York Times* correspondent Carol K. Yoon raised a smile by becoming happily disoriented and wrote a sweet but entirely nonsensical article, together with map, based on the abandoned northwesterly data.[4]

Bird Orientation Testing In 'Emlen' Cages

'Emlen' test cages (fig.1) have been used extensively since the mid 1960s by behaviourists as a means of establishing the 'lift-off' directions of potential avian migrants under all manner of variable conditions. Such apparatus has been used to establish that birds can navigate by stars/star patterns and that they possess a host of lesser mind-boggling navigational attributes.

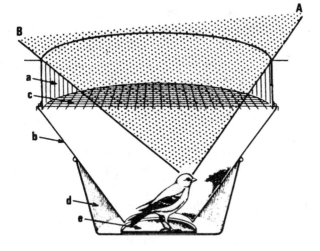

Figure 1. *The 'Emlen' Orientation Cage*

a .. *opaque circular screen/peripheral shield*
b .. *blotting paper/correction paper funnel*
c .. *screen top*
d .. *quart pan or similar*
e .. *inky pad or plain base*

The projected lines of vision (A & B) have been added. *After Emlen & Emlen, 1966.*

During seasonal periods of migratory restlessness, caged inmates scrabble up the sloping sides leaving telltale inky claw marks or scratches on typewriter correction paper. These marks are then translated into a *mean* compass direction with the aid of a certain amount of statistical juggling.

Tens of thousands of individual experiments have been conducted world-wide, despite a number of rather obvious design faults, including the following:

1. The inmate cannot see the complete sky (planetarium or real) until *after* having made its directional scrabble. Akin to taking a sight with the sextant still boxed.

2. Phototactic escape responses cannot be filtered from results. Removal of the peripheral shield ('a' in fig.1) to provide a better view (as was done in the MPI experiments), significantly magnifies this problem.

3. Directionally influencing sights and sounds such as other test birds in adjacent cages, technicians heads, traffic noise, street lighting, tree tops, paper joins etc., are *never* all completely excluded.

4. The *first* recorded choice (as would be the case with a wild free-flying migrant) should be sufficient. It never is.

5. In planetarium experiments, the moon, planets and milky way jointly and severally produce aberrancy (i.e., phototactic escape responses) and have to be excluded. Such tests thus bear no relation to reality.

6. Data from individuals producing 'insufficient' numbers of scratch marks are excluded. The cut-off point is arbitrary and sometimes decided *after* testing, as is the length of time of each individual test and the number of tests.

7. An unknown but considerable number of experiments have failed to produce any 'meaningful' data and thus remain unpublished.

'Emlen' cages can therefore be manipulated so as to produce virtually any directional result desired. These defects were widely publicized in 1981.[5]

Under controlled conditions, no independent worker has ever succeeded in replicating *any* of the many published claims (3 in a recent 9 month period in *Nature*).

The MPI team used between 32 and 35 'Emlen' cages per evening and tested 108 individuals 15 to 20 times each for up to 2 hours per recording session.

The inmates were left *in situ* for varying times, some of the tests were discounted, the basic test apparatus was altered to enhance phototactic directional responses, the number of test per bird varied, already dubious statistical treatment methods were further adapted, views of distant attractive objects and lights were permitted and the birds were *trained* to respond phototactically before tests commenced.

The 1000 word *Nature* letter contained 55 textual errors and omissions, 18 of them major, 6 of the 7 statements made in the opening abstract were incorrect and none of the 18 references supported the new westerly 'discovery.'

Surely some kind of new world record?

NOTES:

1. *Nature*, vol. 360, 17th Dec.1992, p.668-670.
2. T*he Ecology & Conservation of Palaeartic-African Migrants*. Univ. of East Anglia. 4-7th Apr. 1991.
3. *Ibis*, vol.134 supp. 1. 1992, p.38.
4. *New York Times*. 22nd.Dec.1992.
5. *Instinctive Navigation of Birds*. Scottish Research Group. 1981.

"I've evolved a great deal since I met you."

SAGA OF A NEW HORMONE

NORMAN APPLEZWEIG

In recent months we've learned of the discovery of three miracle drugs by three leading pharmaceutical houses. On closer inspection it appears that all three products are one and the same hormone. If you're at all curious about how more than one name can apply to the same compound it might be worth examining the chain of events that occurs in the making of a miracle drug.

The physiologist usually discovers it first—quite accidentally, while looking for two other hormones. He gives it a name intended to denote its function in the body and predicts that the new compound should be useful in the treatment of a rare blood disease. From one ton of beef glands, fresh from the slaughterhouse, he finally isolates ten grams of the pure hormone which he turns over to the physical chemist for characterization.

The physical chemist finds that 95 per cent of the physiologist's purified hormone is an impurity and that the remaining 5 per cent contains at least three different compounds. From one of these he successfully isolates ten milligrams of the pure crystalline hormone. On the basis of its physical properties, he predicts possible structure and suggests that the function of the new compound is probably different from that assigned to it by the physiologist. He changes its name and turns it over to the organic chemist for confirmation of structure.

The organic chemist does not confirm the structure suggested by the physical chemist. Instead he finds that it differs by only one methyl group from a new compound recently isolated from watermelon rinds, which, however, is inactive. He gives it a chemical name, accurate but too long and unwieldy for common use. The compound is therefore named after the organic chemist for brevity. He finally synthesizes ten grams of the hormone but tells the physiologist he's sorry that he can't spare even a gram, as it is all needed for the preparation of derivatives and further structural studies. He gives him instead ten grams of the compound isolated from watermelon rinds.

The biochemist suddenly announces that he has discovered the new hormone in the urine of pregnant sows. Since it is easily split by the crystalline enzyme which he has isolated from the salivary glands of the South American earthworm, he insists that the new compound is obviously the co-factor for vitamin B-16, whose lack accounts for the incompleteness of the pyruvic acid cycle in annelids. He changes its name.

The physiologist writes to the biochemist requesting a sample of of his earthworms.

The nutritionist finds that the activity of the new compound is identical with the factor PFF which he has recently isolated from chick manure and which is essential to the production of pigment in fur-bearing animals. Since both PFF and the new hormone contain the trace element zinc, fortification of white bread with this substance will, he assures us, lengthen the lifespan and stature of future generations. In order to indicate the compound's nutritive importance, he changes its name.

The physiologist writes the nutritionist for a sample of PFF. Instead he receives one pound of the raw material from which it is obtained.

The pharmacologist decides to study the effect of the compound on grey-haired rats. He finds to his dismay that they lose their hair after one injection. Since this does not happen in castrated rats, he decides that the drug works synergistically with the sex hormone, testosterone, and therefore antagonizes the gonadotropic factor of the pituitary. Observing that the new compound is an excellent vasoconstrictor, the pharmacologist concludes that it should make a good nose-drop preparation. He changes its name and sends 12 bottles of nose drops, together with a spray applicator, to the physiologist.

The clinician receives samples of the pharmacologist's product for test in patients who have head colds. He finds it only mildly effective in relief of nasal congestion, but is amazed to discover that three of his head cold sufferers who are also the victims of a rare blood disease have suddenly been dramatically cured.

He gets the Nobel prize.

---

* President, Norman Applezweig Associates, Consulting Biochemists.

THE NOBLE ART

R. KEITH HANSON
909 E. Delaware
Urbana, Illinois 61801

The noble art of Kludgemanship* capitalizes upon the designer's affinity for asinity and deals with the techniques for how to miss the perfect opportunity and succeed in achieving optimum imperfectability. Kludgemanship has many synonyms: Human Foiblesy, Finagleslisity, Gimmickmanship, Glossosophy, Designasininity, etc. However, it basically deals with the design of a Kludge, which according to Granholm[4] is "an illassorted collection of poorly-matching parts forming a distressing whole."

Every good Kludge must be endowed with one or more glitches—an inherent fallibility in the design. The optimized Kludge will have several cleverly conceived glitches, each with maximized unforgivability. However, the development of the maximized glitch requires a degree of finesse. To get carried away will likely produce a totally impossible design, where inept Kludgemanship merely leads to an ordinary design with unidentifiable glitches.

Designing The Optimum Kludge

There are certain fundamental attributes of good Kludgemanship that must be followed if one is to attain eminence as a Kludgemaster:

Avoid Conventionality This is one of the most important rules in Kludgemanship. Tried-and-true systems, techniques, and hardware have been so debugged through years of application that they have degenerated to mundane conventionality and unfailing routine performance. Uniqueness is impossible. R & D projects are impossible.

No one gets excited about a conventional system. You get attention when you have a system that is so totally confounding no one knows what to do or what to expect. Management calls meetings, extra project men are assigned, the labs are alerted to conduct exhaustive tests. Complacency turns into ulcerated worry, and routine is transformed into utter chaos. A successful kludge project generates a great amount of frantic team effort.

*The author is endebted to Jackson W. Granholm[4], Anon E. Muss, and Sue Doenym (2, 3, 5, 6) for their enlightening series of articles, recently published in Datamation Magazine, on the art of Kludgemanship in the computer industry. Since Kludgemanship is such a prevalent aspect of all engineering design activity, we are grateful to the editors of Datamation for allowing us to draw heavily from these articles in our coverage of this vital topic. (Material quoted from Datamation Magazine, Copyrighted 1966 by F.D. Thompson Publications, Inc.)

Capitalize on Cleverness The goal of good Kludgemanship is to become so clever you outsmart yourself, according to Granholm. A well designed Kludge consists of an artful adapton of unusually clever and unique ideas. Use brainstorming extensively for every facet of the system. Choose a "way out" approach that must be reinforced by a host of additional support systems in order to attain any semblance of workability. In this way, you compound the complexity of the kludge and increase the need for even more clever and nonconventional add-ons to the system. The need for cleverness can be enhanced by minimizing the evaluation phase of ideation.

Avoid the Obvious It is considered poor taste and an example of inept Kludgemanship to mix, when there is a choice, several different techniques for achieving similar outputs within the same machine. For example, to transmit rotary motion using V-belt, chain, timing-belt, and flat-belt drives, is merely to display lack of imagination. Stick to one type of drive throughout. In this way, you can subtly generate drive adaption complications because of the inherent incompatibility of a single system for all needs.

A generous variety of clever devices can always be added as back-up systems, fail-safe monitors, system reliability detectors, overload sensors, environmental controls, etc. Every conceivable eventuality under Murphy's Law can be mechanized. There is also the fringe benefit that each of these clever and complex systems can be used as the "gimmick" in an extraordinary sales campaign.

Seek Multiple Response Never provide a singular response to an event in a system. It is customary to design at least three correlated reactions to any event. For example, an interrupt switch should not only deactivate the holding circuits, but should dump the fluid from the main cyclinder, declutch the drive motor from the pump, and throw the main circuit breakers, light up the control board, blow a horn, ignite a flare, and lower the flag.

Capitalize on Redundancy No one can argue against the merits of having an extra identical backup system—after all, symetry is the essence of good design practice, and reliability increases as the square of the number of backup systems. It is a beautiful opportunity to compound the complexity of the system, while at the same time creating an aura of sophistication

Double systems provide an opportunity for self monitoring, especially when the two systems are series coupled. The failure of either or both will provide a warning signal and will render the machine inoperative. Also, preloading one system against the other makes it possible to raise the level of insensitivity above all minor fluctuations. This also results in all components having to work at or above their maximum capacity. Thus, maximum utilization and optimum fallibility are assured.

Avoid Compatibility Every Kludge needs all the competitive edge it can get. Uniqueness is enhanced by assuring that components of other manufacturers will not fit or will be too expensive to adapt. After all, market strength is a function of exclusiveness. All hookup hardware should have specially designed fittings; exclusively unique for each component. Do not standardize your support hardware, for this will only encourage some vendor to cut into the market. Whenever possible, develop inputs that will require a conversion unit. A converter not only provides a clean and specialized input but creates an opportunity to use an exclusive internal circuit system that has unusual requirements, and can be fulfilled only by special apparatus and incompatible system hardware. Incompatibility is the hallmark of a well designed Kludge.

Don't Overlook Antiquity There are many discarded and out-of-date systems, techniques, and hardware items that are rich in kludge potential. Here again there is unlimited opportunity to capitalize on an old Kludge and apply modern techniques to make it an even better Kludge. It could easily catch the industry off-base and start a new trend, with your Kludge in on the ground floor. For example, have you considered the ramifications of a totally automated reciprocating steam engine?

Experimental Kludgemanship

Kludgemanship is not exclusively limited to design activity. This noble art has also been adapted to the laboratory with amazing results. Before we discuss some of the rules of good experimental Kludgemanship, we should acknowledge the fundamental laws of the laboratory from which these rules have developed:

Lowerey's 1st Law:
   If it jams—force it. If it breaks, it needed replacing anyway.

Zumwalt's 1st Law:
   The probability of failure is directly proportional to the number and importance of the people watching the test.

2nd Law of the Laboratory:
   No matter what result is anticipated, there is always someone willing to fake it.

3rd Law of the Laboratory:
   Experiments should be reproductive. They should all fail in the same way.

4th Law of the Laboratory:
   Experience is directly proportional to the amount of equipment ruined.

5th Law of the Laboratory:
   A successful experiment exactly produces the expected data.

Yawning—relief for boredom?

Beware of yawning after you take the antidepressant *Anafranil* (clomipramine), warn three researchers in an article in the *Canadian Journal of Psychiatry*. In four case studies documented in the article, the researchers found that after taking the tricyclic, their patients experienced an orgasm (that's right) upon yawning.

The four case studies involved two women and two men. One woman reported that she could induce orgasm by deliberate yawning, while the other complained of "yawning spells' during which she experienced "unresistable [sic] sexual urges." One of the men overcame the embarrassment of ejaculating at awkward times by continuously wearing a condom; the other man noted that every time he yawned, he experienced such an "intense sense of exhaustion" that he had to lie down for 15 minutes.

Many of the tricyclics produce odd effects, said psychiatrist I.A. Kapkin, one of the authors of the report. He cautioned, though, that their paper merely presents some clinical findings and is not a full-scale study of the drug, which is sold by Ciba-Geigy in Canada and Europe but not in the United States.

A Ciba-Geigy spokeswoman in Canada said, "no cause and effect relationship has been established."

Experimental Approaches to the Date of Origin of Koopmans' Theorem

WANDA A. ST. CYR
L. N. DOMELSMITH
K. N. HOUK
Department of Chemistry
Louisiana State University
Baton Rouge, Louisiana 70803

An unambiguous experimental technique for the determination of the data of publication of a classic article by Koopmans has been devised. Using this technique, the value of this important physical constant has been determined with much greater precision than previously available.

A fundamental physical constant, which is referred to in virtually every paper on photoelectron spectroscopy, and in all literature correlating ionization potentials or electron affinities with SCF orbital energies, is the date of publication of the classic paper by T. Koopmans, wherein the mathematical proof of the identity of SCF orbital energies and ionization potentials was presented.[1] In spite of its fundamental significance, the numerical value of this physical constant is not known with great precision. For example, in five important papers and one book on this subject chosen randomly, the value of this constant is given as "1933", while in five others papers and one other book, the value is quoted as "1934". Thus, the value of this physical constant is apparently known to only three significant figures. The accuracy of most published values may be even less than this, since one recent paper uses the value of "1974". Certainly the use of such an imprecise physical constant may have detrimental effects upon quantitative results of photoelectron spectroscopic investigations. Because of the importance of this physical constant to the area of photoelectron spectroscopy and, indeed, to physical chemistry in general, we have devised a number of ways to measure this constant experimentally. The results of these investigations are reported here.

The most familiar classical method for the determination of physical constants of this kind is to inspect a Xerox of the appropriate article. However, *Physica*, in which this article appears, does not carry the volume number or date at the top or the bottom of the page, so that the Xerox copy in our files was of no help in this case. There was a date--1933--

written in pen on the Xerox, but it had been crossed off, and 1934 was written in pencil next to it. One of us checked the appropriate volume out of the Library, but to our collective horror, we found "1933-34" embossed on the cover. The research literature, another useful source of data of this kind, was similarly ambiguous: 1933 and 1934 were cited as the value of this physical constant with almost equal frequency, although there was a tendency for the acknowledged leaders in the area to use 1934.

A survey of the literature revealed, however, that the confusion about this article is not confined to its date of publication. Thus, there is uncertainty as to whether Koopmans' should be, instead, Koopman's, Koopmann's or Khooppmmaann's, and one monograph on photoelectron spectroscopy even identifies him as a she!

Because of the difficulties with the usual experiments, a more systematic investigation was undertaken with the use of the "Science Citation Index". The analysis of the citation frequency as a function of time is shown in Figure 1. Clearly, the attribution of this article is a time-dependent phenomenon, and violates the well-known "citation non-crossing rules".[2] However, T'Tion's deductions were based on a careful reading of only 5 volumes of "Science Citation Index".[2] Using the information provided by scientists working in this field through citations, we would conclude that 1934 is now the correct date of publication, but before 1975 we would have concluded that 1933 was correct.

From a more general point of view, the general increase in citations to all dates may be considered alarming. Assuming a continuation of the approximately linear increase in citations to this article over the last 10 years, there should be 527 citations to the article in the year 2000, 320 attributing it to 1934, 190 to 1933, and 17 to other dates. Aside from the large space required in "Science Citation Index" to index these citations, which will presumably be taken care of by reducing the print below the invisible size now used, there

---

[1] T. Koopmans, *Physica*, 1, or 7, 104, or 1, or 100, or 105, or 194, or 960, or 404, or 1041 (1934 or 1930 or 1933 or 1939 or 1943 or 1953 or 1974).

[2] C. I. T'Tion, "On Going Blind and Other Aspects of Citation Analysis", *J. Related Phenomena and Related Phenomena*, 1, 104 (1934).

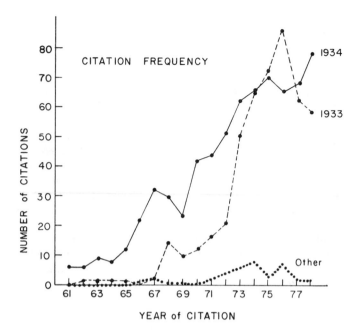

FIGURE 1 (and only): Number of Citations to 1933, 1934, and Other Dates by Year (see caption and footnote to Table I). (We thank Richard Hoffman for preparation of this figure and for illuminating discussions on the size of the L.S.U. football stadium addition.)

TABLE I. Citation Frequency by Citation. (Source: *Science Citation Index*, Institute for Scientific Information, Philadelphia, Pennsylvania, 1961 through First Quarter, 1979).

Citation	Number of Citations
T. Koopmans, *Physica*, 1, 104 (1933)	701
T. Koopmans, *Physica*, 1, 104 (1934)	560
T. Koopmans, *Physica*, 1, 105 (1933)	6
T. Koopmans, *Physica*, 1, 104 (1935)	4
T. Koopmans, *Physica*, 7, 104 (1934)	4
T. Koopmans, *Physica*, 1, 104 (1939)	3
T. Koopmans, *Physica*, 1, 100 (1933)	2
T. Koopmans, *Physica*, 1, 404 (1933)	3
T. Koopmans, *Physica*, 1, 134 (1934)	3
T. Koopmans, *Physica*, 7, 104 (1930)	1
T. Koopmans, *Physica*, 1, 100 (1935)	1
T. Koopmans, *Physica*, 1, 1 (1953)	1
T. Koopmans, *Physica*, 1, 109 (1933)	1
T. Koopmans, *Physica*, 1, 194 (1934)	1
T. Koopmans, *Physica*, 1, 960 (1934)	1
T. Koopmans, *Physica*, 51, 104 (1934)	1
T. Koopmans, *Physica*, 1, 104 (1943)	1
T. Koopmans, *Physica*, 1, 1041 (1934)	1
T. Koopmans, *Physica*, 1, 104 (1974)	2
T. A. Koopmans, *Physica*, 104 (1933)	1
T. A. Koopmans, *Physica*, 104 (1933)	1
T. C. Koopmans, *Physica*, 1, 1041 (1934)	3

will be approximately one-half acre of a forest, for paper, and 5 octopi, for ink, used to print these citations. Considering this example as typical of other important papers, the environmental impact of the printing of citations will be devastating. This aspect of scientific publications is the subject of a separate publication.[3] Table I lists the overall frequency of citations which actually refer to the article in question. Using the traditional technique of averaging data gives a value of 1933.50994036 as the value of the date of origin of Koopmans' theorem. The standard deviation is 1.57. However, some of the data points are clearly the results of faulty measurements. Discarding all values other than 1933 and 1934 gives an average of 1933.42 and a standard deviation of 0.49. Treating the volume and page number similarly, we suggest the following as the form that citations to this article should take in the future:

T. Koopmans, *Physica*, 1.02 ± 0.38, 106 ± 42.4 (1933.4 ± 0.5)

Some of these discrepancies were cleared up through the following experimental tests: A letter was written to Tjalling C. Koopmans, Professor of Economics at Yale University, and winner of the Nobel Prize in Economics in 1975. The letter to Koopmans said, in a nutshell, "Who are you?" The reply confirmed that he was the same as T. Koopmans, the author of the classic paper, and that he received his Masters degree in Physics and Mathematics at Utrecht in the Netherlands, in 1934, and then moved on to the field of Economics. In addition, Dr. P. Tel, technical editor of *Physica*, confirmed that the actual date of publication of Volume 1 by the North-Holland Publishing Company was 1934.

Can conclusions be drawn from this study? Several are obvious: (1) the proofreading expertise of scientists is questionable; (2) many typesetters or typists cannot differentiate between the numbers 4, 7, and 9; (3) scientists apparently frequently trust secondary references; and (4) the very first citation to Koopmans' theorem must have attributed it to 1933, but someone else read the original paper in 1966.

ACKNOWLEDGEMENT. Initial investigations on this subject were carried out with the collaboration of Robert W. Strozier, who showed K.N.H. where the Hill Memorial Library was located. Although Volume 1 of *Physica* was checked out by K.N.H. and R.W.S., the cohabitation of Hill Memorial Library and the Fine Arts Department in the same building caused the investigators to forget what they were supposed to be checking out. Many fine memories of the stacks in the Hill Memorial Library remain. We also thank Professors Koopmans, Mateescu, Heilbronner,[4] and Drs. Tel and U. T. Cobley for helpful advice. No agency saw fit to support this research financially, for obvious reasons.

[3]K. N. Houk *et friends*, "Is Good Science Destroying our Forests and Octopi?", *J. Environment. Impact and Related Phenomena*, submitted, and Editor about to capitulate in the face of badgering by the author.
[4]Professor Heilbronner recounted the facts earlier in a Journal to which reference is forbidden.

RADIOCARBON DATING
A Bootstrapping Fallacy[1]

D. J. HUNTLEY
Physics Department
Simon Fraser University
Burnaby, B. C.
Canada V5A 1S6

Since the pioneering work of Bishop Usher it has long been recognized that the Universe was created in the year 4004 BC. Nevertheless, there is a contrary widespread view that the Universe is of much greater antiquity; this has come about because of measurements and calculations based on the fundamental laws of radioactive decay. For example, the existence of radiocarbon dates extending back to 50,000 years before present would appear to be evidence of such antiquity. A closer examination reveals that this is not the case and that these dates and the associated argument of antiquity form a kind of bootstrapping which is unacceptable as evidence of great antiquity.

Radiocarbon dating is based on a number of assumptions, perhaps the most important of which is that the cosmic radiation, which generates the C-14, has remained constant in time. In this model, matter which was living in excess of 50,000 years ago had an amount of C-14 corresponding to 15 dpm/g when it was alive but an unmeasurably small amount today. In practice, the reverse argument is used, namely that if a sample contains an unmeasurably small amount of C-14 today, its age is in excess of 50,000 years.

Let us examine a different model based on Bishop Usher's conclusions. We shall assume that the Universe was created in 4004 BC. with a cosmic ray intensity the same as at present, and we shall also assume, a priori, that there was no C-14 present at creation. The C-14 content will then grow in time (t) according to

$$C = C_0[1 - \exp(-t/\tau)] \qquad (1)$$

where C_0 is the final equilibrium concentration and τ is the decay constant (8267 years) of C-14. The present value of C is then found by putting the present age, 5979 years, into (1) to obtain $C_P = 0.5148\,C_0$.

In conventional radiocarbon dating the age is calculated from

$$\text{age} = -\tau\,\ell n\,(C/C_P) \qquad (2)$$

---

[1] A paper not given at the party for the 5979th birthday of earth at the Archaeology Museum, S.F.U. at 1 p.m. on October 23, 1975.

On substituting (1) we obtain a relation between the C-14 age T and the time after creation (AC), t,

$$T = -\tau\,\ell n\left\{1.942\,[1 - \exp(-t/\tau)]\right\} - 25 \text{ years} \qquad (3)$$

The following table gives some specific points in this relation.

USHER DATE		C-14 DATE	
BC/AD	AC	BP	BC/AD
AD1975	5979	-23	AD 1973
AD 1950	5954	0	AD 1950
AD 1900	5904	48	AD 1902
AD 1800	5804	145	AD 1805
AD 1500	5504	451	AD 1499
AD 1000	5004	1015	AD 935
0	4004	2403	453 BC
1000 BC	3004	4315	2365 BC
3000 BC	1004	12,414	10,464 BC
4000 BC	4	57,600	55,650 BC
4003 BC	1	69,060	67,110 BC
4004 BC	0	∞	∞

There is no significant difference between the Usher dates and the C-14 dates for the past 500 years. For the C-14 date of AD 935 we consult the tree ring correction graphs of Michael and Ralph (1974) and find it corresponds to a true date of precisely AD 1000; i.e., the Usher date is correct and the radiocarbon date is in error by 65 years.

Beyond this point there is some disagreement. The essential point of this paper is that events occurring during the first few years after creation will yield radiocarbon dates in excess of 50,000 years, and that such dates are an artifact resulting from the assumptions made in radiocarbon dating.

Other dating techniques used in this time span are not of much help in choosing between these models, since they rely to various extents on radiocarbon dates. Both obsidian hydration and racemization dates are based on rate constants determined from C-14 dates. Thermoluminescence dates may be thought to be independent but one should note that this technique was rejected until its dates agreed with radiocarbon dates!

187

I conclude then that the existence of radiocarbon dates older than 4004 BC cannot be used as evidence that the Universe is older than this, because such dates result from an initial assumption of great antiquity. If we remove that assumption and recalculate the dates using different assumptions, consistent with Bishop Usher's conclusions, then we find little conflict with known facts. Radiocarbon dating cannot be used to conclude that the Universe was created prior to 4004 BC.

REFERENCE

H. N. Michael and E. K. Ralph; Radiocarbon 16, pp 198-218, 1974.

Excerpt from
  Robert Louis Stevenson
  "The Philosophy of Umbrellas" in his *The Mind of Robert Louis Stevenson* N.Y., Yoseloff, 1963. p. 114.

"Not the least important, and by far the most curious property of the umbrella, is the energy which it displays in affecting the atmospheric strata. There is no fact in meteorology better established - indeed, it is almost the only one on which meteorologists are agreed- than that the carriage of an umbrella produces desiccation of the air; while if it be left at home, aqueous vapor is largely produced, and is soon deposited in the form of rain. No . . . theory competent to explain this hygrometric law has yet been given (as far as I am aware) by Herschel, Dove, Glaisher, Tait, Buchan, or any other writer; nor do I pretend to supply the defect. I venture, however, to throw out the conjecture that ultimately it will be found to belong to the same class of natural laws as that agreeable to which a slice of toast always descends with the buttered surface downwards."

(Published in 1894)

Sent in by Norman D. Stevens
  143 Hanks Hill Road
  Storrs, Connecticut 06268

Tussock Moths Get Low-Level Air Lift

"Do outbreaks of the Douglas-fir tussock moths spread over long distances because the tiny larvae are air-lifted by the wind? Probably not, says insect ecologist Russ Mitchell of the Pacific Northwest Station, *Thereby answering a long-standing question in forest entomology*." (emphasis added!)

Source: Forestry Research West, USDA Forest Service, November 1979, p. 13.

Common Sense Adjustments of Stellar Parallaxes

From the letters of **LAZLO ARHENNIUS d'STERNUM**
as communicated by **JAN PAUL DABROWSKI**
P.O. Box 910
Fayetteville State University
Fayetteville, North Carolina 28301

Preface

The late Lazlo Arhennius d'Sternum was a scientist's scientist — unafraid of the unknown and with a spirit to delve into any and all facets of scientific investigation. His research included magneto-hydrodynamic field reversals in raising the Andrea Doria and the reverse effect of photocells. In the latter case d'Sternum found that application of a sufficiently large current to the leads of a photocell would cause the device to glow; a property d'Sternum called "pho-tonic emissivity". It was during his attempts to control the problematic melting of the photocell that Lazlo Arhennius d'Sternum met his death. The letter that follows deals with a problem in astronomy and demonstrates d'Sternum's imaginative approach to a hopeless task.

My esteemed colleague,

As you well know, the trigonometrically determined distance to a given star is derived from the angle subtended at the star by the diameter of the earth's orbit about the sun, this angle being called the trigonometric parallax. The angle is inversely proportional to the distance and when the angle (π) is measured in arc seconds, the distance (d) is determined in parsecs:

$$d = 1/\pi, \quad 1 \text{ parsec} = 3.26 \text{ light years.}$$

Catalogues of stellar parallaxes exist, the most extensive being the Yale catalogue and supplement. Since nothing is known perfectly, the parallaxes listed in the Yale catalogue are accompanied by probable errors (σ_n). Roughly, this means that the parallax angle is probably between the limits defined by the probable error:

$$\pi \pm \sigma_n.$$

Since it is always confusing to speak in terms of angles (although it is laudable to know all the angles) it is meritorious to convert the parallax and its probable error to distance and probable error in distance:

$$\pi \pm \sigma_n \rightarrow d \pm \sigma_d$$
$$\text{where } \sigma_d = \sigma_d/\pi^2.$$

For example, if $\pi = 0''020 \pm 0''005$
then $\quad d = 50 \text{ parsecs} \pm 12.5 \text{ parsecs.}$

Again, roughly, this means that the distance to the star is 50 parsecs with a finite probability that the distance is between 37.5 parsecs and 62.5 parsecs. All very straight-forward. But consider the following example. A star has a parallax that is numerically smaller than its probable error. Converting to parsecs we find that the distance is less than the error in the distance:

$$\pi = 0''004 \pm 0''010$$
$$d = 250 \text{ parsecs} \pm 625 \text{ parsecs.}$$

As is known, many stars in the Yale catalogue (>5) fall in this category.

At first glance, nothing seems amiss, until common sense axioms are applied. The distance in the example is 250 parsecs with a finite probability that the distance is between -375 parsecs and $+875$ parsecs. Therefore there is a non-negligible chance that the distance to the star is zero parsecs—in other words, the star is in our solar system! Moreover, if a star has a probability that its distance can change sign (-375 to $+875$) the star has a chance of either being in front of us or behind us! Of course, this is nonsense since the direction of a star is known with precision. In fact most astronomers are capable of specifying the hemisphere of sky occupied by a given star (although there is a report of a cosmologist who once pointed a telescope at the ground). Therefore, it is not at all probable that a star's distance, as inferred from the probable error, can ever be less than zero. Either the probable error of the parallax is too large or the parallax itself is too small. The distance derived from catalogue parallaxes can now be corrected, constraining the limits of the distance to values greater than zero. The details of the calculation of such a correction is left to the investigator's imagination.

Successful application of this method will result in a reduction of the number of meaningless parallaxes in the publications. However no corresponding increase in meaningful knowledge is expected. This paradox of parallax will be treated in future correspondence.

Until sasketoon saskatchewan, I remain belatedly yours,
Lazlo Arhennius d'Sternum

JUST JOSHIN'! OR, APPLICATION OF A NEW PSYCHOMETRIC METHOD TO AN OLD TRIED AND UNTRUE EXPERIMENTAL DESIGN TO IMPROVE THE VALIDITY OF A TAILOR-MADE SCORING KEY

Warren S. Blumenfeld and William L. Godbey
Georgia State University and
Joshua C. Blumenfeld
Cliff Valley Nursery School, Atlanta, Georgia[2]

It is difficult to know where to begin with a study as really special and exciting as this. As suggested by the title, the purpose of the study was to improve the validity of a tailor-made scoring key (a forecasting model) by the application of a new psychometric method to an old tried and untrue experimental design. Let me then first summarize (1) the background and (2) the procedure and results of the study, before getting into the details of the procedure—particularly the new psychometric method.

Background

There has developed over the past several years a body of literature in applied psychometrics that would indicate that the empirical development of tailor-made scoring keys is to be preferred to "store-bought" and/or a *priori* scoring keys. Further, the apparent plateau, or perhaps ceiling, for validity coefficients also seems to suggest the pressing need for breakthroughs in new and innovative psychometric methods and instruments.

However, as Kurtz pointed out so well in 1948, too often the wishes and hopes of the practitioner/developer and/or the consumer manifest themselves in a strange form of selective perception and self-deception in the evaluation of the effectiveness of such tailor-made keys, i.e., the acceptance of self-fulfilling "research" *via* the foldback design (that old tried and untrue design in which the tailor-made key (the forecasting model) is "tested" by re-applying it to the same data base from which it was originally developed).

---

[1]Adapted from a paper read at the meeting of the American Personnel and Guidance Association, San Diego, February 1973, and republished in the *Atlanta Economic Review*, 1973, 23(3),14-16. The paper is a psychological psychometric scientific satire, particularly as satire is defined as "ridicule for the purpose of reform."
[2]Now at Briarcliff High School, Atlanta, Georgia.

Procedure and Results

Regarding the current study, in the data collection phase, 100 special subjects responded to a special instrument (100 2-alternative items) through a special response mode. A new psychometric method was employed extensively in the data collection. Then, an equally special external criterion was developed with which the tailor-made key (the forecasting model) was subsequently developed.

Following data collection, there was accomplished an item analysis utilizing the special external criterion. The item analysis identified 24 of the 100 items for the special tailor-made key (the forecasting model).

Application of this key in the same data base resulted in a biserial correlation of .99+. At this point the authors were extremely encouraged, as one might well imagine, both in terms of the new psychometric method and in terms of the model.

However, it was decided to conduct the "academic nicety" of cross-validation. Application of the key (the forecasting model) in cross-validation resulted in a disappointing biserial correlation of .19.

The first coefficient reported is (clearly) significant beyond the .01 level; the second coefficient reported is *not* significant at the .05 level. Why the descrepancy? How account for the shrinkage? Or better, the inflation?

With this overview, perhaps we can retrace the research methodology so as to explain and better understand this discrepancy.

Purpose

Although the implied purpose of this study was to apply a new psychometric method to an old tried and untrue experimental design to improve the validity of a tailor-made scoring key (the forecasting model), the real purpose was to point out (yes, once again) the specious, self-serving, insidious, suspect, spurious, fallacious, but facinating results that are obtained when cross-validation of a forcasting model does *not* follow model development.

PROCEDURE

With this last revelation in mind, let us now examine in more detail the procedure generally, and the new psychometric method specifically. And, unlike the traditional "senior author," let me give credit where credit is due regarding the relative contributions of the senior author, the second author, and, perhaps most particularly, the junior author.

Data Collection

The subjects, the instrument (the new psychometric method), and the external criterion follow. As previously indicated, the subjects, the instruments, and the criterion were all quite special.

Subjects: Indeed the subjects were special; in fact, they did not exist except in the rich (however bizarre) imaginations of the authors. They are purely hypothetical, science fictional if you will. If credit must be taken, the senior author assumes the credit for the special subjects.

Instrument (The New Psychometric Method) The special instrument I now hold in my hand. As you can see, it is a United States penny, *circa* 1971. (Not being much of a grantsman, the project was run on an extremely modest and limited budget.) You will note that the coin has two sides, i.e., two alternatives. A flip of the instrument by the junior author established the convention as to whether heads would be alternative A or B. (As it turned out, heads was B.) The second author then laid the "instrument" upon his thumb and proceeded to flip the coin 100 times for each of the 100 hypothetical subjects. If the coin came up heads, a B response was recorded; if the coin came up tails, an A response was recorded. The University generously provided the 100 answer sheets (the 100 subjects).

This coin flipping then was the "new psychometric method." As I will give an appropriate name to the new psychometric method later in the paper, I will at this juncture (demonstrating unusual self-discipline) resist the temptation of describing the method as "a series of one-tailed tests," or "the use of a digital computer," or even "one of cumulative side effects."

In this manner, that is, with this special instrument, and its attendant new psychometric method, 100 2-alternative responses were generated for each of the 100 special subjects. Let us now turn to the special external criterion used in the study.

Criterion: Following the development of the 100 100-response answer sheets, a step-wise algorithm was used to develop the special external criterion. Specifically, the senior author (in the pedagological spirit and tradition often suggested by students) stood at the top of an (outside) staircase and allowed the 100 answer sheets to tumble and float to the base of the staircase, littering the various individual stairs in the process. At this point, the junior author (eager to please, as junior authors are wont) recouped the answer sheets in whatever order (i.e., random) they had happened to fall. (I suppose one could refer to this as a "least-stairs solution.")

At this point, the second author stratified the 100 answer sheets into 2 stacks of 50 each, i.e., he sorted, odd-even. Then the junior author flipped another penny (the other half of the budget) to establish which stack of 50 would be the high criterion group and which stack of 50 would be the low criterion group. Following this re-application of then new psychometric method, in a blaze of scientific rigor, the junior author once again flipped the coin to establish which half of the high group and which half of the low group would be the cross-validation (holdout, replication) group (yet another application of the new psychometric method!) In this manner, 4 sets of 25 answer sheets, i.e., high primary, low primary, high replication, and low replication were established for the study. (We had originally planned to use several random tables in the criterion development phase. If we had, I suppose I could have now referred to these tools as "a number of random tables.")

Summary of data collection: Through the application of a "new psychometric method" (coin flipping), a data base of 100 2-alternative responses was generated for 100 (hypothetical) subjects. Utilizing a similarly generated special external criterion, these 100 answer sheets were further sub-divided into primary and replication analysis groups as per any professional item analysis (forecasting model development) project.

Data Analysis

There were three phases to the data analysis of this research, i.e., (1) item analysis (model development) (2) foldback, and (3) cross-validation

Item Analysis: The 100 items in the item pool were item analyzed using the procedure described by Lawshe and Baker (1950) with the special external criterion as previously described. In the item analysis, there were 25 in the high group and 25 in the low group. *Alpha* of .05 was used to identify the "discriminating" items for inclusion in the "special" key, i.e., the forecasting model.

Foldback: The "items" surviving the item analysis (the forecasting model) were (re) applied to the answer sheets of the item analysis group. The predictive validity of the key was documented by biserial correlation.

Cross-Validation: However, for those more interested in the better (rather than the more fulfilling) estimate of the relationship between the derived key (the forecasting model) and the external criterion, the items surviving the item analysis were scored in the replication groups of 25 high answer sheets and 25 low answer sheets. Again, biserial correlation was obtained to quantify the relationship between the forecasting model and the criterion, i.e., the predictive validity.

RESULTS

Item analysis procedure identified 24 items (chance would have been 5) which discriminated between the high and low groups at or beyond the .05 level. No doubt you will be interested in which items "came through." They were "items" (i.e., flips) 7, 10, 12, 16, 20, 21, 27, 31, 34, 35, 41, 42, 43, 59, 64, 66, 68, 72, 77, 81, 84, 88, 91, and 92. These items numbers are as meaningful in context as they are out of context (or vice versa?); and they became the forecasting model.

Applying these 24 items back upon the original sample in which they were derived, the obtained biserial correlation was .99+. No doubt, rounding error prevented the completely self-fulfilling prophecy. This was most encouraging, as this obtained coefficient is clearly off zero beyond the .05 level. (Consider here for a moment those of your acquaintance and/or your employ using this foldback design and at this point mouthing such quasi-professional, but sage, things as "Of course, these results should be interpreted with some caution.")

Unfortunately, when the 24-item model was applied to the replication sample of 50, the encouraging coefficient of .99+ shrank slightly. In fact, it shrank back to .19 (*not* significantly off zero at the .05 level). Too bad; we felt we were on to something—both in terms of a new psychometric method and in terms of the operational utility of the model.

For those of you who are psychometric purists, you will be excited to learn that the obtained odd-even, corrected reliability of the key was .29 (N = 100).

DISCUSSION AND CONCLUSION

At this point, the reason for the obtained discrepancy between the foldback results and the cross-validation (hopefully) should be perfectly clear. The whole thing was a hoax; the old tried and untrue design, i.e. foldback, really did (and does) make something out of nothing—in this case out of something *slightly less than nothing*. Little or no further discussion seems necessary. In a sense (no pun intended) Cureton's classic paper (1952) has been re-executed. At the suggestion of the junior author (still eager to help), I call your attention to the recent treatment of this subject by the senior author (Blumenfeld, 1972). It seems (perhaps cruelly) clear once again that (1) the application of the model to the replication group is the acid test of the quality of the model and (2) the (re)application of the model to the original group is but a half-acid test of the quality of the model.

One would think that this point has been well made often enough, but as an applied psychologist dealing with students and practitioners of business administration and/or educational administration, it is painfully clear to me that the foldback design still remains very much in vogue. (For a recent insidious execution of the foldback experimental design, see, for example, Novak, 1970.) It is for that reason that I continue to believe that it is appropriate to beat home the point of cross-validation, i.e., let's have no more of this half-acid research!

Oh yes, there seem to be two pieces of business yet to be handled. These concern the junior author and the naming of the new psychometric method.

Regarding the junior author, he is now 5½ years old. At the time of the study he was 3½ years old. (The publication lag takes its toll on all of us.)

Regarding the naming of the new psychometric method, you will recall, that the explicit operational mechanics of the procedure were to lay the coin upon one's thumb and flip. Considering the non-consistency between the flippings (i.e., the application of the new psychometric method) of the second and junior authors, and, if you will not think it too flippant of me to re-coin a phrase, I consider it uncommonly—and punishingly—appropriate to call the new psychometric method:

"THE METHOD OF NON-CONSTANT THUMBS"

And, at the risk of losing our place in psychometric history, the future application of this method is not recommended.

Warren Blumenfeld and his son Joshua put into operation their new psychometric method— The method of Non-Constant Thumbs.

REFERENCES

Blumenfeld, W.S. Quasi-successful concurrent validation of a special key for a relatively new and exciting personality instrument in a group of potential managers: or, I am never startled by a fish. Paper read at the meeting of the Georgia Psychological Association, Macon, May 1972. (Republished: *Atlanta Economic Review*, 1972, *22* (5), 14-15. *The Industrial Psychologist*, 1972, *9* (2) 23-26. *The American Psychological Association Monitor*, 1972, *3*(9,10), 3, 14. *The Journal of Irreproducible Results*, 1974, *21* (1), 24-26.)

Cureton, E.E. Reliability, validity, and baloney, *Educational and Psychological Measurement*. 1950, *10*, 94-96.

Kurtz, A.K. A research test for the Rorschach test. *Personnel Psychology*, 1948, *1*, 41-51.

Lawshe, C.H., & Baker, P.C. Three aids in the evaluation of the significance of the difference between percentages. *Educational and Psychological Measurement*, 1950, *10*, 263-270.

Novak, S.R. Developing an effective application blank. *Personnel Journal*, 1970, May, 419-423.

Significantly Entitled

Stephen Kaufman
San Francisco, CA

For years the hallmark of the wine expert has been his ability to read and interpret labels so as to impress others with his expertise. Today in medicine, the sophisticated reader must appreciate the significance of titles and authors appearing in professional journals. For example:

The Diurnal Variation of Erotic Impulses in the Newly Born. VD Birth MD; JC Besmirch MD; WV Besmirch MA and IM DeCynic MD.* From the Divisions of Pediatrics and Psychiatry, University of Hamlin, Frisco, CA 94111

Received for publication November 28, 1982; accepted March 10, 1984
*Reprint requests to IM DeCynic MD, Division of Psychiatry, University Hospital of Hamlin Frisco, CA 94111

To the trained academician the above title, regardless of article content is subject to valuable interpretation. The sheer irrelevance of the topic implies that this paper resulted from an NIH grant and was important to the University because it utilized unoccupied computer time. The use of "Newly Born" rather than Newborn suggests one of the authors is English thus giving the paper an international flavor. It could further be surmised that, as in the middle-ages royal marriages were arranged to unite semi-hostile enclaves, this was an attempt to improve relationships between feuding pediatric and psychiatric departments.

Detailed analysis of the data reveals the year and one-half delay between submission and acceptance. This implies not only were the authors incapable of writing coherent sentences but that the University has a second-rate medical editor (who generally rewrites all articles prior to submission).

The presence of both JC Besmirch MD and WV Besmirch MA indicates that young Dr. Besmirch is a research fellow whose wife, angry that he is never home, is listed as a co-author despite the fact that she was a fine-arts major with no knowledge of medicine. This bit of flattery undoubtedly saved his marriage and gained him time to write a series of grant proposals that will insure his future.

Finally, the appearance of the name of the re-knowned senior author IM DeCynic MD assures the reader that he had absolutely nothing to do with the article from inception to completion. The significance of this is revealed when Dr. VD Birth is invited to Modesto to discuss the paper while Dr. DeCynic will analyze its implications in St. Tropez. ■

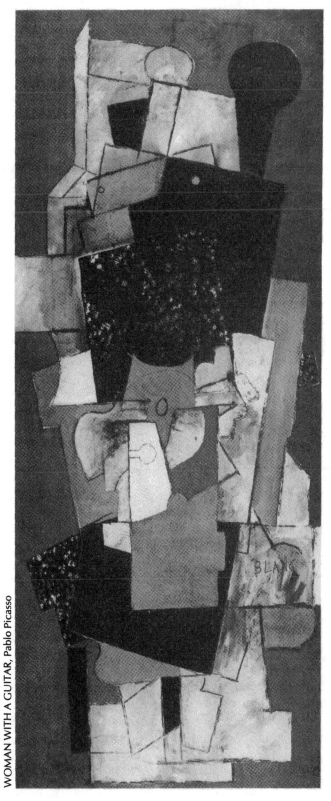

WOMAN WITH A GUITAR, Pablo Picasso

DOUBLE-BLIND CROSSOVER:
A Metaphorical Parable

Nathaniel Haynes
Far Rockaway, NY

One day the Chief Engineer of an electroencephalographic amplifier company received reports that eighty percent of shipments were being returned because of excessive hum. He called in five of his best trouble-shooters and said, "We've got to find the cause of the excessive hum. Our field returns are intolerable.

"As we are selling to the medical profession, let's use their methods in searching for the cure, and apply their validity tests for significance (1) after corrective techniques are applied.

"First, each of you will take one of the rejected amplifiers and search carefully for the cause of excessive hum, and report back to me within ten days."

At the indicated time, each came back with a report on one of the following causes: 1. Unshielded power transformer; 2. Inadequate power-supply filtering; 3. Unbalanced output-stage transistors; 4. Circulating signal and power-supply currents; 5. Unshielded input leads.

"Well now," said the Chief Engineer, "since you are all in disagreement each of you will conduct a double-blind cross-over study. Pick out ten amplifiers from our production. Apply your corrective measure to five of the units and have our test department check the treated and untreated amplifiers for hum reduction without telling them which group was treated. Then undo your treatment on the first five and apply it to the second five. Again have the test department check the units for hum without indicating which group was altered.

"After you've compiled the data, check it on our computer for significance."

Two weeks later the reports came in. The associated probability was not significant and fell far below confidence limits (2).

As a result of the engineering department's inability to find a cure for excessive hum, the manufacturing subsidiary was sold to a competitor. The acquiring company's Director of Engineering looked at the laboratory reports and thought, "What an oversight! Each of the engineers was looking for one cure for all causes. With the five known causes, any one of the amplifiers could have presented thirty-one combination etiologies. Each group of five amplifiers might have

SELF PORTRAIT, by Dürer. Erlangen University Library

presented an array of over twenty-eight million combinative etiologies. There was less than a one in twenty-eight million chance that all five would have presented the same single etiology. What a beautiful technique for producing irreproducible results."

How many medical methodologies test for one or two effects of a pharmacotherapeutic intervention when the procedure is inadequate for counteracting all important etiological factors? How many compliant and refractory subsets (3,4,5) have been identified and specifically treated? How many cures or effective interventions for a specific subset have been discarded because of a statistical ritual? (6).

REFERENCES

1. Ilife RD. The significance of statistical significance. N. Engl. J Med 1983; 308:596
2. Gore SM. Statistics in question. Brit Med J 1981; 283:600-602.
3. Mayeux R, Stern Y, Spanton S. Heterogeniety in dementia of the Alzheimer type: Evidence of subgroups. Neurology 1985; 35:453-461.
4. Mesulam MM. Dementia: It's definition, differential diagnosis, and subtypes. JAMA 1985; 253:2559-2561.
5. Fudenberg HH, Whitten HD, Arnaud P, Khansari N, Tsing KY, Hames CG. Immune diagnosis of a subset of Alzheimer's disease with preliminary implications for immunotherapy. Biomedicine & Pharmacotherapy 1984; 38:290-297.
6. Mainland D. Statistical ritual in clinical journals: is there a cure?-1. Br Med J 1984; 288:841-843.

SOCIOLOGY

BELLE'S CONSTANT

DANIEL McIVOR
and
OSLEN BELLE
Ministry of Corrective & Rehabilitative Services
Building 21, 139 Tuxedo Avenue
Winnipeg, Manitoba R3C 0V8
Canada

While conducting a sophisticated evaluation study of former federal prison inmates who have resided in community release centres, it was noted (Belle, 1976) that one group of 83 men worked a mean of 35 days out of an available 57 days. Two years later, a similar group of 83 men were observed to work a mean of 81 days out of an available 136 days in the community release centre. At first, we were impressed with the differences between the two groups. But when looking at the *proportions* of days worked to days available, we found that 35/57 = .6, and 81/136 = .6. Thus, we concluded that while we had each aged two years, our inmate population had not changed a great deal over time.

Feeling that our initial measures were possibly too gross to catch the true essence of our phenomenon, we converted our measures to hours of work per 24-hour period. Again, we found that, subtracting 8 hours of sleep and 2 hours of rest and feeding, of the 14 hours remaining, the inmates worked an average of 8.4 hours a day, or .6 of the available working time.

Becoming somewhat suspicious of this .6 figure, we turned our investigations upon ourselves, and observed that over a two-year period, we worked an average of .6 of the available time. We were forced to face our data: no matter how we looked at it, the ratio of time worked to time available was always about .6.

Next, we turned to a broader base of observation, and checked with Statistics Canada for further data. According to an obtained report from Statistics Canada (1976), the mean number of daily hours worked on all occupations is about 40 hours per week. According to the .6 constant, the 40-hour work week is quite appropriate. Since there are about 14 hours per day available for work, 8/14 is about .6. Five available work days are 5 x 8 = 40, and 5 x 14 = 70, or 40/70, or .6.

Stepping back to an ever broader speculation about the nature of life itself, we noticed that in North America, man lives about 70 years. Of that 70 years, the first 20 years are devoted to growing up and getting educated. The last 10 years are spent in retirement. The middle 40 years are spent at work. Thus, of an available time of 70 years, 40/70, or .6 of the available time is spent working.

Shifting from the broadest view and focusing again on the fine details of any specific workday and the amount of work actually done, we have observed that in any 8 hour work day, a man spends approximately 40 minutes on coffee breaks, 20 minutes going to the bathroom, 90 minutes figuring out what to do next, and 50 minutes resting, walking, and fiddling around. Thus, in any 8-hour work day, a man works approximately 4.8 hours, or .6 of the time available. Knowing this important constant will help foremen as they plan how long to complete any given task. For example, if it were to take 6 hours to complete a task, the foreman should be aware that the only way the task could be completed in one day would be to hire two men to spend 5 hours working on the task. Each man would work .6 x 5, or 3 hours x 2 = 6 hours. Those who must develop long-term plans for construction projects will instantly see the power of such a constant, which we have named "Belle's Constant."

The implications of "Belle's Constant" are far-reaching. Consider the proposed four-day work week. Clearly, 4/7 is about .6, and is more in accord with Belle's Constant than the present 5/7 working days. But the 40-hour work week is about the right proportion of available time to work time. Thus, manufacturers have wisely chosen to maintain the 40-hour week within the context of a four-day work week. They will succeed.

Furthermore, consider the implications of such a constant when applied to the role of work for inmates in correctional institutions. when the .6 constnat is not observed, frustration levels increase, and violent incidents increase. For example, incarcerated inmates also have 70 hours available for work each week. But the average number of hours worked per week per inmate is about 15 hours, or .21, which is far below the Belle's Constant for normal behavior. When inmates are given the opportunity to work, they generally do, as demonstrated by the junior author's earlier study. Thus, the importance of providing opportunities for incarcerated persons to work is clear. In fact, it may be more beneficial for inmates to work than to be involved in any other form of treatment.

There are numerous other implications for this newly-discovered constant. At this point, some beginning work is being done which will develop the appropriate corollaries to the Belle's Constant. Cooperation is now being sought from broad-based industry to clarify the general effectiveness of this Constant in long-term planning tasks.

In summary, an investigation of a wide range of work behavior has resulted in the formulation of a basic principle called "Belle's Constant." According to Belle's Constant, "The ratio of time involved in work to time available for work is usually about .6." This constant is most useful in the planning of long-term projects and in developing treatment programs for incarcerated persons.

REFERENCES

Belle, O. Outcome studies of federal inmates in community release centres. 1976, in press.

Statistics Canada. Employment earnings and hours. March, 1976, Catalogue no. 72-002, pp. 11-71.

EDITORIAL CORRESPONDENCE

Editor to author:

. . . I should also like to call your attention to referees No. 2 remarks:

"In the experimental section the author writes: *This experiment was carried out in the cold room when the ambient temperature was 4-7°C.*" This gives a temperature fluctuation of 45%! Unacceptable!

Author to Editor:

. . . I quite agree with the remarks of referee No. 2 concerning the temperature fluctuations, and therefore I should like to reword the sentence as follows:

"This experiment was carried out in the cold room, where the ambient temperature varied between 297-300°K."

Temperature variation is thus reduced to only 1%. I hope the paper is now acceptable.

PSYCHOTICS FOR REAGAN:

New Hope For The Republican Party

Laurence B. Guttmacher
Rochester, NY

"Democracy is the theory that the common people know what they want and deserve to get it good and hard."--H.L. Mencken

On Monday November 7, 1984, I was called to our university hospital's inpatient psychiatric unit in order to perform a psychopharmacology consult. Mr. F., a 74 year old, widowed man had been in the hospital for a week. He has a very long, well established history of biopolar affective disorder. He had been hospitalized on an approximately yearly basis, most typically after he discontinued his lithium carbonate. His current hospitalization had been precipitated by his usual manic behavior; he had begun to impulsively spend large amounts of money that he did not have, was wandering around downtown Rochester propositioning young women, had utter disregard for his own safety, had stopped sleeping, had developed grandiose delusions, etc. He had made little progress during his brief hospitalization. He had spent most of the week in restraints due to several assaults on other patients.

When called to his room I encountered an elderly man in full leather restraints. He was dressed in a ripped grey flannel suit coat and pants, but bore no shirt. His fly was unzipped. He was unshaven. Spittle could be seen coming from his mouth. He was covered with several other forms of human excreta. His speech was quite pressured and he exhibited flight of ideas. He announced to me that while he had always considered himself a working man and a Democrat he now thought it high time for a change and that he was about to become a gentleman and a Republican. He was demanding television air time in order to publicly announce this fact.

Recent court rulings have underscored the rights of psychiatric patients (c.f. Jiffy v Alabama). I felt that these decisions left us little alternative but to attempt to heed his request. I was also hopeful that Mr. F. might singlehandedly turn the electoral tide. My calls to all three networks were rebuffed; they simply would not grant Mr. F. airtime. Public Broadcasting thought that he might be fit for William Buckley's Firing Line, but that was not scheduled to air until after the election.

TABLE 1.

| | New York Times CBS Poll | | Rochester Psych Center | | | |
	Reagan	Mondale	Reagan	Mondale	Other*	Significance**
Males	59%	41%	96%	1%	3%	P<.001
Females	57%	42%	95%	2%	3%	P<.0001
Whites	66%	34%	98%	2%	0%	P<.001
Blacks	9%	90%	94%	1%	5%	P<.0001

*Write-in votes were recorded for: Haile Sellasie, Evita Peron, Van Halen, Mickey Mantle, Mickey Mouse, the Ayatolah Khomeni, and the former dean of the local medical school.
**Student's t-test, one tailed.

The events surrounding Mr. F's curious political conversion prompted me to explore the question of psychotic voting behavior in general. Rochester Psychiatric Center is a 1050 bed hospital whose charge is the care of the chronically mentally ill in the Rochester community. During elections a special polling place is set up for inpatients at the Psychiatric Center. The vast majority of residents vote, in large measure because if affords them an opportunity to leave their wards. By offering respondents free cigarettes and coffee we were able to conduct exit polls with a 97.8% response rate. Basic demographic data were accumulated as well as the patient-voters' electoral choice. Data are presented in Table 1 and compared with The New York Times-CBS News national data.

As can be seen psychotic patients were overwhelmingly Republican. There are no previous data to compare with, but this response is surprising for a disenfranchised and therefore traditionally Democratic group. It seems inescapable then that there must be something peculiar about psychosis which predisposes to Republicanism. The implications of this are staggering. Recent data accumulated by the National Institute of Mental Health's Collaborative Project on the Epidemiology of Mental Illness indicate staggering prevalences for major psychiatric disorders. More than

1% of the population will carry a diagnosis of schizophrenia, another 1% will be psychotically depressed. In short, at any given moment more than 20,000,000 Americans, mostly adults, will be suffering from a major psychiatric disorder. Despite this neither party has made a significant attempt to mobilize this vote. The Democrats even took Mr. Eagleton off the ticket because of past treatment for a depressive episode. The Republicans clearly have a solid foothold with the psychotic vote.

Several correlative questions remain unanswered. Psychotics voted for Reagan. Did you have to be psychotic to vote for him? Is the psychotic-Republican alliance a state or a trait phenomenon? If the latter case is true, successful psychotherapy might well convert many patients into Democrats. Would either party do well to run an active psychotic for the presidency? These and many other related questions can only be answered through further research. ■

A VENEREAL APPROACH TO EDUCATIONAL TERMINOLOGY

Paul J. Zingg
Philadelphia, PA

The expansion of higher education over the past few decades has effected an explosion of educational terminology. The National Center for Higher Education management Systems has published a *Glossary of Standard Terminology for Post-Secondary Education* in an attempt "to help promote standardization and consistency in communication throughout post-secondary education, at the institutional, state, and national levels."

As helpful as the *Glossary* may be, however, it lacks a certain definition for many of the *dramatis personae* who inhabit the halls of academe. Rather than rely on traditional educational jargon to develop terms for these individuals

and groups, perhaps a more appropriate approach would be to resurrect a once authentic and authoritative source of nomenclature for our contemporary lexicon.

The medieval exercise of venery with its accompanying coinage of imaginative collective nouns provides many guidelines. As collected by James Lipton in *An Exaltation of Larks or, The Venereal Game* (Second edition, New York: Penguin, 1977), these venereal terms are often as witty as they are strikingly appropriate.

The list which follows represents a combination of original, medieval terms and some modest additions suggested by Lipton and myself.

Students

A Dilation of Pupils
A Plentitude of Freshmen
A Platitude of Sophomores
A Fortitude of Graduate Students
An Avunculus of Alumni
A Clutch of Pre-meds
A Herd of Pre-Vets
An Acne of Adolescents

Professors

A Tenure of Associate Professors
An Entrenchment of Full Professors

An Ex Cathedra of Professors Emeriti
A Drift of Lecturers
A Brood of Researchers
A Wrangle of Philosophers

Academic Areas

A Doctrine of Doctors
An Escheat of Lawyers
A Liter of Chemists
A Family of Biologists
A Nucleus of Physicists
A Recession of Economists
An Era of Historians

An Essay of English Teachers
A Case of Sociologists
A Column of Accountants
A iamb of Poets

Administrators

An Execution of Officers
A Bored of Trustees
A Penury of Budgeters
A Dilemma of Deans
A Frown of Advisers

NonRelatives

Kenneth Kaye
Lawrence, KS

To social antropologists, the kinship terms of a particular society's language reveal the whole structure of that culture. The Yuukliu Eskimos, for example, make a distinction between *mukluk,* the uncle who is one's mother's brother, and *lukmuk,* one's father's brother. We speakers of English lump both those collateral male relatives into the same category, and we toss the husbands of our aunts in as well. In our culture it is the person himself, and what he can do for you, that matters; not his blood relationship.

Kinship terms are especially revealing when they designate relationships that one culture deems unimportant, and therefore nameless, while another culture deems them so important that a special term is needed. For example, one's married children's parents-in-law are thought of so rarely in the Anglo-Saxon culture that no term for them is needed; the fact that they have a special name in Yiddish, *machetunim,* indicates their importance as mutual objects of cordial contempt.

Societies change over time, however, and sometimes language is a little slow to keep pace with changes in the culture. Anthropologists need a new set of kinship terms to capture the complexity of family relationships in America. Some examples:

Ex-husbands-in-law. One's wife's previous husbands. (Similarly, one's husband's previous wives are one's *ex-wives-in-law.)*

In-husband. One's ex-wife's current husband. This person is the counterpart of the ex-husband-in-law: I am one of my in-husband's ex-husbands-in-law. However, the relationship is not symmetrical because each in-husband may have several ex-husbands-in-law. Usually only the most recent ex-husband-in-law matters to an in-husband, unless the more remote ex-husbands-in-law's children are still living with their mother and the in-husband (their stepfather). (The children's step *mother* is her ex-*wive's*-in-law's in-*wife.* Henceforth, such obvious gender reversals will be omitted in the interest of brevity.)

First husband once removed, etc. This set of terms refers to the changes in person A's ex-spouse's status with each subsequent remarriage of A. If I am my wife's third husband, for example, there may be considerable animosity between her *second* husband and us, especially if she left him for me or if she hasn't forgiven him for leaving her. But her *first* husband, now the first husband once removed, is off the hook. The second husband will become the second husband once removed when and if I cease to be the in-husband.

Step-grandparents vs. Grand-stepparents. The former are the parents of one's stepparents, who enter one's life later than one's blood grandparents, often depart sooner (see next entry). The latter are one's parents' stepparents, who, if one knows them at all, may be the only grandparents one has.

Ex-step-grandmother. The mother of one's ex-stepfather or ex-stepmother. Sometimes called the disappearing grandmother, this person stops sending sweaters from Lord & Taylor and is never heard from again. However, one is not expected to return her previous gifts, and the ex-stepparent should not claim them in the settlement.

Step-step-grandfather. One's stepfather's stepfather. He may be acquired at the time one acquires the stepfather, or later (if the stepmother remarries after her son does).

Ex-step-step-grandparents. There are two kinds: one's stepparents' ex-stepparents, and one's ex-stepparents' stepparents. The distinction is trivial, since all disappear upon acquiring this status.

Step-ex-step-grandfather. A non-grandfather whom a child's new stepfather's mother divorced prior to her son's marriage to the child's mother. The set is empty on the stepmother's side unless the children live more than half the year with their father and stepmother, and the stepmother's ex-stepfather had married her mother while she (the stepmother) was still a child.

Half-children once removed. One's ex-spouse's children by subsequent marriages, but only if one or more of one's own children also live with that ex-spouse. The latter children are then the in-husband's or in-wife's stepchildren, which is why this term is needed for the relationship between oneself and one's children's half-siblings.

Stepchildren twice removed. The children by *previous* marriages, of one's in-spouse. The paradox: Your step-children (not removed) are not related to you by blood. Your half-children once removed *are* related to you (*sort of:* by blood once removed), because they are half-siblings of your own natural children. Nonetheless, one sees them rarely if ever, whereas one sees far too much of one's step-children not removed. Step-children *twice* removed are not related to you (unless your in-husband or in-wife happens to be either your own relative or an ex-in-law), yet you may see more of them than of your step- and half-children *once* removed, because the twice removed are likely to be closer in age to your own children, live with them for part of the summer, and can't very well be left behind when you pick up your natural children for a day at Great America. (A friend of mine found himself at the top of the Hell Drop strapped into a cabriolet with two screaming step-children twice removed, his glasses falling off, his wallet missing, without the faintest idea where his step-children once removed, his step-children not removed, his children, half-children, and ex-children were. His girlfriend, it turned out, had picked up a sailor and gone home.)

Ex-brothers and ex-sisters. The offspring of a child's ex-stepparents, but only those who lived in the same household with the child and were called "brothers" and "sisters" for at least a month prior to their parent and the child's parent separating. Children are remarkably tolerant of such kithship updates, but problems occasionally arise if they happen to run into their ex-siblings later, and fall in love. If an ex-brother marries his ex-sister, each one's parent (on that side) becomes the in-law once removed of his or her own ex-spouse, and that parent's current spouse (if any) becomes stepparent-in-law to his or her own step-children twice removed. However, if the ex-brother and ex-sister live together without marrying (as who can blame them?), then their four closest parents remain their ex-stepparents as well as stepfathers-in-common-law to one member of the couple and stepmothers-in-common-law to the other. ∎

Lenoir, L., A. Bebarge, M. Willott, and **P. Muller.,** (Inst. Med. Legale et Med. Sociale, Lille, Fr.) Une recente et brusque modification des lesions de charriage dans la submersion dans les canaux du nord de la France. *A recent and abrupt change in the lesions caused by barges in the canals in northern France.* MED LEG DOMM CORPOR 3(3): 261. 1970.—The canals in this area are now being used by larger and more powerful boats. These boats have propellers which not only create rapid movements of water but have the capability of being extremely destructive to the human body. These boats have recently caused a largely increased amount of human body segments in the water, incapable of being identified.—L.C.S.

HOPE IT'S FRESH:
THE ARMADILLO AND LATE-PLEISTOCENE HUNTERS

Richard L. Stromberg
Toronto, Canada

Ever since the discovery of chipped stone projectile points in association with giant bison and mammoth remains, most archaeologists have been confortable with the picture of North American Paleo-Indians relying on vast herds of large Pleistocene ungulates to provide a stable, suitable supply of food. However, the actual number of these sites remains small and there has been controversy over how one kills and then brings home a dead mammoth. The most common explanation is that the "schlepp effect" (put simply, you only bring home cuts of meat you can carry (Daly, 1969)) distorts the relative frequencies of archaeologically recovered skeletal elements and thereby reduces the "visibility" of megafauna in the archaeological record. Recent research in the southern United States, however, suggests that larger ungulates may have played an altogether different role in the hunting patterns of Paleo-Indians.

A brief survey of a large open section of the Willis ranch, located about 24 km southeast of Cognito, Texas (Rand-McNally, 1980), was conducted while searching for a bolt inadvertently tossed while changing a jeep tire. Archaeological materials were sparse but included a long-neck Lone Star bottle, an Oldsmobile hub cap, and a pre-pop-top pop can (Stromberg, 1984). Bleached bones and other zoological evidence were left behind by the Willis beef cattle.

Noteworthy among the faunal bones was a smashed skeleton. Analysis showed it to be the remains of an armadillo which had its spine crushed. Dead armadillos in themselves are not particularly uncommon in southern Texas, except that this one was not a roadkill. It was lying among hoof prints where it had obviously been trampled by a herd of cattle. The location and circumstances of this armadillo's death have implications which allow one to generate a model of a late Pleistocene food procurement strategy.

During the Pleistocene, several species of giant armadillo and glyptodont ranged widely through North and South America (Colbert, 1980). It is unlikely that these beasts were any more adept at getting out of the way of others than are their modern descendents, so it is fairly certain that armadillos were trampled to death by bisons, mammoths, or other large game. We can call these events "spoor kills" to encompass the variety of species and localities possible worldwide. The general paucity of spoor kill sites can be explained by the "schlemiel effect:" only a schlemiel would get hit by a herd of thundering bison while standing in the middle of nowhere. Spoor kills as large as giant armadillos would have been an attractive source of food requiring a modest output of energy. Assuming that 50-70% of the armadillo was useful meat, the average Paleo-Indian family of four could have dined 2-5 days on a single spoor kill, but it is probable that several families would have shared the kill, thereby ensuring that little went to waste through spoilage. Evidence for cooperation in food procurement is preserved today in Texas folklore where it is often asked how many are needed to eat an armadillo (ans: 2, one to eat and one to watch for cars). A Pleistocene family would have eaten in comfort knowing that another family was standing guard watching for more herd "traffic." Guards would have had to fend off some animals with their spears; spear points would have been occasionally dislodged and left in the flanks of larger game animals who would then carry them as shrapnel until their death. This explains some of the occurrences where points and skeletal remains are associated but little other human activity is discernable. It is also important to note that while ungulates were still relied on to provide food, it is possible that they were unwitting partners in the chase rather than the objects of the chase.

ACKNOWLEDGEMENTS

The preparation of this research report was facilitated by a grant from the Ontario Research Council and an 18" snow storm which made it impossible to do anything else. Tim Kaiser and Cathy Duncan read the manuscript and should have caught any errors. ∎

REFERENCES

Colbert EH. 1980 *Evolution of the Vertebrates* (3rd ed.). John Wiley, New York

Daly P. 1969 Approaches to Faunal Analysis in Archaeology. *American Antiquity* 34:146-53

Rand-McNally. 1980 *Road Atlas.* Chicago

Stromberg R. 1984 An archaeological reconnaissance of the Willis ranch. Ms. filed with the Communicado County Historical Society, Cognito, Texas

Disco Music Makes Mice Turn Gay

Ankara, Turkey

Disco music causes homosexuality in mice and may make no exception where men are concerned, a study at the Aegean University maintains.

The Milliyet newspaper said yesterday that researchers at the Izmir-based university "discovered that high-level noise—such as that frequently found in discos—causes homosexuality in mice and deafness among pigs."

"The researchers think that there is a caveat in these studies for human beings as well," the Milliyet said.

The paper did not offer any explanation as to how mice were judged resistant to deafness or why pigs kept their sexual identities.

United Press

Notes On The Sociobiology Fracas

David Weinberger
Brookline, MA

RESTORATION OF A NEANDERTHAL GROUP, Chicago Natural History Museum

The debate over sociobiology flares up each time a sociobiologist claims to have explained another social phenomenon. The sociobiologist thinks there are genetic-evolutionary explanations of most (if not all) enduring social phenomena. Consequently, when he offers a new explanation, he thinks he is just confirming the validity of his science. His opponents, however, take it to be a further encroachment on the range of human freedom. Further, the opponents worry that the general public, if not the sociobiologists themselves will take the explanation as a justification for the social practice concerned. Since sociobiologists have so far offered explanations for slavery, rape, war, and cannibalism, the opponents claim that their inherent politics are reactionary. It is in the interests of all concerned to see how far the list of topics treated sociobiologically can be extended. The following are some recent sociobiological explanations of lesser social phenomena; it is on issues such as these that the outcome of the debate rests.

1. *Don't talk with your mouth full.* Sociobiologists point out that those cavemen who attempted to talk with their mouths full were understood less frequently than those who chewed thirty times, swallowed, and then articulated their demands. Someone who says, "Please pass the mastadon" with a mouth full of food liklier than not will receive a bowl full of tarragon or nasturtiums as a result of his temporary speech impediment. But a diet of tarragon and nasturtiums is considerably less wholesome than one of thick slabs of mastadon. Thus, the gene for talking with one's mouth full would have become rapidly extinct.

Opponents argue that those who could success-fully combined the arts of eating and talking simultaneously were better able to request more food passed to them. It was in the interest of all cavepeople to say "Please pass the mastadon" as often as possible. Those who talked with their mouth full got more to eat, were healthier and better able to reproduce.

2. *Don't slouch.* Standing perfectly erect confers a distinct evolutionary advantage, enabling those with straight backs and good posture to see further. They would then be the first to begin running from any sabre-toothed tigers in the vicinity. Further, when walking under cliffs the straight-standers presented a smaller target for precarious boulders and rogue pterodactyls.

Opponents argue that those that did not slouch were more likely to hit their heads on the ceilings of low caves, resulting in a befuddlement which could only encourage the onslaught of wily sabre-toothed tigers. And by straightening up the caveman's pelt was likely to become untucked, exposing his unprotected midriff to harsh weather and further tempting predators.

3. *Children should be seen and not heard.* Consider two cave families, the Grunks and the Spocks. Mr. and Mrs. Spock believe that their children should be encouraged to talk as much as possible. They will not lay a hand on them, believing it might inhibit their growth and development as whole and fulfilled people. As a result, the Spocks spend a lot of time cleaning up after the young Spocks and listening to childish twaddle. Not only could this time be better spent devising barriers against sabre-toothed tigers, but if a child is talking, the Spocks will not interrupt even to yell, "Watch out! There's a glacier coming!", resulting in many tragic deaths, particularly on holiday weekends. The Spocks do not live as long as the Grunks who regularly thrash their children for venturing opinions.

Opponents argue that sabre-toothed tigers are less like to invade caves which they know are occupied, and the endless chatter of the Spock tots would be a primitive equivalent to the modern practice of leaving a light on in order to scare off potential burglars. Sociobiologists retort that all the din would make the sabre-toothed tiger's lot easier. Opponents counter-retort by putting sabre-toothed tigers on the endangered species list.

4. *Vote Republican.* Societies that do not as a whole vote Republican suffer from increasing crime rates, skyrocketing inflation, devastating national debt, a weakening of defense capabilities, slackness of moral fiber, and a lack of drive and will. Those that vote Republican, however, are strong, self-assertive, healthy, untroubled by hooligans and malingerers, re- pected by other societies, feared by their enemies, and proud of their own heritages.

Opponents claim that those who vote Republican tend to be fat cat industrialists sitting on their butts, living off the honest sweat of others, suffering from heart disease and cirrhosis of the liver.

At this point the sociobiologists and their oppo- nents square off and engage in a struggle for survival.

DOUBLES TROUBLE

Muscular Feminate
Masters and Johnson mate
folk who've forgotten what
needs to be done.

There are some who get worse
polymorphousperverse
they never discover
sex can be fun

Barry Blackwell
Milwaukee, WI

**United States
Department of
Agriculture**

January 21, 1986

TO: All Divisions
FROM: Deputy Administrator for Management, AMS
SUBJECT: Changes in Government Travel Policies Due to Gramm-Rudman Bill (Affecting Accomodations and Meals)

1. Beginning March 1, 1986, the government has arranged for all Federal employees on detail orders to make use of low cost accomodations while traveling to areas where government accomodations are not available.

2. Arrangements have been made to house government personnel in YMCA's halfway houses, mental institutions, resident drug treatment centers, public shelters, and various correctional institutions available in most larger cities throughout the United States.

3. Certain designated bath houses which have recently been closed down by the local boards of health because of the AIDS epidemic are being made available for use by government employees on detail orders to the greater San Francisco area. These employees will be required to pass a rigorous physical examination, given by the bath house management prior to admittance due to the recent outbreak of various highly infectious diseases in the area.

4. Detailed travelers to any other city will be required to report to the local police department where they will receive an assignment to one of the many designated public housing facilities, possibly including the police station itself. If no quarters are available, the traveler will be issued a Statement of Nonavailability. This will authorize the traveler to stay at a low cost men's or women's shelter in which adequate comfortable dormitory style facilities are available. Travelers will be advised to leave all personal belongings, shoes, and wallets at the police headquarters overnight if they make use of these facilities.

5. Arrangements have also been made with major airlines to make unused airline meals left over from each flight available to government employees on detail orders. These meals will be issued to travelers as they depart the aircraft and are to be used exclusively during the detail. All unused meals are to be turned in when boarding the return flight. In the event that a traveler cannot be given enough meals to cover the entire detail period, McDonald's gift certificates will be issued to make up the difference.

6. If the above procedures are followed, no advance payment will be required and all travelers should be able to live within government-allowed per diem rates.

Agricultural
Marketing
Service

On the Incidence of Contra-Stripe Ties in the Transportation Consulting Industry

Diane Kravif
Los Angeles, CA

Traffic engineers use the term "contra-flow lane" to designate a street or highway lane dedicated to traffic travelling opposite to the prevailing direction of flow, for example, a northbound bus lane on an otherwise one-way southbound street. This paper examines a tangentially related phenomenon, the incidence of "contra-stripe" ties among male staff members of a large transportation engineering consulting organization.

A *contra-stripe tie* is hereby defined as a tie with diagonal stripes running from upper right to lower left, in the frame of reference of an observer facing the wearer of the tie. Such stripes are 90° offset from the prevailing direction of diagonal stripes, which on the vast majority of diagonally striped ties run from upper left to lower right.

This phenomenon first came to the author's attention as her thoughts wandered, during a meeting attended by herself and 26 others, from the topic at hand to what initially appeared to be a piece of sartorial trivia. Of the 27 people present, 25 were wearing ties. Of these, 5 wore solid-color ties and 6 wore ties with an all-over pattern (polka dots, small trains or other motifs arranged along both diagonals, or axially symmetric plaids). The remaining 14 wore ties with diagonal stripes, and of these, not one was of the type the author and her associates have since come to know as "contra-stripe." At the end of the meeting, the author announced her initial hypothesis to the assembled company, to wit:

All diagonally striped ties are striped from upper left-hand corner to lower right-hand corner.

The road to a monumental scientific achievement is rarely free of potholes. The following day, a colleague of an inquiring turn of mind reported the results of a survey of his closet: of 17 diagonally striped ties, 15 were striped in the prevailing direction (upper left to lower right), but the other two were contra-stripe. Confronted by this evidence, the author stated an amended hypothesis:

The vast majority (85-90%) of diagonally striped ties worn by consultants within the U.S. transportation industry are striped in the prevailing direction.

This version has been confirmed time and time again by the author and her most scientifically minded colleagues.

The obvious remaining question is, what motivates wearers of contra-stripe ties to act with such flagrant nonconformity? For some time, the author's only co-worker who did so consistently was the highest-ranking architect in an organization of some 75 engineers. His contra-stripe ties are clearly a subconscious flaunting of his minority (and in his eyes, superior) status.

However, several members of a British firm have recently become consultants on the project. The author's observation that all of them wear contra-stripe ties almost exclusively has given rise to a new hypothesis of stunning generality and power, which the author hereby makes public for the first time:

In countries where people drive on the X-hand side of the road, whether X equals left or right, the stripes on 85 to 90% of the diagonally striped ties worn by transportation consultants permanently resident in those countries run from upper opposite-X-hand side to lower X-hand side.

The author is in the process of gathering final confirmation of this theory in the form of eye-witness accounts of mass disposals of contra-stripe ties on the part of Swedish transportation consultants, closely followed by mass purchases of prevailing-direction ties, when the country converted from left-hand to right-hand drive some years ago. The author will also be pleased to entertain proposals from potential sponsors of research forays to Japan for further observation, and will respond promptly and courteously to all offers submitted along with a stamped, self-addressed envelope.

ACKNOWLEDGEMENTS

Thanks to Bob Vance and Piers Connor for their helpful suggestions.

207

FOOD AS A STATE SYSTEM

A.M. Ruder
C.T. Ruder
Rechovot, Israel

PORTRAIT OF RUDOLF II AS VERTUMNUS, by Giuseppe Arcimboldo

TABLE 1. Religious (Other Than Jewish) Dietary Laws*

Religion	Law(s)	Comments
Buddhists, Hindus, Zorastrians, Seventh-Day Adventists	no meat products	Food of a higher-caste Hindu unfit if handled by member of a lower caste
Latter-Day Saints	no alcohol, tea, coffee	
Roman Catholics	no meat eating on Fridays or during Lent	no longer need be observed
Jains	no food that involves taking life	tubers, roots, honey and alcohol prohibited as well as animals
Moslems	no pork or alcohol	

*Additional laws prescribe periods of fasting

Living organisms are the most conspicuous example of systems combatting the universal tendency toward entropy and disorder in the closed system of the universe. This is possible because living organisms are open systems interacting with the rest of the universe (von Bertalanffy, 1968).

If living systems are first-order anti-entropy items, classifications imposed upon the natural world are second- and higher-order anti-entropy items. These classifications include taxonomic systems, national identity numbers, and dietary laws. In addition to the almost universal law that "eating people is wrong" (Flanders M, Swann D, 1959), almost every religion has imposed some dietary strictures upon its adherents. Table 1 lists some of these. To examine how such strictures function as higher-order anti-entropy rules, we will examine in detail one such set of laws, the Jewish system of *kashrut* (kosherness). In this system, all food (or potential food) is classified as *tref* (unclean; only to be eaten under extraordinary life-threatening circumstances, if ever), milk and meat (which may not be eaten together), or *parve* (can accompany either milk or meat).

Everything in the universe can be considered as food or potential food, in one of ten states (Table 2). The transitions from state to state are well-defined in this system of laws. They are presented graphically in Figure 1. Table 3 lists the permissible state transitions and gives examples of each.

One of the laws of *kashrut* is that hitherto permissible foods can become *trafish* by coming in contact with a *trafish* item. The intentional addition to a kosher mixture of a *trafish* item, no matter how small, or the inadvertent addition of such an item ≥ 1.67 (1/60th) of the total changes the state to *trafishness*. The juxtaposition of otherwise kosher meat and milk items, assuming neither is less than 1.67% the quantity of the other, renders both of them *trafish*.

TABLE 2. The State System of Jewish Dietary Laws

State	Items Included
1. *parev* candidate	plants, yeasts, fish with movable scales, and ova of birds in meat-candidate category
2. *parev* food	vegetables, eggs without bloodspots, and fish healthy when killed, prepared without any milk, meat, or *tref* additions
3. milk candidate	lactic secretions of mammals in meat-candidate category
4. milk food	milk candidate processed/prepared without any meat or *tref* additions
5. meat candidate	ungulate mammals and gallinaceous birds
6. meat food	meat candidate correctly killed and processed without any milk or *tref* additions
7. tref candidate	all living animals not mentioned above
8. tref food	killed tref candidates; other food or food candidates incorrectly processed
9. previously inanimate	minerals, etc. never before in the food chain
10. digested/decomposed	molecules and atoms of any of the above

TABLE 3. Permissible State Transitions

From	To	Examples
1	2	an apple is picked
2	4	flour added to a cheese souffle
2	6	onions added to liver and onions
2	8	lettuce added to shrimp salad
3	4	cow milked into milk-only container
4	8	cream added to beef stroganoff
5	6	an unblemished animal is properly killed
5	7	an animal becomes sick or blemished
6	8	beef added to beef stroganoff
7	8	a lobster is boiled
9	1,3,5,7	Na- incorporated in living tissue
9	2,4,6,8	NaCl sprinkled on a food item
10	1,3,5,7	Uptake/incorporation of organic molecules

Because of these rules, at any isolated point in time, flow between states will appear to be undirectional, toward *trafishness*. If this were indeed so, there would be no kosher items left in the universe long before entropy ran down (because *kashrut* is a higher-order organization than life). However, *trafishness* is not defined at an atomic level. It is defined only for biochemical molecules (e.g. porcine proteins) and larger items. Once *trafish* substances are no longer fit even for animal consumption, i.e. have decomposed, *trafishness* no longer exists, and the substances could be eaten (presumably, only in case of dire necessity) by an observant Jew. In addition, catabolized *tref* molecules can be incorporated in potentially kosher organisms. For example, frogs are *trafish*. Frog atoms, incorporated in the molecules of a duck which eats the frog, become potentially meatish (still potentially *trafish* until the duck is properly slaughtered and prepared and served on meat-only dishes). What of recognizably *tref* items inside otherwise kosher items (a shrimp in the gut of a fish; a fly in the trap of a Venus-flytrap)? The *traf* is discarded; the fish or plant can be eaten.

Before and during certain festivals and holy days, particular foods are prescribed or proscribed. These ad-

	Starting State									
	1	**2**	**3**	**4**	**5**	**6**	**7**	**8**	**9**	**10**
1	O	—	—	—	—	—	—	—	Y	Y
2	Y	O	—	—	—	—	—	—	Y	—
3	—	—	O	—	—	—	—	—	Y	Y
4	—	Y	Y	O	—	—	—	—	Y	—
5	—	—	—	—	O	—	—	—	Y	Y
6	—	Y	—	—	Y	O	—	—	Y	—
7	—	—	—	—	Y	—	O	—	Y	Y
8	Q	Y	—	Y	—	Y	Y	O	Y	—
9	—	—	—	—	—	—	—	—	O	—
10	Y	Y	Y	Y	Y	Y	Y	Y	Y	O

O = homeostasis, Y = permissible transition.

FIGURE 1. State Transition Table.

ditional restrictions, such as abstaining from leavening (and food grains, in Ashkenazi culture) during the Passover holiday can be considered as higher-order states of *kashrut*.

The implications of organizing systems such as the laws of *kashrut* are great. If we consider entropy the objective equivalent of philosophic anarchy, and higher-order physical organizations the objective equivalents of moral guidelines, then increasing the number of rules governing the use of physical objects—placing them in higher-order states—increases the subjective organization of the universe. In addition, for those who believe in such systems (whether or not they follow them), the greater the number of rules the greater the number of free-will decisions available to the individual, and the more opportunity the individual has to demonstrate his adherence to a philosophy by following, or by not following, the rules.

REFERENCES

Von Bertalanffy, L.: 1968. *General Systems Theory: Foundations, Developments, Applications.* New York: George Braziller, Inc., p. 21 ff.
Flanders, M., Swann, D.: 1959. "The Reluctant Cannibal," from *At the Drop of a Hat.*

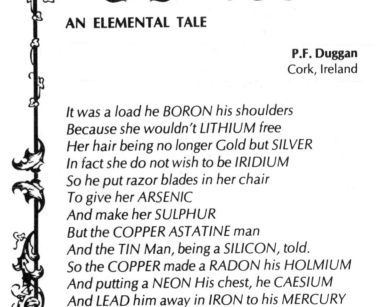

AN ELEMENTAL TALE

P.F. Duggan
Cork, Ireland

It was a load he BORON his shoulders
Because she wouldn't LITHIUM free
Her hair being no longer Gold but SILVER
In fact she do not wish to be IRIDIUM
So he put razor blades in her chair
To give her ARSENIC
And make her SULPHUR
But the COPPER ASTATINE man
And the TIN Man, being a SILICON, told.
So the COPPER made a RADON his HOLMIUM
And putting a NEON His chest, he CAESIUM
And LEAD him away in IRON to his MERCURY
It was a great SCANDIUM to see someone
ZINC so low
I have XENON worse
   MoRaLi
Better to pay ANTIMONY
Than BISMUTH your character.

209

Heggie's Objection To The Peter Principle *

Jack Heggie
Boulder, CO

In 1969 Dr. Laurence J. Peter, working with Raymond Hull, elaborated his now famous Peter Principle in a book of the same name. (1) The Principle states: In a hierarchy, every employee tends to rise to his level of incompetence. An important corollary, Peter's Corollary, immediately follows from this Principle: In time, every post in a hierarchy tends to be occupied by an employee who is incompetent to carry out its duties.

The Peter Principle explains "Why things always go wrong."

It has been over a quarter of a century since Dr. Peter expounded his Principle, and in that time many, many more people have had a chance to rise to their level of incompetence. This may explain such anomalies as why, in times of apparent prosperity, there are more homeless people than ever; why, after the dissolution of the animosity between the two former superpowers, there are more wars than ever; why, after various environmental groups have been active for years there is a growing hole in the ozone layer, and many species of both plants and animals are dying out: why, in a time of peace, "militias" are rising up against the government, and so on.

At this point we must ask a question: If Dr. Peter is entirely correct, why hasn't civilization ground to a complete halt? Why have not the vast majority of those employed in a hierarchy (which means, of course, the vast majority of mankind) risen to their Level and thus ceased to perform any useful work? Why have we not slid into the abyss to be replaced by some species that has yet to achieve Life Incompetence, as Dr. Peter refers to the situation wherein so many people have achieved their Level that the entire species is no longer viable?

Is it possible that there is a flaw in Dr. Peter's Principle? There is indeed such a flaw, which may be denoted *Heggie's Objection*. This flaw is so simple, and, in fact, so blatantly obvious, that it seems passing strange that someone hasn't pointed it out before.

Observe Figure 1. Peter's Pyramid, which illustrates a simple pyramidal hierarchy. This pyramid is at the base of all of Dr. Peter's analyses of hierarchies. At the apex is the boss, and below him, in layer after descending layer. are his subordinates. then the subordinates' subordinates, then the subordinates' subordinates' subordinates, and so on, till we reach the workers at the very bottom of the pyramid.

Figure 1: Peter's Pyramid

Now this is all well and good, but notice that this Pyramid is just an *outline* of the hierarchy — it contains no details of the internal organization. (Dr. Peter also mentions some alternate form of hierarchy, such as the "Flying T Formation," but the diagram for this also conceals an important detail, under the heading "Divisions." Whether this concealment is deliberate or only an accidental slip, I must leave to the reader to decide.)

Now look at Figure 2, Peter's Pyramid, Enhanced Version. Here we can see a crucial element that is not easily discerned in Dr. Peter's original Pyramid. For the sake of simplicity and space, I show a Pyramid with an *Index of Subordination* of three. This means that each person above the lowest level of the hierarchy has three subordinates. Now the problem with Dr. Peter's analysis becomes obvious: *There is a vastly insufficient number of slots above any given level in the hierarchy for everyone to rise to his Level. In fact, there is insufficient number for even a majority to rise to their Level.*

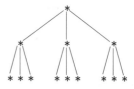

Figure 2: Peter's Pyramid, Enhanced Version

Consider: In a typical hierarchy, any supervisor will have more than one subordinate. Although the number of subordinates will very greatly from one hierarchy to another, and even within a given hierarchy, there will very rarely be a case where a supervisor has only one subordinate.

As an example, let us suppose that each supervisor in a certain hierarchy has ten subordinates. Then, at a particular level, only one in ten employees is eligible for promotion to the next level above, because there is only one slot available at the next supervisory level for each ten employees. Thus, initially it would seem that the way is clear for only some 10% of the employees to rise to their Level.

However, even this is too great an estimate. To see this, consider, as a simple case, a company with seven employees, a boss, two supervisors, and four workers. The boss is at the highest level, and the two supervisors report to him. In turn, each supervisor has two workers who report to him. To make the analysis, we must introduce one more technical term, the Hierarchical Echelon Integer, which is the number of levels in the hierarchy. For this very simple company the Index of Subordination is two, and the Hierarchal Echelon Integer is three. This company is illustrated in Figure 3.

Figure 3: A Simple Example Hierarchy, With IS = 2, and HEI = 3

As long as the boss remains where he is, the hierarchal structure is stable. No one is eligible for promotion. But suppose that the boss gets his "Final Promotion" (that is, he dies or retires). Now one of the two supervisors at the level immediately below him, assuming that he hasn't reached his Level, is eligible for promotion, and should get his job. In turn, one of the four employees at the lowest level of the hierarchy, also assuming that he is not already at his Level, is now eligible for promotion to supervisor. Finally, a new employee is added at the lowest level to replace the employee who has been promoted to supervisor.

Thus, in this small hypothetical company, with seven employees, an Index of Subordination of two, and a Hierarchal Echelon Integer of three, in one promotion cycle, only two out of the seven employees, or about 29%, can be promoted, and thus have at least a chance to reach their Level of Incompetence. If we take into account the fact that a large hierarchy has many levels and a varying number of workers reporting to each supervisor, the mathematics involved in calculating the percentage of employees who will at least have the chance to be promoted to their Level, which we may call P(L)max, becomes quite complex. In an unpublished (and possibly unpublishable) monograph entitled "Variation of P(L)max on the Basis of Index of Subordination, Hierarchal Echelon Integer, and Time." I give a formula for making such a calculation, which may be called Heggie's Theorem.

For our purposes here it is only necessary to note that P(L)max, the Percentage of workers in a given hierarchy who at least have a chance to rise to their level of incompetence, is fairly small, and, in the maximum theoretical case can only be as IMUM great as 1/3, or 33%. In the real world (such as it is), P(L)act, the percentage of people who actually reach their Level, will always be considerably less than this.

For example, in a fairly simple hierarchy with a Hierarchal Echelon Integer of four, and an Index of Subordination of three, application of the Theorem reveals that P(L)max is only 3/40, or 7.5%, for one promotion cycle. Thus, in a given time period only 7.5% of the employees have a chance to be promoted to their Level, and it is by no means certain that every promotion will result in an employee attaining their Level of Incompetence. Thus, the actual percentage of those who reach their Level, P(L)act, will almost invariably be less than 7.5%.

There is yet one final problem with the Principle. Once an employee has been promoted to his Level, he is ineligible for further promotion, and thus he forms a block to all those below him. This condition, Peter's Plug, will prevent all those employees below the Plugee from being promoted, and thus prevent them from reaching their Level. Thus, we may state that Peter's Plug Prevents Promotions, and paralyzes Peter's Principle.

If a Plug occurs fairly low in the hierarchy, the effect will be small, because only a few people, those working directly for the Plugee, or for his subordinates, will be blocked. If the plug is higher up, more people will be blocked, and the effect will be more serious. If the Plugee is the CEO, and thus is at the very top of the hierarchy, he may block all promotions, and thus inhibit the operation of the Principle altogether, at least for a time, and at least in that one particular hierarchy. And, it should be fairly obvious that the more people who reach their level of incompetence in a given hierarchy, the more who are blocked from promotion, and thus from reaching their Level. Thus, Peter's Plug forms a kind of natural antidote to the Peter Principle itself. This consideration reduces P(L)act even more, and ensures that there will be a fairly large percentage of people in any given hierarchy who are below their Level, and that are able to do some useful work. At any rate, the Peterists' alarmist ideas on the rapidly approaching demise of the human race, or our promotion to Life incompetency, as they style it, while they should not be dismissed entirely, may now be viewed with much less trepidation. In any event, those who, fearing the end, are maintaining bomb shelters, living "off the grid," or, in general, are preparing for the imminent collapse of civilization, can slack off a little and enjoy life.

I have heard of people who, upon reading Dr. Peter's book, decided that, since all was soon to be lost, there was no reason to carry on at all, and who then dropped out altogether. This phenomenon, which may be dubbed Peter's Predicament, quite possibly may at least partly account for the increasingly large number of homeless and those who are on welfare today. To these wretched souls we may now say, "Take heart! All is not lost! Heggie's Objection reveals the flaw. Pick up your burden and carry on, there is still hope! Return to the world and once again put your nose to the grindstone — and someday, given enough time, you, too, can reach your Level."

REFERENCES:
(1) Peter, Laurence J., and Hull, Raymond: The Peter Principle: Why Things Always Go Wrong. NY: William Morrow, 1969.

*   This article is excerpted from the forthcoming book *Heggies's Rule: How The Experts Ruin Your Life*

Economics 101[10]

William Haber, professor emeritus of economics at the University of Michigan.

"Slowing up of the slowdown is not as good as an upturn in the down curve, it is a great deal better than either a speedup of the slowdown or a deepening of the down curve; and it does suggest that the climate is about right for an adjustment to the readjustment. It is hard to tell, before the slowdown is completed, whether a particular pickup is going to be fast. At any rate, the climate is right for a pickup this season, especially if you are about 25, unmarried and drive a red sports car."

FROM: Rockwell International

A Social Science Experiment Designed to Assess the Effect of Degrees of Acculturation Upon Musical Oicotypification

KEITH CUNNINGHAM
Box 5905
Northern Arizona University
Flagstaff, Arizona 86011

ABSTRACT: *An attempt to assess the effect of degrees of acculturation upon musical oicotypification (or to quantify the Kola tea of mercy [which is not strained]) ending in failure. The study turned instead to the study of certain complex legal questions concerning fieldwork.*

INTRODUCTION

As one of the few genuine, certified students of culture alive and well in Arizona, I long regretted the regrettable fact that my field of study regrettably, relative to its syntagmatic structures, is looked down upon by other disciplines because of its lack of graphs and charts and phems and is even a little shaky as to the number of incomprehensible theories it has produced. (I feel this sorry state of affairs came about because too long we have been content with mere observation and have avoided the experimentation which is the heart and kidneys of true scientific research and because social scientists don't wear lab coats [there is, by the by, an interesting tale about folklorists to the effect that early blues collectors did wear lab coats but discontinued the practice when they were pelted with watermelons by certain subjects (taboo, of course) who mistook them for klansmen]).

At any rate (editor, could you run a rate chart here?), Europe is not so unfortunate. France has its Levi-Strauss, Germany its Grimm brothers (I didn't really think that their collecting was all that bad), and Sweden its von Sydow (to say nothing of Saul his thousands). All of these gaints (including the Grimm brothers who are affectionately known to their students as "Snake" and "The Eighth Drawf") produced incomprehensible theory in abundance. Unfortunately, they did not engage in experimentation (the well known tale about snake in the grass aside). This regrettable lackency the principle researcher resolved to remedy with this study.

REVIEW OF RELEVATN LITERATURE
Oicotypification

Since the investigator speaks or reads almost no Swedish (except, of course, for such basic terms as saki and pizza) he decided to limit the relevant literature to that which has been translated into American. Writing in some weird Irish magazine, von Sydow introduced the concept which, slightly altered by high altitude, became the household word we all know and love today—oicotypification. He defined this gumbuster as "the almost predictable alteration which takes place when an item of folklore is changed to fit the cuturally preferred pattern of an area."[1]

Roger Abrahams included an introduction and appendix concerning oicotypification in his spiffy collection of dirty jokes from Philadelphia, and these sections of his book had lots to say about oicotypification.[2]

The researcher's dissertation was also about this stuff.[3]

Momus Culture

Throughout the long and honorable involvement of that fearless scientist the anthropologist with Momus culture, lots of people have written lots of things. From the point of view of the study, the most important things they have written concerned the fact that the Momus' have really far out music and a matrilineal and materfamilias society.

DESIGN OF THE EXPERIMENT

The experiment was designed to put von Sydow's theory of oicotypification to the test using Momus music in Momus culture. The plan was to introduce an oicotypical and non-oicotypical version of an Anglo American folk song from the Southern Mountains into Momus culture and predict the acceptance or rejection of the two forms in terms of the degree of acculturation of the informants.

First of all, "Pretty Polly," a well known Southern Mountain folk song was chosen (sure, you know the song, dummy. It's the one in which Polly's boyfriend knocks her up, takes her for a ride [on horseback no less] to a place where there just happens to be "a new dug grave with a spade lying by." bangs her in the head and kills her thus exemplifying a primitive but effective form of birth control). Two forms of the song were arranged and recorded. One was translated into Momus and set to a well known Momus melody (or at least that's what my assistant told me; it just seemed to me that he went "oo wah wah" a lot). The other form was a version by that fountainhead of tradition the Kingston Trio.

After the oicotyical and nonoicotypical forms of "Pretty Polly" were prepared, Momus singers were located (this turned out to be a real pain; at first the researcher just asked people standing around outside Flagstaff's Club 66 [the local Indian bar where local Indians bare their troubles] and was inevitably directed to a Singer shop on the reservation which has a bunch of peddlepushers in stock; finally the researcher said to hell with it and looked up "Singer" in the Yellow Pages).

After the singers had been located, they were given recording of the two versions of "Pretty Polly" (this also was a problem; the researcher had planned to distribute the songs on 45 rpm records, but one sagacious, venerable medicine man spoke for the whole group when he said, "If it ain't eight track stereo, just forget it").

The final step in the investigation was to classify the singers as to their degree of acculturation. The researcher had planned to administer the MMPI, TAT, and the Ink Block tests; but since he couldn't understand any of the directions, a very ingenious index of acculturation was developed as follows:

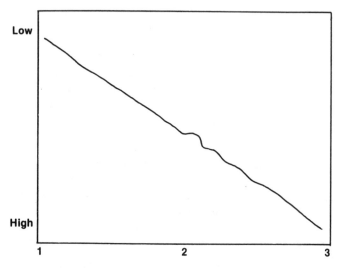

The explanation of this magnificent chart above is as follows below: the up and down thingies stand for degree of acculturation and range from high (represented by low) to low (represented by high). The across the page whatumacallits are the factors used in determining the degree of acculturation. They are, reading from right to left, 3: three or more color pickup, woman driving, sister and kids and grandmother in cab, man riding in back with laundry; 2: same as one but man is riding in cab with grandma riding in back with laundry or the pickup is only two toned; 1: same as two except the man is driving the truck or it is a solid color.

HYPOTHESIS

The researcher predicted that the most acculturated, or one-color-pickup Indians, would adopt the nonoicotypical form or "Pretty Polly" while the least acculturated, three-toned-pickup-with-man-riding-in-back, Indians would adopt the more nearly oictypical form in Momus set to a Momus melody and would sing it at Squaw Dances (a sort of primitive sock-hop without socks or gymnasia).

RESULTS OF THE EXPERIMENT

1.) In a direct reversal of the predicted behavior, the most highly acculturated singer (he had a black car instead of a truck and thus was completely off the acculturation scale) thought the Momus language version of "Pretty Polly" was "neat;" and his band, Spider Rock, started playing and singing it at sock-hops (a primitive kind of Squaw Dance with socks and gymnasia).

2.) In a further reversal of the hypothesis the least acculturated singer said that he "dug" the Kingston Trio version of "Pretty Polly" and started singing this nonoicotypical form at the Rock Rock High School Squaw Dances held at the gym with socks required.

3.) A third result (which perhaps might have been predicted, but that is up to the courts to decide) was that both the English language and the Momus Language versions of "Pretty Polly" oicotypified further in subtle ways. The texts were changed so that "Pretty Polly" became "Lucy Begay" and "Sweet Willie" was called "Little Billy Brokeshoulder." The plot also developed so that in the emerging oicotype Lucy killed Billy by the banks of the Little Colorado when she became pregnant although he pleaded, "I am not prepared to die."

4.) Sales of spades are reported up 37.41% on the reservation.

5.) Six young Momus men and one really old guy (coincidently all named Billy Brokeshoulder) have disappeared in the past few weeks.

QUESTIONS FOR FURTHER STUDY

1.) What did that fella mean by "an accessory before the fact"?

2.) With that kicker as question one who needs a question two?

[1]If you want to know more see Carl von Sydow, "Folktale Studies and Philology: Some Points of View" in Alan Dundes, ed., *The Study of Folklore* (Englewood Cliffs, Prentice-Hall, 1965).

[2]Roger Abrahams, *Deep Down in the Jungle.* (Hatboro, Folklore Association, 1964).

[3]Keith Cunningham, *A Study of the Southern Folk Song Style Area Sweetheart Murder Ballad: The Search for an Oicoclass,* unpublished dissertation, all American dissertations have been reduced to the size of a pinhead by microphotography in order to make them easier to swallow and are kept somewhere in Michigan.